Islam:

In Light Of History

Dr. Rafat Amari

A Religion Research Institute Publication

Printed in the United States of America.

First Edition, November 2004

This book can be purchased directly through
www.**religionresearchinstitute**.org , or by contacting RRI
through e-mailing to: info@religionresearchinstitute.org

Contents

Preface

It was 20 years ago when I began studying Islam and its sources. At the beginning, I thought the study would require me to dedicate two years of my time. Also, because I preside over a Christian organization which requires that I travel from time to time to conduct prayer and teaching conferences in various countries of the world, I thought that my study of Islam should be limited to only a few years so that it would not conflict with my travel plans. However, the study continued for twenty years, compelling me to dedicate eight to nine hours a day, except for Sundays. There was no time for vacation. I researched various books written about the life of Mohammed and his sayings, called the Hadith. I read, re-read and studied the Qur'an several times in the light of the famous expositors of the Qur'an. I studied other Islamic and non-Islamic texts describing the history of Arabia before Islam and the Arabian mythology. Then, I found it necessary to study the classical Greek and Roman authors who visited Arabia and wrote about its geography. I wanted to know if they mentioned Mecca.

My residency in The United States of America gave me access to many of the major libraries of the world which were instrumental in my study of the most important texts. Unfortunately, competent scholastic work was very limited. For example, I estimate that the total pages about Zoroastrianism in the Qur'an in these texts can be estimated at not more than twenty pages. When I thought that my study was complete, and wanting to publish some of my works, I realized that the Lord was urging me to do my own research on the sacred Zoroastrian texts, such as the Zenda Avest and the Pahlavi Texts, and not to depend only on what I had studied. This meant more years of study and research. My study was further extended to examine the sacred literature of other religions at the time of Mohammed.

I was surprised by the similarities I found in the comparative study between the Qur'an and sacred texts of various sects and religions at the time of Mohammed, including: Zoroastrianism,

Mandaeanism, Harranism, Manicheism and Gnosticism. (Mohammed had connections with all of these religions and sects, mainly through the group called "Ahnaf," which he joined in his youth.)

I asked myself: "What material from other religions was used in the Qur'an?" I discovered that much research had been connecting the Qur'an with Judaism and Christianity, but almost nothing had been connecting the Qur'an with Mandaeanism and Harranism. Even what had been done was inadequate and trivial when it came to examining Manicheism and Zoroastrianism as major sources for the Qur'an. My own research showed that these pagan religions had a major impact on the Qur'an, much more than Judaism, Christianity and heretical Christianity at the time of Mohammed. Suleiman al-Farsi was a priest of Zoroastrianism who embraced Islam and became a close counselor of Mohammed. His contact with Mohammed made Zoroastrianism a major resource for the Qur'an. Since Arabic is my native language, I used Arabic to write 800 pages on Zoroastrianism as a resource for the Qur'an.

The study of Mandaeanism from their many sacred books allowed me to detect the roots of Mandaeanism in the Qur'an, which enabled me to prepare a volume of references about this study. I prepared the same thing for Manicheism, Harranism and Gnosticism as roots of the Qur'an.

I continued my research with the occult religion of Arabia called the Jinn religion, or the religion of Kuhhan, the priests of the Jinn–devils. The affiliation of the family of Mohammed with this religion, and the existence of many of their doctrines in the Qur'an, makes this religion an important root of Islam.

These religions were not alone. Another Arabian local religion has obvious roots in the Qur'an. It is the Arabian Star religion, in which Allah was the head; Ellat, the sun, was his wife; and al-'Uzza and Manat, representing two planets, were his daughters. These studies also gave birth to the Religion Research Institute, a scholarly ministry which endeavors to help Christians better understand Islam and its true sources. While this book is still being written, I am in the process of preparing a study course to help those who want to serve among Muslims, and for those who want to help their Muslim friends understand the roots of Islam. I want it to be easier for Muslims to make intelligent choices and avoid the trap of the untruthful data which they have inherited.

The present text, *Islam: In Light of History*, has been prepared as an introduction to Islam. It will be part of the Religion Research Institute course to be presented in the first year of our curriculum. Though I mention some of the sources of the Qur'an in this book, this present text is not intended to cover the sources of the Qur'an, something that I am going to treat in a future publication.

I am indebted to all those who edited, reviewed and stood behind me in this work. Finally, the book would never have been written without those who held me before the throne of grace continually in prayer. May the Lord use this effort to enlighten many to the truth.

Dr. Rafat Amari, 2004

Introduction

More than 1.5 billion people of the world's population face toward Mecca when they pray. They believe that the city of Mecca was visited by Abraham with his son, Ishmael, who, according to Mohammed's claim in the Qu'ran, built the first temple, called Kaabah. According to his claim, Mecca would have been a flourishing city in western Arabia ever since the 21st century, B.C., which was the time in which Abraham lived, although there is no historical documentation to support this claim.

The claim itself was conceived at the time of Mohammed by four people who called themselves "Ahnaf." We read in the narration of the life of Mohammed, called Ibn Hisham, and written during the 8th century A.D., that the Honafa', or Ahnaf, was a small group "started when four persons at Mecca agreed on some ideas. Those four were Zayd bin Amru bin Nafil, Waraqa bin Naufal, Ubaydullah bin Jahsh and Uthman Bin al-Huwayrith. They all died as Sabians."[1]

The four founders of Ahnaf were relatives of Mohammed, descendants of Loayy, one of Mohammed's ancestors. Furthermore, Waraqa bin Naufal and Uthman Bin al-Huwayrith were cousins of Khadijah, the first wife of Mohammed. Ubaydullah bin Jahsh was a close relative of Mohammed; in fact, his mother was Umayya, daughter of Abdel Mutaleb, the grandfather of Mohammed. In other words, he was a cousin of Mohammed. Ubaydullah's sister was Zainab Bint Jahsh, one of the wives of Mohammed who was previously the wife of Zayd bin Harithah, the adopted son of Mohammed.[2]

When Ibn Hisham says the group died as Sabians, this is because the group often went to Sabian territory, especially Zayd bin Amru bin Nafil, who was known to travel extensively to Musil in northern Iraq, and to Jazirah in the northeastern part of Syria near the border with Asia Minor (which is Turkey today); and to Iraq, to inquire about religion.[3] Sometimes Zayd was accompanied by Waraqa bin Naufal on these inquiry trips. Nafil Bin Hashim, a grandson of Zayd bin Amru bin Nafil, mentioned the travels which his grandfather made to the city of Musil and to the district of Jazirah accompanied by Waraqa bin Naufal. Their journies were to search for religion.[4]

The area of Musil has been known since the 2nd century A.D. as the residence of the Sabian Mandaeans, a pagan Gnostic sect which worshipped a complex of polytheistic deities of Persian origin under influence of Mesopotamian polytheism. Harran, the residence of the Sabian Harranians, who were known as worshippers of the god Sin, the moon, the stars, planets and the Jinn, was in the district of Jazirah.

The close relationship between the Ahnaf and the Sabians, who were Mandaeans and Harranians, reveals how Mohammed incorporated many myths and rituals of those sects into the Qur'an. For example, the ritual of Ramadan was known to be a Harranian ritual. (See Part V, Section 3, about Ramadan.) The Islamic prayers, their movements, and the ablution before each prayer were known originally as Mandaean rites. Unfortunately, we must leave the size of the myths, as well as the teaching and rituals which were incorporated into the Qur'an from Mandaean and Harranian sources, for another book, since this study focuses on the history of Mecca and Ishmael and the rise of Islam.

The fact that the Ahnaf were considered to be Sabians by the people of Mecca shows that the Sabians were distinguishable in their teaching, myths and rituals at Mecca to such a degree that, when the Ahnaf presented similar teachings and rituals, they were classified by the Meccans as within that group.

Mohammed joined the Ahnaf in his early youth. He used to spend time with them in the caves of Harra'. Zayd bin Harithah, Mohammed's adopted son, mentioned that Mohammed presented food to Zayd bin Amru bin Nafil when Mohammed spent months with him in the caves of Harra'. Thus, Zayd bin Harithah confirmed the relationship between Mohammed and Zayd bin Amru bin Nafil.[5] Ibn Darid, an Islamic historian, mentioned the encounter between Mohammed and Zayd.[6] This confirms that Mohammed was taught since his youth by Zayd.

Waraqa, the cousin of Khadijah, was another leading figure in the Ahnaf. He used to make Tahnuf, which meant he spent time in the caves of Harra', separating himself from the society for months at a time. (Such practices were known among heretics, as we learn from the early Christian fathers.[7]) Khadijah, the cousin of Waraqa who became the first wife of Mohammed, used to make Tahnuf at the same caves.

Waraqa embraced the Christian cults, such as Ebionism. While Zayd refused any form of religion that was related to Christianity or Judaism, he insisted on the ideas he obtained, mainly from the Mandaean and Harranian Sabians. Some Kuhhan, who were priests of the religion of the Jinn in Arabia, joined this group. There are signs of the involvement of the group of Ahnaf in occultism, such as: their relations with the Jinn which are devils; their secret and occult retreats in the caves of Harra' near Mecca; and their promotion of the Jinn as agents for the prophets, replacing the angels. All these things are included in the Qur'an and in the life of Mohammed.

The claim of this group (called Ahnaf) that Abraham was the founder of their sect originated at the time of Mohammed, and influenced him. Mohammed, in one of his Hadith, said, "Zayd will be considered as the chief founder of a nation between Jesus and me."[8] This claim of Mohammed reveals that Zayd was believed by Mohammed, and other members of the group of Ahnaf, to be the founder of the Ahanf, just as Moses was the head of Judaism, and as Jesus was the head of Christianity. This is a further proof that, before Zayd, nobody claimed to be of the "religion of Abraham." Such claims were born at the time of Mohammed through the claims of Zayd.

Historical data shows that Mecca was not founded before the 4th century A.D. One of the goals of this book is to follow the classical Greek and Roman historians who visited the area of west central Arabia where Mecca was eventually built. We'll see that none of them mentioned Mecca. The area where Mecca was later built is easily identifiable as uninhabited before the Christian era.

This book will also discuss the archaeology of Arabia and archaeological references in the records of the nations who occupied north and west central Arabia. Archaeologists provide important proof that Mecca could not be an ancient city, as Islamic tradition and the Qur'an claim. The cities, tribes and nations on the routes of Arabia that reach the markets of the Fertile Crescent are clearly shown in the Assyrian and Chaldean Inscriptions, without any mention of Mecca, which was built on a main route between Yemen and northern Arabia.

We will look at the Bible, an important source for our study of ancient history. The Bible describes the trade routes through Arabia and mentions various cities on the routes through western Arabia leading to Palestine and Phoenicia on the Mediterranean coast of Lebanon.

We will discuss who built the Kaabah and the dates it was built. We will also refute the excuses Islamic tradition gives for the absence of the Black Stone in Mecca before the 5th century A.D.

Islam is also founded on the claim that Mohammed was a progeny of Ishmael, that Ishmael lived at Mecca, and that his descendants, the Ishmaelites, also lived at Mecca and established monotheism in Arabia. In Part IV of this book, we will follow the history of the Ishmaelites from the time of Joseph, and show their true residency. Then we will follow the emigration of the Ishmaelite tribes from Sinai after the 11th and 10th centuries B.C. All this is confirmed by Assyrian inscriptions which show that the Ishmaelite tribes never reached the area where Mecca was eventually built.

We'll discuss the origin of the family of Mohammed. He was from a Sabaean family who lived in Yemen and had nothing to do with the Ishmaelites. We will also examine, and refute, the false genealogies which try to connect Mohammed to Ishmael.

In Part V of this book, we will look at the pagan roots of the Pilgrimage, called the great Hajj, which was originally a ritual for a few pagan local tribes. It was designed to plead for rain with the sun, the moon and Manat, one of the daughters of Allah. Although the great Hajj had nothing to do with the city of Mecca,

Mecca did have a small Hajj called "Umra." We'll discuss the true nature of that Hajj and its affiliation with the occult worship of Mecca and Medina. Ramadan, as a Harranian rite, will also be discussed in the third section of Part V.

Other arguments which we will treat briefly are the Kaabah as an expression of the Arabian Star Worship. We will discuss the relationship between Mecca's temple and Arabian Star Worship. We'll examine Allah's origin in Thamudic and Arabian tribal inscriptions. Mohammed's concept of deity is rooted in Arabian Star monotheism based on Venus which, in the past, was worshipped as Athtar, the planet which snatched the title of Allah from the moon.

Finally, we will discuss: how Islam arose; the true forces which enabled Mohammed to dominate Arabia; the role of the Jinn religion of Arabia in begetting the Islam of Mohammed; the tipe of adherents who became Muslims at Mecca; and how Mohammed, after seeing that only a few people believed in his claims at Mecca, changed his strategy and sought to convince an Arabian tribe to wage wars behind him so that he might dominate the other Arabian tribes and, in return, offering his filthy bargain of killing the males and giving their females and riches to the tribe who would accept this bargain.

We'll also see how the two tribes of Medina accepted his bargain and began the terrible, violent trend the world is facing today at the hand of the Islamic militants. It is not a new phenomenon, but it is a simple and authentic imitation of what was taught and practiced by Mohammed in his own time.

Before going into detail on these different topics, the first part of the book tells why Mohammed and the Qur'an can't be trusted. I'll prove that his followers rewrote Muslim history and invented a new chronology. How can the Qur'an be trusted when it affirms that Abraham built the Kaabah when, in actuality the Qur'an reveals its author's ignorance of basic history and historical chronology. He mixed the events which took place over thousands of years with those that took place in one generation. He inserted Biblical and other historical figures into different countries and ages. He removed nations from history with a magical cry, applying Zoroastrian and other myths to Biblical and historical figures. How can a book with such primitive confusion of historical facts reflecting the ignorance of the author be a dependable resource for us today to teach us about the 21st century B.C., the time in which Abraham lived? A book without any prior documentation supporting its deviation from recorded history cannot be reliable today.

Why did men like Ibn Ishak rewrite history for Muslims? The answer is simple. They wanted to corroborate the false claims of Mohammed in the Qur'an. In Part I of the book, I'll show you how they created genealogies to back the claims of Mohammed; how they demonstrated that their writings are of no historical value, consisting of cheap myths and statements without any historical chronology; and why they should be disqualified as men of reference for historical facts. The sad fact is that Muslims today still depend on their writings. Believing the false historians only separates Muslims from official documented history, and imprisons them within a false, primitive literature born in Medina in the 7th and 8th centuries A.D.

I understand that to separate a man from the religious beliefs he inherited from his fathers is not an easy task, even though he was taught myths about the Cosmos and about history that even an elementary school student would not accept today. The persistence of many people in certain religious beliefs is due to many factors, but a major consideration is ignorance. Often adherents fail to study to verify historical facts claimed by their religion. The prophet Isaiah tells us that the Lord blames those who are ignorant. God has given us the gift of intelligence to research His will and discover His truth. Ignorance does not excuse us when we sentimentally embrace all that we hear without reasoning in our mind and weighing the truthfulness of what we hear. The fact that our fathers may have accepted what the religion teaches is no excuse.

Another reason many people blindly follow the religious doctrines of their fathers is that they are not honest with themselves. They endeavor to defend the enormous mistakes which contradict reality and history by trying to justify them. Abu

Baker, the first assistant of Mohammed who became his first Caliph, endeavored to support Mohammed when Mohammed claimed to fly on a winged camel to visit the Temple of Solomon in Jerusalem, even though the Temple was not in existence at that time. Yet, Abu Baker claimed he also visited the Temple and asked Mohammed to describe it. When Mohammed began describing the doors and other details about the temple, Abu Baker claimed that Mohammed described it correctly according to what Abu Baker himself had seen when he visited the same Temple.[9] Nothing could stop Abu Baker from defending Mohammed, even at the cost of presenting lies and claiming to visit a place which did not exist in his time.

Today, I see many Muslims on the Internet with the same spirit as Abu Baker. Rather than seek the truth, they are willing to create historically inaccurate excuses to justify Mohammed and his writings. They easily invent false claims which oppose the truth, and they defend what is obviously false. This book is an attempt to warn them that they are deceiving themselves and will be accountable in the day of judgment for deceiving others.

Finally, this book is designed to help those who are true seekers. I invite anyone to verify the information I present by reading the references I quote. I urge thinking Muslims to pray to God that He may enlighten their minds in order to understand the truth and be saved. The true seeker who asks God for help will never be left without illumination. The Lord promised in Jeremiah 29:13, "You will seek me and find me when you seek me with all your heart."

REFERENCES AND NOTES TO THE INTRODUCTION

[1] *Ibn Hisham*, 1, page 242

[2] Ibn Kathir, *Al Bidayah Wal Nihayah*, II, Dar Al Hadith, Cairo, 1992, page 242

[3] Ibn Kathir, *Al Bidayah Wal Nihayah*, II, pages, 243-244

[4] Ibn Kathir, *Al Bidayah Wal Nihayah*, II, page 244

[5] Ibn Kathir, *Al Bidayah Wal Nihayah*, II, page 244

[6] Ibn Darid, *Al-Ishtiqaq*, 84; Qastallani Ahmad ibn Muhammed, *Irshad al-Sari*, 6:171; cited Jawad Ali, *Al Mufassel Fi Tarikh Al Arab Khabel Al Islam*, Dar Al Ilem Lialmalain, (Beirut, 1978), Volume vi, page 473

[7] Hyppolytus, *The Refutation of all heresies*, book VIII , Chapter XIII

[8] Ibn Kathir, *Al Bidayah Wal Nihayah*, II, Dar Al Hadith, Cairo, 1992, page 245

[9] *Ibin Hisham* 2, page 31

Fig. 1 The Sinai at the time of Moses

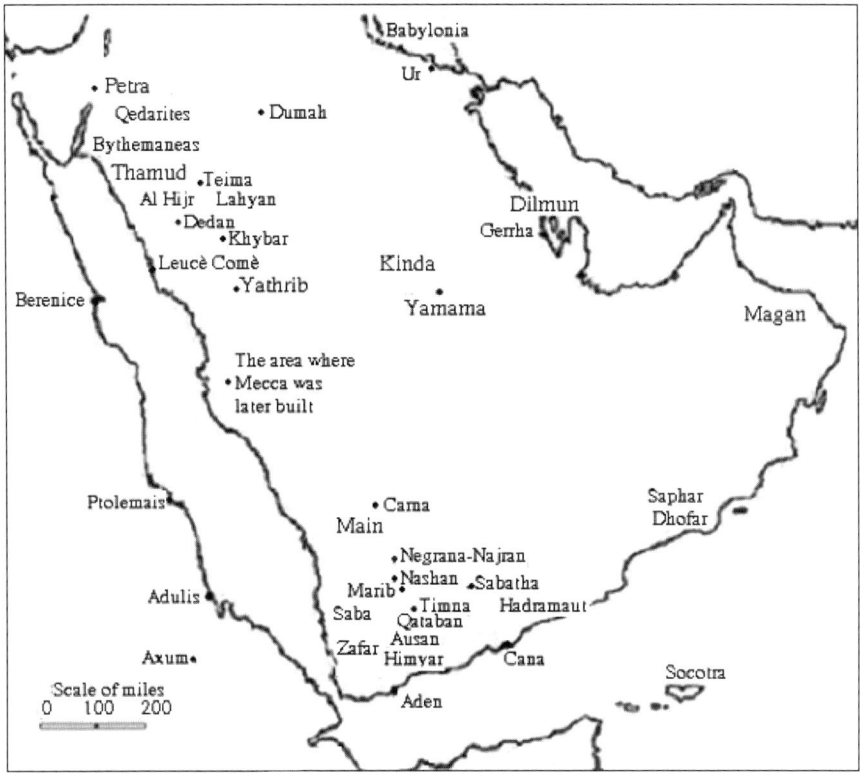

Fig.2 Arabia in ancient times.

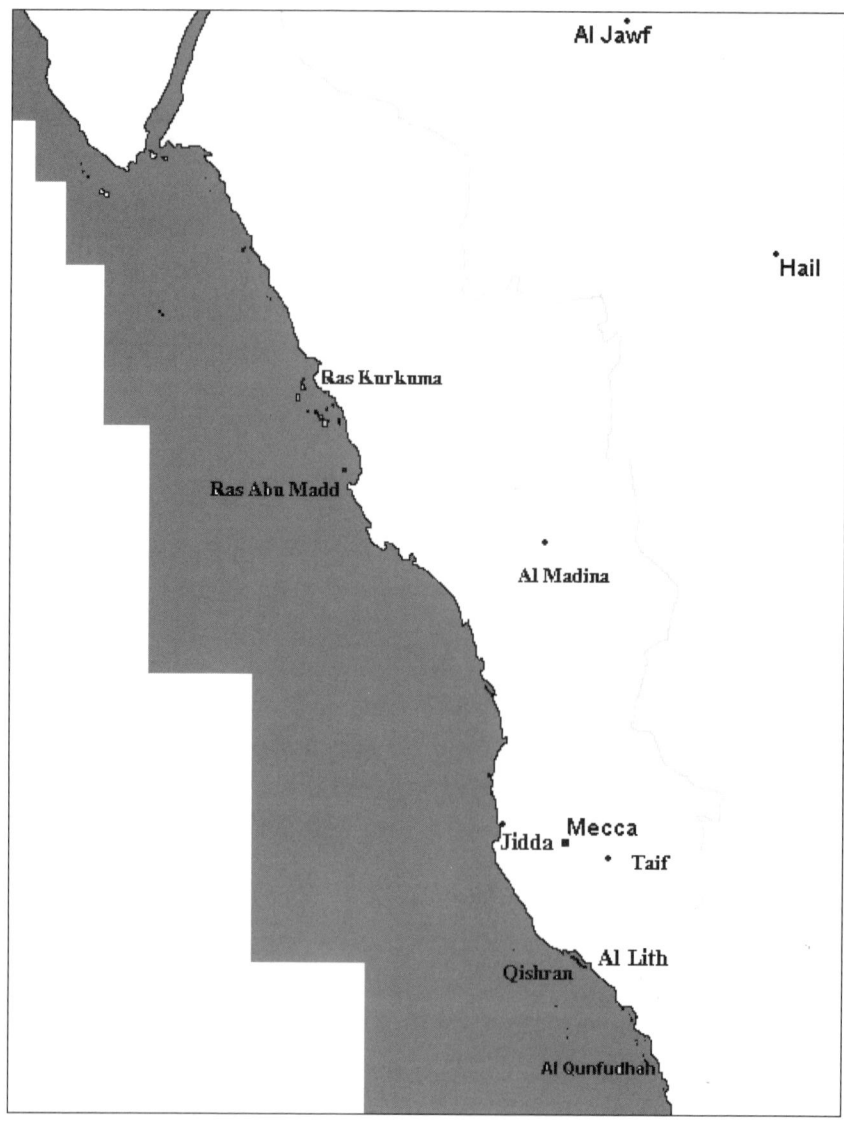

Fig. 3 North-central Western Arabia.

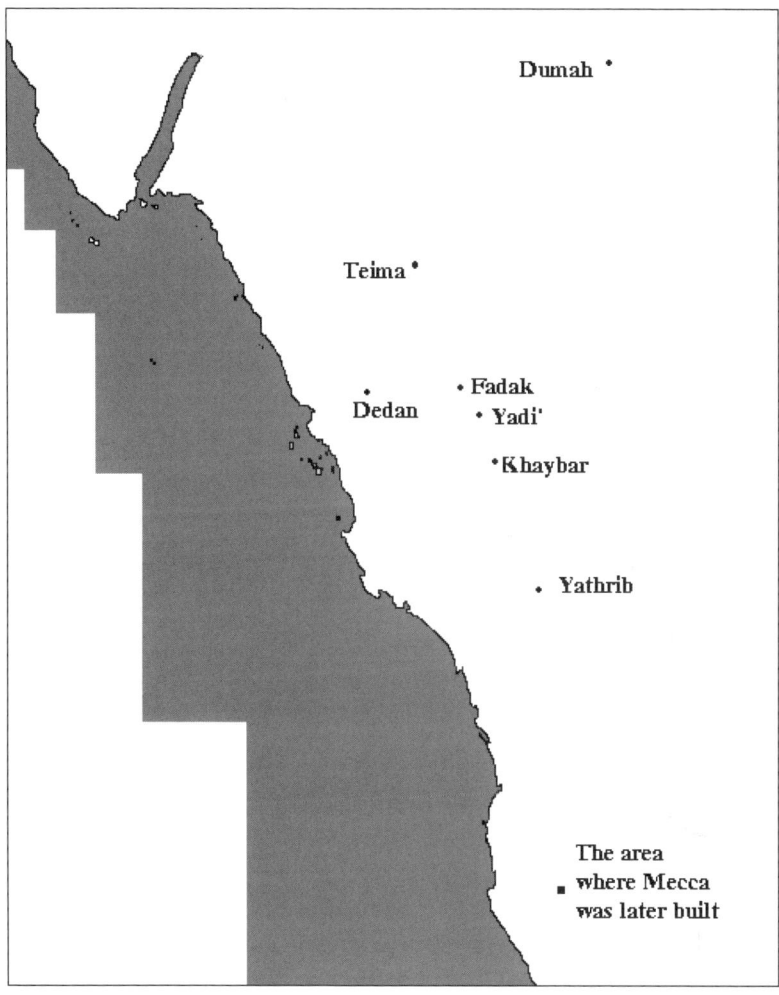

Fig. 4 The cities occupied by Nabonidus, king of
Babylonia, during his 10 years' sojourn in north and central
western Arabia; Mecca is missing in his records.

PART I

The Unreliability of the Qur'an and the Writers of the Islamic Tradition Regarding History

1 _____

AN ANALYSIS OF THE QUR'AN IN THE LIGHT OF DOCUMENTED HISTORY

What is the Documented History?

To begin, we'll address the question, "What is documented history?" History is based on documented narration, which is information provided by historians through what they wrote in books during the times in which they lived.

One example of documented narration is the writings of the Greek historian, Herodotus, who was born in Asia Minor and lived in the 5th century B.C. Cicero considered him the father of history. He wrote a history of the world, especially focusing on the Persian Wars. His work simply titled, *Histories,* covers a period from the middle of the 6th century B.C. to the early part of the 5th century B.C. Ancient historians such as Herodotus not only can be a reliable source for information on the era in which they lived, but their information can be vital to our understanding of the previous century. Other Greek and Roman historians who came after Herodotus also wrote valuable works which can be considered reliable sources of documented history.

Still others who contributed to documenting history are written records or chronicles of kings and nations. The chronicles of the Assyrians, Chaledeans and Persians are especially helpful. The most ancient chronicles come from the Assyrians and date back to the 8th or 7th centuries B.C. These sources would be enough in themselves, but we have more resources for documenting history, including the annals, and the inscriptions on stones and other archaeological findings.

The Bible as a Valid Resource for Ancient History

It is true we have all of these resources to validate ancient history, but the single most reliable resource is the Bible. The books of the Bible were written by various prophets who lived at various times. Moreover, they were inspired by God to ensure accuracy. Most of the inspired writers of the Old Testament lived and wrote before the historians themselves.

The first Biblical writer was Moses who lived in the 15th century B.C. Moses chronicled the nations as they branched and grew from Noah's sons after the flood. Moses' writings make up Genesis, the first book of the Bible. Though in the past, scholars doubted some of the Biblical narrations, today, we have found archaeological discoveries which confirm the historical accuracy of the Bible. Although the Bible covers a period in history where there were no historians, archaeology has increased our knowledge through its excavations in different sites throughout the Middle East. Since archaeology has never contradicted the Biblical narration, the Bible is considered a valuable resource, especially for ancient history.

The Unhistorical and False Chronology of the Narration Found in the Qur'an

On the other hand, Islam does not have a single resource to document its claims. Mohammed wrote in the 7th century A.D., a long time after the documented histories which had preceded him. He never presented a chronology of history like we find in the Bible because he never had one. All he had were stories which he mixed with the personalities he borrowed from the Bible. In some cases, Mohammed inserted these accounts in other time periods hundreds, and sometimes thousands, of years from the time in which those personalities lived.

The Qur'an Placed Haman and the Tower of Mesopotamia in Egypt at the Same Time as Moses

For example, he placed Haman, the prime minister of the Persian king, Ahasuerus, and the tower of Mesopotamia in Egypt, at the same time as Moses. Ahasuerus has been identified by most scholars as Xerxes, who became king in the year 486 B.C., not at the time of Moses who lived in the 15th century B.C. Mohammed claims Pharaoh asked Haman to burn bricks and build a tower so that he could go to heaven and see the God of Moses. Here is Mohammed's account in Surah al- Qasas, 28:38,

> Pharaoh said, "O people, I know no god except me. Therefore, Oh Haman, light me a kiln to bake bricks out of clay and build me a lofty tower, that I may mount up to see the God of Moses because I think Moses is a liar."

Mohammed borrowed this story from Genesis, 11:3, 4. After the flood:

> They said to each other, "Come, let's make bricks and bake them thoroughly." They used brick instead of stone, and tar for mortar. Then they said, "Come, let us build ourselves a city, with a tower that reaches to the heavens, so that we may make a name for ourselves and not be scattered over the face of the whole earth."

We know that the Pharaohs never built towers which were characteristic of the towers of Mesopotamia. The Egyptians didn't use burnt bricks until the Roman occupation of Egypt. They used stones for the pyramids and for their temples. For houses, they used bricks which were dried with the sun's heat.

Mohammed Applied the Name "Samaritan" to the Time of Moses, Even Though the Samaritans did not Appear Before the 6th Century B.C.

One example of a misapplied title is found in Mohammed's narration concerning the golden calf, which the book of Exodus says Aaron made in the wilderness. This occurred when Moses went to the mountain to receive the Ten Commandments. Due to pressure from the Israelites who saw that Moses was delayed for 40 days, Aaron submitted to the Israelites' demands and made the golden calf idol for them to worship. Mohammed reported the event in Surah Ta Ha 20:85-97 when he wrote:

> Allah said, "We have seduced your people in your absence. The Samaritan had led them astray." Moses returned to his people in a state of anger and sorrow. He said to them, "Oh people, did not your lord make a good promise to you? Did the promise seem too long for you, or did you want the wrath to come down on you from the lord, and so you broke your promise to me?"
>
> They said, "We broke not the promise to you, as far as it lay in our power, but we were made to carry the weight of the ornaments of the people, and we threw them into the fire, and that's what the Samaritan threw. Then he brought a lowing calf before them. So they said, "This is your god and the god of Moses."
>
> Then Moses said, "What is the matter with you, O Samaritan?" He replied: "I saw what they saw not, so that I took a handful of dust from the footprint of the Apostle, and threw it into the calf" ... "Go," Moses said to him. "Your punishment in this life will be that you will say, 'Touch me not.' And you will have a day of punishment that will not fail. So look to your God from whom you have gone astray and whom you have worshipped."

When Mohammed attributed these words to the Samaritan, he certainly had Simon, the Samaritan magician in the book of the Acts of the Apostles, in mind. Simon deceived the people of the city of Samaria with his magic and was rebuked by the Apostle Peter. The similarity between the rebuke of Moses to the Samaritan in the Qur'an and the rebuke of Peter to the Samaritan in the book of Acts, indicates Mohammed wanted to use the Samaritan in the book of Acts to place him at the time of Moses, even though there were 1,500 years between the two events.

The city of Samaria was built by Omri, King of Israel, around the year 880 B.C., but the name "Samaritans" was not coined until the 6th century B.C., when it was given to the people whom the Assyrians brought to Samaria after Sargon II occupied the city in year 721 B.C. Mohammed, who was ignorant of the history of the Samaritans, was caught in a major historical mistake.

Mohammed in the Qur'an Confused Mary, the Mother of Jesus, with Mary, the Sister of Aaron and Moses.

Another example of Mohammed's confusion of the historical facts was in the Biblical chronology concerning Mary. Mohammed was misled by the Mandaeans when he considered Mary, the mother of Jesus, to be Mary, the sister of Aaron and Moses mentioned in the Bible. Mary, the mother of Jesus, in Arabic is called Miriam, the same name as the sister of Aaron and Moses as found in Numbers 26:59. In Sura Maryam 19:28, the text addresses Mary, the mother of Jesus, "Oh sister of Aaron, your father was not a man of evil, nor your mother a woman unchaste."

Mohammed intended in this Qur'anic verse to show that Mary, the mother of Jesus, was the same Mary who was the sister of Aaron and Moses. This is confirmed in another Surah in which Mohammed contends that Jochebed, the wife of Amram, who was the father of Aaron and Moses, dedicated Mary, the mother of Jesus, when she was born. This we read in Surah 3 al-I'Imran: 35 and 36:

> Oh my lord I am delivered of a female child. And Allah knew best what she brought forth. In no way is the male like the female. And I have named her Mary.

Mohammed made these statements even though Mary, the sister of Aaron and the daughter of Amram, was born near the end of the 16th century B.C, while Mary, the mother of Jesus, was born between 26-20 B.C.

Mohammed's confusion resulted from the fact that he was misled by the Mandaeans, a sect that appeared for the first time in Mesopotamia in the 2nd century A.D. The Mandaeans were known in Arabia as Sabians. Mohammed was acquainted with their teachings, and sometimes called Sabian by his contemporaries because they saw him practicing many Sabian rituals, such as:

praying five times a day; preceding each prayer with ablution like the Sabian Mandaeans did; adopting the same movements during prayer; and other rituals. The Mandaeans thought that Mary, the mother of Jesus, was a member of the family of Moses and Aaron. In their book, *Haran Gawaita*, dated in the 3rd century A.D, we read about Jesus who, according to their book:

> was placed in the womb of Mary, a daughter of Moses. He was hidden in her womb for nine months. When the nine months were fulfilled, she entered labor and brought forth the Messiah.[1]

Mohammed was called a Sabian by his co-citizens. For example, on his return from one of his campaigns, he was thirsty. His companions asked a woman who carried a water skin to carry water for him. The woman asked, "Where?" They said, "To the prophet of Allah," to which she replied, "To that one who is called a Sabian?" They answered, "Exactly, to the one you call a Sabian." The woman returned to Mecca and said, "Two men whom I encountered brought me to the one called Sabian."[2] We see that Mohammed was recognized by the people of Mecca as a member of the Sabian community. Earlier Islamic literature says that the tribe of Quraish called Mohammed a Sabian, and they called the followers of Mohammed Sabians, as well,[3] demonstrating to us that the Arabians at the time of Mohammed were acquainted with the Sabian sects, including their rituals and teachings. They knew the relationship Mohammed enjoyed with the Sabian sects of Mecca, so when Mohammed came out with new religious claims, it appeared to the Quraish tribe as coming from the Sabians who lived among them.

When Hasin, the father of a Muslim named Umran, became Muslim, the tribe of Quraish said he "Saba,"[4] which means he converted to the doctrines and religion of the Sabians. When Hamzeh, the uncle of Mohammed, entered the mosque to support Mohammed, they said to him, "We see only that you became a Sabian."[5] Abu Lahab, an uncle of Mohammed who disagreed with Mohammed, called Hamzeh "the stupid Sabian."[6] All these historical facts show that the tribe of Quraish classified Muslims as a Sabian sect.

Not only did the tribe of Quraish make this judgment, but other Arabian tribes followed suit as well. A man named Labeid went to visit Mohammed and became a Muslim. He returned to Bani Amer, his tribe, doing ablutions. Ablutions were ceremonial washings like the Sabians performed. He adopted Sabian slogans such as the cry, "Allah Akber," which means, "Allah is greater." Labeid began bowing and kneeling like the Sabians, praying like them and saying the Fatihah. All the rituals of prayer known to the Arabians as Sabian rituals became incorporated into Islam. Sirafa Bin Auf Bin al- Ahwas, the poet of the tribe of Bani Amer, saw Labeid's Sabian rituals and mocked him in a poem in which he described Labeid as "one who came to them with the religion of the Sabians."[7]

Confusion on the Timing of the Tribes of Ad and Thamud.

Another example which shows Mohammed's ignorance of historical chronology is where he placed the Arabian tribes of Ad and Thamud. Ad was a small Arabian tribe which lived in northern Arabia in the 2nd century A.D. Claudius Ptolemy of Alexandria, Egypt, was born in the year 90 A.D. and died in 168 A.D. He wrote his famous book of geography in the first part of the 2nd century A.D. Among the tribes he mentioned in one of his maps was Oaditae, which many identify with Ad. Ptolemy placed Oaditae in the area east of Gulf Aqaba. No other geographer had previously mentioned this tribe, although classical authors like Pliny (who wrote around the years 69-70 A.D.) had mentioned all tribes in the region, yet he did not mention this tribe. Prior to him, Strabo wrote about the same region without mentioning this tribe. Other classical Greek authors, such as Agatharchides of Alexandria who wrote between 145-132 B.C., described the region, but he did not mention this tribe. All this shows that the tribe of Ad was a small tribe which appeared in the 2nd century A.D. It is not known how long it existed there; most probably it was absorbed by greater tribes in the area, such as Thamud.

Mohammed claimed members of this tribe inhabited of the earth in the second generation after Noah. We read in Surah al-A'raf 7, 69:

> Call to your remembrance that he made you inheritors after the people of Noah, and gave you a stature tall among the nations.

And in Sura 23:32:

> Then we raised another generation after them - by which he means after the people who died in the flood at the time of Noah - and we sent a messenger to them from among themselves saying, "Worship Allah."

Mohammed claimed that the tribe of Ad was destroyed by a cloud or wind which Allah brought against it.

The phrase "stature tall among the nations" in Sura 7:69 indicates that Mohammed was influenced by Manichean literature, which claimed that the people who lived on earth at the time of the flood were giants, and very tall in stature. Mani, the founder of Manicheism, wrote a book which he entitled "*The Giants*." We also find this idea in other Gnostic literature embraced by the Manicheans in the 4th century A.D. In I Enoch we read that the angels married the human women "and the women became pregnant and bore great giants, having heights of three thousand cubits"[8] (about 4,500 feet). The idea in the Qur'an of the two angels Harut and Marut who came down to Babel and taught magic to people is taken from the book of *Giant of Mani*.[9] The connection between Mohammed and the Manicheans is affirmed by the fact that many people in the tribe of Quraish, from which Mohammed came, embraced Manicheism. The Manicheans were called Zandik at Mecca.[10]

Mohammed created a dilemma for Muslims by placing the Arabian tribes, Ad and Thamud, in a period connected with that of Noah, that is, 5000-6000 B.C., so they searched for a remedy or a way out from this problem. The first Muslim who proposed a remedy for this contradiction was Ibn Ishak, who died around 774

A.D. (152 years after Mohammed's emigration to Medina).[11] Ibn Ishak changed the genealogies in Genesis to fit the Qur'an's historical mistakes. He added names to the genealogy of Shem, son of Noah; Arabic names of his generation style that were not known as style even in four or five centuries prior to his times. He inserted the name of Ad as son of Uz who is mentioned in Genesis 10:21-24. "as son of Aram, son of Shem, son of Noah."   He then changed the genealogy of Noah, arabizing it.[12]

Ibn Ishak was considered by the educated people of his time as one "who fabricates false genealogies" and as a "liar and deceiver." Since no one before him had mentioned such modified genealogies, his educated Islamic contemporaries considered him to be a false historian. Yet, in the generations which followed, Ibn Ishak's writings became the foundation for a new history which backs the Qur'an. Based on the genealogy that Ibn Ishak invented, Ibn Khaldun (1332-1406 A.D.) claimed that Ad occupied the south of Arabia and part of western Africa. [13] He invented this claim without any precedent from history to draw upon. We find no support for his historical fabrication in any archaeological find or writing. The Muslims found an old tomb in Hadramot among the tombs of southern Arabia, and attributed it to Hud as his tomb, without any evidence to support such a claim prior to the Islamic era.

Muslims today look to Surah 53, verse 50, where it says "he destroyed the ancient Ad," to claim that there were two Ads: the ancient one (which they placed in southern Arabia) and another Ad that appeared in the north in the area of the Gulf of Aqaba. But the Qur'an called Ad "ancient" because Mohammed placed it as second generation after Noah; he did not intend to distinguish it from another more recent Ad.

Muslims also look to Surah 46, verse 21, where it says "mention the brother of Ad who warned his people about the winding sand–tracts;" in Arabic the "winding sand tracts" is Ahqaf. They say the first Ad lived in Al-Ahqaf, which they considered as a place in southern Arabia in the desert of Rub al-Khali at the border of Hadramot. But the Qur'an spoke about Hud as a prophet who, according to the Qur'an, was a prophet to Ad, and who warned Ad of a destruction which would come to Ad through winding sand-tracts. This is what the Qur'an intended by this verse. In verse 24, we find the Qur'an describing the coming of this wind over the tribe of Ad which, according to the Qur'an, destroyed every thing.

The earlier Islamic writers understood the word of Ahqaf not as a place, but as windy sand. Among these writers I mention al-Feiruzabadi.[14]

The Qur'an intended in this ancient Ad a place in northern Arabia and not in the south. The Qur'an intended that this ancient Ad inhabit the same area that Thamud inhabited immediately after Ad's destruction through wind. The Qur'an specified the area where ancient Ad and Thamud lived by describing the area where houses are being hewed in the rock of the mountains, which we know existed only in a certain place in northern Arabia near the city of Hegra. In reality, it was a Nabataean city where some Thamud lived in northwestern Arabia. In Surah 7, called al-A'raf, verse 69, we see that Mohammed spoke of Ad existing one generation after Noah, and he dealt with destroying them. Then, immediately in verses 73 and 74, he began speaking about the tribe of Thamud as coming a generation after Ad and inheriting their land:

> To the Thamud we sent Salih, one of their brothers... Remember how he made you inheritors after the Ad people and gave you habitation in the land; you build for yourselves palaces and castles in the plains and hew homes from the mountains.

It is clear that Mohammed placed this ancient Ad (which he placed after Noah) in the area where houses were hewed in the rocks which, in Surah al-Hijr 15:80, he specified that the area was the city Hegra (known also as Hijr):

> The inhabitants of Hijr have rejected the messengers. We sent them our signs, but they turned away from them. Out of mountains they hewed homes where they were safe. But the cry seized them one morning and gave them no avail.

We know that Hegra is in northwestern Arabia, and was built by the Nabataeans, who alone were known as people who hew their houses in rocks. So we see that Mohammed meant by the "ancient Ad" a tribe who lived before Thamud in the area of Hegra in north-western Arabia, and not a tribe who lived in southern Arabia. He placed such a tribe as second generation after Noah, though we know that Thamud appeared in the 8th century B.C. (as I will discuss in the coming paragraphs). Ad appeared in the same area of Thamud only in the 2nd century A.D.

Muslim writers claim that the "ancient Ad" lived in southern Arabia and disappeared two or three centuries before the Christian era. But there is no tribe or nation who lived in southern Arabia whose history lacks archaeological documentation. Not even one archaeological finding supports this Islamic position. No inscriptions in southern Arabia speak of Ad, though the southern Arabian Inscriptions are the richest in the whole world. Even the smallest nations are richly attested to with hundreds of inscriptions.

Serious Historical Mistakes of Mohammed About the Tribe of Thamud

This brings us to the tribe of Thamud. Mohammed claimed the inhabitants of Hegra, a city built in the 1st century B.C. whose houses were hewn from the rock by the Nabataeans, were Thamudic. Mohammed placed them in the third generation of history after the people of the flood, immediately after Ad and Noah. He also claimed that they would be removed from history through a magical cry. Again, verses 73 and 74 of Surah7 al-A'raf tell us:

> To the Thamud we sent Salih, one of their brothers... Remember how he made you inheritors after the Ad people and gave you habitation in the land; you build for yourselves palaces and castles in the plains and hew homes from the mountains.

Historically, Thamud was an Arabian tribe that did not appear before the 8th century B.C. During the end of that period, they attacked the Assyrian borders with other Arabian tribes, and they were defeated by Sargon II, who brought some of them to live in Samaria.[15]

Mohammed in Surah al-Hijr 15:80 placed them as inhabitants of an Arabian city called Hegra. I quote again the verse:

> The inhabitants of Hijr have rejected the messengers. We sent them our signs, but they turned away from them. Out of mountains they hewed homes where they were safe. But the cry seized them one morning and gave them no avail.

At the time of Mohammed, Hegra was called Hijr. Today the term Hijr is still used for the ruins of Hegra. Hegra is about 24 kilometers from the old city of Dedan.[16] The city of Hegra was hewn from solid rock by the Nabataeans in the 1st century B.C.[17] The Nabataeans were the only ones to practice building this way. The place the Nabataeans occupied was originally a small Lihyanite village. The Lihyanites appeared in the 6th century B.C. Although the city was built by the Nabataeans in the 1st century B.C., Mohammed assigned the city to the third generation after Noah's flood.

Mohammed attributed this city and its construction to the Thamud tribe, even though the Thamud never hewed their houses in rocks as did the Nabataeans, although some Thamuds lived in tents in the city when the tribe flourished after the Christian era began. What happened to the tribe of Thamud? Mohammed claimed that they were judged through a cry, and removed from history, as we see in Sura Hud 11: 67, 68:

> The cry overtook the wrongdoers, and they lay prostrate in their homes before morning. As if they never dwelt and flourished there. Behold, the Thamud were removed.

Yet, we know that Thamud continued to live as an organized tribe until the 5th century A.D.

THE CASE OF THE MIDIANITES

Mohammed placed the Midianites close to the time of Sodom and Gomorrah and eventually removed them completely from history.

The Thamuds were not the only people for whom Mohammed claimed extinction. Mohammed placed the Midianites close to the time of Sodom and Gomorra and eventually removed them completely from history. In Surah Hud 11, verse 89, Mohammed invented the prophet Shuyeb to speak to the Midianites. Shuyeb addresses his people:

> "Oh my people. Let not my dissent with you cause you to suffer a fate similar to what occurred to the people of Noah or of Hud or of Salih nor are the people of Lut far off from you."

Hud and Salih were the names of prophets which Mohammed assigned to the tribes of Ad and Thamud. He dated Midian very close to God's judgment of Lut, only one or two generations from the destruction of Sodom and Gomorra which happened around 2070 B.C. According to Mohammed's chronology, the Midianites would have lived around 2040-2010 B.C.

The Bible tells a different story. The Midianites came from Keturah, whom Abraham married after Sarah died, as reported in Genesis 25:1-6:

> Abraham again took a wife, and her name was Keturah. And she bore him Zimran, Jokshan, Medan, Midian, Ishbak and Shuah. Jokshan begot Sheba and Dedan. The sons of Dedan were Ashurim, Letushim and Leummim, and the sons of Midian were Ephah, Epher, Hanoch, Abidah and Eldaah. All these were the children of Keturah.

It was not until the 18th century B.C. that the descendants of Midian became a nation.

Here's Mohammed's account from Surah Hud 11: 94, 95, where we read about the cry that removed the Midianites from history:

The cry seized the wrongdoers and they lay prostrate in their houses in the morning. As if they had never dwelt and flourished there. Behold, this is how the Midianites were removed just as were the Thamud were removed.

Removing the Midianites from history at a time close to when Lut lived shows how Mohammed simply dealt promptly and quickly with the people of the world by using magical cries. He was completely ignorant of their history. Not only did he display total ignorance about the chronology of the people as to when they appeared in history, but he also completely removed nations from history who lived close to his time. He claimed that they had been exterminated in ancient times.

On the other hand, the Bible tells us a lot about Midian. Moses lived among them 40 years when he was in south Sinai. He married a Midianite woman. Though he had contacts with Jethro, his father-in-law who was a priest of the Midianites, Moses never reported what the Qur'an alleges to be the extermination of the tribe of Midian. Nor did Moses ever mention Shuyeb, the prophet whom Mohammed said was sent to the people of Midian. History tells us that the Midianites continued to exist in the Sinai and north Arabia during the time of the Old Testament, and into the Christian era, as well.

In the Qur'an, Mohammed Claimed a Magical Cry Destroyed the City of Antioch in the 1ˢᵗ Century A.D.

In the Qur'an. the use of a cry to destroy people and to remove them from history was used by Mohammed to exterminate the people of Antioch in the 1ˢᵗ century A.D. We read the text of the Qur'an in Surah Ya Sin, Surah 36, starting from verse 13:

By way of a parable, I set forth the story of the inhabitants of the city. Then the messengers came to it. We sent to them two messengers whom they rejected, but we strengthened those two with a third. They said to the inhabitants, "We have been sent on a mission to you." The people replied, "You are only men like ourselves, and the Rahman sent no sort of revelation. You do nothing but lie." They replied, "Our lord does know that we have been sent on a mission to you, and our duty is only to proclaim the clear message." The people replied, "for us, we conjured an evil omen from you. If you desist not, we will certainly stone you and we will inflict a grievous punishment on you."

The reporters of the Hadith of Mohammed and his biographers confirmed that the city intended by the Qur'an is Antioch in Asia Minor. Al-Khurtubi was among the oldest expositors of the Qur'an who said that Antioch was the city meant by the Qur'anic verse.[18]

The Qur'an text surely demonstrates that Mohammed had in mind Barnabas and Paul, the two apostles who preached and taught in Antioch. Then their testimony in the city was strengthened by the arrival of Silas, which the Qur'anic text expresses clearly by the words "we strengthened them with a third."

The threat of stoning the apostles did not occur in Antioch as the Qur'an portrays, but in another Antioch, the Antioch in Pisidia. Evidently Mohammed failed to accurately remember the early mission to Antioch, and the rest of the missionary trips, as reported in the Book of Acts. We read in the Book of Acts that the Holy Spirit sent Paul and Barnabas on a mission trip where they were joined by Mark. In Antioch of Pisidia, the people wanted to stone them. Evidently Mohammed, thinking that Antioch of Pisidia was the main city Antioch, combined the events of the mission to Antioch with the events of Antioch of Pisidia to form one event which he expressed in one paragraph. He had a habit of reporting great chapters of the Bible in small confused sentences and paragraphs.

Then we read in the same Surah 36, verse 29, that the magic cry which judged and destroyed the inhabitants of Antioch "was just one cry, and behold they were quenched like ashes." The main reporters of the Hadith of Mohammed confirm that the city of Antioch was destroyed with its king and inhabitants because of this cry. One of the reporters was Khutadeh, a main reporter of the Hadith of Mohammed. Another was Abdullah Ibn Abbas,[19] the cousin of Mohammed. His sayings are considered by Muslims to be next to the Qur'an in importance.

The city of Antioch in the Christian era was full of Greek philosophers and geographers, as well as Christian fathers. We have much literature coming from Antioch which relates even secondary things that happened in the city. We have Roman historians who precisely recorded the deeds done in each city in the empire. Although Antioch was the third most important city in the empire after Rome and Alexandria, no one mentioned a magical cry which destroyed the inhabitants, or even part of them. Mohammed, when he applied his habitual cry to destroy and remove nations in ancient times, was unaware that Antioch in Asia Minor was ineligible to receive his claims. This reveals the ignorance of Mohammed's companions who accepted his claims. They were ignorant of the civilized world which was in existence in their time.

The Qur'an displays an inadequate knowledge of historical chronology when it presents unsubstantiated statements, confuses the personalities of the Bible, and adulterates history. Mohammed took advantage of his local environment at Medina where the people were generally deficient in the knowledge of history. Mohammed was able to use the ignorance of his companions who were unable to compare his narrations with the true facts of history. Will Muslims today continue to defend the Qur'an in our generation when the knowledge of documented history reveals the obvious mistakes it makes?

THE HOOPOE, AND SOLOMON AND THE QUEEN OF SABA

A Comparison Between the Biblical Narration of the Visit of the Queen of Saba to Solomon and its Mythological Narration of the Qur'an

We will compare the Qur'anic position about the visit of the Queen of Saba to King Solomon with the Biblical and historical facts about the same visit.

First of all, I'd like to turn your attention to the trading relationship between Saba, called Sheba, in Yemen and the Mediterranean countries such as Israel.

God gave Solomon a great gift of wisdom. So much so, that other rulers heard about his wisdom and came to him bearing gifts. The Queen of Sheba was among them. In I Kings, chapter 10, we read about the visit of the Queen of Sheba to King Solomon. The Bible says:

> Now when the Queen of Sheba heard of the fame of Solomon concerning the name of the Lord, she came to test him with hard questions. She came to Jerusalem with a very great retinue, with camels that bore spices, very much gold, and precious stones, and when she came to Solomon, she spoke with him about all that was in her heart. So Solomon answered all her questions; there was nothing so difficult for the king that he could not explain it to her. Then she gave the king one hundred and twenty talents of gold, spices in great quantity, and precious stones. There never again came such abundance of spices as the Queen of Sheba gave to King Solomon.

When did the Queen of Sheba visit Solomon?

The book of I Kings specifies that King Solomon had completed most of his important accomplishments before the visit of the Queen of Sheba. Among the things he did was the construction of the Temple at Jerusalem, the construction of his palace, and the building of his marine fleet with the help of Hiram, King of the Phoenician city of Tyre. (Solomon later married Hiram's daughter.) Solomon ascended to the throne in the year 971 B.C. Five years later, he began building the Temple, which he finished in seven years. That takes us to around 959 B.C. Then he started building his palace. According to I Kings 7:1, "Solomon took thirteen years to build his own house." The completion of his palace brings us to about 945 B.C. Then he wanted to trade gold with Ophir on the Persian Gulf, so he built a fleet of ships in Ezion Geber near Elath on the Red Sea. We read about this in IKings 9: 26-28, which says:

> King Solomon also built a fleet of ships at Ezion Geber, which is near Elath on the shore of the Red Sea, in the land of Edom. Then Hiram sent his servants with the fleet, seamen who knew the sea, to work with the servants of Solomon. And they went to Ophir and acquired four hundred and twenty talents of gold from there.

According to the Bible, all these accomplishments were made before the Queen of Sheba visited Jerusalem. When we add all the numbers, we conclude that the visit of the Queen of Sheba was between 940 and 935 B.C.

How the Queen of Sheba knew of the wisdom of Solomon.

We could ask ourselves how the Queen of Sheba heard of the wisdom of Solomon. Perhaps Sabaean merchants were already traveling the land route through northern Arabia by the 10th century B.C. If so, the cities on the oases of northern Arabia, such as Teima, Dedan and Qedar, may have been only small villages, which facilitated trade along the land route from Yemen to Israel. This is probably the reason the Queen was convinced to travel by land to Jerusalem rather than by sea. In the previous century, it was impossible to make the trip by land.

I believe that Solomon's name was famous in Saba many years before the visit of the Queen of Sheba because of his ships, built many years before her visit. The fleet traveled across the Red Sea to Ophir on the Persian Gulf and made many stops along the way, many of which were to Sabaean ports, the most important ports on the Red Sea. The Sabaean ports were places where ships traded merchandise and re-supplied themselves with water and food. This made the King of Israel well-known among sailors for his wisdom and the beauty and greatness of his Temple which, along with the Great Wall of China and the pyramids, was already considered one of the greatest marvels of the ancient world. What else, other than the wisdom of Solomon, which impressed Israel and other kings of the earth, would have been the reason for the servants of Solomon, who served in the ships, to speak to the Sabaeans about him?

Many years before Solomon's fleet was constructed, King Hiram, the Phoenician king of Tyre, began sailing his fleet on the Red Sea to the Persian Gulf. Hiram traveled to Ophir, passing through the Sabaean ports. As we saw previously, Hiram traded in the Mediterranean and even provided Solomon, his son-in-law, with gold, special wood and precious stones. Mediterranean nations were connected to the Gulf region, where there were important kingdoms, such as Dilmun (which is present Bahrain) and Magan (which is present Oman). There were also rich ports, such as Jerra, which traded with India and made far-away Asian products available to the Phoenicians. So the main news of kings, like the wise and famous Solomon, was spread to many kingdoms through this international marine trade. This allowed other rulers to learn about the wisdom of Solomon and, consequently, prompted them to try to create friendships with him. We see this in the Biblical narrative of I Kings 4: 31, 34, where it is written:

> For he was wiser than any other man....Men of all nations came to listen to Solomon's wisdom, sent by all the kings of the world who had heard of his wisdom.

All the marine traffic from India to the Persian Gulf passed through the ports of Saba, carrying with it all the news of the Mediterranean, especially news of the famous King Solomon who was given special wisdom from God. He became known in the ports of Saba. So how would the Queen of Saba (Sheba) be the only woman in Saba to not hear about the wise king of Jerusalem? How would she be the only monarch of the earth who did not hear about him? The marine connection between Solomon and Ophir on the Gulf region through Saba leads us to believe that the Queen of Saba was the first monarch of the earth to hear about Solomon's kingdom. Also, this leads us to believe that the kingdom which Solomon was most acquainted with was the kingdom of Saba and her Queen.

The mythological Qur'anic narration regarding the visit of the Queen of Sheba to Solomon, copied from the II Targum of Esther.

You will find this difficult to believe, but the Qur'an claims that King Solomon never heard of the Kingdom of Saba or its famous Queen until a bird, a hoopoe, told him about her. The Qur'an in Surah 27, called al-Naml, or the chapter of ants, gives us a mythological narration of the visit of the Queen of Saba to Solomon. Solomon gathers his army composed of Jinn (meaning devils), men, and birds to fight the ants. Afterward Solomon missed the hoopoe and threatened to execute him. The hoopoe returned to announce the discovery of the Kingdom of Saba and its Queen. Then Solomon sent a message with the hoopoe threatening to wage war if the Queen didn't submit to him. The Queen submitted but before she arrived, the Jinn, under the order of Solomon, brought her throne to Jerusalem in only one second.

This Qur'anic myth is copied with little variation from the mythological Jewish book called the Second Targum of Esther. The bird in the Targum is a wild rooster, while in the Qur'an it is the hoopoe. The Targum uses eagles as carriers to the throne, while the Qur'an uses the Jinn. Other than this, the Qur'anic narration is identical to the Targum.

The Second Targum of Esther was written before Christ and was widespread among Arabian tribes who embraced Judaism. We find this myth in Arabian poems written before Mohammed's time, and in the poems of people claiming to be prophets in Arabia before Mohammed's time. One of these was Umayya bin abi al-Salt, a cousin to Mohammed on his mother's side of the family.[20] Prior to Umayya, Tubb'a, the Yemeni leader who

42

occupied Mecca around the year 425 A.D., spoke about the hoopoe, and Solomon and the Queen of Saba.[21] This is because Tubb'a, when he occupied Yathrib (Medina), took two rabbis from the Jewish communities there and brought them to Yemen. They instructed Tubb'a with many Judaic myths, which he then incorporated into his poems.[22] Among such myths was the myth of the hoopoe which discovered the kingdom of Saba and announced such discovery to Solomon. This proves that the book of II Targum of Esther at the time of Tubb'a (in the first part of the 5th century A.D.) was spread among the Jewish communities of Arabia.

This Qur'anic myth is copied from the II Targum of Esther, with little variation. As I mentioned above, most of the details are identical; for example, the Targum mentioned that the Queen, when arriving at Solomon's palace, thought that the King was sitting in water and she raised her dress. The Qur'an copied this particular incident from the narration of the Targum. I quote first the words of the Targum:

> Now when King Solomon heard that she was coming to him, King Solomon arose and went to sit down in a bathhouse. When the Queen saw that the King was sitting in a bathhouse, she thought to herself, "the king must be sitting in water." So she raised her dress to wade across. Whereupon he noticed the hair on her legs, to which King Solomon responded by saying: "Your beauty is the beauty of women, but your hair is the hair of men." Now hair is beautiful for a man but shameful for a woman.

Mohammed copied the same idea from the Targum. We read in Surah 27, called al-Naml, verse 44:

> She was asked to enter the palace, but when she saw plenty of water she raised her dress uncovering her legs.

NIMROD IN THE QUR'AN

According to Genesis 10:8-11, Nimrod was the first builder of the old cities of Mesopotamia. He was the son of Cush, the son of

Ham, the son of Noah. We can date him to between 5000-4500 B.C. Islamic genealogies correctly state that Nimrod was the son of Cush but incorrectly state that he lived around the time of Abraham.[23]

This false claim about Nimrod was made to conform to a mistake in the Qur'an, which made Nimrod reign at the time of Abraham. The Qur'an says Nimrod persecuted Abraham and cast him into a fire that did not harm him. We read this in Surah al-Anbiya' 21:51-70 and Surah al-Safat 37:95.

Midrash Rabbah, a mythological Jewish book, is the source of the Qur'anic narration about Nimrod and Abraham.

Many Jewish books were widely spread among Arabian tribes who embraced Judaism. At the time of Mohammed, the myth of the Qur'an regarding Abraham and Nimrod was taken from a Jewish book called Midrash Rabbah. The narration of the Qur'an corresponds perfectly to chapter 17 of this Jewish book. A Jewish writer found in the Bible that Nimrod built the oldest Mesopotamian cities, but the writer incorrectly applied a story from the book of Daniel to Abraham. The book of Daniel told of the three Jewish young men who refused to worship a statue of Nebuchadnezzar, King of Babylon, and were cast into a fire that didn't harm them. However, the writer of Midrash Rabbah ignored the fact that 3,000 years separated Abraham from Nimrod.

The confusion of Mohammed regarding the history of Alexander, Nimrod and Solomon.

In his Hadith, Mohammed claims that Nimrod reigned over the entire earth and that Solomon, Nebuchadnezzar and Dhu al-Qarnayn ruled over the entire earth, as well. Dhu al-Qarnayn means the "one with two horns," a title for Alexander the Great, as shown by Aramaic literature. Mohammed stated that two were believers: Solomon and Alexander the Great, and that two were infidels: Nimrod and Nebuchadnezzar.[24]

This assertion is clearly incorrect because not one of these men ruled the whole earth. Alexander the Great did occupy a small part of Europe, in addition to his conquests in the Middle East and parts of Asia. Solomon extended his domain from Israel into parts of Syria and Trans Jordan. Nebuchadnezzar occupied the Fertile Crescent and Egypt. Nimrod's reign was limited to Mesopotamia. So none of them ruled the entire earth.

Mohammed's Hadith is also clearly incorrect in its claims about who were believers and who were infidels. Alexander the Great was known to be a pagan king with a passion for the idols of his conquered cities. In spite of this, Mohammed claimed Alexandar was a Muslim leader who made a holy war, or Jihad, to spread Islam throughout the world. (I will refute in detail this claim of the Qur'an in the next section.) Such myths of the Qur'an about Alexander the Great and Solomon are derived from many Arabian resources, especially from poems recited by men of the time, many of whom claimed to be prophets.

ALEXANDER THE GREAT AND THE MYTHS OF PERSIA

Alexander the Great was known to be a zealot pagan and polytheistic worshipper of idols. But Mohammed claimed Alexander was a servant of Allah who made Jihads, or holy wars, to spread Islam in the ancient world.

In Addition to Mohammed's confusion with historical chronology, he attributed magical judgments to nations and removed them from history, even though these nations continued to exist throughout history until close to his own time. Like the prophets of the Arabian Jinn religion, Mohammed wrote important historical figures into the religion of Islam.

For example, Mohammed claimed Alexander the Great was a Muslim leader who made Jihads to spread the religion of Allah throughout the world. At the time of Mohammed the Qur'an called him "Dhu al- Qarnayn," which means "the one with two horns." This term is used in *The Romance of Alexander*, an Aramaic book which spread among Nastoric Christians before Islam. Old versions of *The Romance of Alexander* were found which carry the title of "Dhu al-Qarnayn."

Alexander the Great was portrayed on the coins of the kingdom with two horns to symbolize the conquests of the West and the East. Alexander was known to be the most polytheistic pagan worshipper in history. He consulted the priests of the Greek gods before any military campaign, and worshipped the idols of each city he conquered. He claimed that he was a god, the son of the Greek god, Zeus. When Alexander heard that Philotas, the commander of the Companion Cavalry, had mocked his claim to be son of Zeus Ammon, Alexander was so angry that he arrested Philotas, put him on trial and condemned him to death. Alexander's claim to be deity was something mentioned by all the classical writers. The historian Agatharchides said:

> Alexander, who was invincible on the battlefield, was completely helpless in his personal relationships. For he was ensnared by praise, and when he called himself the son of Zeus he didn't think he was being mocked, but thought he was being honored for his passion for the impossible and his forgetfulness of nature.[25]

Aristobulus, an eyewitness working as an engineer for Alexander, gives us the reason why Alexander was planning to conquer Arabia. Aristobulus says:

> When Alexander knew the Arabians worshipped two main deities, he took it for granted that they would worship him as a third deity if he conquered them and allowed them to keep their ancestral independence.[26]

Yet, Mohammed still claimed that Alexander was a Muslim devoted to Allah. Mohammed said Alexander's campaigns were Jihads for Allah in order to justify Mohammed's own campaigns against innocent Arabian and Jewish tribes.

Mohammed took a Zoroastrian myth and applied it to Gog and Magog, two Biblical figures. He replaced the mythological Zoroastrian hero of the myth with Alexander the Great.

Mohammed incorporated other well-known myths from the religious sects of his time into the Qur'an by exchanging the names of the main figures with other Biblical and historical people. For example, he copied the Zoroastrian myth about Azi Dahak, a diabolic personality whom the Zoroastrians believed was chained to a mountain in the east by Fredun, another one of their mythological heroes. Zoroastrians believed Azi Dahak would remain there throughout history. At the last day, he would be freed to attack the world.

According to Dinkard, book 7 and chapter 13, later in the Zoroastrian myth, Azi Dahak became responsible for the diabolical inhabitants whom they called Mazendarans.[27] The Khvaniras lived adjacent to the Mazendarans. They complained to Fredun about the Mazendarans, saying they were dangerous.[28] With a magical movement of his nose, Fredun split the land of the Mazendarans by establishing natural barriers between the two parts. They would remain separated until the last day[29] when they would attack the world. The Zoroastrian myth developed further after the Christian era. The Mazendaran demons eventually were called Mazonik demons. Kai-Us, another mythological figure, built metallic structures to hold them until the last day, because they were dangerous to the whole world.[30]

The Persian myths of the 5th and 6th centuries A.D. expressed the way in which kings imprisoned people by building dams or barriers between two mountains. We find, for example, in a myth attributed to Kesrah, the Persian king, that he built a barrier between two mountains where he imprisoned people in his region.[31] This is consistent with the myth about Alexander the Great who, according to the Qur'an, imprisoned Gog and Magog in a metallic dam he built between two mountains.

Mohammed copied the entire Persian myth about the imprisonment of Azi Dahak and his Mazendarans. According to Mohammed, while campaigning in Asia, Alexander encountered people about whom the Qur'an said, "they did not understand any saying." The people complained to Alexander about Gog and Magog, saying they were wicked people who threatened the world. Alexander then built a dam of metal between two mountains and wrapped the dam in molten copper. In this dam he imprisoned Gog and Magog for the rest of history until it will be demolished in the last day, and Gog and Magog will be liberated to attack the world. You can find this teaching in Surah 18, al–Kahf, verse 98. Mohammed copied the same Zoroastrian myth, but he changed the names of Azi Dahak and his diabolic people to Gog and Magog, and he exchanged Fredun for Alexander the Great.

Where did he get the names Gog and Magog? He simply borrowed them from the Old Testament book of Ezekiel where the prophet Ezekiel speaks of Gog and Magog as people who did not exist in his time, nor did they remain throughout history, as the Zoroastrians portrayed the diabolic people of the Mazendarans. Ezekiel refers to Gog and Magog as a "people of the north," which some scholars think of as a modern-day Russia, European country, or a country from the old Soviet Union. According to the Bible, the country from the north will attack Israel when Israel returns to Palestine after it has been dispersed to various countries of the world. We know this prophecy started to be fulfilled in the year 1948 when Israel again became a nation in Palestine. The attacking country, according to the prophecy of Ezekiel, will be accompanied by other countries whose names we recognize like Iran, Libya and Cush, which, in the past, have included Ethiopia and Sudan. The prophecy might indicate that Sudan is the primary country. The attack against Israel will be endorsed mainly by Islamic countries.

However, Mohammed, unable to understand the prophecy of Ezekiel, presented the Zoroastrian myth, instead. Zoroastrians believed that Azi Dahak and his people are fettered to the mountain until the end of time. Mohammed believed the same. Gog was imprisoned by the dam between two mountains, as we are told in the Qur'an, Surah 18:96, but Mohammed put his eschatology to the test when he combined it with Zoroastrian teaching. He placed the dam near the rising of the sun, at a spot on the earth where Mohammed claims that Alexander the Great visited. Obviously, Mohammed did not expect someone to live a great number of years and travel so far to reach the place where mythology placed the sunrise. According to some primitive ideas advanced in Mohammed's time, the sun rises each day from a spring of water, a concept which the Persians used to explain the difference in the length of the days.[32] Mohammed shared this view. [33]

Kes Bin Saideh, the Arabian orator to whom Mohammed listened before he (Mohammed) claimed the role of a prophet, claimed that Alexander lived 2,000 years.[34] Since the Arabians made the diameter of the earth so great that one needs 500 years to reach the extremity of the earth, only Alexander, who lived 2,000 years could go and visit the extremities of the earth and return. Mohammed claimed that he, also, visited the western edge of the earth where the sun, according to the Qur'an, was seen by Alexander setting in a spring of mud. Mohammed could only accomplish his allegation by mounting the Baraq, which was the winged camel on which he also visited the extremity of the East where the sun rises. There, he attested to the imprisonment of Gog and Magog in the metallic dam, and he claimed to hear the noise that the sun made when it rose from one of the springs of water in the East, and when it set in the muddy spring of the West.[35] At the time of Mohammed, Arabians believed that the sun makes a noise when it enters or exits the springs of muddy water.[36]

Mohammed was confident no one would refute him or disbelieve his teachings about the sun, or about Gog and Magog, because no one could live long enough to reach that distant place. But these stories, made up by Mohammed, need not be accepted by blind faith today, since the Qur'an claimed the metallic dam will remain throughout history until the last day. If that's true, the metallic dam should be available for people to see today. Why wouldn't Muslims travel to the far end of the East and easily verify the narration if it is true?

Another important thing to keep in mind concerns the campaigns of Alexander the Great. Many of Alexander's assistants were eyewitnesses who wrote in detail about his campaigns. One witness was Callisthenes, who wrote around the year 330 B.C. Others were: Onesicritus, Alexander's chief helmsman; Nearchus, Alexander's naval commander; and Chares, a chamberlain of Alexander. Nearchus wrote some years after the death of Alexander. These writers were all eyewitnesses. Ptolemy, one of Alexander's four main commanders, and the one who founded the Ptolemy dynasty in Egypt, wrote about the expeditions of Alexander. Another historian who wrote about Alexander's life and military expeditions was Aristobulus, an engineer for Alexander. He was also an eyewitness to the events he wrote about. Many classical writers depended on these eyewitnesses who wrote in detail about the campaigns of Alexander the Great in Asia. No one ever mentioned the legendary metallic dam. If Alexander would have built such a dam, it would have been a significant item mentioned by everyone.

As irrational as the Zoroastrian myth sounds, Mohammed made it more a product of fantasy. Even a child would question imprisoning an inhabitant of a land in a dam built between two mountains. What would keep Gog and Magog from burning an opening in the dam? Could they not climb the two mountains and avoid the dam altogether? Could they not avoid the mountains, go another direction and avoid the legendary imprisonment altogether, which would imprison them throughout history?

THE LEGEND OF THE SEVEN SLEEPERS OF EPHESUS

Mohammed incorporated the Syriac legend of the "Seven Sleepers of Ephesus" into the Qur'an. The legend is about seven Christians who slept in a cave for 150-200 years. This was in the year 250 A.D., at the time of Decius, the Roman emperor who persecuted Christians. Decius, according to the legend, came to Ephesus to persecute Christians. He met with seven young, noble Christians and tried them in court. He then gave them time to consider the gravity of the situation and renounce their faith, but they decided to give what they owned to the poor, except for a few coins which they took with them. They did not deny their faith. They went to a cave in Mount Anchilos to prepare themselves for death. When Decius returned to Ephesus he inquired about them, and his soldiers found them sleeping in the cave. Decius ordered his soldiers to seal the cave with big stones burying them alive.

At the time of the Christian emperor – either Theodosius the Great who lived between 379-395 A.D., or Theodosius the Younger, who lived between 408-450 A.D. – there was a controversy about the resurrection which many heretics denied. When a landowner opened the cave to use it as cattle stall, the sleepers awakened from their sleep and thought they had slept only one night. So the seven sent one of their number to buy food. The one sent by them went with the coins of Decius which they had kept when imprisoned in the cave. He was amazed to see the Cross over the churches and the name of Christ openly on the lips of everyone. The people were astonished to see the young man with the coins of Decius. They assumed he had found a treasure in the cave. The man then revealed the story of their sleep. Emperor Theodosius went to the cave to see the seven men, and used this miracle to confirm that bodies indeed can be resurrected. When the seven men eventually died, the king wanted to make tombs of gold for them, but the men appeared to the king in a dream asking him to bury them in a normal cave.

The story had pagan origins before the Christian era. The Greek philosopher, Aristotle, tells a similar story about sleepers at the city of Sardis,[37] a city in the same region as Ephesus in Asia Minor, or what today is Turkey. Since Aristotle was born in 384 B.C. and died in 322 B.C., the Syriac version depended mainly on the old pagan version but replaced Ephesus with Sardis. Koch, a scholar, demonstrated that there were other old pagan versions of the legend including Indian, Jewish and Chinese versions.[38] Today, the tale is considered a classical myth of wide-spread pagan origin, known in many parts of the world before Christianity.

The legend was Christianized by the Syriacs, probably translated by the Syriacs from the pagan Greeks because the Syriacs were known to have translated the works of Greek philosophers, such as Aristotle. The tale was known among Syriac resources before it was translated into other languages, proving that they had translated it from pagan Greek resources. The tale also appeared in the Homily of Jacob of Saruq, or Sarugh. He was a Monophysite priest, Syrian poet and writer who lived in the city of Edessa, a Syriac city in North Iraq. He studied in the Syriac school Raha. In the year 519 A.D., he became bishop of Batnan and died in 521 A.D. Known to the Arabs as Yakub al- Saruji, Jacob of Sarugh had connections with Najran, a city between Yemen and Mecca. From the 3rd century A.D. until the time of Mohammed, Najran was home to many Christians. At one point, Jacob of Sarugh wrote a letter to the Christians at Najran.[39] We can only conclude that the spread of the legends to Najran, and then later to Mecca, was probably through Syriac sources connected to Jacob of Sarugh and his version of the Seven Sleepers of Ephesus.

The legend grows.

The story remained within a limited circle of oriental Syriacs until it was translated into Latin in the late 6th century A.D. by Gregory of Tours, and it gained legendary status. The legend is found in the 95th chapter of his book, *De Gloria Martyrum*, which means "the Glory of the Martyrs." Gregory says that he heard the legend from "a certain Syrian or Syriac." Gregory recorded the story as legend. The story is a legend because it originated in pagan circles before the Christian era. It was translated from the Greek pagan literature into Syriac, and spread among limited number of Syriacs in north Iraq.

Before Gregory translated it into Latin and popularized it, the legend was never mentioned in Ephesian literature, even though Ephesus was the city where the Syriacs say the story happened. This is an important criteria in refuting its history. Only after the legend was popularized by Gregory, a church was built over the tombs in the city of Ephesus, claiming they were the tombs of the Seven Sleepers of Ephesus. There is not one historical account in all of Ephesian literature to substantiate this legend. On the other hand, if we had such scant evidence on the life of Christ from

Palestine, the land where Jesus lived, then we would have reason to doubt the existence of Jesus. But most of the authors of the New Testament were disciples of Jesus, men who accompanied him and observed His works and teachings. Moreover, we have evidence of the miracles and the death of Jesus from Josephus Flavius, the Hebrew writer who lived in Jerusalem. We also get information from the Talmud. But when it comes to the legend of Ephesus, though the city was full of philosophers and historians during the 4th and the 5th centuries A.D., no one ever mentioned such an event. Neither the Roman records of Theodosius the Great, nor of Theodosius the Younger, say any thing about the legend of the Seven Sleepers of Ephesus, which says that Theodosius met them personally and constructed a tomb for their burial.

Nather, a Relative of Mohammed, Tests Mohammed on Where he Got his Legends

Mohammed copied the legend of the Seven Sleepers of Ephesus, as though it were historical fact. Mohammed included the legend in Surah 18, called al-Kahf, or "the chapter of the cave." Some leaders of Quraish, the tribe from which Mohammed came, got together. Among them was Nather Bin al-Hareth. As a result of suggestions from some of the Jews, Nather Bin al-Hareth sought to expose the ignorance of Mohammed concerning history. They were concerned about his trend to incorporate all the myths he heard into Suras in his Qur'an. This incident was reported by Ibn Hisham.[40]

Nather Bin Hareth was known for exposing the origin of Mohammed's Persian myths. Every time Mohammed recited verses from the Qur'an which were of Persian origin, Nather would stand and recite the same Zoroastrian myths with more accuracy. We read about this in the book of Ibn Hisham. He writes:

> When Mohammed used to sit and recite the Qur'an to the tribe of Quraish, Al-Nather would speak after him and narrate the stories

and myths of Rustam, Isfendyar and the Persian kings. Then, al-Nather would say, "Mohammed's narration is not better than mine. His narration is just ancient myths. He wrote it as I wrote it."[41]

Nather was able to say this because he studied Persian history and mythology in Hira, a city governed by the Lakhmids, an Arabian tribe who were vassals to the Persians.[42]

Included in the questions Nather asked Mohammed was a question about the legend of Ephesus. The Jews and those who were well educated in Mecca knew the story was a myth popularized by Gregory. Thus, expecting that Mohammed would incorporate it as genuine history in the Qur'an, they would use this to prove to others the habit of Mohammed to include myths in the Qur'an and falsely claim them as historical fact. Nather and his companions also posed other questions of basic history to Mohammed. One of the questions concerned Alexander the Great, called Dhu al-Qarnayn, which means "the one with two horns." It was a topic which the average person at the time of Mohammed knew well. Greek Byzantine education was prevalent in the Middle East, especially at Mecca, where the inhabitants were rich traders in continuous contact with the Byzantine Empire in Syria and Palestine. Selecting Alexander, the most known figure of their history, became a test to Mohammed's integrity. It was not a random choice. Nather wanted to challenge Mohammed's ignorance concerning basic elements of history. He wanted to confirm the way in which Mohammed dealt with elements of history. Either Mohammed condemned ancient historical figures through magical ways such as a cry, or he made them devoted Muslims who embraced his myths. He did so after he consulted the primitive resources which provided him with the mythological narrations. We have seen, in part, how Mohammed answered the question about Alexander the Great. It only confirmed the idea which the Jews and the educated citizens of Mecca had about him and his claims.

Our Muslim friends must learn to evaluate Mohammed, not on sentimental religious claims which imprison their minds and mislead their intellects, but on historical facts. The test put to him by Nather and his companions revealed Mohammed to be one who accumulated myths from primitive sources to appear as though he had all knowledge because, according to his claim, he was sent by Allah.

The Qur'an lacks spiritual understanding. When he failed the test, Mohammed proved that he was unable to respond to the simplest spiritual questions.

The third question posed to Mohammed was, "What is the spirit?" This is a simple question every Jewish or Christian man should answer immediately by quoting the Bible. God created man with a body, soul and spirit. The spirit is the human entity which communicates with God and enables man to worship God.

The Jews composed the third question when they noticed that the verses from the Qur'an quoted by Mohammed lacked spirituality, and focused on earthly things. For example, Mohammed claimed an unusual sexual relationship with all women, including the wives of his followers. The Qur'an claims he had the prerogative to marry anyone, and each Muslem female was to offer herself to him. This is the 50th verse in Surah 33, called al-Ahzab. It reads:

> Oh prophet, we made it lawful to you to take the wives for which you have paid their dowry. What your hand possesses from the prisoners of war that Allah gave you, and the daughters of your uncles and the daughters of your aunts, and the daughters of your maternal uncles and aunts, those who migrated with you, and any believing woman that gives herself to the prophet, if he wants to wed her, are yours. These privileges are only for you and not for the believers at large, we know what we have appointed for them as to their wives and the females whom they captured in the wars. We established this so no embarrassment would come you.

The Arabic word used for "wed" in this verse is "Nakaha," derived from "Nikah." Aisheh, the youngest wife of Mohammed, explained that, among the applications of Nikah, was that a woman must offer herself for a limited period of time, perhaps several months, to a man for sexual enjoyment.[43] We can only assume from this verse that Mohammed had special sexual prerogatives. As a result, many women left their husbands to offer themselves to Mohammed.

A considerable part of the Qur'an revolves around Mohammed's campaigns and those of his followers who must respond to Mohammed's call for Jihad. The distribution of the spoils allowed for him to have a fifth of everything. The Jews, seeing the lack of spirituality in Mohammed's sayings, wanted to reveal his inability to answer when asked the simple question, "What is the spirit?" Mohammed did not answer questions about the spirit immediately, but he promised to answer them the following day. Mohammed did not show up for two weeks. Evidently he went to look for help. He returned, claiming Allah inspired him. Surah 17, called Isra', verse 85 says, "When they ask you about the spirit, tell them, 'the spirit is the affair of Allah.'" Mohammed did not enter into discussion. He was completely ignorant about the argument, showing that he lacked a spiritual education and was unable to express an opinion.

Concerning the question of Alexander the Great, Mohammed returned with mythological ideas expressing thoughts embraced by some superstitious Arabians of his time. Alexander became a legendary person, visiting the ends of the earth and confirming Yemeni myths that the sun sets in a spring of mud. They expressed the idea espoused by some Persians who identified Alexander with their mythological hero, Fredun, who imprisoned Azi Dahak, another mythological character, and his diabolical followers until the last days. Azi Dahak, according to Zoroastrians, was descended from Ahriman, who was the devil in their sacred books.

Mohammed's misinformed understanding of the Legend of the Seven Sleepers of Ephesus.

When questioned concerning the seven young people who slept for centuries, Mohammed naturally turned to his Christian-Byzantine friends, among whom was Jaber. We read in Ibn

Hisham, the book which contains the most significant narration on the life of Mohammed:

> The prophet of Allah very often sat with a Christian named Jaber. Jaber was a slave to the children of al-Khathrami. The people of Mecca often said, "Many things that Mohammed teaches, were taught to him by Jaber, the Christian slave to the children of al-Khathrami."[44]

This accusation by the Meccans to Mohammed was not without foundation. Why would Mohammed sit with a poor slave almost every day? Another thing to consider is that Mohammed despised slaves. He said that a slave can't testify in a court unless he is beaten.[45] If one of his followers wanted to free a slave, Mohammed objected, insisting that his follower sell the slave instead of freeing him.[46] But here is a Christian slave who never became Muslim, yet Mohammed took the time to go to him every day. Mohammed came to Jaber. It was not Jaber who came to Mohammed. This reveals Jaber's importance as a source of information (for Mohammed) on the Bible, Christian doctrine, and the Christianized myths of the Byzantine period. Arabic sources speak of Jaber as a "Roman." The term was used in Arabia for the citizen of the Byzantine Empire. They also say that Jaber gathered books. Old narrations mentioned the family of al-Khathrami had two slaves, Jaber and Yasar, and when they read the Bible, Mohammed would pass by them and listen to their readings.

Another contact for Mohammed was "Balaam," also called "Yaish," or "Addass."[47] Balaam was a Byzantine Christian who was a slave to Huitab Bin Abed al-Uzei. The people of Mecca often saw Mohammed when he met with Balaam, and they said Balaam used to teach Mohammed.[48] But it seems Jaber and Balaam were superstitious men, not like the Christian-educated people in their time who distinguished between legends and historical facts.

The Qur'an's version of the Legend of the Seven Sleepers shows that Mohammed failed to understand the legend and its purpose.

In the Qur'an, Surah 18, al-Kahf, or the Cave, we find Mohammed's answer about the sleepers. He presented the legend as historical fact, yet his variations reflected his lack of understanding and the unreliability of his legendry sources. In verse 17, Mohammed said:

> You would have seen the sun when it rose to the right from the cave, but when it set, it turned away from them toward the left while they were in the open space of the cave.

This verse says the sun entered the cave, but avoided them. It may be a variation of the legend, indicating that no one could have seen the sleepers during the centuries they slept because the sun had avoided them. This contradicts the original legend which said that the cave was sealed with stones, in a way that neither the sun could penetrate the cave nor could any one see the sleepers.

In verse 18, we read another development in the legend which only a primitive environment like Arabia at the time of Mohammed could support:

> Their dog stretched his two forelegs on the threshold of the cave. If you had visited them (the Sleepers) and looked, you would have fled from them, filled with terror.

The Qur'an, through the dog, protected the sleepers during those hundreds of years. According to Mohammed's account, anyone who came toward the cave was filled with terror and fled, because a fierce dog guarded the entrance.

Mohammed picked up on the original legend, which said that after these young people arose from their sleep, they sent one of them with money to buy food for them, thinking that they had slept only one day. The Qur'an tells us that the people knew about the case of the seven sleepers, but they prevailed against them, and decided to construct a mosque over them to prevent them from coming out from the cave. According to the legend, Mohammed thought that the sleepers arose when the inhabitants of the city and the authorities were angry at the sleepers, to the point they prevailed over them and constructed the place of worship over them to assure that they would be imprisoned in the cave. This shows us that Mohammed failed to understand the Christian purpose of the legend, which was to show how these seven sleepers were protected when the Roman Empire was persecuting Christians, and arose during a time when the empire espoused Christianity. According to the original legend, the seven were considered saints.

When the Byzantine Church found tombs in the city of Ephesus, they wanted to use the legend to convince atheists of the resurrection, and to profit by making it a popular sacred place. So, they built a church over the tombs. But Mohammed thought the church was built by people who wanted to prevent the legendary sleepers from coming out from the cave.

Mohammed knew his sources about the legend were inferior to the knowledge of those who presented the test to him, so he advanced the argument that Allah prohibited him from discussing the legend.

Mohammed could not come up with a definite number of sleepers in the Ephesian legend. There are two versions of the original legend. One presents seven sleepers and the other, eight. But, among Mohammed's various friends, it seems there were many thoughts about the number of sleepers, which discouraged Mohammed from presenting a specific number for the fear he would be ridiculed by those who tested him. In this case, Mohammed withdrew his claim to present information as coming from Allah, as he always did in the past. Instead, he said Allah ordered him not to discuss the number. In verse 22, he says:

> They will say there were three sleepers, the dog being the fourth. They say there were five, the dog being the sixth. Guessing at the unknown, they say there were seven, and their dog is eight. You should say, "My lord knows best their number." Those who know

their number are few. Therefore, do not enter into controversies concerning them, except on a matter that is clear, nor consult any one regarding the sleepers.

We ask ourselves: if only a few people, according to the verse, knew the exact number, why was not Mohammed one of them? If he is in contact with God who knows everything, why was not Mohammed among those few who knew the number? We can only conclude that Mohammed was afraid to come with a definite number because he knew the ones who presented the test were more knowledgeable than he was about the legend, and he discovered his sources could not provide a definite number. Thus, he claimed Allah prohibited him from discussing the case.

Mohammed made the sleepers wake up more than 300 years after the authors who Christianized the myth and spread it had died.

Also, in verse 25 of the same Surah (18), we read, "They stayed in their cave 300 years. These years increased by nine." By this reasoning, the sleepers awoke around the year 559 A.D., when the earlier Syriac translators of the legend from the Greek language were all dead. Even Jacob of Sarugh, who included this legend in his writings, was dead. He died in the year 521 A.D.

Mohammed felt free to establish dates, thinking that no one had the right to refute him. He included myths and legends in the Qur'an which were spread in his generation, without considering the dates when they were actually spread. Then, he defended the years of sleep he established for them by saying in verse 26, "Say, 'Allah knows best how long they stayed. Allah has the secrets of heavens and earth.'" By this he claimed 309 years as the period they slept as indisputable, because Allah had inspired it. But how did the claim of Mohammed fit into reality? First, the whole tale is well known as legend, or myth. Second, the Christianized legend was well known in Syriac literature for more than a century before the date established by Mohammed.

Mohammed with his enormous historical mistakes can't be a reliable source for ancient history. Neither can we trust the Islamic writers who came after Mohammed and invented stories without any support of written documentation.

The summary which I have presented concerning the historical mistakes of the Qur'an confirms Mohammed's lack of education regarding official history. Muslims can't depend on his assertions to establish truth. Since what Mohammed said about historical figures and nations is incorrect, it cannot be backed up by the official documented history. Because of its primitive mythological character, how can Mohammed expect us to believe that Mecca was an ancient city, and that its temple was built by Abraham and Ishmael? How can we trust his claim that Abraham and Ishmael built its temple, and that Ishmael lived there with his progeny?

We know that no source in history confirms what Mohammed claimed about Mecca, Abraham and Ishmael. On the other hand, we also know that official documented history shows the contrary to Mohammed's claim. If we can't trust Mohammed to tell us the truth about the issues we have been discussing, how can we trust him to tell us the truth about anything?

2

THOSE WHO REWROTE HISTORY FOR MUSLIMS

Mohammed said in Surah 2, called al-Baqarah, verse 127, that Abraham and Ishmael built the temple. His claim is backed up by the writers of so-called "Islamic tradition." But such tradition was born many years after Mohammed died. The Islamic tradition writers never quoted a written document earlier than Mohammed, nor did they quote any document before Islam which supports their claims. They simply created their stories as one creates fiction. To make matters worse, the writers who came after them depended on what Islamic tradition writers wrote, and considered their writings to be true. This shows us that the writers who depended on the first writers (who invented the stories) did not find any historical document on which to support their claims, so they adopted the inventors' stories as if they were well-documented history, and they added their own stories to them. Eventually, a huge false tradition was formed.

The Inventors of the "Islamic Tradition" Were Also Ignorant of Basic History

The development of the Qur'an goes beyond ignorance of historical fact. It involves deception by the first fathers of the Islamic tradition. Educated people don't consider their writings valid, since their stories were born in the generations in which they were written, and there is no written document in history which supports their claims. Unless a person is writing pure fiction, it is clear that he has no right today to insert a story into events that happened 3,000 years ago and claim he is writing truth. Yet the fathers of Islamic tradition wrote stories which they created in the 7th and 8th centuries A.D., and inserted them into events that happened in the time of Abraham, which was about 2,900 years earlier.

IBN ISHAK

Ibn Ishak and his Prevaricated History and Ignorance of Basic Historical Fact

Ibn Ishak was the first person to assign names to the tribes living in Mecca and create a history for Quraish, the tribe of Mohammed. Yet, Ibn Ishak was born in Medina around 725 A.D., 85 years after Mohammed immigrated there. Ibn Ishak died 150-153 years after the emigration of Mohammed to Medina.

Ibn Ishak, and others who depended on his writings, thought this was the only way to authenticate the narration contained in the Qur'an. In order to contradict documented history and the events of the Bible, he wrote a new history which respected the Qur'an's narration. He tried to tell the world he was writing truth, when he was actually writing creative fiction. He didn't fool the Muslim scholars of his time. They knew he was a fake, writing a fabricated history. They said he was writing without the support of prior historians and geographers. He was accused by his contemporaries of fraud, deception, forgery and creating false genealogies. It was common knowledge that Ibn Ishak was a womanizer which led to the Caliph criticizing and scourging him for his immorality. [49]

It's a matter of credibility too important to let stand without exposing its true nature. Muslims today are trusting their lives and their destinies to these claims. They must not trust their eternal destiny to literature born in the 7th and 8th centuries A.D. which presents primitive and mythological stories as documented history.

The unreliability of Ibn Ishak's writings and the other main Islamic writers who endeavored to back his unhistorical claims concerning Mohammed.

The so-called "fathers of Islamic tradition" rewrote history, separating Muslims from documented truth and keeping them from reading the Bible.

As I mentioned previously, Ibn Ishak is accepted today as the chief biographer of Mohammed and of Islam, the religion he founded. The writer of Halabieh, a book that narrates the life of Mohammed, reports that Ibn Ishak recorded some of Mohammed's Hadiths without anyone previously telling him what was contained in those Hadiths. This means that Ibn Ishak invented the Hadiths and reported them as fact. The writer of Halabieh tells us that respected Islamic scholars, such as Ibn al-Madani and Ibn Main, said that Ibn Ishak was not trustworthy, and Malek Bin Uns accused him of lying and forgery. Malek said:

> Ibn Ishak is one of the most dishonest frauds. Therefore, we expelled him from Medina, the city of Ibn Ishak.[50]

Other Islamic scholars have also commented on Ibn Ishak. The modern commentator on Ibn Hisham wrote:

> We find trustworthy reporters of the Hadith, such as Malek Bin Uns and Hisham Bin Urua Bin al-Zubeir, all of whom eliminated Ibn Ishak from the list of the trustworthy reporters of the Hadith. They never hesitated to accuse him of lying, forgery, knavery, depending upon untrustworthy reporters, inventing poetry which he inserted in his book, and creating false genealogies.[51]

It is interesting to note that, among the accusations against Ibn Ishak which were made by the major reporters of the Hadith, there is a concern about the poetry he wrote and introduced into his book. He wrote poetry in the Arabic language of his time, but he attributed it to the 21st century B.C., at a time when there was no Arabic language at all. The Arabic language began in the 10th century B.C. The Arabic before the rise of Christianity was totally different from the Arabic of the Qur'an, which was the language spoken by Quraish, the tribe from which Mohammed came. This Arabic developed after their emigration from Yemen to Mecca a few centuries into the Christian era.

Another accusation against Ibn Ishak, as we saw, was creating false genealogies. These very genealogies became the official genealogies which Muslims follow today. They state that Mohammed descended from Ishmael. This claim is unsubstantiated outside their writings. Mohammed, himself, refused to allow his own genealogy to go back prior to his 21st ancestor, certainly not back to Ishmael.

The commentators on the biography of Mohammed quote Muslim scholars commenting on Ibn Ishak. "Meki Bin Ibrahim abandoned the Hadith reported by Ibn Ishak and never returned to it. Yazid Bin Haroon reports that Ibn Ishak spoke to the people of Medina about a certain tribe, but Medina's citizens opposed his sayings. Evidently, they knew about the tribe better than did Ibn Ishak, and they detected his forgery. Ibn Numeir said that Ibn Ishak narrates false claims about unknown people."[52] Ibin Numeir criticized Ibn Ishak for making false claims and making up stories about people that didn't exist. Ibn Ishak gave details about Biblical people which the Bible never gave. For example, Ibn Ishak invented stories about those people, such as whom they married. He created Arabic names for them taken from names common in Ibn Ishak's own time and gave them Arabic wives, even though the people lived in Palestine.

One of the most serious things which Ibn Ishak did was to create stories and give details to support the false claims of the Qur'an. One example of this perversion concerns the flood. The Qur'an states that God sent a flood to Egypt as one of the plagues against Pharaoh. Ibn Ishak said the flood covered all of Egypt, and he gave details about it as though the Qur'anic claim were true.[53] We know that the words of Mohammed about the alleged flood are historically false. Egypt never had a flood–not during the reign of any of the pharaohs, nor at any time in history since the flood of Noah.

Ibn Ishak also had much to say about the origin of nations. For example, Ibn Ishak tells us where the Romans came from. From the Bible he found that Esau, the son of Isaac, son of Abraham, married Basmath, a daughter of Ishmael. But he also said Basmath begot Rum who became, according to him, the father of all Romans.[54] Ibn Ishak created genealogies for many Biblical people, giving Arabic names to them and their ancestors. He created Arabic names for the daughters of Adam.[55] No one besides Ibn Ishak ever named a daughter of Adam. By so doing, Ibn Ishak made himself a pillar of inspiration more important than Moses, who was inspired to write the book of Genesis and record the names of the sons of Adam and their progeny. Ibn Ishak created stories for the offspring of both Adam and Noah. His genealogies connected Arabic tribes with Noah and with his son, Shem. One of these tribes was Thamud. He claimed that Thamud was the third generation after Shem.[56] He did this to support Mohammed's claim in the Qur'an that Thamud was the third generation after Noah, but the tribe Thamud did not appear until the 8th century B.C. Ibn Ishak created genealogies for other figures, some of which were mentioned in the New Testament. Among them, he gave Arabic names to the ancestors of John the Baptist. Just to make him a Muslim, John became the son of Adi, son of Muslim, son of Saduk.[57]

Ibn Ishak was the person who originated the idea that Abraham mounted the Baraq, or winged camel, to travel between Damascus to Mecca every time he wanted to visit Ishmael,[58] whom Mohammed claimed built the temple of Mecca and lived there. We know this is a Persian myth built on the book of Dinkard. Kai-Khusrois, mythological prophet, transformed Vae, the god of the air, into the shape of a camel. Then, Kai-Khusrois mounted the camel and went where the immortal mythological Persians were dwelling.[59] Ibn Ishak skipped the distance between Palestine and Mecca on this Persian mythological camel.

Ibn Ishak said that the son whom Abraham placed on the altar as a sacrifice was Ishmael,[60] rather than Isaac, although the Islamic narrators before him said it was Isaac.[61] It's ironic that Ibn

Ishak's idea was accepted by the Islamic world in which Ishmael became more prominent than Isaac.

Ibn Ishak claims that a people descended from Shem were transformed into guenons [62] (small monkeys with long tails) to justify the Qur'an's claim the Israelite inhabitants of Ilat on the Gulf of Aqaba were transformed into monkeys. This also supports Mohammed's Hadith which says that one tribe of the twelve tribes of Israel was transformed into mice.[63]

Ibn Ishak, depending upon Wahab Ben Munabbih, says that in Antioch there was a pharaoh named Antikos, son of Antikos, son of Antikos. This pharaoh practiced the worship of idols. Ibn Ishak claims that Allah had sent three missionaries to Antioch and to the pharaoh; their names were S'adik, S'aduk and Shalum. At first, Allah had sent two missionaries, but the inhabitants of Antioch did not believe in them, so Allah strengthened the testimony by sending the third missionary. These three missionaries were supposedly disciples of Christ. When Pharaoh and the people of Antioch decided to kill the missionaries, Allah is said to have intervened and exterminated Pharaoh and all the inhabitants of Antioch; no one survived.

These narrations of the fathers of Islamic tradition are claimed to be strengthened by the testimonies of others, such as Khutadeh and Abdullah Ibn Abbas, [64] both of whom were major contributors to the story and to the Hadith of Mohammed. Ibn Abbas was also the cousin of Mohammed. These narrations attempt to justify and prove the myth of Mohammed. Actually, these narrations demonstrate incoherence of the claims of the founders of the Islamic tradition and how these claims contradict true documented history. These narrations also illustrate the naiveté of the people who listened to these claims and believed them.

The line of pharaohs disappeared many centuries before the Christian era. The city of Antioch was built around the year 300 B.C. by Selecus Nicator, one of the four leaders who succeeded Alexander the Great. Therefore, the pharaohs disappeared centuries before the city of Antioch was built. Moreover, the pharaohs' capital and primary residence was in Egypt, not on the border between north Syria and Asia Minor where Antioch is located. The name given for the pharaoh whom the fathers of the Islamic tradition assigned as king of Antioch was: "Antioch, son of Antioch, son of Antioch." This is actually a series of titles of kings of the royal family of the Greek Selecus dynasty, which controlled Syria after Alexander died.

This demonstrates the ignorance of the fathers of the Islamic tradition with respect to true documented history. They were extremely uninformed when they attempted to rewrite history to support the myths of the Qur'an. They mixed ancient times with more recent times. They misplaced the pharaohs – very important historical figures – in countries or cities which were not known at the time of the pharaohs. Such inconsistencies would be readily apparent to many of their contemporaries, such as students of history in other contemporary civilized countries. Yet, Muslims today still refer to the Islamic tradition, and its fathers and founders, as reliable resources for history, and as a fundamental "proof" in confirming the unhistorical claims of the Qur'an.

Besides Ibn Ishak, Other Narrators of Islamic Tradition Also Rewrote Islamic History

Ibn Ishak can't be trusted when he writes about ancient history. He never based his claims on historical proof or historical documents. he invented most of the narration. Although he quoted some narrators who related some stories before his time, those upon whom Ibn Ishak depended were Muslims who lived years after Mohammed died. They cannot be reliable sources for ancient history. How can Muslims build their history on his claims? Those upon whom Ibn Ishak depended were ignorant of basic history. In rewriting history for Muslims, Ibn Ishak, and others who came after him or preceded him by one or two generations, rewrote history to accommodate what Mohammed had written. I will briefly discuss and comment on some of the inventors of the so-called "Islamic History."

AL-SHAABI

Al-Shaabi, a major source for Ibn Ishak, confessed that the tribe of Quraish began recording history only after the year of the elephant, which was 570 A.D., and he advised his readers to turn to Jewish history for the facts.

Ibn Ishak often mentioned things he heard al-Shaabi say. Sometimes, Ibn Ishak asked questions to al-Shaabi,[65] yet al-Shaabi said:

> Muslim history must be viewed according to the Jewish history–meaning as it appeared in the Old Testament–Muslims never recorded history before Mohammed's emigration to al-Medina. They never recorded anything before that. Quraish didn't begin recording history until the year of the elephant.[66]

The year of the elephant is defined as the year when Abraha, the Ethiopian, occupied Mecca, using the elephant to gain victory. This occured sometime around 570 A.D., the same year Mohammed was born. Look at all the evidence. First, al-Shaabi, Ibn Ishak's main source for his history, confessed that Muslims should follow the history of the Jews. Second, Muslims didn't begin dating and writing history until after around 622 A.D., when Mohammed emigrated to the Medina. Third, the tribe of Quraish, which lived in Mecca, didn't write their history until 570 A.D., the year of the elephant. Then, what is the significance of Islamic writers trying to date history at all? What right do Ibn Ishak and others have to compose a history for Mecca showing dates 2,600 years before the year of the elephant?

To justify their accounts, Muslims claim the Bible is corrupt; that's why it doesn't agree with the accounts of Islam. Yet, when we compare the reliability of the Bible to that of the Qur'an, we see a great difference. There are copies of portions of the Bible that go back as far as the 2nd century B.C., such as the manuscripts of the Dead Sea Scrolls, found in a cave at Qumran, near Jericho. Scholars think these portions of the Bible originated many centuries ago. The Old Testament of the Bible was translated from the Hebrew language into Greek by Ptolemy II Philadelphus, King of Egypt, in 287 B.C. Ptolemy II established a library in Alexandria which he enriched by adding the Bible to it. Ptolemy invited 70 Jewish scholars to Alexandria to translate the Bible into the Greek language, which became known as the Septuagint. Many ancient copies of the Septuagint still exist. Even Jesus and the apostles quoted from it. In addition, many translations of the Bible were done at various times and in various languages. So many are in existence today that there is little doubt concerning its accuracy.

Even al-Shaabi, one of Ibn Ishak's most important sources, and other Muslim writers of his time, said it was time to return to the "Jewish history" of the Bible, and that any research in religious things must be according to that history. We can only conclude that we should not give credence to what has been written about the history of Quraish and Mecca before 570 A.D., the year of the elephant. Nor can we rely on Islamic writings before the emigration of Mohammed in 622 A.D.

AL-SUDI'

Al-Sudi' was an inventor of stories to justify sin.

Another creator of Islamic history was al-Sudi'. Like many Islamic narrators, al-Sudi' attempted to justify Mohammed in what he did. For example, al-Sudi' made up a story which said the wind lifted up the garment worn by the daughter of Jethro, the priest of Midian, while she accompanied him to her father's house.[67]

Al-Sudi got the idea for his account from an incident in the life of Mohammed. When Mohammed visited his adopted son, Zayd Bin Harithah, who was called Zayd Bin Mohammed or "the son of Mohammed," Zayd was not in his house when Zainab, Zayd's wife, opened the door for Mohammed. The wind lifted up her clothing before Mohammed and, as a result, Mohammed desired her and expressed this openly to her. When Zayd returned back home, his wife told him about Mohammed's desire for her. Zayd, knowing that every female whom Mohammed desires should be given to him, went to Mohammed and told him that he would leave his wife for Mohammed's sake.[68] The next day Mohammed brought a verse from the Qur'an, the 37th verse of Sura 33, called al-Ahzab, which claimed that Allah gave Zayd's wife to him. He also authorized Muslims to marry their daughters-in-law if their adopted sons leave their wives. All this, to justify his desire to marry his daughter-in-law. Verses Mohammed read also attacked the practice of adoption. He called on the Muslims to renounce adoption and to call those who were adopted by the names of their biological fathers, not by the names of those who adopted them (Surah 33: 5).

As I mentioned, Zayd was his adopted son. When Zayd was a child, his Syrian father came to beg Mohammed to return his son whom Khadijah, the first wife of Mohammed, had bought as a child to be a slave, then adopted him. When Mohammed refused to return the son to his father, his father wrote a sad poem in which he described his continuous grief for his son.[69]

Al-Sudi' intended to make the story of Mohammed and Zayd's wife, Zainab, less embarrassing by intimating that this(the wind lifting the garment of the woman) had happened to people other then Mohammed. Al-Sudi' claimed that the wind had also lifted the garment of the woman whom Moses married. Where did al-Sudi' obtain this story? It is not recorded in any Judaic literature, nor anywhere else, for that matter. To try to minimize the sin of Mohammed by fabricating a story and attributing it to Moses can fool only the naive.

In another instance, al-Sudi' claimed that Balaam, son of Beor, was an Israelite.[70] The Bible states that Balaam was not an Israelite, but was from "the sons of the East." Al-Sudi also claims that Balaam's donkey said to him, "You have sex with me at night and ride me during the day."[71] The Bible does not mention such a thing.

Many narrations written by the fathers of Islamic tradition are like this. They add ridiculous stories, taking advantage of people who fail to understand or ignore the Bible. How can Muslims continue to depend on these stories when they seek to establish the truth?

WAHAB BIN MUNABBIH

Wahab Bin Munabbih, one of the main authors who rewrote history for the Muslims.

Wahab Bin Munabbih, a Yemeni of Persian origin who embraced Islam, is another writer among the major authors of Muslim history. Ibn Ishak often quoted him. Wahab wrote about the campaigns of Mohammed. He died 114 years after Mohammed emigrated to Medina,[72] and Ibn Ishak died about 40 years after Wahab.

Just as Ibn Ishak had done, Wahab created many stories which had never been written before him, nor which had ever appeared in any documented sources. All histories were mythological and exaggerated. Wahab was confused in his understanding of historical events and Biblical chronology. He claimed that Ezekiel led Israel immediately after the death of Joshua,[73] the servant of Moses who led Israel into the Promised Land. Wahab didn't know that 1,000 years had passed between Joshua and the prophet Ezekiel, and that Ezekiel was a prophet, but never became a leader in Israel.

Wahab claimed that Ezekiel raised an army of Israelites from the dead. The Qur'an, in Surah 2:243, mentions this incident without mentioning the name of Ezekiel. Wahab, like Mohammed, did not understand the Biblical book of Ezekiel (chapter 37), in which God showed Ezekiel a vision of numerous bones strewn in a valley. God showed Ezekiel that the bones took on flesh and nerves. The Spirit of God came upon them, and in the vision they stood as an army. The vision which God showed to Ezekiel is a symbolic prophecy depicting what God promised to accomplish in New Testament times. God promised to revive the people who are dead in sins, like He revived the dead bones. After

72

saving them through the redemptive death of Christ on the cross, God promised to pour his Holy Spirit on them. But Mohammed, not understanding the meaning of the prophetic vision which the Lord showed Ezekiel, thought Ezekiel raised an army of Israel from the dead bones. No prophet who came after Ezekiel believed this, nor does any Judaic book mention a miracle like this. If it happened, it would have been among the greatest miracles recorded in the Old Testament, like the parting of the Red Sea.

Ibn Ishak used another of Wahab Bin Munabbih's narratives when he wrote the following account of the Ark of the Covenant in the Old Testament:

> Inside the ark there was the 'Shekhinah' glory, and it was the head of a dead cat. When the dead cat's head issued a loud cry from inside the ark, the Israelites had assurance of victory and knew they would conquer the lands of others.[74]

We know there were no dead cats in the ark. This mythological narration is never mentioned in the Bible because it never happened.

Ibn Ishak depended on Wahab Bin Munabbih for another far-fetched story. He says that the Queen of Sheba came to Solomon with an army of 12,000 kings from Yemen. Under each of the kings were thousands of soldiers.[75] This exaggerated number meant Yemen had 12,000 kings and over 50 million soldiers at a time when all the inhabitants of the world did not exceed this figure. We know (through the Roman expedition to Sheba) that the Sabaean army was small in comparison to the Ethiopian or the Egyptian army. Ibn Ishak, depending on Wahab, says that Solomon caused the Queen of Sheba to marry "Tubb'a King of Hamdan," and that Tubb'a became King of Yemen through the marriage.[76] This demonstrates the ignorance of Wahab to the history of Yemen, his own country. The Tubb'a title only applied to the Himyarite kings of Yemen which appeared around 115 B.C. and occupied Sheba around 275 A.D. Thus, we can conclude that "Tubb'a" was used as a title for some kings of the Himyarites in Yemen later than 275 A.D., but King Solomon lived in the 10th century B.C. Wahab's claim that Tubb'a married the Queen of Sheba, and became King of Yemen at the time of Solomon, only shows how much Wahab and Ibn Ishak were ignorant of historical data and chronology.

Wahab claims that Raseh, the Ethiopian who marched against Asa, the King of Judah, was an Indian king. He further said that Raseh was helped in his expedition by the people of Gog and Magog.[77]

Depending on Wahab again, Ibn Ishak says that Job was a Roman citizen and he (Ibn Ishak) created a genealogy for him which connected him with Isaac, the son of Abraham.[78] Wahab says that Samson was from a Roman village, and he was a Muslim.[79] But we know that Samson was an Israelite judge who was born in the 13th century B.C., before the city of Rome was built in 753-748 B.C. Wahab, like all the creators of Islamic tradition, wanted to support Mohammed in claims he made in the Qur'an. Wahab tried to give Mohammed's religion, Islam, ancient roots. Mohammed, in the Qur'an, claimed that Islam was an ancient religion embraced by historical figures, such as Alexander the Great, and the Queen of Sheba who came to visit Solomon. He also made Muslims of the magicians who opposed Moses in Egypt; of Pharaoh and the wife of Pharaoh, whom he named Assia; and he claimed that Allah gave Assia to him in a marriage in heaven along with Mary, the mother of Jesus.[80]

Wahab Bin Munabbih's perversion of history continued in an attempt to justify the mistakes of the Qur'an. Wahab Bin Munabbih wanted to justify the mistake of the Qur'an that Mary begot Jesus under a tree of dates. Unfortunately, there are no date trees in Bethlehem, because the tree grows only in very hot weather. It is ridiculous what Wahab stated: that Jesus was born at the border of Egypt "near a tree of dates."[81]

HISHAM BIN MOHAMMED

Hisham Bin Mohammed continues the confusion of history.

There were other writers who, like Wahab, rewrote Islamic history to justify Mohammed's outlandish claims. One was Hisham Bin Mohammed. Hisham said that one of the sons of Tubb'a, the King of Yemen, once occupied China. Another son conquered Constantinople and then laid siege against Rome. After failing to occupy Rome, he went to Samarkhind and occupied it after defeating the Turks. He then marched toward China and found his brother, who had occupied China three years earlier. Both men stayed there until they died, claims Hisham.[82] So, Hisham claimed that a Yemeni king of the 5th century B.C. dominated China, which we know is not true. He also claimed that his brother conquered the Oriental Byzantine empire by occupying its capital, laying siege to Rome, and occupying Asia all the way to China. Stories like this can be accepted only by ignorant people.

Hisham's distorted history also says that Nebuchadnezzar was a Persian. His leaders were Darius, Cyrus, and Ahasuerus, who all became kings of Babel after Nebuchadnezzar died.[83] History tells us that Nebuchadnezzar was not Persian, but Chaldean. The kings of Persia whom Hisham listed as commanders of Nebuchadnezzar's forces came centuries after Nebuchadnezzar died. Hisham was influenced by the claims of Mohammed in his Hadith which says that Nebuchadnezzar, Solomon and Alexander the Great became rulers of the whole earth, each in his own time.[84] Hisham claimed that even the known Persians kings were commanders for Nebuchadnezzar.

Hisham, like Mohammed and all inventors of Islamic history, lacked the historical background to accurately write history. The mistakes contained in the Qur'an, which the Islamic writers endeavored to defend, are enormous. In trying to defend Mohammed's original mistakes, they only added to them. Yet, their writings were accepted in environments where true knowledge and history were viewed as infidel literature which should be fought and eliminated. They insulted the education of the Islamic people for generations with the ridiculous and false history they created, based on Mohammed's claims. Will Muslims today remain victims of such cheap, primitive and false stories? Or will they think for themselves?

IBN ABBAS

Ibn Abbas, the authoritative scholar of the nation of Islam and an expositor of the Qur'an, was a superstitious mythological narrator who failed to understand historical chronology.

One of the main creators of "Islamic tradition" is Ibn Abbas. His first name is Abdullah. He was the son of Abbas, the uncle of Mohammed. He was 13 years old when Mohammed died. He was called "Heber al-Ummah حبر الامة , which means "the scholar of the nation of Islam." Ibn Abbas reported many Hadith of Mohammed, and is considered a significant authority interpreting the Qur'an. He died in the year 690 A.D.

The narrations of Ibn Abbas failed to consider history when he endeavored to support Mohammed's ideas. For example, he claimed that all the progeny of Adam, up to the time of Noah, were Muslims.[85] He claimed that the Babylonians were Muslims.[86] Like Mohammed, who claimed that many ancient historical figures were Muslims, Ibn Abbas believed Mohammed's assertions without comparing them to history. Ibn Abbas was believed in environments where people were without any education in history.

Ibn Abbas created false stories about Biblical figures. His stories are numerous. For example, he invented a story about the rod of Moses. Ibn Abbas said the rod was given to Moses by an angel about the time he was in Midian. The priest of Midian, who became his father-in-law, argued with him about who should get the rod, until an angel came and decided it was to belong to Moses.[87]

The myths of Ibn Abbas are replete with Old Testament names. I will give an example so that the reader may have an idea

76

of the man: Ibn Ishak (relying on the narration of Ibn Abbas) related many myths about Og. Og was the King of Bashan, a land in Trans-Jordan which Moses defeated with his people before entering the land of Canaan. You can read the account in Numbers 21. Ibn Abbas claimed that Og was 800 ells tall. Since each ell is about 3 feet, that makes him 2,400 feet, or 800 yards, tall, the length of 8 football fields. Ibn Abbas also claimed that Moses was 10 ells tall, or 30 feet. His rod was also 30 feet tall, and Moses could jump 30 feet high. But even though Moses could reach only the heel of Og, he was able to kill him(Og). Og was so big that his body became a bridge over the Nile for the people of Egypt to cross. Although no one in the Bible lived longer than 969 years, Ibn Abbas claimed that Og lived 3,000 years.[88]

Like Mohammed, Ibn Abbas got by with this because his readers were ignorant of history. They were superstitious, and tended to believe in exaggerated measurements for heroes and historical figures, something that we often find in ancient Persian and Arabian myths.

Ibn Abbas Failed to be Historically Accurate in his Chronology

Also like Mohammed, Ibn Abbas lacks the basic knowledge of historical chronology. He tells stories about Biblical figures without knowing the dates of those figures. This happens more times than I can count. For example, Ibn Abbas says there were 179 years between Moses and David.[89] We know from both history and the Bible that Moses was born about 1525 B.C., and that David became King around the year 1004 B.C., not less than 500 years later.

Where did Ibn Abbas get these dates? Some of his stories came from the friends of Mohammed. Most probably they heard the stories from Mohammed themselves. At one point he told them the story of a man in Israel who dreamt that the destruction of Jerusalem would lie in the hands of a poor boy, the son of a widow. The name of the boy was Nebuchadnezzar. So, the Israeli dreamer went to Babel in search of Nebuchadnezzar. The Israeli dreamer came to Nebuchadnezzar's mother and he found Nebuchadnezzar gathering wood, like a woodsman or bushman would do. Over his shoulders he carried a bundle of wood. The Israeli took the wood away from Nebuchadnezzar's shoulder and gave him three Roman denarii, which was a day's wages, and asked him to buy food. Nebuchadnezzar bought bread, meat and wine with the money, and they ate what he bought. On the second and the third days, the Israeli did the same. Then he said to Nebuchadnezzar, "If you someday become king, would you grant my safety?" Nebuchadnezzar answered, "Do you make fun of me or mock me?" The Israeli said, "No, but give me a sign that you will not destroy me." The mother of Nebuchadnezzar said to her son, "You will not lose anything, so write him a letter of safety."

Ibn Abbas' story is entertaining and, for Arabians who don't know history, it can be impressive. It also gave Ibn Abbas a reputation of being a great scholar, reporting the sayings of Mohammed and his friends and explaining events in history. But for the average person today, these narrations are just made-up Arabian stories told in an amusing way. In fact, Nebuchadnezzar was the son of Nabopolassar, the King of Babylon, who liberated Babylon from the Assyrian domain, destroyed the Assyrian empire, and reduced Nineveh, its capital, to ruins.

Ibn Abbas goes on to say that the King of Israel wanted to marry the daughter of his wife (his step-daughter). But John the Baptist said to him, "It is not lawful for you to marry her." This is incorrect, according to history and the New Testament of the Bible which say that King Herod was the one who killed John the Baptist. Since Herod was an Edomite ruler under the Romans, it was not an Israeli king who killed John the Baptist. Israel was conquered in 721 B.C. It was King Herod, who married the wife of his brother, Philip, who ordered John's death when John rebuked Herod for telling him it was not lawful for him to marry the wife of his brother.

Ibn Abbas says the daughter of the king's wife gave him a drink. When the king wanted to sleep with her, she asked that the head of John the Baptist first be cut off. He granted her request. But when the head of John the Baptist was brought to him, Ibn Abbas says that the head continued to say to him, "It is not lawful for you to marry her." Then he ordered the head to be buried in the ground. But when the head was buried, blood came out of the ground and the head continued to cry, so they added more and more dirt to cover the blood until the level of the ground reached the top of the walls. Still, the blood continued to cry. When Nebuchadnezzar heard the call of the blood, he retaliated for the killing of John the Baptist by destroying the city with the help of the Romans.[90]

The New Testament gives us quite a different picture of how John the Baptist was beheaded. When the daughter of Herod's brother's wife danced for him, she was instructed by her mother to ask for the head of John the Baptist on a platter. But, Ibn Abbas added many myths to the story, such as the severed head of John crying from the ground and the blood continuing to cry after the head was buried. Ibn Abbas breaches history when he makes Nebuchadnezzar a contemporary with John the Baptist. He also confuses the destruction of Jerusalem by Nebuchadnezzar in 586 B.C. with the destruction of the same city by the Romans in 70 A.D. Neither of these two events has anything to do with John the Baptist, who was killed around 33 A.D.

These are only a few of the many examples of the stories made up by one whom Islamic tradition considers the "scholar of authority." These examples express his style of narrating Biblical events using primitive myths, with no respect to any historical chronology.

Ibn Abbas served as a resource to confirm the legislation of Mohammed regarding free sex.

As a Muslim historian, Ibn Abbas confirmed many laws which Mohammed enacted or legislated. For example, Mohammed legislated free sex, especially for those who do Jihad, conducting a holy war in order to impose Islam on others. They were given the license to have free sex with any female who belonged to the people they defeated. For example, when Mohammed occupied Mecca, he permitted Muslims to have free sex with the females of Mecca.[91]

The free sex idea became lawful for Muslims during Mohammed's time, not only during wars but also in times of peace. According to Sahih Muslim, an authoritative book of Hadith of Mohammed, during the time of Mohammed and the Caliphs (civil and religious leaders who came after Mohammed), Muslims were permitted to have sex with women on the condition that they give the woman dates and flour.[92] Sahih Muslim reports that free sex was allowed for Muslims and spread among them especially during the time of Mohammed and the two consequent Caliphs, who were Abu Baker and Umar.[93] The Sahih Muslim also reports the testimony of many companions of Mohammed whom Mohammed allowed to go and have free sex with women for a few days, with the condition that they give to the women their charge or fees.[94]

There are many verses in the Qur'an which allude to free sex. One is found in Surah 4, verse 24:

> Also prohibited are women already married except those whom your hands possess. I license to you beyond that to possess with your money ... Therefore, with whom you enjoyed sex give them their fees or charges, in order that you do not sin in what you agreed upon.

The first part of the verse, "Also prohibited are women already married," prohibits Muslims from having sex with married Muslim women. He is not speaking here about marriage, because it is illogical to prohibit marriage with an already married woman, but this verse clearly establishes how free sex should be governed. The verse gives them permission to have sex with any woman "their hands possess." That includes war or buying concubines with money. The verse also allows them to go "beyond that," allowing them to go beyond the limit of buying concubines, to enjoy sex by paying women for it. This is what we would call forced prostitution. Many Islamic scholars interpret this verse to say that Mohammed is allowing them to have a provisory contract with women for free sex for a limited period of time, with the condition that they give money to the women. Mohammed allowed his followers to participate in these immoral practices. How could Mohammed allow his followers to commit such immoral practices? This also gives us insight into the role of subjection which women in Muslim societies face today.

Al-Bukhari refers to the words of Umar bin Hasin, a companion of Mohammed:

> The verse granting free sex came in the book of Allah – by which he means the Qur'an – and we practice free sex during the time of the prophet of Allah. There never was a verse in the Qur'an that prohibits it nor warns against it before Mohammed died.[95]

This shows that during the time of Mohammed, Muslims, citing the Qur'an, practiced free sex with women. Ibn Abbas legitimized the free sex practice because Mohammed allowed it during his lifetime, and because verses in the Qur'an sanction it.[96]

Today, Muslim Shi'ites legislate free sex for their adherents by quoting some verses of the Qur'an, such as the one we already discussed, and because Mohammed allowed it during his lifetime. Shi'ites allow a provisory contract between a man and a woman for sexual enjoyment lasting a few hours or a few days. It is prostitution legalized by the Shi'ites.[97]

Ibn al-Nadim, the famous Arabic historian, mentioned many Islamic writers who wrote books defending free sex based on the example of Mohammed, who allowed it during his lifetime and the lifetimes of the Caliphs who came after him. Among the writers which Ibn al-Nadim mentioned was al-Safwani, who wrote a book on "The free sex and its legitimization, and the refute to those who would make it unlawful."[98]

The immorality which Mohammed allowed for Muslims, and which Ibn Abbas legalized, became something to be defended throughout Islamic history. Jamal Il-Banna', a contemporary Islamic Egyptian writer, defended the Nikah regarding sex enjoyment in a recent book he published in Egypt, claiming that this provisory contract between a man and a woman for sex enjoyment helps the man to avoid fornication.[99] People, such as il-

81

Banna', are following Mohammed in his legislation to such fornication.

Finally, the provisory contract between a man and a woman, which Mohammed legalized for sex enjoyment, was known in Arabia as a costume. Ammianus Marcellinus wrote around the year 378 A.D., mentioning the costume practiced by many Arabian tribes to have a provisory contract with women for sex enjoyment.[100] Thus, we see that Mohammed transferred to the Qur'an the immoral habits and customs of some Arabian tribes.

Ibn Abbas is an Important key to Confirm the Identification of Many Qur'anic Myths

The command to the seven Earths.

Ibn Abbas played an important role as he confirmed the identification of many Qur'anic myths. Often, the myths Mohammed told were in a summary form, sometimes as little as a sentence or two. They couldn't be understood without either a Hadith of Mohammed, or a statement by Ibn Abbas or some other reporter. Ibn Abbas usually presented details which help us to see the original myths which Mohammed abbreviated in the Qur'an. One reason for this is that Ibn Abbas belonged to the intimate environment where Mohammed lived, so he was acquainted with the stories which Mohammed told in the Qur'an. One example is Ibn Abbas' interpretation of Surah 65, called al-Talaq, verse 12. Here the Qur'an says:

> Allah who created seven heavens and of the earths the same
> number, the command of Allah descends down through the midst
> of all.

This verse reflects Mohammed's idea that the heaven is formed of seven layers. When dying, those who believe in Islam go to a certain layer according to their works. According to this verse and other Hadith of Mohammed, there are also seven earths, one over the other. Our earth is superior. The angel Gabriel descends between the seven skies and the seven earths carrying the commands of Allah. Mohammed copied this idea from the Mandaeans in which Pthahil, one of their "personalities of light," is the creator of the seven heavens.[101] Pthahil is called Gabriel by the Mandaeans.[102] The seven earths were created by Hibil Ziwa, who was also called Gabriel by the Mandaeans.[103]

Ibn Abbas explained this verse from the Qur'an saying that Gabriel descends carrying the commands of Allah to each of the seven earths. Ibn Abbas claims:

> In each earth there is creation like this earth, even an Adam like your Adam and an Abraham as your Abraham.[104]

So the command of Allah as explained by Ibn Abbas is the inspiration which Gabriel carries to the prophets in each of the seven earths.

Mohammed used a Mesopotamian myth about a furnace which caused the earth to flood at the time of Noah. Ibn Abbas has located its place.

Mohammed claims in the Qur'an that the flood of Noah occurred because "the furnace boiled and fermented." Such mythology finds its origin in Sumerian mythology which teaches that there are unclean waters which are boiling in the underworld, overflowing from time to time and flooding the Euphrates and Tigris Rivers, making the rest of the Sumerian lands unproductive for agriculture. There are Sumerian Inscriptions which say that the waters of the underground world came from a place called "Kur," replacing the waters in the rivers and killing the crops.[105]

The Sumerian mythology claims that Ninurta, the god of the stormy south wind and the son of Enlil, the famous Sumerian god of the atmosphere, blocked the unclean waters by piling up stones in a certain place in Mesopotamia.[106] The piles of stones became like a hot furnace, underneath which the boiling waters tried to overflow and flood the land. This myth became the base from which the Qur'an explained where the flood of Noah came from, as we see in Surah 11, verse 40, called Hud:

Our command came, and the Tannur effervesced or bubbled.

The Tannur in Arabic means "furnace of stones." The myth of the Tannur was spread among Arabians. Most of the Arabic narrators, such as al-Shaabi, located the Tannur in Kufa,[107] a place in the old Sumerians' land, confirming the origin of the Qur'anic myth. Ibn Abbas says that the Tannur, which flooded the whole earth at the time of Noah, is found in India.[108] Ibn Abbas expressed what Mohammed intended in the Qur'an by the word "Tannur." We understand from his words that the flood came from a furnace located east of Babel, but he placed it more distant than that. Though the narration of Ibn Abbas is less accurate than that of Shaabi, it reveals the same Mesopotamic myth as the origin of the Qur'anic verse.

The Sumerians have seen the muddy waters which flood their land from time to time, thinking they were from the hostile underworld. In reality, the muddy waters happened when the Euphrates and the Tigris Rivers flooded, bringing the muddy soil from the mountains of Northern Mesopotamia and Turkey. Thus, this muddy water became the enemy of the Mesopotamians, a hostile enemy which they thought existed under the earth. The mythological concepts developed by the Sumerians thrived in subsequent generations and were adopted by many religions and sects who lived in Mesopotamia. Among such sects were the Mandaeans, who were also called Sabians. In their sacred books, we find "personalities of light" descending to the underworld, which is formed of the seven earths. They brought the commands of the "King of Light" to people living there. In the Ginza Rba, the main sacred book of the Mandaeans, we read about Mandadahi, one of their "personalities of light." He testified that, after returning from the underworld, he saw the "black waters boiling and trying to effervesce."[109]

From this we know that the underworld was seen as full of hostile, black, muddy, dirty water. This corresponds exactly to the description of Tubb'a, the Yemeni leader who described the sun setting in a spring of black, dirty, muddy water. His view was consistent with the ancient idea that the sun goes down to the underworld to illuminate its inhabitants before it goes upward to heaven to illuminate the foremost layers of heaven, or to rest in a room in heaven in order to worship the superior gods.

The Babylonians believed that the sun, Samas, or Utu, enters through a gate in heaven and rises from a corresponding gate in the East. Yet, there is another tradition which the Babylonians believed, which is the sun goes to the underworld during the night to illuminate it. The Egyptians also believed the sun goes down to illuminate the underworld.

Agatharchides of Cnidus reported the belief of the Yemeni that the sun sets in the sea,[110] which means that it sets in the water at night in order to illuminate the underworld. Tubb'a, the Yemeni leader who occupied Mecca, held to the idea that the sun sets in a muddy spring of water – consistent with the mythology that the underworld has hostile muddy waters – and when the sun goes to the underworld, the first thing it encounters is the muddy water. When Mohammed approached the subject of the muddy water, he incorporated many of these ideas into the Qur'an, making Alexander the Great see the sun setting in a spring of mud.

How can a book which is filled with mythological stories and unimaginable events be relied upon to give you the facts relating to death and preparation for eternity? These fanciful stories can only lead people away from the truth, and from the God who spoke the truth in the Bible.

Ibn Abbas helps us identify the city of Antioch, which Mohammed claimed was condemned and then destroyed by a loud cry during the early days of the Christian era. Nothing could be further from historical truth.

As we saw previously, in the Qur'an, Mohammed spoke about the mission of two disciples who went to a city where they were joined by a third person. By studying the Qur'anic text, we know that Mohammed was alluding to the mission of Barnabas and Paul when they went to Antioch. Their ministry was then strengthened with the arrival of Silas, who was sent there by the apostles in

Jerusalem. You may remember that Mohammed claimed that the inhabitants of the city were condemned and destroyed by a "cry." We know this was a perversion of history. Ibn Abbas confirms that the city was Antioch.

The Primitive, Mythological and Historically Inaccurate Literature of Islam Found Acceptance in the Superstitious Environment of Medina.

Ibn Abbas presents a good bridge between the original myths and their counterparts in the Qur'an. The Qur'anic narrations express the confusion Mohammed had about history. But neither Ibn Abbas, nor Mohammed, nor any of the fathers of the Islamic tradition, nor the people who built their sayings on their writings, could be considered reliable sources on the history of Mecca, especially before 570 A.D., the year of the elephant. That's the year in which the tribe of Quraish, the inhabitants of Mecca, began recording history. We already saw that al-Shaabi, one of the most important sources for Ibn Ishak and others who depended on his writings, admitted this.

What the inventors of Islamic history wrote is similar to Mohammed's writings which were recorded in the Qur'an and in his Hadith. What they each wrote contains significant mistakes when they try to account for elements of historical chronology. They transported the myths which spread in Arabia, Persia and other parts of the Middle East and inserted them or combined them with the figures and personalities of the Old Testament. Every one of the men who invented their own histories could have been the founder of their own Arabian religion like Mohammed was.

The period in which these men lived, including Mohammed, was the 7th and 8th centuries A.D. It was a time when Arabia was under the influence of many sects and religions, such as: Zoroastrianism, Sabianism – which was a combination of Mandaeanism and Harranism – Manicheism, Gnosticism, and mythological Judaism, which was embraced by some of the Arabian tribes. Genuine Judaism was spread by Judaic tribes. Christianity grew as Jews became Christians, and Gentiles joined them. Arabian religions, the most important of which was Family Star Worship and the occult Jinn religion, were all part of that mix. All these religions and sects influenced others, especially in the areas around Mecca and Medina. The myths of these sects and their philosophies were soon embraced by the newer groups, and became source material to which Mohammed and his companions added, eventually forming the Qur'an.

The inhabitants of Medina, where Mohammed emigrated, were less educated than the people of Mecca, but those of Mecca had connections with the Byzantine Empire through their rich commerce. The mythical accounts of the sects found acceptance in the city of Medina, but in Mecca the myths of Mohammed were recognized as the "myths of the ancients,"[111] a phrase often recorded in the Qur'an to give credence to Mohammed's claims over the claims of those in Medina.

But in Medina, home to the primitive tribes of Oas and Khazraj, the myths of Mohammed found the greatest acceptance. Medina presented a superstitious environment that viewed Mohammed as a great prophet, and accepted his primitive unhistorical narration which was based on Middle Eastern mythology. Ibn Abbas became known in Medina as a great scholar, due to the myths which he heard from his father, who was the uncle of Mohammed and embraced Islam. He was a continuous companion of Mohammed. Certainly, the myths which Ibn Abbas narrated were heard from his father, who learned them from Mohammed himself. Ibn Ishak, another significant Islamic historian, grew up in Medina. He exaggerated what Ibn Abbas failed to mention. He invented many genealogies and told many stories about Mecca, but he was disbelieved in the city of Medina.

This literature, though primitive, mythological and significantly misinformed, was accepted in the city of Medina, and later was imposed on Arabia and the Middle East with the sword. It was presented as the true history of the world, and the truth which can't be challenged or subjected to doubt. Since Allah had inspired it to Mohammed, it had to be defended, even to the extent of creating a new history which connected them to a past that they had never experienced. They followed Mohammed's teachings, even though there were no documents that would support any connection between their invented history and the Bible, or any other ancient recorded history. The writings of Ibn Ishak and Ibn Abbas, and other men such as Wahab bin Munabbih, were eventually accepted as true. Their undocumented stories replaced documented history because they wanted to fill the great gap between the claims of Mohammed and the facts of history.

Because there were no archiving methods and no printing such as we have today, it is commonly accepted that tradition can be considered accurate only if it was written within four centuries of the writers. We have some writers who wrote about Arabia between the 7th and 9th centuries A.D. That means we may have accurate information about Arabia extending four centuries before they wrote, but what they wrote presented information that was in stark contrast to what Ibn Ishak, Ibn Abbas, and others who were born in Medina, presented about Mecca and its temple.

By comparing the writings of these two groups of historians, we can deduce some truth about the history of specific Arabian tribes and their emigration patterns from Yemen to other parts of Arabia and the Fertile Crescent. But, even here, we can't claim credibility on information before the 2nd century A.D., since the writers lived between the 8th and 9th centuries A.D. However, from their information, we can conclude that the true builder of the city of Mecca was the tribe of Khuzaa'h in the 4th century A.D., and the true date, in which Quraish occupied the city, was in the 5th century A.D. We can also conclude that the true builder of the temple of Mecca was a Himyarite, pagan, and Yemeni leader named Asa'd Abu Karb. He is also called Abu Karb Asa'd, and he reigned in Yemen from 410-435 A.D.

From their information, we also know when the Black Stone was brought to Mecca from Yemen. Islamic writers presented illogical explanations for the absence of the stone in Mecca before

Quraish occupied the city, because they wanted to support the Islamic claim that the stone descended from heaven, and existed at the time of Abraham.

As we seek to uncover the historical facts about the temple of Mecca and its true worship, we discover illogical interpretations as to why the Black Stone was absent, and the absurdity of the myths which were invented. We discover what took place in the temple of Mecca, the origin of the pagan Hajj around Mecca, and other information about the nature of the worship of the Temple of Mecca and its occult Hajj, which became known as Umra' Hajj.

Important research should be based on documented data. We have many such sources. Greek historians and geographers who visited western Arabia wrote books about what they observed. The records of the nations who occupied the region in many epochs give us more reliable information. The archaeology of Arabia itself, and the archaeology of other nations who uncovered information about Arabia, provide us with further information. Finally, the Bible provides information on how many of the Arabian tribes sprang up in ancient history. It gives us the trading routes which they took when they traveled from Arabia, and lists the main nations and cities on these routes.

These important sources help us see which cities existed in western Arabia before the Christian era. All the sources definitely exclude the existence of Mecca before the 4th century A.D. These documented historical sources also give us the history of the Ishmaelites – where they lived and where they emigrated. It is a study which excludes the Ishmaelites from living in Mecca, or being the heirs or founders of a monotheistic faith, as Muslims claim.

Why Muslims should study history.

Muslims should study credible history and compare it to what Ibn Ishak, Ibn Abbas and others wrote in the 8th and 9th centuries A.D. to support the claims of Mohammed. To illustrate the importance of this kind of study, we need only to look at African history. We know that many African tribes believed in magic and turned to magicians or medicine men as their doctors until they came in contact with true modern medicine. The false was abandoned only after the true emerged in all its effectiveness.

I know that many Muslims look to the literature born in Medina as something sacred and indisputable, even though the writers of this literature were unreliable sources who started from Mohammed and extended to others who wrote afterwards in their attempt to back his writings. Not only did they write in the 7th and 8th centuries A.D. without any prior documentation to support their claims, but they also miserably failed the tests of chronology and history, and embraced well-known myths. They proved to be more primitive in their writings than writers in other sects who wrote the pagan and false histories in the Middle East.

As we continue our studies, I'll present more on the documented history of Mecca, its temple, and the Ishmaelites. This study is necessary to help our Muslim friends discover what is historical and true, and compare it with what was born in the city of Medina in the 7th and 8th centuries A.D.

REFERENCES AND NOTES TO PART I

[1] *Haran Gawaita* , Citta del Vaticano, Biblioteca Apostolica, page 3

[2] *Al-Bukhari*, (Dar al-Kutub al-Ilmiyeh, Beirut-Libenon), 1:89

[3] Ibn al-Athir, *al-Kamel Fi al-Tarikh*, 2: page 86; *Tarikh al-Tabari* 1, page 126 ; Al-Asbahani, *Al Aghani* 17, pages 15-17

[4] *Halabieh*, (Dar al-Maarifah, Beirut-Lebanon), 1, page 456

[5] *Halabieh* 1, page 477

[6] Halabieh 1, page 508

[7] Ibn al-Athir, *al-Kamel Fi al-Tarikh,* 2, page 86

[8] *I Enoch* 7:2

[9] John Reeves, *Jewish Lore in Manichaean Cosmogony*, Hebrew Union College Press, Cincinnati, 1992, page 88

[10] al-Ya'akubi 1, page 226

[11] *Ibn Hisham*, I, page dal

[12] *Ibn Hisham*, I, page 8

[13] Ibn Khaldun, Kay's edition, quoted by Wilfred Schoff in his comments on *The Periplus of the Erythraean Sea*, Munshiram Manoharial Publishers Pvt Ltd, 1995, page 142

[14] al-Feiruzabadi, *Al-Khamus al-Muheet*, (Cairo, year 1913), 3, page 129

[15] Inscriptions of Sargon, (*Ta-mu-di*, Lie, *The Inscriptions of Sargon II, King of Assyria,* 20:120; Lyon 4:20; *Iraq* 16 {1954}, 199: 18); quoted by *The Ancient Arabs*, I. Eph'al, E.J.Brill, Leiden, 1982, page 230

[16] F.V.Winnett and W.L.Reed, *Ancient Records from North Arabia*, University of Toronto Press, 1970, page 130

[17] F.V.Winnett and W.L.Reed, *Ancient Records from North Arabia*, University of Toronto Press, 1970, page 130

[18] Al-Khurtubi, *Al Jama' al-Ahkam al-Quran*, 15, page 14; Abu Hayyan Al-Andalusi, *Tafsir al-Baher al-Muhit*, 7, page 327

[19] Tabari Abi Jaafar Bin Jarir, *Tarikh al-Tabari*, Dar al-Kutub al- Ilmiyeh, (Beirut-Lebanon, 1991), first Volume, pages 379 and 380

[20] *Diwan Umayya Bin Abi al-Salet*, page 26; quoted by Jawad Ali, *al-Mufassel Fi Tarikh al-Arab Khabel al-Islam,* Dar al-Ilem Lialmalain, (Beirut, 1978), Volume vi, page 490

[21] *Tarikh al-Tabari*, Abi Jaafar Bin Jarir al-Tabari, Dar al-Kutub al-Ilmiyeh, (Beirut-Lebanon, 1991), I, pages 426- 429

[22] *Tarikh al-Tabari*, I, pages 426-428; al-Ya'akubi I, 226

[23] *Tarikh al-Tabari*, I, page 128

[24] *Tarikh al-Tabari*, I, pages 142 and 143

[25] *Agatharchides of Cnidus, on the Erythraean Sea*, book I, 17, translated and edited by Stanley Burstein, The Hakluyt Society London, 1989, page 52

[26] *The Geography of Strabo*, Book XVI .I. 11

The Geography of Strabo, Volume VII, Harvard University Press, 1966, page 211

[27] *Dinkard*-Book VIII, Chapter XIII, 9, *Pahlavi Texts*, Part IV, Translated by E.W. West, *The Sacred Books of the East*, Volume 37, Published by Motilal Banarsidass, Delhi, 1969, page 28

[28] *Dinkard*-Book IX, Chapter XXI, 17- 19, *Pahlavi Texts*, Part IV, Translated by E.W. West, The Sacred Books of the East, Volume 37, Published by Motilal Banarsidass, Delhi, 1969, page 216

[29] *Dinkard*-Book IX, Chapter XXI, 22-23, *Pahlavi Texts*, Part IV, Translated by E.W. West, *The Sacred Books of the East*, Volume 37, Published by Motilal Banarsidass, Delhi, 1969, page 218

[30] *Dinkard*-Book IX, Chapter XXII, 4-9, *Pahlavi Texts*, Part IV, Translated by E.W. West, *The Sacred Books of the East,* Volume 37, Published by Motilal Banarsidass, Delhi, 1969, pages 220-222

[31] *Tarikh al-Tabari*, I, page 424

[32] *Bundahis*, chapter V:5

[33] *Tarikh al-Tabari*, I, page 48

[34] *Halabieh* I, page 321

[35] *Tarikh al-Tabari*, I, pages 48 and 49

[36] *Halabieh* 2:104

[37] (Phys., IV, xi); Quoted by the Adrian Fortescue, *The Catholic Encyclopedia*, Volume V

[38] Koch, Die Siebenschlafereigende, ihr Ursprung u. ihre Verbreitung (Leipzig, 1883), pp. 24-40, Quoted by the Adrian Fortescue, *The Catholic Encyclopedia*, Volume V

[39] Wright, *A Short History of Syriac Literature* (London, 1894); Duval, *La Literature Syriaque*, 3rd ed. (Paris, 1907), pp. 351-854; Assemani, *Bibliotheca Orieritalis*, I, c. XXVII; H. Hyvernat, Transcribed by Joseph P. Thomas, *The Catholic Encyclopedia*, Volume VIII

[40] *Ibn Hisham*, I, page 240

[41] *Ibn Hisham*, I, page 282

[42] *Ibn Hisham*, I, pages 239 and 282

[43] *Sahih al-Bukhari*, 6, page 132; Halabieh 1, page 69

[44] *Ibn Hisham* 2, page 26

[45] *Sahih al-Bukhari*, 3, page 150

[46] *Sahih al-Bukhari*, 3, page 86; 3, page 135

[47] *Tafsir al-Tabari*, 18, page 137

[48] al-Allusi, *Ruh' al-Maani*, 14: 233; *Tafsir al-Tabari* 14:119

[49] Commentators on *Ibn Hisham* I, page L

[50] *Halabieh*, I, page 93

[51] Introduction to *Ibn Hisham*, page mim

[52] Introduction to *Ibn Hisham*, page nun

[53] *Tarikh al-Tabari*, I, page 247

[54] *Tarikh al-Tabari*, I, page 190

[55] *Tarikh al-Tabari*, I, page 102

[56] *Ibn Hisham* 1:8;Tabari, I, pages 133-138

[57] *Tarikh al-Tabari*, I, page 348

[58] *Tarikh al-Tabari*, I, page 165

[59] *Dinkard*-Book IX, Chapter XVIII, 2-7, *Pahlavi Texts*, Part IV, Translated by E.W. West, *The Sacred Books of the East*, Volume 37, Published by Motilal Banarsidass, Delhi, 1969, pages 224-225

[60] *Tarikh al-Tabari*, I, page 165

[61] *Tarikh al-Tabari*, I, page 164

[62] *Tarikh al-Tabari*, I, page 125

[63] *Sahih al-Bukhari*, 4, page 98

[64] *Tarikh al-Tabari*, first Volume, pages 379 and 380

[65] *Tarikh al-Tabari*, I, page 171

[66] *Tarikh al-Tabari*, I, page 120

[67] *Tarikh al-Tabari*, I, page 236

[68] *Halabieh*, 2, page 484

[69] *Ibn Hisham*, I, page 200

[70] Tabari, I, page 259

[71] *Tarikh al-Tabari*, I, page 260

[72] *Tarikh al-Tabari*, I, page 496

[73] *Tarikh al-Tabari*, I, page 272

[74] *Tarikh al-Tabari*, I, page 274

[75] *Tarikh al-Tabari*, I, page 292

[76] *Tarikh al-Tabari*, I, page 292

[77] *Tarikh al-Tabari*, I, page 308

[78] *Tarikh al-Tabari*, I, page 194

[79] *Tarikh al-Tabari*, I, page 381

[80] *Halabieh* 1, page 106

[81] *Tarikh al-Tabari*, I, page 350

[82] *Tarikh al-Tabari*, I, pages 420 and 421

[83] *Tarikh al-Tabari*, I, pages 317 and 318

[84] *Tarikh al-Tabari*, I, pages 142 and 143

[85] *Tarikh al-Tabari*, I, page 118

[86] *Tarikh al-Tabari*, I, page 125

[87] *Tarikh al-Tabari*, I, page 237

[88] *Tarikh al-Tabari*, I, page 254

[89] *Tarikh al-Tabari*, I, page 496

[90] *Tarikh al-Tabari*, I, page 346 and 347

[91] *Sahih Muslim* 9, page187

[92] *Sahih Muslim* 9, page 183

[93] *Sahih Muslim* 9, page 183

[94] *Sahih Muslim* 9, pages 184, 185 and 187

[95] *Sahih al-Bukhari*, 5, page 158

[96] *Sahih Muslim* 9, page 190

[97] Alessandro Bausani, *L'Islam*, Garzanti Milano, 1980, page 117

[98] Ibn al-Nadim, *al-Fahrisit*, page 197

[99] Jamal Il-Banna', *Masuliat Fashal al-Dalah al-Islamiah*, quoted by *al-Hayat*, Arabic Magazine

[100] Ammianus Marcellinus, *Historiae*, XIV, 4, 4

[101] *Ginza Rba*, book 13, translated by Yousef Matta Khuzi and Sabih Madlul al-Suheiri, Bagdad, year 2001, page 220

[102] *Diwan Masbuta d Hibil Ziwa*, from *Haran Gawaita and the Baptism of Hibil Ziwa*, Citta del Vaticano, Biblioteca Apostolica, page 34

[103] *The Canonical Prayerbook of the Mandaeans*, translated by Drower, Leiden 1959, page 295

[104] Ibn Kathir, *al-Bidayah Wal Nihayah*, I, page 20

[105] *The Sumerians Their History, Culture, And Character*, Samuel Noah Klemer, page 151

[106] *The Sumerians Their History, Culture, And Character*, Samuel Noah Klemer, page 152

[107] Ibn Kathir, *al-Bidayah Wa Nihaiah*, I, page 114

[108] Ibn Kathir, *Al Bidayah Wa Nihayah*, I, page 114

[109] *Ginza Rba*, book 3, first Hymn, translated by Yousef Matta Khuzi and Sabih Madlul al-Suheiri, (Bagdad, year 2001), page 51

[110] From book 5 of *Agatharchides of Cnidus, on the Erythraean Sea*, excerpt from Photius, *Bibliotheca*, cited by Burstein, page 171-fragment 107a ; from book 5 of *Agatharchides of Cnidus, on the Erythraean Sea*, excerpt from Diodorus, *Library of History,* cited by Burstein, page 171, fragment 107b

[111] Qur'an 16:24; 27:68 ; 23:83 ; 25:5; 68:15

PART II

True History Of Mecca

Objectives of This Study

Mecca is widely known as the city to which Muslims take the religious pilgrimage known as the "Hajj." As we better understand what Muslims have been taught about Mecca, we can better understand Islam.

This study has special meaning to Christians because we are facing a religion which is trying to appear as having a reciprocal root to the Old Testament, claiming to have connections with the father of faith, Abraham. It presents itself to countries with Christian roots and foundations as the last revelation of the God of the Bible to mankind, relying on the false claim that Abraham, with Ishmael, built the Temple at Mecca. Our study helps Christians to know the historical and Biblical proofs that refute such a claim, so that they can help those who are under the influence of Islam.

This study will equip Christians to better dialog with Muslims, who are convinced by the false claims of the Qur'an that they are the true heirs of the faith of Abraham. In order to witness effectively to Muslims, Christians need to understand these claims of Islam and learn how to refute them.

This study is important to Muslims because Mohammed replaced Jerusalem, where Christ was crucified on Golgotha, with Mecca, the pagan place. This replacement was aimed at canceling the geographical and historical place where the Son of God paid sin's penalty on the cross, and where Abraham prophetically was ordered to offer his son, Isaac, as a symbol of the Father offering His Son 2,000 years later. This replacement was aimed at canceling important Biblical heritage with all its prophecy about Christ the Savior, and shifting the focus of Muslims to the pagan Mecca, thereby depriving his followers of the gift of God which is connected with the belief in the Cross of Jesus, which all prophets had foretold. This study will help Muslims to not base their eternal hope on a false historical claim, but to embrace the Bible and its main subject, which is Jesus Christ.

DID HAGAR FLEE TO MECCA ?

***Hagar went with Ishmael to live in the Wilderness of Paran, but
was the city of Mecca even in Paran as Muslims claim?***

Muslims claim that the temple at Mecca was built by Abraham
and Ishmael. They also claim that from the time of Abraham,
Mecca has been a famous center of monotheistic Arabian religion
which continued throughout history until Mohammed was born.
We want to discuss these claims in light of the Bible and of
history.

When Ishmael was a child, Abraham sent away Ishmael and
his mother, Hagar. The Bible says Ishmael and Hagar, Abraham's
Egyptian servant, went to the wilderness. The Bible doesn't say
they went to the heart of Arabia. Here's what we read about
Ishmael in chapter 21, verse 20, of the book of Genesis:

> God was with the lad and he grew and dwelt in the wilderness, and
> became an archer.

We are told the name of wilderness in the following verse:

> He dwelt in the Wilderness of Paran; and his mother took a wife for
> him from the land of Egypt.

Paran is close to the border of Egypt. Numbers 10:12 refers to that
location as it describes the journey Moses and the people of Israel
took as they wandered in the wilderness after God delivered them
from Egypt:

> And the children of Israel set out from the Wilderness of Sinai on
> their journeys; then the cloud settled down in the wilderness of
> Paran.

It is clear from this verse that Paran is part of Sinai. It's the closest
wilderness to the Mount of Sinai. When some Islamic writers read
in the Bible that Ishmael lived in the Wilderness of Paran, they try
to convince their followers, called Muslims, that Paran is Mecca.
But the Bible is clear. It identifies Paran as part of Sinai, close to
Mount Sinai.

The book of Numbers specifies the location of the Wilderness
of Paran. It is not south of Mount Sinai, but north of it, and very
close to the border of South Palestine. When Moses sent spies
into the Promised Land, he had his men depart on their journey
from the Wilderness of Paran, because it was the closest part of
Sinai to the cities of Palestine. In the first three verses of the
thirteenth chapter of the book of Numbers, we read:

> And the Lord spoke to Moses, saying, "Send men to spy out the
> land of Canaan which I am giving to the Children of Israel; from
> each tribe of their fathers you shall send a man, every one a leader
> among them." So Moses sent them from the Wilderness of Paran
> according to the command of the Lord.

In verse 22 of the same Chapter, the spies entered Hebron, the
main city of South Canaan. This demonstrates clearly that Paran
was part of Sinai, which is on the border of South Canaan. Not
only in Numbers, but other verses from the Bible confirm the
location of Paran. In the first verse of the book of Deuteronomy
we read:

> These are the words which Moses spoke to all Israel on the side of
> the Jordan in the wilderness, in the plain opposite Suph, between
> Paran, Tophel, laban, Hazeroth and Dizahab.

This shows that Paran is between the River of Jordan and the
south border of Canaan. Its proximity to the south of Israel made
it a refuge place for those persecuted by the kings of Israel. In fact,

because Paran is on the border of Israel, closer to Hebron and to other southern cities of Israel, David went to Paran when Samuel died, as we read in I Samuel 25:1.

Because of Paran's location, it is no wonder Ishmael could easily participate with Isaac in the funeral of their father, Abraham, as we are told in Genesis 25:9:

> Abraham's sons, Isaac and Ishmael, buried him in the cave of Machpelah which is before Mamre in the field of Ephron, the son of Zohar the Hittite.

The cave of Machpelah is in Hebron, located about 1,000 miles from the place where Mecca was built in the 4th century A.D. If Paran were in the heart of Arabia, as Muslims claim, it would have taken Ishmael four months to reach Hebron. Burial laws and weather conditions required Abraham to be buried the same day as his death. To make it in time for the funeral, it is clear that Ishmael must have been living in Paran near Hebron, which was indeed at the border of Canaan.

However, Muslim tradition found a way to explain the travel problem. Aware of the huge distance between Mecca and the area where Abraham lived in Canaan, tradition says that a Baraq, which is a camel with two wings, carried Abraham from Hebron to Mecca. There, they say, Abraham visited Ishmael. It is interesting to me that Islamic tradition tries to resolve this huge distance problem with a winged camel. This mythological creature is not new to literature. The winged camel was used in Persian mythology before the time of Mohammed.

Previously, I mentioned the winged camel. We find it in Persian Zoroastrian mythology. The Pahlavi Texts of the book of Dinkard are Zoroastrian canonical comments on the Avesta, considered part of the Zoroastrian scriptures. It mentioned Kai-Khusrois, a mythological prophet who transformed Vae, the god of the air, into the shape of a camel. He then mounted him and went where the immortal mythological Persians dwelt. According to the same chapter of Dinkard, the Kai-Khusrois would return to revive and establish the Zoroastrian religion over all the earth.[1] So we see that the winged camel is the glorious transportation vehicle to carry and ensure the movements of the champion prophets of Zoroastrianism, as they moved toward heaven and other places hidden in the extremity of the earth and the universe. Later, Mohammed claimed he mounted the same Persian mythological Baraq to go to heaven. Islamic tradition, as we saw previously, used the winged camel to bring Abraham from Canaan to this unknown desert place. Many other events in the Bible show that Ishmael continued to live out his entire life in Paran.

The well which God showed to Hagar in the Wilderness of Beersheba was not the well of Zamzam at Mecca.

We can read in Genesis that Ishmael lived in the region south of Canaan near his nephew, Esau. In fact, the Bible goes into some detail about their relationship, showing that they were in constant contact with one other. And Ishmael would have had to live there for many years, because Esau married Ishmael's daughter, according to Genesis 28:9. At that time, when Ishmael and his mother were sent away from Abraham's house in Beersheba, South of Palestine, they could not have walked more than 50 or 100 miles before the skin of water she carried was empty. Let's read the story as told in the book of Genesis:

> So Abraham rose early in the morning, and took bread and a skin of water; and put it on her shoulder. He gave it and the boy to Hagar, and sent her away. Then she departed and wandered in the Wilderness of Beersheba.

> And the water in the skin was used up, and she placed the boy under one of the shrubs. Then she went and sat down across from him at a distance of about a bowshot; for she said to herself, "Let me not see the death of the boy." So she sat opposite him, and lifted her voice and wept. Then God opened her eyes, and she saw a well of water. And she went and filled the skin with water, and gave the lad a drink.

> So God was with the lad, and he grew and dwelt in the wilderness, and became an archer. He dwelt in the Wilderness of Paran; and his mother took a wife for him from the land of Egypt.

These words are from Genesis, chapter 21, verses 14 through 21. Look at the facts concerning Ishmael and his mother. The well which God showed Hagar was in Beersheba, not very far from where Abraham had previously lived. It was in South Canaan. The well that the Lord showed to Hagar could not have been the well of Zamzam at Mecca, as Muslims claim, because the well of Mecca is more than a thousand miles from Beersheba. Obviously, Hagar could not possibly have been carrying a water supply for a thousand-mile walk. Even if she had food and water, the great distance between Hebron and Mecca was through an uninhabited desert, untraveled in her time, without any city or village for her to rest in. She would have needed more than a year to walk to her destination. She would have been an unescorted woman, traveling by foot. She would have had no caravan to carry her, and no directions from previous travelers.

We know that the first record of the Egyptians about Yemen was in the 14th century B.C., centuries after Hagar's time. It was only in that 14th century B.C. that the Egyptians knew there were people living in Yemen. Those Egyptians gave us the first historical record about that land. The oldest report on southern Arabia came from the times of the Pharaoh, Tuthmosis III, in the middle of the 14th century B.C.[2] It was not until the 12th century B.C. that the first kingdom in Yemen started. That was called the Sabaean Kingdom, about nine centuries after Abraham lived. So you see, before the appearance of the Sabaeans, the desert between Palestine and Yemen was never crossed by any caravan. Also, the cities which were built on the caravan road appeared very late in history, because the land route was not adopted by the Yemeni until much later. According to scholars and historians, a marine route was adopted before a land route, because marine travel was faster and less dangerous than land travel. Scholars do not believe the marine route was adopted before the 12th century

B.C., and the land route along the Red Sea was not developed until the 3rd century B.C.

Thus, saying that Hagar and Ishmael crossed the desert to Mecca is a ridiculous statement, which can be accepted only by persons who ignore completely the history of Arabia. In Hagar's time, there was no relationship between Palestine and Yemen; there was no kingdom known in Yemen; and no civilization which existed in Western Arabia in the regions where Mecca was eventually built. As I stated before, the land route from Yemen toward the North of Arabia by the Red sea started only in the 3rd century B.C. Since then, some villages have been built as stations for the caravans to refresh themselves. Prior to that time, caravans avoided that dangerous desert. The Yemeni used to sail the Red Sea, avoiding this long and dangerous deserted segment to reach ports near Ilat, which is now a seaport in Israel near Aqaba, the Jordanian port. Some cities along the Red Sea were established only after the land route flourished around the 1st century A.D. But not Mecca.

Greek and Roman geographers walked the land route after it started in the 3rd century B.C. They mentioned the villages and cities which were established along the Red Sea, where Mecca was eventually built. They mentioned the tiny and trivial villages and stations where caravans stopped. They mentioned each temple which existed in the regions of West Arabia. Not one mentioned Mecca, or that a temple existed in the area where Mecca was later built.

Geographers also described the tribes and people living in West Arabia. But, when describing the area where Mecca was later built, they all said that it was an uninhabitable region of sand where only dangerous nomads moved from time to time. There were no real settlements or villages. We have a clear picture of this fact from the times of Herodotus, the famous Greek historian and geographer who lived in the 5th century B.C., and throughout all consecutive centuries after Herodotus until the 4th century A.D. During this span of time, several Greek and Roman historians walked that route, and also wrote about it.

We clearly see historical documentation that Mecca didn't exist before the Christian era, nor in the first few centuries after Christ lived on earth. This definitely refutes the Islamic claim that Mecca was in existence at the time of Abraham, and also refutes the claim of the Qur'an that the temple at Mecca was built by Ishmael and Abraham. Thereby, history excludes any connection between the pagan temple and the Biblical monotheistic faith which Abraham and his son Isaac, and Isaac's descendants, were entrusted with until the coming of Christ, who is the fulfillment of the revelation given to Abraham and to all the prophets of the Old Testament.

STUDIES BY CLASSICAL WRITERS SHOW THAT MECCA COULD NOT HAVE BEEN BUILT BEFORE THE 4TH CENTURY A.D.

Accurate data from Greek geography also excludes the appearance of Mecca before the 4th century A.D.

There is no mention of Mecca in the writings of any classical writer or geographer. This fact is an important argument against Islam's claim that Mecca has existed since the time of Abraham. We have complete records of Greek and Roman writers, as well as many geographers who visited Arabia from the end of the 5th century B.C. through the 3rd century A.D. Some of these people drew maps of Arabia telling us about every city, village, mountain, and temple existing there, yet none mentioned Mecca. If Mecca did indeed exist at the time of any of these geographers and writers, surely someone would have told us about this city.

To give you a better understanding, we'll look at the work of some of these classical writers. Greeks were well known for their accuracy in geography. So much so, that they didn't put much stock in reports provided by merchants. We can see this in the writings of Strabo, a famous Greek geographer and historian of the 1st century A.D. He emphasized how important it is to not depend on reports from merchants, but to depend upon the official findings provided by geographers and historians who visited the regions themselves.[3] This makes the research on the geography of Arabia provided by ancient Greek geographers and historians a valuable resource, especially when they tell us which cities existed in West Arabia since the end of the 5th century B.C. through the 4th century A.D. We see, then, that facts gathered by Greek geographers and historians are extremely important in establishing the dates when these cities first appeared. Since those geographers provided us with accurate reports dated between the end of the 5th century B.C. and the 3rd century A.D., scholars can easily determine within approximately 20 years the date of each city built in West Arabia. With reliable accuracy, we find that Mecca is absent from all the years documented by the Greek and Roman geographers. How ironic it is to claim that a city like Mecca existed as early as the Muslims claim, when it was never mentioned by the historians who documented that time period. So, the case for Mecca existing as a city since Abraham's time is more than a lost cause. It's the most unhistorical assertion that anyone could claim or insert into history.

Herodotus, an Ancient Greek Historian, Visits Arabia

Greeks have been interested in the Red Sea and its Western coast region since the 6th century B.C.[4] One valuable geographical survey, which describes in detail the geography of Arabia, first appeared with another important document provided by Herodotus, the famous Greek historian of the 5th century B.C. Living between 485 B.C. and 425 B.C., Herodotus traveled throughout the ancient World. His main work, *Histories*, describes the countries he visited. He visited Arabia around the middle of the 5th century B.C. and wrote about the geography of Arabia. In his writings, he mentioned the names of the cities in the Arabian Peninsula. He did not mention Mecca.

Any religious city would be worthy of note, because those cities were critical to the culture of the times. Jerusalem, in Israel, and other religious cities were mentioned by Greek historians and geographers in their writings, as were religious cities in other parts of the world, such as Europe, Asia, the Middle East, and parts of Africa. Due to its importance, Mecca would have been the first city to be mentioned in any survey or writing about Arabia. Yet, we find that an attentive historian like Herodotus mentioned all the cities known at his time in Arabia – but he didn't mention Mecca.

THE GEOGRAPHERS OF ALEXANDER THE GREAT AND ARABIA

A survey prepared by two geographers commissioned by Alexander the Great also excludes the presence of Mecca from accounts in the 4th century B.C.

We come to the 4th century B.C. Alexander the Great sent two Greek geographers to make a survey of Arabia in preparation for an invasion Alexander was planning. Although his death in 323 B.C. stopped the invasion, the classical historians and geographers whom Alexander sent succeeded in providing the Greeks with detailed information about Arabia. Those two men, Batlimos Bin Lagos and Aristopolos, developed an important survey which came to us through the Greek classical writer, Arianos, and the famous historian, Strabo. In their survey, they mention important details about the coast of the Red Sea and the surrounding region. If Mecca existed in the 4th century B.C., they couldn't have missed it. But there's no mention of Mecca in their reports.

The expedition of the two Greek historians sent by Alexander the Great is of special importance, because Alexander is known to have studied the cultural, historical and religious aspects of each country before battle, in order to determine how to deal with its inhabitants. If Mecca had existed at the time of Alexander's expedition, it would have attracted attention from the Greek geographers and historians whom he sent ahead.

If the Muslim's claim that Mecca, as the center of a monotheistic religion, had existed since the time of Abraham, it would have attracted worshippers from tribes in Arabia, including Yemen. Therefore, it would have been the subject of Alexander's two scholars. No other city would have been more important to present to their master, Alexander the Great, who doted passionately on religion and the history of religions. But the fact that they mention every detail of Arabia, without mentioning Mecca, is a clear demonstration that Mecca did not exist in the 4th century B.C. This leads us to the conclusion that the Qur'an and the Muslim claims about this city are historically inaccurate.

When comparing the historical claims of the Qur'an with those of the Bible, we find that the Biblical claims are true and historically accurate. I cannot find a single critic in history who argued about the existence of Jerusalem. Records concerning Jerusalem and its monotheistic faith have come from each generation since the time the Israelites entered into the Promised Land, in the 15th century B.C. Records from Mesopotamia and Egypt all contain important entries about Jerusalem. We find in Hebrew literature complete records about the kings who reigned in the city of Jerusalem. Much literature attested to by both internal and external records tells about the monotheistic worship by the Jews in the Temple of Jerusalem.

These facts should convince our Muslim friends to return to the historical legacy of a monotheistic worship as proclaimed in the Bible and known throughout documented history – and not to give heed to claims which create a worship without any historical foundation housed in a pagan temple built in the 5th century A.D.

THEOPHRASTOS' SURVEY

Theophrastos' survey also excludes the existence of Mecca during the end of the 3rd century B.C.

We continue our study by looking at the works of other classical writers who wrote on the geography of Arabia. If we really study these works, we'll learn that they prove that Mecca did not exist until after the 4th century A.D.

An important Greek historian, Theophrastos, lived in the 4th century B.C. He wrote about the Sabaeans – their trade, their land and their marine routes. He wrote in detail about the region but he never mentioned Mecca. That is significant, because Muslims claim that, in ancient history, Mecca was a center of commerce with Yemen and the Sabaeans. In spite of this claim, we find that Theophrastos, who specialized in describing details about the region – especially all trade connections and the routes – did not mention Mecca.

After the death of Alexander the Great, many classical writers and historians arose who were concerned about the geography and history of Arabia. Most of these historians and geographers lived in the city of Alexandria, which was the capital of the Ptolemies. The first university in the world was established in Alexandria, and it boasted of a famous library, the Library of Alexandria. One of the most important historical figures of Alexandria was the famous geographer, Eratosthenes. He lived between 275-195 B.C., he contributed greatly to documenting the geography of Arabia. Eratosthenes gathered important information from various resources. He examined the data obtained by the explorers who were sent by Alexander the Great, and data by geographical expeditions initiated by the Alexander Ptolemaic successors.[5] These Greek expeditions continued through the 3rd century B.C.[6]

Information from the expeditions of Ptolemy II in 278 B.C. encompassed the southern regions of the Red Sea and the African coast. They were used to help in the control of the spice route coming from India and Yemen. This information was also used to facilitate elephant hunts. Elephants were used in the Ptolemies wars against the Seleucids, the royal Greek family which dominated Syria. These factors opened the door for a systematic collection of geographical data of the African coast of the Red Sea and the Arabian coast. The results of this geographical activity was the book of Eratosthenes, and an important map.[a]

Eratosthenes measured the length of the Red Sea. He also gave a complete survey of the land and marine routes which connect southern Arabia with Aqaba, or Ilat on the north, which is the Israeli port on the Red Sea. He described all the people and centers in the region, but he didn't mention Mecca, even though

---

[a] Many of the reports upon which Eratosthenes based his map were lost, but much of the contents survive in the fragments of Agatharchides' work "*On the Erythraean Sea,*" Burstein, page 12

he followed the land route upon which Mecca was eventually built.

Classical Geographers Describe the Area Where Mecca was Eventually Built as "Uninhabitable."

Among the things which Eratosthenes described is the Arabian region, which corresponds to Africa's coastal region along the Red Sea called the Troglodytic Land.[7] The Troglodytic Land is an important region for our study because there is a huge desert area opposite it on the Arabian coast of the Red Sea. This was described by the classical geographers. The southern part of the Troglodytic Land was an arid area without cities or villages. It was a dangerous region where savage nomads roamed from time to time, attacking caravans. This area was described by the classical writers as uninhabitable, dividing the region of Northern Arabia from Southern Arabia. We know of nothing that was built in that area until Mecca was built there around the 4th century A.D. Yet, it was the most fearful tract in the land route. During the 3rd century B.C., around the time of the Sabaeans of Yemen, they began using the land route in commerce with Israel and Syria. It continued to be the most dangerous tract of land until after the Christian era.

Eratosthenes mentioned the area of Arabia, opposite to the African Red Sea region called Troglodytic Land. While geographers, who came in the centuries following Eratosthenes, described some areas near this one, Eratosthenes did not. This tells us that in 275-195 B.C., at the time of Eratosthenes, many areas around this one were not inhabited. They were part of a huge desert. Since the land route beside the Red Sea from Yemen toward Palestine was scarcely used in Eratosthenes' time, we conclude that no villages were yet established along it.

We know that Eratosthenes' report expresses not only his time – starting from the end of the 3rd century B.C. – but also the various geographers who ventured and visited the area before, starting with the two explorers of the Alexander the Great during the last part of the 4th century B.C. If Mecca had existed in

109

Eratosthenes' time, how had he failed to put it on his map of that region? It would have become a refuge for the travelers and their caravans, and would have become the pride of the Red Sea. No villages or cities were described by him, or by those who explored before him, because no villages or cities existed. Mecca would have become a center of rest and hope for the geographers and those who crossed that arid and terrible tract of the desert. Mecca, if it had existed in Eratosthenes' time, would likely have been the main reference point for his map – it is logical that he would have used Mecca as the point of reference from which distances to other regions were estimated and measured. But, unfortunately, geographers such as Eratosthenes did not have any city or village to use as a reference in the area where Mecca was eventually built. Nor was there a temple in that arid and desert region, to be a pride for such desert. Nor were there religious or non-religious tribes which would require a temple to be built for their worship.

How ironic it is to build a historical, monotheistic faith on this arid uninhabited tract of the desert. And how strange that it shifted people's attention from the Truth to Arabian paganism in the centuries following the Christian era.

If this is the picture of this neglected part of the desert in the 4th and 3rd centuries B.C., even when the initiated land route had just scarcely started, then how unrealistic it is to conclude that this part of the desert was a center of the monotheism in the 21st century B.C. at the time of the patriarch Abraham, where no land routes were known, Yemen, itself, was unknown to the contemporaries of the patriarch. To build an eternal hope on this tract of sand, which did not express life through history to help anyone create a religious legacy, is fatal for the soul. However, the tribe of Mohammed came to live on this unimportant region of sand in the 5th century A.D. After emigrating from Yemen, and after Mohammed claimed himself as prophet of Allah, he wanted to shift the legacy of the Bible to his tribe's new location; yet, it did not affect the historical reports about such tract of the desert. Our Muslim friends need to return to the real legacy of monotheism known in history. They need to acquire a Biblical view, where it is prophesied many times that the true Savior of the world is Jesus Christ. This is the only trustworthy legacy through which all people are called by God to seek Him and His salvation. Many, many people in every generation have received salvation when they have believed in the atoning death of Christ as prophesied in the Old Testament.

Isaiah, who prophesied in 750 B.C. concerning the suffering of Christ, said in chapter 53, verse 5:

> He was wounded for our transgressions, He was bruised for our iniquities; the chastisement for our peace was upon Him, and by His stripes we are healed.

This is an invitation for every person who longs to be healed from his or her sin, to look to the righteous Lamb who was slain for us on the cross. Jesus did not refuse to be led to the place where He would be slain, as Isaiah also prophesied in the next verse:

> He was led as a lamb to the slaughter, and as sheep before its shearers is silent, so He opened not His mouth.

He was willing to be slain, though He is the all-powerful One about whom Isaiah said in chapter 9, verse 6:

> For unto us a Child is born, unto us a Son is given; and the government shall be upon His shoulder. And His name shall be called Wonderful, Counselor, the Mighty God, the Everlasting Father, and the Prince of Peace.

The powerful God went to the Cross – though He was able to avoid it – because He was willing to pay the penalty for our sins so that we can live forever.

AGATHARCHIDES' SURVEY ON WESTERN ARABIA, AND THE ACCURACY OF HIS SURVEY AS A RELIABLE SOURCE FOR OUR STUDY.

In our study, we now come to the 2nd century B.C. Without doubt, the most important geographer and historian of the time was Agatharchides of Alexandria, who wrote between 145-132 B.C. He was believed to be a major figure in compiling Egypt's political history in the late 2nd century B.C.[8]

Because he was very close to the royal palace of the Ptolemies, he had first-hand knowledge of the results of the expeditions which took place throughout the 3rd and 2nd centuries B.C., especially in the regions around the Red Sea, the African shore and West and South Arabia. He had access to sources which documented the achievements of the Ptolemies. These were mainly reports presented by the envoys of the kings during the 3rd and the beginning of the 2nd century B.C.[9] Agatharchides coordinated all the information as a keen synthesizer and analyzer. He documented the names of the explorers who visited the region. Among those he mentioned was the name of the geographer, Ariston. That geographer is the one whom Ptolemy dispatched in the 3rd century B.C. to explore Arabia, especially the regions of West Arabia near the Red Sea where Mecca was later built.[10]

Agatharchides mentioned the name of other explorers, such as Simmias, whom Ptolemy III sent to explore the region. Agatharchides told how Simmias described the region, and how this had become an important resource.[11]

Agatharchides also studied books written by other geographers sent by the Ptolemies.[12] Scholars think he drew heavily from Anaxicrates' voyage to South and West Arabia.[13] We know of at least seven authors who visited and wrote about the Red Sea region during the 3rd century B.C. Among them are: Pythagoras,[14] who was an admiral under Ptolemy II, Basilis, Dalion, Bion of Soli, Simonides the Younger, Aristocreon, and Philon. Scholars assert that Agatharchides consulted all of their writings. Those books were available in the famous Library of Alexandria. In fact, we understand from the narration of Strabo, that Eratosthenes made a collection of these books.[15] Agatharchides synthesized and gathered information from reports and books which explorers and geographers had written before his time. He also depended upon people he encountered whom he called "eyewitnesses." Among them were envoys of the king – traders and explorers who visited the regions surrounding the Red Sea.[a] Unfortunately, the original documented survey of Agatharchides on the Erythraean Sea disappeared, but almost the entire book has survived in the writings of three classical writers: Strabo, Photius and Diodorus. The most significant summary of Agatharchides' book is found in Photius' book, *Bibliotheca*.[b]

The accuracy of his survey is very much accepted by scholars. The expeditions and discoveries from the 7th and 8th centuries A.D. confirmed the accuracy of the writings of Agatharchides, as they corresponded completely to his writings. Burstein, in his book *Agatharchides of Cnidus, on the Erythraean Sea*, describes it this way, "they have vindicated its basic accuracy so that, once again, it is recognized by scholars as one of the most important sources for the study of the history and human geography of ancient northwest Africa and western Arabia to survive from antiquity."[16]

One example scholars give to defend Agatharchides' accuracy is how he described the shores and adjoining water. Agatharchides tells us that the color of the water opposite Saba Land, South

---

[a] Many passages in *On the Erythraean Sea* clearly point to the fact that Agatharchides consulted eyewitness merchants and others who visited the region. See especially fragment 41.

[b] Although the book of Agatharchides is no longer in existence, it has been preserved through the synopsis of the classical authors Photius, Diodorus and Strabo. We find a good summary of the 5th book of Agatharchides in the work of Diodorus *Library of History*, chapters 12-48. The summary of Photius in his work *Bibliotheca*, especially Codex 250, is very important.

Arabia, was white, like river water. The phenomenon is still true today.[17] Another element which proves the accuracy and value of his writings is the similarity between his descriptions of tribes and people living in the area, and the description of the same people in later reports.[18] Agatharchides gives measurements of various tracts along the shores of the Red Sea in West Arabia. This tells us that his writing depended on testimony from expert geographers who examined the shore and the regions of Arabia connected to it.

Ptolemies wanted an exact study of the region to protect their trade in the Red Sea, and to know how to deal with various groups of population or tribes living in regions connected with the Red Sea. They also wanted to know the exact lengths of regions where the trade might find uninhabited areas, or areas with savage tribes or Bedouins. This justified the quantity and the quality of a prolonged, intensive and accurate study through the 3rd and 2nd centuries B.C., where the Ptolemies started to control the movement of trade on the Red Sea, and deal with piracy which threatened such trade coming from the interior Arabian regions. The book of Agatharchides reflected the success of the Greek geographers in providing to the Ptolemies accurate and detailed geographical and geographical information of the region of West Arabia.

Although Agatharchides wrote about locations along the Red Sea, including all the temples and routes which pass through the area where Mecca was eventually built, he never mentioned Mecca, nor its temple.

In his description of West Arabia, Agatharchides mentions each of the populations present in the 3rd century B.C. and the first half of the 2nd century B.C., in the regions adjacent to the Red Sea. He began with the Nabataeans, who had their capital in south Jordan and then penetrated into north Arabia, and he went on to describe each population, city, port, temple and mountain, until he reached Yemen. Here's what we learn from Agatharchides' accounts: He passed through the region where

114

Mecca was later built, but he never mentioned Mecca, nor did he mention a single temple in that region, although temples were a central subject in his study. We find him stopping to give the origin of the Poseidon Temple, in the northwest coast of Sinai. He tells who built it and for whom it was built. We find him also giving much attention to the temple located in the Negev desert, saying:

> There is also an ancient altar that is made of hard stone and bears an inscription in lettering that is archaic and unintelligible. The sanctuary is cared for by a man and a woman who occupy their sacred office for life.[19]

Agatharchides accurately reports the Greek trend to know about the temples existing in each region, especially in Sinai and West Arabia, where a temple is a rarity. The Greeks had a passion to know the origin of each temple. In the temple in the Negev, the Greeks made an effort to analyze the archaic inscription carved in the stone altar. They also described the source of the priesthood who served in the temple.

Agatharchides describes a temple along the Gulf of Aqaba.

Agatharchides told about another temple close to Ilat in the Aqaba gulf area. It is in a land belonging to a tribe called "Batmizomaneis." Agatharchides emphasizes that the temple, in his own words, "is highly revered by all the Arabs."[20]

Many Muslims claim that Agatharchides' temple was actually the Temple of Mecca. To fix the exact place of that temple, let's follow the narration of Agatharchides, as reported by Photius and Diodorus. Agatharchides began to describe regions north of this temple, including the Nabataeans around the Gulf of Aqaba, which was called the Laeanites Gulf. In Photius and Diodorus, Agatharchides says:

> One encounters the Laeanites Gulf around which there are many villages of the so-called Nabataean Arabs. They occupy much of the coast and not a little of the adjacent country which extends into the interior and contains a population that is unspeakably great as well

115

as herds of animals that are unbelievably numerous. In ancient times they led a just life and were satisfied with livelihood provided by their flocks, but later, after the kings in Alexandria had made the gulf navigable for merchants, they attacked those who suffered shipwreck. They also built pirate vessels and plundered sailors, imitating the ferocity and lawlessness of the Tauri in the Pontus. But later they were caught at sea by quadriremes and properly punished. After what is called the Laeanites Gulf, around which Arabs live, is the land of the Bythemaneas.

Notice that the land of Bythemaneas is connected to the south of the Nabataeans' region, close to Gulf of Aqaba (see fig. 2). Musil, a famous scholar on Arabia, declared that this land was the "lower portion of the Wadi al- Abjaz, namely the so-called Wadi al 'efal[a], a lowland 50 Km long by 20 km wide just east of the Gulf of Aqaba."[21] The narration of Agatharchides continues:

> Next after this section of the coast is a bay which extends into the interior of the country for a distance of not less than five hundreds stades. Those who inhabit the territory within the gulf are called Batmizomaneis and are hunters of land animals.

The stade, or stadia, according to the system of Eratosthenes, equals one tenth of an English mile,[22] thus making the land of Bythemaneas only about 50 miles. He is placing the inhabitants of Batmizomaneis within the gulf region, as we see from his statement, "Those who inhabit the territory within the gulf are

---

[a] The geographical book *Western Arabia and the Red Sea*, specifies the area of Wadi al- 'efal in the following area adjacent to the Gulf of Aqaba: "East of the Gulf of Aqaba two important watersheds lie, roughly parallel to one another and to the gulf; immediately behind the coastal lowlands the Ridge of al- Farwa separates the Wadis, which cut westward through the coastal ridge to the gulf, from those which drain southward to the Red Sea east of Ras Fartak. The chief of the latter wadis is Wadi al-Abyadh which, in its lower reaches, broadens and is called Wadi Efal- behind to be the plain inhabited by the Bythemani- Bythemaneas-....."; *Western Arabia and the Red Sea*, Naval Intelligence Division, Geographical Handbook Series, 1946, page 40; see also footnote 3

called Batmizomaneis." He means that these people lived within the Laeanites Gulf, which was the old name for the Gulf of Aqaba. The narration of Diodorus is parallel to that of Photius because both copied the writings of Agatharchides in his fifth book *On the Erythraean Sea*. Diodorus says:

> The people who inhabit the country beside the gulf, who are named the Banizomenes, support themselves by hunting and eating the flesh of land animals. A very sacred temple has been established there which is highly revered by all the Arabs.

We see that both Photius and Diodorus placed the people of Banizomenes (or Batmizomaneis) beside the gulf of the Laeanites, or the Gulf of Aqaba, many miles from where Mecca was eventually built. Mecca is in central western Arabia, very close to Yemen. Following their comments on Banizomenes, the two authors speak of another area in the south, the Thamud territory. They describe it in these words, "after these it is the territory of the Thamoudeni Arabs." [23] The Thamud tribe was known in history to inhabit northern Arabia close to the Aqaba gulf; they never reached to the south, toward the area where Mecca was later built. So the temple described by Diodorus was between the Thamud region and the city of Petra, within the Gulf of Aqaba region.

After Photius mentioned the Thamud region, he mentioned the next segment to the south of Thamud. [24] Scholars have identified this segment as the portion of the coast between Ras karama (25 54 N, 36 39 E) and Ras Abu Madd (24 50 N, 37 08 E). [25] Ras Abu Madd is about 450 kilometers (280 miles) north of Mecca. This accurate study shows clearly that the temple mentioned by Diodorus was in the Aqaba Gulf region, north to the Thamud region, and could not be identified with the Temple of Mecca (see Fig.2).

Nonnosus, another classical writer, seems to speak about the same temple at the same place close to Petra. This temple is built to honor the Arabian deities. Nonnosus says:

> Most of the Saracens, those Phoinikon and those beyond the
> Taurenian mountains, consider as sacred a place dedicated to I do
> not know what god and they assemble there twice a year. [26]

The Saracens are a people mentioned by Pliny in *Natural History*,
Book V, chapter 12, as people who live in the Gulf of Aqaba not
far from the city of Petra. Crone studied the locations and tribes
who venerated this temple. Crone has located the temple in the
northern region of the Gulf of Aqaba. The Saracens are people in
northern Arabia. Since the Taurenian Mountains are Jabal Tayyi',
the sanctuary is located in the northern area of the Gulf of
Aqaba.[27] This leads us to assume that Nonnosus was speaking
about the same temple mentioned by Diodorus.

This temple mentioned by Diodorus is built to honor the
Arabian deities. The remarks of the Greek historians and
geographers about this temple, though situated within the
secondary tribe's domain, is very significant. They remark that the
temple is highly revered by all the Arabs. The Greeks are very
careful to distinguish the temple, which has special importance
and is revered by many, in a land, regardless of where it is located.

With such propensity of the Greek historians and geographers,
it seems impossible that they could fail to mention a temple with a
special claim such as to draw worshippers from all tribes, as Islam
claims, for the Temple of Mecca. The fact is that neither Mecca,
nor its temple, is mentioned by Agatharchides, although he
pursued with such passion all temples existent until his time. This
is a clear indication that Mecca, and, its temple, did not exist
during such times.

Agatharchides covered the narrations of geographers of the 3rd
century B.C., and of his time, which was the first part of the 2nd
century B.C. Scholars today confirm the fact that the temple near
the Aqaba Gulf, close to the border with South Jordan, was
revered by Arabian tribes, just as the classical authors had written.

Scholars today believe that even Quraish, which is the tribe of
Mohammed, traveled north every year to a revered temple. There
are many proofs that Quraish neglected the temple of Mecca and
made their Hajj to the north. Wellhausen quotes the words of al-

Kalbi, "people would go on a pilgrimage and then disperse, leaving Mecca empty." [28] In their thinking, another temple had pre-eminence over Kaabah, the temple at Mecca.

Verses in the Qur'an tell us that the citizens of Mecca used to make a trip "far away," but later the Qur'an put a stop to the practice. Mohammed also prohibited people from making this religious trip after he occupied Mecca. Quraish used to go to Taif in the summer. This is attested to by a saying of Ibn Abbas, as reported in the Tabari. [29] The other trip may be toward a northern temple.

Agatharchides' survey, along with what we have discussed, confirms the fact that Mecca and its temple didn't exist during the 3rd and 2nd centuries B.C. Even when the temple was eventually built in later centuries A.D., it was a local temple of secondary importance, disregarded even by the tribe to which Mohammed belonged. Mohammed's tribe used to make a pilgrimage with other Arabian tribes to a temple in the far northern part of Arabia.

It is unhistorical to believe the Islamic claim that the temple in Mecca was built by Abraham and Ishmael as a center of monotheistic worship for Arabia. Muslims today need to renounce this claim and return to the true monotheism of history, the revelation of God, which the Bible alone represents. Such Biblical revelation has been documented in all epochs since the time Moses received the first five books of the Bible until Revelation, the last book of the New Testament.

Nonnosus reports on the temple in the Gulf of Aqaba area.

This temple mentioned by Agatharchides in northern Arabia in the Aqaba Gulf region is attested to by Nonnosus. Previously, I quoted the words of Nonnosus regarding this temple, as we find them in the book of Photius:

> Most of the Saracens, those Phoinikon and those beyond the Taurenian mountains, consider a place dedicated to I do not know what god as sacred, and assemble there twice a year.

The first of these gatherings lasts a whole month and goes on until the middle of Spring. The other lasts two months. While these gatherings last, they live in complete peace not only with each other, but also with all the people who live in their country. They claim that even the wild beasts live in peace with men and, what is more, among themselves.[30]

This tells us that the northern temple was a place where many tribes would perform a pilgrimage twice a year. During this pilgrimage, the tribes abstained from fighting each other. If one of the religious trips of Quraish was to this temple, it is clear that Mohammed tried to stop this famous and historical Arabian temple pilgrimage. He directed Quraish, the tribe of Mecca, as well as other tribes, to make the pilgrimage to Mecca instead.

From the quotation of Nonnosus, we see that the northern temple had similarities between their rituals and the rituals we encounter in the temple at Mecca and in other temples of Arabia. These rituals included the Hajj, and abstinence from war during the Hajj. These rituals performed in the temple of Mecca reflect those of pagan Arabian religions. The Temple of Mecca was built in the 5th century A.D. by Tubb'a, the Himyarite leader of Yemen. However, the Quraish tribe, like many Arabian tribes, continued to make a pilgrimage twice a year. The word "Hajj" means pilgrimage. Scholars think the Quraish were regularly traveling on these pilgrimages to the temple at Taif and to a temple located in the far north of Arabia. These travels were performed long before Mohammed imposed worship at the Temple of Mecca on all Muslims and annulled worship at the other temples of Arabia. Therefore, with the accuracy of Agatharchides and the geographers of that time, we see that neither the temple of Mecca nor the city of Mecca existed at that time. Instead, there was another temple, which attracted the Arabian tribes. That temple was located near the border between northern Arabia and Jordan.

Quraish, the tribe of Mohammed, occupied Mecca after it was built around the 4th century A.D. by another tribe called Khuzaa'h which had come from Yemen. So the Quraish tribe did not find a revered ancient temple in the city. Even after the Temple of Mecca was built in the city later, the Quraish continued the practice of many Arabian tribes and made a pilgrimage twice a year.

The Qur'an in Sura Quraish 106, verses 1-3, prohibits the tribe to do their "covenant" for two journeys. I think the two pilgrimages to a northern temple and to the temple of Taif are intended in the Qur'anic verse and, instead, compel them to worship Allah in the Temple of Mecca. Sura Quraish 106, verses 1-3, says:

> for the covenants by the Quraish; their covenants covering journeys by winter and summer. Let them adore the lord of this house.

Islamic tradition confirms that Quraish used to have two religious Hajj to other places in northern Arabia. Scholars think that Quraish were traveling on these pilgrimages to a temple located in the far north of Arabia and to the Taif temple. These travels were regularly performed before Mohammed imposed worship at the temple of Mecca, called Kaabah, on all Muslims. Mohammed annulled worship at the other temples of Arabia, many of which were also called Kaabah.

The kaabah of Mecca was part of a religious system involving many kaabahs of Arabia that belonged to Arabian Star Worship.

In the worship before Mohammed's time, "Kaabah" was the name given to all the temples of the so-called "Family Star Religion" of Arabia. The Kaabah of Mecca was no exception. Each Kaabah had the same basic cubic form, with the same structural details on the inside as are found in the Temple at Mecca. For example, each temple had a well where gifts were placed. Also, each temple had a well which provided holy water for use in the rites of the pilgrimage. In the case of Mecca, this well is called Zamzam.

The Main element in the Kaabahs are the black stones, a key element in worship. These stones are meteorites which the Arabians found and revered. Wherever one of these stones was found, a temple was built around it. So each Kaabah has one black stone which is held in esteem as a deity representing the family star. Pilgrims visiting any of these Kaabahs perform many of the same rites we encounter in the rites at Mecca. For example, men and women wearing special clothing circle around the black stone. The Kaabahs originated in Yemen and were dedicated to "The Star Family." Hilal, the moon, was the father and Ellat, the sun, was his wife. The Kaabahs spread across Arabia with the emigration of many Yemeni tribes in the north. The tribe of Khuzaa'h emigrated from Yemen in the 2nd century A.D. to the area where Mecca was later built. In the 4th century A.D., they built the city of Mecca. Asa'd Abu Karb, the Yemeni leader who occupied Mecca during his reign in Yemen from 410-435 A.D., built the Temple of Mecca with the same specifications as Yemeni existing temples. They worshipped the daughters of Allah, and his wife, Ellat, the sun, just as in every Kaabah in Yemen and in regions of northern Arabia.

Through the report of Agatharchides, we know that the area where Mecca was eventually built was uninhabited during his time.

We will now return to our discussion of the works of Agatharchides. He is known for describing in detail the regions of Arabia along the Red Sea. He identified all the peoples that lived along the entire Arabian coast of the Red Sea. Agatharchides described the geography from the coast of the Red Sea to 100 miles inland. He mentioned cities like Petra, located about 80 miles from the coast. This was the area that the caravans begin to use in the 3rd century B.C. as their land trading route along the Red Sea.

The Greek and Roman geographers were very interested with the strip of land which extended in depth from the shore of the Red Sea to about 100 miles inland, and in length from Sinai to Yemen. This strip of land is important to our study, because this is the place where Mecca was later built – about 40 miles from the shore. Although sites in this area were well documented, Mecca is absent in the descriptions of all the Greek and Roman geographers from this time who explored and described this strip of land.

There is another historical strip of land which starts about 150-200 miles from the Red Sea in northwestern Arabia. A few cities were built on some of the oases in this region around the 9th century B.C. Among the first cities built were Dedan and Qedar. Other cities were built later, when a trading route developed between the oasis cities and Yemen in the 8th century B.C. Among these cities were Yathrib and Khaybar, which are mentioned in various records of the kings and the people who occupied northwestern Arabia, an area also called Hijaz. The location where Mecca was later built is also located in Hijaz. Mecca is not mentioned in these different records.

One of the kings who ruled in the area of northwestern Arabia, known as Hijaz, was Nabonidus, the Babylonian king. Nabonidus transferred his residence to the city of Teima in northern Arabia for 10 years (550-540 B.C.). In what has been called, the "Verse Account of Nabonidus" we read:

> Nabonidus killed the prince of Teima and took his residency and built there his palace like his palace in Babylonia.[31]

From an inscription which Nabonidus left at his original city Harran, we know that during his sojourn at Teima he also ruled the cities of Hijaz existing at that time. Among them were Yathrib (Medina) and Khaybar,[32] but he did not mention Mecca (see Fig. 4). Mecca, if it existed at that time, would have been the only city of Hijaz which he did not conquer. This would have been strange for a strong Babylonian king to conquer so deep and far into the land of Hijaz, reaching as far as Yathrib, and then spare Mecca. The fact is that he did not mention Mecca because it did not exist in his time, which was the middle of the 6th century B.C. Therefore, Mecca is absent from the historical picture of the events of northern Arabia during the aforementioned times.

This strip of land bordering the Red Sea holds yet another key to the dating of Mecca. The land is historically attested to by expeditions of Greeks and Romans. It is also attested to by kingdoms that tried to control the trade across it from Yemen toward Palestine and Syria. One of these kingdoms is the Nabataean kingdom, situated on the border between Arabia and Jordan. Another is the Main Kingdom in Yemen. In all their reports, Mecca is absent from the archaeological records.

Agatharchides' survey covered, in detail, this strip of land along the Red Sea where Mecca was built in later times. He started systematically with the Nabataeans and mentioned a body of water called the Laeanites Gulf. This confirms the influence of the Lihyan kingdom on the region of Aqaba Gulf. This influence extended from the 4th century B.C. until the 2nd century B.C.

Agatharchides also tells us about the land inhabited by people called the Batmizomaneis. He says:

> Next after this section of the coast is a bay which extends into the interior of the country for a distance of not less than five hundred stades. Those who inhabit the territory within the gulf are called Batmizomaneis and they are hunters of land animals.[33] (A "stade" is one eighth of an English mile.)

Fig. 2 shows the Gulf of Aqaba where the land of the Batmizomaneis is located – south of the Nabataeans and north of the Thamud.

In this land Agatharchides mentioned the temple which all the Arabs used to revere, the temple that I discussed previously. This temple is not the Temple of Mecca; geographers had placed the temple in the land of the Batmizomaneis, close to Petra, about 700 miles distant from where Mecca was built. It is interesting to note that Agatharchides describes each group of people living on the strip along the Red Sea, and he explicitly mentions how far each one's territory extended into the interior. As a careful Greek geographer, he documented, in detail, all the people and the geography of the strip, mentioning places at least 100 miles into the interior of Arabia.

After describing land along the Red Sea, Agatharchides turns to the Thamud region, which covered a section north of the strip about which we've been talking. He says this area is inhabited by

"Arabs called Thamoundeni," or Thamud, a tribe which first appeared in the 8th century B.C. and continued until the 5th century A.D. The existence of the Thamuds is also reflected in Assyrian records, whose inscriptions on rocks proved that the Thamuds were scattered through a wide part of northern Arabia, including the strip along the Red Sea. Agatharchides describes many details about this part of strip – the length of the Thamudic coast, and other particulars. This helped scholars to identify the coasts which come next after this Thamudic coast, corresponding to today's maps of the Red Sea. In fact, the next coast he described has been identified by geographers as the coast between the following current locations in Arabian peninsula: Ras Karkama located at 25 54' N, 36 39' E, and Ras Abu Madd located at 24 50' N, 37 08 E.[34] Ras Abu Madd is about 450 kilometers (280 miles) from Mecca.

After describing the place identified today as Ras Abu Madd, Agatharchides seemed to pass through uninhabited areas. Previously, he would stop to describe the inhabitants of each area, but after leaving the area which the geographers identified with the region that ends with Ras Abu Madd, there are no descriptions of inhabitants. It is unusual for Agatharchides and the other geographers upon whom he depended to fail to describe an area if it was inhabited. To fail to tell about the inhabitants of an area allows us to conclude that the area was uninhabited. This segment without inhabitants corresponds to the strip where Mecca was built in later times. This fact is reconfirmed by other geographical facts not only by scholars recognizing the tract that precedes it, namely, the tract between Ras Karkama and Ras Abu Madd, the two cities which we find today on the map of Arabia. It is also identifiable by the tract, which follows in the description of Agatharchides, which he describes with the following words:

> The next part of the coast is dominated by dunes which are infinite in their length and breadth and black in color.

This is identified by scholars with the black basalt Harat Shama half way between Jeddah and the lagoon of al-Sharifa.[35] Today,

Jeddah is considered as the port of Mecca – it is about 40 miles distant from it. Al-Sharifa is described by the geographical books as "a very long inlet, parallel to the coast immediately northwest of al-Lith, shut in by a long narrow island, Jezirat Qishran."[36] (See Fig. 3.)

After the area where Jeddah and Mecca were built, Agatharchides described another arid, uninhabited area in his time which extended about 86 miles to the south. From his description, we can see a long tract, starting from Ras Abu Madd until half-way between Jeddah and the Lagoon of al-Sharifa, which was uninhabited in the time of Agatharchides. It is the tract where Mecca was built in later times. This tract is estimated to be about 460 miles in length. Mecca was built in the 4th century A.D., in the middle of this tract which divides northwestern Arabia (particularly where some of the Thamuds came to live along the Red Sea) from other tracts which connect central west Arabia with southern Arabia. It was a huge arid geographical barrier between northwestern Arabia and the southwest, where no inhabitants lived at the time of Agatharchides, who wrote about the 3rd century B.C., and about his times, the middle of the 2nd century B.C.

This observation of Agatharchides about this tract located in central western Arabia is understandable historically, because the tribes which inhabited the north of Arabia along the Red Sea were mainly Lihyanites and Thamuds, along with the Nabataeans who extended their dominion (sometimes) over Northwestern Arabia. None of these tribes were known in history to have lived toward the central western portion of Arabia where this uninhabited tract (that later became the city of Mecca) is situated. All this tells us is that it would be easier for the people of Alaska to claim that Abraham went to the frozen north and built a temple to establish a monotheistic religion, than for Mohammed to claim that Abraham built a city in an arid tract along the Red Sea in central west Arabia – an area which never attracted people to inhabit it, even the closest tribes of North Arabia. None of the tribes and nations closest to such tract from the southern direction had ever inhabited such tract of central western Arabia.

ARTEMIDORUS' SURVEY

Artemidorus' survey showed that the tract on central western Arabia, where Mecca was later built, was still uninhabited as late as 103 B.C.

Another Greek geographer and historian, Artemidorus of Ephesus, wrote a total of eleven geography books. He lived around 103 B.C. and was quoted by the historian, Strabo. Although Artemidorus included extensive excerpts from the book of Agatharchides in his eleven-book survey of world geography,[37] he also included additional information gathered by others in his time, and from his own travels, as well.[38] Consequently, Artemidorus, as well as Agatharchides, described the strip of land along the Red Sea. Just like Agatharchides, Artemidorus described the nature of each tract along the coast of the Red Sea and the population who lived there. When he came to the same central western Arabian tract where Mecca was later built, he didn't mention any people living there, making it clear that around 103 B.C. this tract was still uninhabited. He mentioned some islands near that area which were also uninhabited.[39] He has to walk very much more to the south of this region in order to find a small port. To the south of this port was a land inhabited by the so-called "Debae" people. There were Bedouins traveling in the area and a few farmers, but no cities were seen in that area. Artemidorus had to travel much further south to near the border of Yemen to find, as he said, "more civilized" people.[40] In other words, the tract of central western Arabia where Mecca was built later was still uninhabited as of 103 B.C. This tract is divided from Yemen by an area, which is inhabited only by uncivilized Bedouin tribes.

THE ROMANS EXPLORE WESTERN AND SOUTHERN ARABIA

The Roman Expedition into western and southern Arabia accurately described the villages which were built in the area of central western Arabia, but a city called Mecca was never mentioned.

Our history doesn't end here. In the year 30 B.C., Egypt became a Roman province. The Romans then wanted to control the Arabian regions along the Red Sea, especially south of the city called Leuce Kome on the shore of the Arabian Red Sea. From there, through the central western shore, were places where savage tribes were acting as pirates and threatening sea navigation. The Romans also wanted to control Yemen and, subsequently, the spice trade coming from India through Yemen.

Rome trusted the military campaign to Gallus, the governor of Egypt. He was unsuccessful, but his campaign provides more historical accuracy for us. Gallus departed from the Egyptian shore of the Red Sea with 10,000 Roman soldiers, 1,000 Nabataean soldiers, and some other Roman allies in the region. The Nabataeans were ruled by the Roman Empire at that time, so they promised to help the Romans in this expedition as soldiers and guides. The Nabataeans were ideal as guides because part of northern Arabia along the Red Sea was under the Nabataean domain. Strabo, the famous geographer and historian, took part in the expedition and wrote about it in his 16th book. This gives to the expedition a special value in terms of geography; it is a highly-documented expedition, and not a narration of any kind.

The expedition had special importance for a geographer, because it was not the journey of a traveler who might have missed cities deeper inland. It was a military expedition, intended to control all the villages and cities which might threaten Roman trade within this strip of land. The Romans were very thorough and would not have missed a city. The Roman Expedition went through the strip of land which geographers used to explore along the Red Sea, which I defined previously as extending from the shore to at least 100 miles inland. The Romans wanted to subdue every village because of the continuing piracy which originated from central western Arabia. Therefore, no city or village was left alone in this military expedition.

The expedition arrived at Leuce Come, which means the "white village." This village was part of the Nabataean territory at the time of the expedition. Strabo attested to the flourishing of the land route through this village to Petra, and from there to Egypt and Syria. This village is placed in the today map of Arabia at El Haura, 25 7 N., 37 13 E.[41] Leuce Come is about 280 miles from the place where Mecca was later built. To the south of this village lay the central western part of Arabia along the Red Sea, which we previously saw was uninhabited in 103 B.C. But now, because the land route along the Red Sea had started to flourish, there had been a few villages built since 103 B.C., which Gallus occupied. These villages are mentioned in the narration of Strabo, who was an eyewitness to this important expedition.

After Leuce Come, Gallus marched to the south, through Nabataean-controlled lands. Strabo describes the nature of the region with these words:

> Gallus moved his army from Leuce Come and marched through regions where water had to be carried by camels.

Gallus marched until he reached the desert assigned to Aretas, his kinsman, by King Obodas of Nabataean. We assume that Gallus was marching toward the village of Egra about 1,100 Greek stadia from Leuce Come (about 137 miles). Strabo described this part under Aretas, as follows:

> It afforded only zea, a kind of coarse grain, a few palm trees and butter instead of oil.[42]

It is a description of a deserted tract of land with few stations on the caravan route coming from the south. These stations are mainly Nabataean stations to protect and control the trade passing through this area.

Then Strabo described the next segment of the central-western Arabian campaign with these words:

> The next country which Gallus traversed belongs to nomads and most of it was truly desert; and it was called Ararene, and he spent fifty days arriving at the city of Negrani.

That was a city of Najran on the border of Yemen about 385 miles south of Mecca, and about 125 miles from the shore of the Red Sea. We understand from the description of Strabo that the central western tract of Arabia along the Red Sea during the time of the expedition had few changes since the 3rd and 2nd centuries B.C. This region was described by previous geographers as uninhabited in its northern part, and inhabited by Bedouins in its southern part, until reaching the more-civilized people near Yemen. At least three of the stations which the Nabataeans had built on the caravan road became small villages, which were mentioned in this expedition. The situation was likely similar to that of the 2nd and 3rd centuries B.C.

Gallus wanted to subdue the region to protect the trade from the piracy coming from this area. His plan was to occupy all the cities found in this dangerous tract, but he did not find any city until he reached Najran. This demonstrates that Mecca was not yet built in those times – that is, around 23 B.C. Gallus occupied Najran, then Asca (within Yemeni territory). Going south, he occupied a city called Athrula, then advanced toward Marsiaba (probably Ma'rib, the capital of Saba). He assaulted and besieged the city for six days, but desisted for want of water. He lost only seven soldiers in war against the Arabians of Najran and in the battles south of it. Most of the losses in his army came from lack of water and supplies, and disease.

If Mecca had existed at the time of the Roman Expedition, it would have been impossible to be missed by a weary army which needed a city in which to rest and replenish supplies.

The hardships of Gallus' army were because of the huge distances, which existed between the small few villages in this tract of central Arabia where Mecca was built in later times. This caused many soldiers to die from a lack of water and supplies. The Romans accused Syllaeus of not helping them as a guide because he chose paths between the villages and cities that were longer than they should have been. This did not affect the plan of passing through all the villages which existed in the area, since the villages and cities were known by all contemporaries to the expedition, and confirmed by the inhabitants. In other words, each village or city knew the name of the next city or village which Gallus needed to visit on the way to Najran and the other cities of Yemen.

Since subduing all of central western Arabia was an important goal for the expedition, Gallus would not have missed a city like Mecca, if it had existed then.

Another thing to consider is that after Gallus failed to occupy the Yemeni city of Marsiaba, he replaced Syllaeus as a guide, and instead depended on native experts to return to Negrana and then to the Nabataean village of Leuce Come. Consequently, he made the return trip more quickly, passing through the few villages which were built on the caravan road where Mecca was eventually built. Strabo mentioned them by name, but never mentioned Mecca.[a] Ultimately, Gallus withdrew from the war. The huge

---

[a] Regarding the expedition of Gallus; He returned to Negrana in nine days after he failed to occupy Marsiaba in Saba. Negrana is Najran, about 650 kilometers south of Mecca. On the 11th day he reached a village called Hepta phreata, then he went to another village named Chaalla, then on to another village named Malotha which, most probiblay, was Malothan located close to the actual city of Jadda, which is about 30 miles from Mecca. But between Malotha or Malothan and Egra (north of where Mecca was later built) there were no villages mentioned by Strabo who accompagned the expedition. Gallus badly needed urgent supplics of water and food, but he could not find villages which could give him rest, and re-supply his troops in the area where Mecca was eventually built.
See *The Geography of Strabo*, Book XVI. 4 . 24

distances between the villages, which were built on this central Arabian tract, created a logistical travel problem for an army of more than 11,000. Gallus lost thousands of his soldiers because of lack of water and supplies.

The Roman historian, Dio Cassius, described the failure of the expedition in his book, *The History of Rome*. Here's what he wrote:

> At first Aelius Gallus encountered no one, yet he did not proceed without difficulty; for the desert, the sun, and the water (which had some peculiar nature) all caused his men great distress, so that the larger part of the army perished.[43]

This advances our argument. If Mecca had existed as a city, it would have been Gallus' main goal to control it. No cities are described by any of the historians, except for the few villages I mentioned previously which were built on the caravan road. If Mecca had existed, it would have been an important place to rest, to replenish supplies and to prepare a person to traverse the rest of this terrible tract toward Najran and the other Yemeni cities. No one who planned to occupy a desert would abandon its main city. But that desert had no city in existence like Mecca; that is why the expedition had its hardships and problems with supplies.

What this ultimately shows us is that the claims of Islam which state that Mecca was a city that flourished during the time of Abraham, are unsubstantiated and false. All the records of the historians of the time show that Mecca was not in existence until the 4th century A.D., certainly not in the time of Abraham. If Islam is wrong on this key assertion, how can we trust it in other assertions?

MECCA WAS ABSENT FROM THE HISTORICAL TRAVELS AND WRITINGS OF STRABO.

The historian, Strabo, shows us clearly that the city of Mecca could not have existed during the time of Christ and, therefore, not when the Muslims claim.

We will continue to refute the Islamic claim that Mecca has existed since the time of Abraham. To this end we will now study the works of Strabo, a Greek geographer who lived between 64 B.C. and 23 A.D. In his geographical study, Strabo summarized the most important works written by geographers before him and reported writings done by his contemporaries. Among those whose work he referenced were: Artemidorus, Eratosthenes and Agatharcides.[44] I have mentioned these men in the past.

Athenodorus was a geographer who accompanied Strabo in some of his travels. In Strabo's own words, he was "a philosopher and companion of mine who had been in the city of the Petraneans."[45] By "Petraneans" Strabo means the city of Petra, and he quotes some of Athenodorus' writings about the city and its government. Strabo also passionately and accurately gives us a detailed survey of Arabia during his lifetime. He visited the region with other Greek historians, philosophers and geographers and described the region, relying on his own first-hand research and the observations of those who accompanied him in the region. I mentioned previously that as a geographer and historian, Strabo accompanied Gallus on the Roman Expedition. Strabo's purpose was to personally verify information about the region which he had gathered from various sources. He discussed the goal of the expedition in these words:

> Many of the special characteristics of Arabia have been disclosed by the recent expedition of the Romans against the Arabians, which was made in my own time under Aelius Gallus as commander. He was sent by Augustus Caesar to explore the tribes and the places.[46]

So we see that one of the aims of the expedition was to explore the "tribes and the places" of Arabia. Strabo mentioned Augustus Caesar's particular interest in western Arabia when he said:

> Caesar saw that the Troglodyte country, which adjoins Egypt, neighbors upon Arabia, and he saw also that the Arabian Gulf, which separates the Arabians from the Troglodytes, is extremely narrow. Accordingly, he conceived the purpose of winning the Arabians over to himself or of subjugating them.[47]

From this we see that one main goal of the Romans was the pacification of the northern and central regions of Arabia, which lay opposite to Troglodytes on the shore of the Red Sea and the regions around it. This is also where the city of Mecca was later built. Notice, also, that the control of this area was important to the security of the land trade, which was beginning to flourish around the start of the Christian era. Caesar, also, needed to protect the marine route from piracy which was coming from the Arabian regions adjoining the Red Sea.

Strabo's work is important to my argument that Mecca didn't come into existence until many, many years after Abraham lived. Although this region was documented thoroughly by Strabo's participation in the Roman Expedition, Mecca was not mentioned at all. Though his survey quoted heavily the intensive research by other geographers, Mecca was not mentioned in all of this. Neither was any tribe mentioned that, according to Islamic tradition, was supposed to have lived in Mecca since the time of Abraham, nor was any temple found in that area. Strabo's survey is also important because it verified the description given by other geographers who wrote about the tribes and places along the Red Sea, starting from the far north of Arabia and reaching south to Yemen.

Why doesn't Strabo make any mention of Mecca or its temple? This cannot be accidental. If a tourist with far less interest in exploring a region had failed to mention the name of a main city, we might be able to consider this an accident. But when a geographer, who is entrusted to make a survey for a great empire

134

like Rome, fails to mention a city like Mecca, there is no possibility that he accidentally missed it. Add to that all the geographers and experts who described the area, and didn't mention once a city like Mecca, and you can reach only one conclusion: Mecca did not exist in about 23 B.C. when Strabo wrote his reports.

"THE PERIPLUS OF THE ERYTHRAEAN SEA"

"The Periplus of the Erythraean Sea" confirms Mecca didn't exist during the end of the 1st century A.D.

I have mentioned Artemidorus, Eratosthenes and Agatharcides, as well as Strabo – none of whom acknowledged the existence of Mecca in their time, which was prior to Christ. Now I'd like to take you to another source. This time, to a book considered to be one of the most reliable historical documents on trade routes and the regions of Arabia. The book, written between 58- 62 A.D.[48] by an unnamed author, is *The Periplus of the Erythraean Sea*. It was written by a resident in the city of Berenice, opposite to central Arabia, and located about 200-220 miles from the place where Mecca was later built.

The dating of the book is important to our study, and many external evidences attest to the dating. For example, Pliny copied some of the ideas of Periplus into his book, *Natural History*. *Natural History* was written between 72-76 A.D.,[a] so we can conclude that Periplus was written before that. Another important element in determining the date of Periplus is that the author, in Chapter 57, mentions the monsoon on the Indian Ocean, which

---

[a] Scholars agree that Pliny wrote his *Natural History* after the compilation of *The Periplus of the Erythraean Sea*, because Pliny seems to include many elements in the description of *The Periplus of the Erythraean Sea* of Arabia Felix. It is known that Pliny accomplished his work *Natural History* between 72-76 A.D.

Hippalus documented around 47 A.D. Because Hippalus noticed the periodic weather behavior, he was able to sail to India at just the right time, thus shortening the time required for a round-trip voyage to India. His discovery allowed trade with India to flourish.

The author of Periplus mentions the monsoon discovery, proving that the book was written after 47 A.D. Some other proofs more accurately determine that the book was even written a little later than that – somewhere between 60-62 A.D.

It is certain that the author of Periplus was a Greek merchant, and that he traveled the Arabian regions as far as India. We also assume that he lived in the city of Berenice on the Red Sea, opposite the Arabian ports of Leuce Come, and not in the larger city of Alexandria. How do we know this? Because the author didn't describe the usual voyage as going from Coptos in the interior of Egypt, along the Nile, and through the Egyptian desert. Strabo and Pliny both describe this voyage in such a way which causes scholars to assume that the writer of Periplus lived in Berenice.

The city of Berenice is on the western coast of the Red Sea, opposite the Arabian ports of Leuce Come and Egra. We know that Egra is about 137 miles away from Leuce Come, and only 62 miles from the village of Malathan, which is the closest village to the place where Mecca was later built. This is important to us because the author lived on the African shore of the Red Sea, not too far from the tract of land on which Mecca was later built. Being very familiar with the central tract of Arabia where Mecca was built in later times, he wrote about the regions close to where he lived, making his book an extremely important document. We also know that the book was not written by a person who only visited the region, or made a survey during his lifetime, but by a person who knew in detail the cities and villages near the area where he actually lived.

The distance between the city in which he lived and the place where Mecca was built is between 200-250 miles. His knowledge of Mecca, if it had existed in his time, is analogous to a contemporary resident of Paris knowing about the city of Rome. Assuredly, the author would have known about the city if it had actually been there. The accuracy of Periplus is corroborated by many geographical and historical evidences. We find that descriptions in the book agree with descriptions in the later book which Pliny wrote describing the Arabian coasts.

Also, we find historical facts corresponding with those narrated by *The Periplus of the Erythraean Sea*. For example, the author of the book, in chapter 19, mentioned Malichas as king of the Nabataeans. Josephus, the Jewish Roman historian, mentioned this king, under the name of Malchus, in more than one place.[49] The author of *The Periplus of the Erythraean Sea* mentioned Eleazus as a title of the king of Frankincense country, that is, Hadramuot.[50] He also mentions Charibael as title for the king of two Yemeni tribes, the Himyarites and the Sabaeans.[51] This information is attested to be true by inscriptions discovered in southern Arabia by archaeologist Glaser.[52]

The author mentioned many other cities which were distant from the shore of the Red Sea. One example is Coloe, which he said is "a three days' journey" from Adulis, a city on the African shore.[53] The author mentioned many other cities which were similarly distant from the Red Sea. Therefore, not mentioning Mecca, which is only 30-40 miles from the Red Sea, is a significant matter. While the author mentioned many cities in the region which are of little importance, and are two or three times as far from shore as Mecca, the author still does not mention the city of Mecca at all. Think about it .The author of *The Periplus of the Erythraean Sea* described the regions adjacent to the Red Sea and Indian Ocean, which were the western and southern regions of Arabia. He mentioned the names of kings, tribal chiefs, and cities distant from shore, but he did not mention Mecca. His report has significant importance because he is a resident in the city of Berenice, opposite to central Arabia, and a distance of about 200-220 miles from the place where Mecca was built in later times. As an expert merchant and geographer, which his book clearly shows, it cannot be attributed to him to be ignorant of the cities close to his home when he described the Red Sea coastal regions. In fact, if he did succeed in describing with such accuracy the cities, tribes and trade as far as India, how, then, could he be ignorant of a city such as Mecca, which would be only 200–220 miles from his home? The fact is that he does not mention Mecca because, in his time, Mecca did not exist.

PLINY'S SURVEY

Pliny's Survey covered all of Arabia, mentioning all the cities, villages and tribes of Arabia, but he never mentioned Mecca, or any tribe which the Islamic tradition claims inhabited Mecca since ancient times.

Previously, we looked at an important military campaign during the time of Caesar. The Roman geographer and historian, Strabo, documented the campaign, but nowhere did he mention the city of Mecca. This causes us to conclude that Mecca had not been built during the time he lived, which was 64-23 B.C.

We move ahead in history to another important Roman author. We know him as Pliny, the Elder. Pliny was born at Como, in northern Italy, in 23 A.D. He became a commander of a Roman cavalry squadron, studied the law, became the Procurator – the financial manager – in Spain, then returned to Rome and became part of the Emperor's intimate inner circle.[54] This gave him access to the Roman documents, especially about the expedition into Arabia under Gallus, which Pliny mentioned in his work. He then received a naval commission. He died in 79 A.D.

Pliny completed his book, *Natural History*, in 77 A.D. It is his most important contribution to the knowledge we have about Roman life and times. It is an encyclopedia covering a wide variety of subjects, including: geography, astronomy, botany, zoology, meteorology and mineralogy. In the preface to this book, Pliny writes that he deals with 20,000 matters selected from 100 different authors. One of the authors Pliny consulted was Juba, a king in Mauritania, who did a survey of Arabia, documenting various locations and tribes in Arabia.

Pliny, in *Natural History*, Book Five, chapter 12, deals with "the coasts of Arabia, situated on the Egyptian sea." Then, in the book six, in the lengthy chapters 32 and 33, he focuses with detail on Arabia. The work of Pliny is considered a true encyclopedia. He mentioned approximately 92 nations and tribes in Arabia. Though he mentioned the least and most insignificant tribes of Arabia which existed in his lifetime, he does not mention any of the tribes which the Islamic tradition claims lived in Mecca during the first centuries after Christ. Although he mentioned 69 cities and villages in Arabia at this time, including villages of insignificant tribes, he did not mention Mecca. This adds to all other documented proofs that the Islamic claims regarding Mecca are unhistorical and without any foundation.

Pliny's survey has significant value, because he covered all the regions of Arabia. The survey starts in the far north, proceeds to the eastern gulf region, then proceeds south until it reaches the southeastern corner of Arabia. He goes west to the Red Sea, then north to the Gulf of Aqaba, and finally returns by proceeding south, all the while describing the interior land of Arabia. It is easy to see that the survey didn't overlook any area of Arabia which was inhabited at that time. Pliny was so detailed that he mentioned tribes which inhabited the desert, called the An-Nafud Desert today, such as the tribe of the Agraei, but still he didn't mention Mecca or any tribe living in the area where Mecca eventually was built.

Considering that Pliny's research covered all regions of Arabia, it is significant that there is a total absence in Pliny's work of any mention of any of the tribes, which were claimed by the Islamic tradition to have existed, and which had an important role in the affairs of Arabia. I firmly believe that the absence of such tribes confirms that Islamic tradition wanted to back the Qur'an in its false claim concerning Mecca. Consequently, the Muslims created false names of tribes, and a false history which doesn't correspond with the true documented history of men like Pliny, Artemidorus, Agatharchides and Strabo. One of the tribes that the Muslims created an imaginary history about is Jurhum. It is claimed that the people of Jurhum existed in Mecca since the time of Abraham and that, for a period of time, those people dominated Arabia. If these claims were true, Jurhum would have been superior to the documented nations of Arabia, such as Saba. Neither Greek nor Roman historical or archaeological records mention or allude to a tribe called Jurhum, even though archaeology over many centuries B.C. had uncovered many nations and tribes who lived north and south to the area where Mecca was later built. Jurhum might have been an insignificant tribe which appeared only after the Christian era.

Pliny's research also refutes the Islamic tradition concerning Quraish, the tribe from which Mohammed, himself, came. Islam claims that Quraish was an old tribe which lived in or around Mecca. Islamic tradition also claims that Quraish held a pre-eminent role over the other Arabian tribes in the region. Pliny, along with his Greek predecessors, demonstrates clearly that the Islamic history of Mecca is completely untrue and unhistorical. It wasn't until the 8th century A.D. that Islamic writers began to claim a special history for Mecca of great prestige in the region. Of course, the work of both Pliny and the Greeks shows that these claims can't be substantiated.

Furthermore, the early surveys disprove the claim that Quraish, the tribe of Mohammed, was an old tribe which had religious prestige among the other Arabian tribes. When compared to the well-documented Greek and Roman histories, the claim is proven to be without historical foundation. In fact, the survey of Pliny, with other Greek and Roman surveys, confirms the fact that Quraish, Khuzaa'h, the tribe which first built Mecca, and other tribes which inhabited Mecca did not yet exist in the 1st century A.D. in the region where Mecca was eventually built. This is a further confirmation that these tribes appeared and emigrated from Yemen in later times, and built Mecca some time after they emigrated from Yemen.

Ibn Ishak invented false history, and revealed his ignorance.

Previously, I mentioned that the person who first attempted to assign names to the tribes living in Mecca, and to create a history for Quraish, was Ibn Ishak. He lived in the 8th century A.D.

I also mentioned the ignorance of Ibn Ishak, his limited knowledge of history, and his confused chronology. In spite of this, the Muslims still follow this man's writings today, although he showed ignorance in his narration about history and lack of any historical basis for his writings. Ibn Ishak wrote about the life of Mohammed, and Ibn Hisham was the one who later edited the writings of Ibn Ishak. Therefore, the biography written by Ibn Ishak was named *Ibn Hisham*. This is the oldest and primary narration of the life of Mohammed. The writings of Ibn Ishak, in addition to the sayings of men like Wahab Bin Munabbih, al-Shaabi and Ibn Abbas who wrote in the 8th and 9th centuries A.D., became the foundation which other Muslim historians depended upon for Islamic history.

Ibn Ishak's work is filled with examples of historical ignorance in relation to documented and indisputable historical facts. For example, he claims that King Solomon, the son of David, dominated the entire earth before Alexander the Great did.[55] We know that this was not true of the true historical King Solomon.

According to Ibn Ishak, Christianity originated in Rome through a Roman emperor who was converted to Christianity by the twelve disciples of Christ. Ibn Ishak thought that the Roman emperor, Constantine, who lived in the 4th century A.D., was a contemporary of Jesus.[56] We know that these claims about Christianity, Constantine and Jesus are not true. Ibn Ishak says that one of the leaders of Yemen, named Tubb'a Asa'd Abu Kareb, who reigned in Yemen between 410-425 A.D., occupied China.[57] History does not mention this occupation of China. An occupation of China by Yemen in the 5th century A.D. would have been recorded as a great event; however, there is no evidence of this event happening. How could all other historians miss such a major event if it had truly happened?

The writings of Ibn Ishak are full of enormous mistakes which less-informed and ignorant elementary students would not make.

How can he be considered a reliable historian for Muslims when he writes a narrative which disagrees with documented history? And he did all this in order to convince people that Ishmael lived in Mecca and built the temple with Abraham's help! Sadly, this untrustworthy person became the father of a false history which has kept many Muslims from reading true and documented history. He has also kept many Muslims from reading the Bible, a dependable source for understanding ancient history.

It is time for Muslims to think for themselves, to go beyond false claims, and to challenge what they have believed for years. Once they find the truth about Islam, they will also find the truth about Jesus Christ, the One who died as the sacrifice for sin, and the only way to heaven.

PTOLEMY'S SURVEY AND THE LOCATION OF MACORABA

The Greek geographer, Claudius Ptolemy of Alexandria, Egypt, was born in the year 90 A.D. and died in 168 A.D. He wrote *Almonagest*, a chief astronomical work, and another work about astrology called *Tetrabilos*. Around the year 150 A.D., he dedicated himself to the study of the earth's geography – more specifically, cartographical representation, or mapping of the earth. He was inspired by the work of several other geographers who lived before him, including Marinus, who lived from 70-130 A.D. These geographers pioneered the concept of latitude and longitude lines for world maps. Ptolemy enhanced the concept of the latitudes and longitudes. Ptolemy reduced the latitude and longitude that Marinus has established before.[58] Ptolemy tried to document in his geographical work, simply called *Geography*, the latitude and longitude coordinates, also called meridians lines, for the important locations marked on the maps of his time. Most scholars doubt that the maps which included his latitude and longitude coordinates were actually drawn by him. But they do believe that other geographers used his information when making their maps.[59]

142

Ptolemy's geography provides valuable help in locating places that existed in his time, but we should consider some disclaimers which he mentions in his work. In his second book, Ptolemy mentions that the locations of some of the places or cities that were documented more recently, with respect to his time, are actually estimated regarding their proximity to more established places or cities.[60]   When compared to the latitude and longitude system we use today, his system seems crude and inaccurate. Yet, it is still helpful to know about the recently-discovered places which didn't appear in previous geographical surveys. We can establish where newer cities are located in relation to older ones. It's helpful to know whether the cities in question are south or north of an old city, or whether they are east or west.

From a practical standpoint, Ptolomy's criteria proves valuable when looking for other cities in the Middle East mentioned by him, or even by those in his own country, Egypt. Based on these facts, his work helps us resolve the location problem for some cities, such as Macoraba, which appeared in his generation.

In book six, chapter seven, of his work titled *Geography*, Ptolemy documents the latitude and longitude coordinates of several landmarks in Arabia.[61]   By studying these locations and coordinates, we notice once again that the city of Mecca is never mentioned. In fact, Ptolomy doesn't mention any cities in the strip of land where Mecca was eventually built.

Macoraba was a city in the Arabian interior which was mentioned by Ptolemy. Some people wanted to assume that Macoraba was actually Mecca. Macoraba had appeared recently, with respect to Ptolemy's time. This assumption would result in the conclusion that Mecca was built around the middle of the 2nd century A.D. However, even if this were true, it wouldn't support the claim that Mecca was an old city existing from the time of Abraham. Upon further study of the facts concerning Macoraba, we can conclude with certainty that Macoraba cannot be Mecca, and we can refute the idea that Mecca was built in the 2nd century A.D. All the facts point to the historical argument that Mecca was constructed in the 4th century A.D. Since Macoraba is not pronounced like Mecca, the scholar Crone suggested that the

143

location of Maqarib, near Yathrib, was actually Macoraba. Maqarib is mentioned by Yaqut al-Hamawi, an Arab geographer who lived from 1179-1229 A.D., in his geographical dictionary *Mujam al-Buldan*.[62] This location is more acceptable than Mecca for the modern-day location of Macoraba, because Maqarib is closer in pronunciation to Macoraba than to Mecca. Another reason is that Maqarib, though it does not exactly fit the documented location of Macoraba, is closer to the location, according to the latitude and longitude of Ptolemy, than Mecca is to the documented location of Macoraba.

In order to determine the exact location of Macoraba, scholars have looked to the city of Lathrippa, mentioned by Ptolemy at a longitude of 71, as a reference. Lathrippa is accepted by most scholars as the city of Yathrib, a city documented in the historical record. Ptolemy placed the city of Macoraba at 73 20 longitude, which means about three-and-a-third degrees east of Yathrib, while Mecca is west of Yathrib. So Macoraba cannot be the city of Mecca, nor a city in the direction where Mecca was later built. Macoraba should be located deeper into the interior of Arabia, or toward the eastern coast of Arabia.

We have just analyzed the longitude; now let's turn to the latitude. When we study latitude we find more data concerning the historical location of Macoraba. Ptolemy described Macoraba, not as the next city south of Lathrippa, or Yathrib, but the sixth city to the south. While the city of Carna is the first city to the south of Lathrippa, Macoraba is the sixth city to the south. Carna was a well-known Yemeni city, belonging to the Minaean kingdom mentioned by Strabo. This is significant, because Strabo described the main tribes of southern Arabia in these words:

> The extreme part of the country is occupied by the four largest tribes; by the Minaeans ... whose largest city is Carna; next to these, by the Sabaeans, whose metropolis is Mariaba; third by the Cattabanians, whose royal seat is called Tamna; and the farthest toward the east, the Chatramotitae, meaning Hadramout, whose city is Sabata.[63]

In the past, Carna was known as the most important, and the largest city of the Yemen Kingdom of Ma'in. Carna was a significant city of Arabia which Ptolemy couldn't miss. Because Macoraba was listed as the fifth city south of Carna, we understand Ptolemy used Carna as a reference point for the five cities he listed south of Carna, included Macoraba. We can't make Lathrippa a reference point for locating Macoraba, since Lathrippa is farther north of Macoraba, but Macoraba's location is south of the famous old Minaean city of Carna. We can only conclude that by latitude, Macoraba is in south Arabia, south of the Yemeni city of Carna. However, by longitude, Ptolemy placed it closer to Carna. By any measure, Macoraba must be near Carna, in Yemen.

I think we should go more east of Yathrib to identify Mocoraba mentioned by Ptolemy. In fact, Pliny mentions a city with the name Mochorba, and he said it was a port of Oman on the Hadramout shore in South Arabia. It's also possible that Macoraba is derived from Mochorba.[64]

Since Macoraba never appears in any literature other than the narration of Ptolemy, it must have been a small settlement or tiny village which disappeared in Ptolomy's time during the 2nd century A.D. Probably a small Omani tribe emigrated from the port of Mochorba toward the north of Yemen, near Carna, the old Minaean city of Yemen, and established a small settlement which they named after their original city. The tribe would then have moved to another area in search of better living conditions, a usual migratory occurrence in Arabia. The fact that Macoraba never appears again in any other classical survey confirms the fact that it was a small provisional settlement of a small tribe, and not a significant town.

If a case for the name of Machorba should be opened, it should be seen in relation to the southern Arabian city of Mochorba, and not to Mecca. In the same manner, we see the city of New London in the United States as being named after the original city of London. We can't open a case for the origin of the name of the American city apart from the English city after which it was named.

THE ABSENCE OF MECCA IN THE ETHIOPIAN, SYRIAN, ARAMAIC AND COPTIC LITERATURE

The absence of Mecca in the Ethiopian, Syrian, Aramaic and Coptic literature points to the fact that it couldn't have been founded during the 3rd century A.D.

Let's look at Ethiopian literature. The Ethiopians were also concerned with documenting Arabian cities on the opposite coast of the Red Sea, especially in the area where Mecca was eventually built. Again, we see that there is no mention of Mecca in their surveys. Neither do we find any mention of Mecca during the 2nd, 3rd or 4th century A.D. This also demonstrates that Mecca did not exist at the time of Ptolemy; we have to place its origin at a later date.

That Mecca was not built before the 2nd A.D. century is an indisputable fact. The question now is whether we can determine if Mecca was built in the 3rd or 4th century A.D. The absence of records in Syrian, Aramaic and Coptic literature makes the dates for the existence of Mecca later than the 3rd century A.D. Crone, whom I mentioned earlier, did a survey of the Coptic and Syrian literature which was concerned with Arabia, but none of these works mentioned Mecca.[65]

We also have other reasons to assume that the date for Mecca's founding was after the beginning of the 4th century A.D. We find some help in Christian evangelistic and missionary activities in Arabia and Christian literature. They do not mention Mecca, either.

We also know that the Christians under the Byzantine Empire tried to evangelize Arabia. The Byzantine emperor targeted the main cities of Arabia and sent missionaries to evangelize and establish churches. This evangelism was so successful that, at the Nicea Convention around 320 A.D., an Arabic bishop participated.[66] The church in Najran, a city on the border of Yemen toward Mecca, was established before the Nicea Convention. In 354 A.D., Constantine the Second sent Theophilus Indus to Arabia to evangelize the region. He established churches in Eden, Thafar and Hermez. The Ethiopians sent missionaries to Arabia to evangelize the cities around the Red Sea. The Nestorians sent missionaries to Hijaz; into northern and central western Arabia where Mecca was eventually built. Arabia was also the main target of missionary activity for the church of Hira in southern Iraq.

It is significant that we don't find any mention of Mecca in all the Christian records of this time. This suggests that Mecca did not exist in the 3rd century A.D., or at the beginning of the 4th century. Because it was inhabited by many tribes, and built by a big tribe, like Khuzaa'h, Mecca could not be a small village which would not have attracted the attention of the missionaries and the Christian churches of Mesopotamia, Ethiopia and Byzantium.

Once again, we see the writers of history confirming our research which shows that Mecca was built long after Muslims claim it was. This simple truth should challenge Muslims to take a fresh look at the teachings of the Bible and seek after the truth, which Jesus said, "...will make you free."

3 _____

THE HISTORY AND ARCHAEOLOGY OF ARABIA SHOW THAT MECCA DID NOT EXIST BEFORE THE ADVENT OF CHRISTIANITY.

The richness of the archaeological findings and inscriptions of many regions of Arabia.

Islam claims that Mecca is an ancient historical city which existed long before Christ, dating as far back as the time of Abraham. A powerful argument against this claim is the absence of any inscriptions found on monuments, or in any archaeological records dating back to those times. The ancient cities and kingdoms of Arabia do have rich histories which survive to this day through monuments, the inscriptions they bear, and in other archaeological documents. These historical records have given archaeologists a highly-integrated and, in some cases, complete record of the names of kings who ruled these cities and kingdoms. These records have also given archaeologists important information about the history of the wars fought over the kingdoms and cities of Arabia. In most cases, inscriptions and monuments in various cities – especially in the western and southwestern portions of Arabia – even give the names of coregents who ruled with the kings. Yet, even with this rich collection of historical and archaeological information, there are no inscriptions or monuments, or other archaeological findings whatsoever, that mention Mecca.

Regarding the richness of the archaeological findings in Arabia, Montgomery says that Assyrian inscriptions did not provide as much detailed information as the Arabian inscriptions did.[67]

If Mecca existed in ancient times, it should have more archaeological findings than did regions south and north of it, whose history is richly documented through archaeology.

This lack of mention of Mecca is especially interesting, given the fact that Mecca was built on the caravan routes between the kingdoms of Arabia, and that these kingdoms had written historical records several centuries before Christ. In fact, Mecca is built on what was the famous commercial route between southern Arabia and the northern Arabian cities of Qedar and Dedan. In addition, Mecca was built alongside the Red Sea trading route.

It is claimed by archaeologists that the Sabaeans of southwestern Arabia had utilized the skill of writing since the 10th century B.C.[68] Inscriptions on rock formations in southwestern Yemen are among the richest archaeological finds among Middle Eastern civilizations. Many thousands of these ancient inscriptions are available to historians today. Most of these inscriptions have survived without serious degradation, due to the small amounts of rain in that area of the world.

In northern regions of Arabia, some hundreds of miles north of where Mecca was later built, many cities had rich inscriptions carved in stone, and the inscriptions give us the names of various dynasties which ruled those cities. Dedan and Teima are examples of cities situated on famous trade routes. Located north of what became the site of Mecca, their stone, rock and monumental inscriptions are enough to reflect their history since the 8th or 7th century B.C.

What about Mecca? Mecca was built on a location between the documented civilizations (the Sabaeans, Dedan and Qedar), yet these civilizations do not have any known inscriptions whatsoever which mention Mecca. Mecca, if it had existed at the time of those civilizations, would have contained more intact inscriptions than the civilizations which lived in the regions south of it – for example, in Yemen. The region around Mecca is known for its very low amounts of rain, even compared with the other regions of Arabia. The lands of Yemen have ten times more rainfall than the area around Mecca. Also, the cities of northern Arabia have much more rain than the region of Mecca. So, if Mecca existed several centuries before Christ, then its inscriptions in stone and rock would have been more intact than the thousands of inscriptions remaining from the cities to the north and south of it .

Over the years, historians and archaeologists have identified a series of rulers and kings for every Arabian kingdom before the 7th century B.C., and continuing through subsequent centuries. Based on thousands of inscriptions and other archaeological findings, historians have drawn tables listing the rulers, and the kingdoms which they controlled. We find such tables in the works of K. A. Kitchen, Von Wissmann and others.

Today, we can trace the history of each kingdom or city which existed in the first millennium before Christ, and in the years that followed. Although there are a few unattested names, for many locations we also can easily connect the names of the rulers with their cities, using virtually certain information.

NORTHWEST ARABIA IS ATTESTED TO IN ARCHAEOLOGY

The Cities of Qedar, Dedan and Teima

Let's look first at northwest Arabia and the cities of Qedar, Dedan and Teima. The series of rulers over some of the northern cities of Arabia, such as Qedar, is almost completely documented as far back as the 9th century B.C. Major contributing factors to this are the many annals of the kings of Assyria and Babylonia who had relationships with the Arabian cities. The Assyrian and Babylonian kings traded with the cities of Arabia, and sometimes subdued them or had wars with them. Some of the Mesopotamian kings who occupied the cities of Qedar and Dedan had royal chronicles which provide detailed information. For example, we have the Nabonidus Chronicle, a history of the Babylonian king who occupied northern Arabia and made the city of Teima his residence for about ten years, from 550-540 B.C.

Some historical records were carved into bowls. We have one silver bowl dedicated to the shrine, Han Ilat, on which we see the name of King Qaynu of Qedar, who reigned between 430-410 B.C.[69] Other records are provided by graffiti, with writings on the walls, such as the Graffito of Niran at Dedan, at al-Ula, where we find mention of Gashmu I, son of Shahr I, King of Qedar.[70] This confirms the Biblical narration found in Nehemiah 6:6 about this king who opposed Nehemiah in the rebuilding of the city of Jerusalem, after the Babylonian exile. In fact, the Hebrew Biblical name for this king is Gashem, a variation of the name Gashmu, who reigned from the Arabian city of Qedar from 450-430 B.C.,[71] at the same time that Nehemiah returned from the Babylonian exile to rebuild the walls of the city of Jerusalem. We know that Nehemiah took a small contingent of Jews and returned to Palestine around the year 445 B.C. This is one of hundreds of historical proofs of the accuracy of the Bible.

When we put the records together, we have a series of fourteen kings and queens who ruled in northern Arabia. Although historians are uncertain about the period between 644-580 B.C., there are no other gaps in the listing of rulers between 870-410 B.C.

The accuracy of inscriptions found at the archaeological site of El-Ula, in the area of the ancient city of Dedan, was written in Minaean language. It shows that the city was in subjection to the kings of Main. Many of these kings who were mentioned in the inscriptions were identical to the Minaean inscriptions of Yemen.[72]

In the old ruins of Teima, there are many inscriptions, showing the names of their gods, and their wars with other cities and tribes in the region, including their wars with the city of Dedan. The moon in Teima was represented by a crescent.[73] In the inscriptions of Teima, there is mention of a god called Lame'h. Lame'h is described as a brilliant shining star. One of their deities is given the title of Rahim, whom I believe is the star deity, Lame'h.[74] The same title is given to Allah in the Qur'an, which shows that Islamic worship has its roots in ancient pagan Arabian worship.

The North Arabian Tribes of Thamud, Lihyan and the Nabataeans are Richly Attested to in Archaeology

Next, I want to look at the Thamud tribe of north Arabia, which appeared for the first time in the 8th century B.C. and continued until the 5th century A.D. There are hundreds of Thamudic stone or rock inscriptions found in many places in north Arabia which tell about the life of the tribe, their deities and their wars.

Second, we have the Lihyan kingdom of northern Arabia. We have an abundance of records about this kingdom. With the exception of the founder of the Lihyanite line, we have complete documentation of the rulers and the periods in which they ruled; the inscriptions also chronicle other important information about historical events concerning their reigns and their gods. Some of these records are in royal monuments, statues, dedications, tomb inscriptions, tomb-building texts, stone texts, and graffiti.

The founder of the Lihyan kingdom reigned approximately from 330-320 B.C. Information concerning the kings which followed him is well-documented. King Shahru II reigned between 320-305 B.C. The line ended with the tenth king, Mas'udu, who reigned from 120-100 B.C. There are no historical gaps in the inscriptions in this series.[75]

The third kingdom we want to look at is the Nabataean Kingdom, which penetrated into many regions of Hijaz. It has special importance in the history of northern Arabia because it controlled the road used in the spice trade which connected the south of Arabia with Syria and other Mediterranean countries. This is the same route which passed through the region where Mecca was built in the 4th century A.D. Records of the Nabataean Kingdom are very complete, both externally and internally. In the external records, historians wrote about the Nabataeans. Some Jewish literature tells about them, and other works have been found in various archaeological sites outside Nabataean territories. Internally, an important means of identifying the rulers of the Nabataean Kingdom are from their many coins. Also, dedications of buildings, statues dedicated to kings, private and royal monuments, and tomb inscriptions all provide historical text. The inscriptions on tombs are abundant and are found in different sites, such as Petra, Madain Salih, and other places. Based on these records, historians came to understand with great detail about the series of rulers of the Nabataean Kingdom who ruled after 175 B.C. Rulers before this date are still unknown, though there are many records about the kingdom since the first stage of its dominion. With the exception of the second ruler in the series from 175 B.C., other rulers of the series are well-documented, starting from Aretas I, who ruled from175-150 B.C. until the twelfth (and last) ruler, Rabbel II, who reigned from 70-106 A.D.[76]

After examining all the records concerning the kingdoms and cities located north of Mecca, we conclude that the reigns of most of the rulers are well-documented. We know about the wars in which they were engaged, and the names of their gods. Mecca is conspicuous by its absence. Even though Muslims claim Mecca dates back to the time of Abraham, not one record indicates its existence at any time before Christ.

It is impossible to introduce a city like Mecca and claim that it has the longest life in the history of Arabian cities, unless you have some record. In this case, the region was well-documented, even for cities which lasted only a few centuries. But, there was no record of any city called Mecca.

Did you notice that none of the kingdoms which were north of Mecca had been in existence before the 10th century B.C.? Some of them, like the Lihyanite kingdom, first appeared in the 4th century B.C. and disappeared near the end of the 2nd century B.C. Some cities had limited roles in Arabian history. Many came into existence after the 10th century B.C. and disappeared around the beginning of the 4th century B.C. All of them had an abundance of records for most of their existence, but none of these records mentions Mecca.

Muslim tradition would give an early and long life to Mecca, from before the time of Abraham, who lived around 2080 B.C. If this claim were true, then there should be many more archaeological records surviving for Mecca than for any of the northern cities and kingdoms which we have examined. In reality, there is not one known record mentioning the existence of Mecca, even for a small time, before the time of Christ. We find this lack of historical records about Mecca, in spite of its proximity to regions where, because of lack of rain, archaeological records would not be eroded by water. We find this, in spite of Mecca supposedly existing in a region and time where the historical existence of cities and kingdoms is documented in more clarity than in any other place in the ancient world. There are very few regions in Europe which have clear documentation of their rulers as far back as the 1st millennium B.C. One reason for this could be the weather conditions. Heavy European rains tend to wash away valuable ancient inscriptions. This is in stark contrast to the regions of dryer Arabia surrounding the location of Mecca, where the lines of succession are well-documented. So, with these criteria, it is impossible to claim that a city like Mecca would have existed in Arabia throughout its ancient history, without any mention of it in any of the known historical records of the region. The real history in Arabia is abundantly expressed by its records. It is impossible to introduce a city like Mecca into a history so well-documented.

According to the Muslim claim, Mecca had the longest existence of any major city in Arabia; it is claimed to have existed as a major city since the 21st century B.C., and well into the Christian era. It means Mecca existed, without historical mention, in an area where even cities with a short existence are documented in the many historical records of the region. Every city in the region has abundant historical records, while Mecca is silent. To claim Mecca's existence since the time of Abraham, without support of the historical record, is not logical. The dating of the city of Mecca may sound like a simple thing, but it should challenge Muslims today to ask if they are following other teachings which are inaccurate, misleading and untruthful. It should also challenge Muslims to read the Old and New Testaments of the Bible, and to ask themselves if what the Bible says about Jesus is true.

KINGDOMS AND CITIES SOUTH OF MECCA MAINTAINED PLENTY OF HISTORICAL RECORDS

Previously, we have examined the kingdoms and cities north of where Mecca was later built. We saw how some of these kingdoms as far as 500-600 miles away maintained plenty of historical records. What about the kingdoms and cities south of Mecca's eventual location? The southwestern portion of Arabia has even clearer records than kingdoms to the north. In some cases, thousands of records, many of them stone inscriptions, have been discovered. This makes southwestern Arabia one of the most abundant archaeological regions in the world. In addition to stone inscriptions, writings have also been found on royal and private monuments, building texts, decrees, dedications, temples, and more. Based on such records, historians and archaeologists have followed the succession of rulers for each kingdom and each city. In most cases, these genealogies of the various rulers can be mapped without any gaps in the chronology.

The Rulers of the Kingdom of Main

A line of rulers for the kingdom of Main, in southern Arabia, starts with King Abkarib I, who reigned from 430-415 B.C. He began an unbroken line of 26 rulers, which ended with Ilyara' Yashur II. He reigned from 65-55 B.C. Their records include the names of many of the kings' brothers and sons who reigned alongside them. Consequently, we know for certain the names of rulers of the kingdom of Main for the time between 430 and 55 B.C.[77]

Small kingdoms south of where Mecca was eventually built are documented with great accuracy in the ancient history of Arabia, yet Mecca has no records to support the Islamic claim about its ancient existence.

Many small kingdoms near the kingdom of Main also have documented royal lines with very few gaps. Some of these small kingdoms are located close to where Mecca was later built. These small kingdoms existed in the centuries before Christ as modest, but not prominent, kingdoms. Yet, there are historical and archaeological records which clearly testify about their existence and their lines of kings.

These records present an obvious challenge to the claims that Mecca existed in the centuries before Christ – because there are no such similar records for Mecca. This challenge to the existence of Mecca is further supported by the fact which I emphasized previously: the lack of rain in Arabia allows archaeological records to remain intact for long periods of time. Therefore, no city or kingdom in southern Arabia is left without a wealth of inscriptions describing it. This is true, whether the kingdom had a short or long existence, and whether it was modest or important in the region. The inscriptions bring to light the nature of the cultures, the lines of rulers, and the main wars and events in which the kingdoms were involved.

Let us look at some of the small kingdoms. First, there was the kingdom of Haram, which had a line of rulers starting with King Yaharil in 600 B.C.,[78] and ending with King Maadikarib Raydan, who ruled from 190-175 B.C.[79] Next was the kingdom of Inabba. Its most prominent ruler was King Waqahil Yafush, who reigned from 550-530 B.C.[80] The kingdom of Kaminahu started with King Ammiyitha, who reigned from 585-570 B.C.[81] The line continued through eight more documented rulers to King Ilisami II Nabat, who reigned between 495–475 B.C.[82] Records show that this kingdom flourished under the rule of Wahbu, son of Mas'ud, around 160-140 B.C. Then there was the kingdom of Nashan, whose first documented ruler was King Ab'amar Saqid. He reigned around 760 B.C.[83] Another line of three kings is documented to have ruled between 520-480 B.C. The last of these three kings was Yadi'ab Amir, who reigned between 500-480 B.C.[84]

Thus, we see that there is substantial documentation of the chronology of these kingdoms, even though they were small and had little influence when compared to other kingdoms in the region. This shows that even small kingdoms near where Mecca was eventually built are documented with accuracy in the ancient history of Arabia. Islamic tradition claims that Mecca was a prestigious and pre-eminent religious city throughout the history of Arabia. The tradition also claims that this pre-eminence of Mecca extended back to even before the time of Abraham. Yet there are no historical records regarding Mecca, similar to the examples above, which can support these claims of the Islamic tradition. These claims about Mecca have absolutely no support in the historical and archaeological record.

We Have an Amazing Amount of Records for the Kingdom of Qataban

But our study doesn't stop there. In the kingdom of Qataban, we find more proof that Mecca did not exist before Christ. This kingdom was located in southwestern Arabia. We have amazing amounts of knowledge about the sequence of events and the name of the rulers of this kingdom. There is line of 31 rulers whose reign started in 330 B.C. and continued through the last ruler, Marthadum, who reigned at the very end of the Qataban kingdom (150-160 A.D.). Historians have documented all but two of these 31 rulers: they are numbers 2 and 27. This reflects the completeness of the inscriptions and records of the kingdom of Qataban.[85]

SABA AND HIMYAR

Saba and Himyar present a series of 102 kings which started in the 9th century B.C. and ended in the 6th century A.D. This is a proof that Mecca did not exist in ancient times. If it had existed, it should have had archaeological documentation for each generation of its history.

Even more impressive than the kingdom of the north which we have studied, is the kingdom of Saba and its successor in the region, the kingdom of Himyar. Many archaeological records document a series of rulers, beginning with Karibil A., who ruled around 860 B.C. The series continues with 31 Makrab. The Makrab were kings who not only ruled Saba, but other nearby regions. The last Makrab king was Yitha'a Amar Bayyin II, who reigned between 360-350 B.C. Saba then lost control of its surrounding states, and its rulers could no longer enjoy the title of Makrab, but were kings, instead.

After the Makrab, the line of kings continued with number 32, Yadi'ubil Bayyin, who reigned between 350-335 B.C. And the line goes on to number 55, a king of Saba named Yada'il Dharih IV. He reigned between 0–15 A.D. The kings of Saba and Dhu-Radydan followed this series of rulers.

But the documentation doesn't end here. We have continuing records of the kings of Himyar and Saba. King Dhamar'alay Warar Yahan'ifm was the 56th ruler in the series. He was followed by a line of kings which ended with ruler number 79, the last king of Saba. His name is Nasha'karib Yuhamin II Yuharhib, and he reigned between 260-275.

Then the line of rulers shifts to the first king of the empire of Himyar, Yasir Yuhan'im I, who reigned between 275-285 A.D. The kings of Himyar reigned over the kingdoms of Saba, Himyar and other states in the region. This series finally ends with Maadikarib III, who reigned between 575-577 A.D. Maadikarib was ruler number 102 in a long series of kings which covers a period of 1,437 years, starting in the 9th century B.C., just a few decades before the Queen of Saba had visited Solomon, and ending in the 6th century A.D.[86]

A study of these kings has something significant to tell us. The abundance of records over such a long period of time shows us that southern and western Arabia are some of the most well-documented regions in the ancient world. We could not document such a series of rulers for any European country in the 1st millennium B.C. with the same degree of accuracy. Here we have a series of kings in Yemen dating back to the 9th century B.C., with very few gaps in the lines of documented rulers, especially when we look at the long series of rulers in Saba and Himyar. Therefore, the claim that a central religious city, like

Mecca, could have been present, without any records to substantiate it, is implausible and unacceptable.

THE KINGDOM OF KINDA, EAST OF MECCA, AND ITS ARCHAEOLOGICAL RECORDS

We've looked at the north and south, now let's come to the regions east of Mecca. We have the kingdom of Kinda, which dominated central and northern Arabia. The capital was Dhu-Kahilum, known today as Qaryat al-Fau, near the old city of Yamama, about 500 miles from Mecca. The ancient site of Dhu-Kahilum is abundant in archaeological findings from which we can discern important information about the kings of Kinda and their wars. The first king was Rabi'a, who ruled from 205 to 230 A.D. He is mentioned in the Sabaean inscriptions as "King of Kinda and Kahtan."[87] We know about the history of Kinda, particularly through inscriptions. For example, in the year 290 A.D., Kinda lost its domain to the kingdom of Saba. In fact, we read in Sabaean Inscriptions from Mahram Bilqis–Ma'rib, the following statement about a Sabaean king: "Saadta Iab Yatlaf, descendant of Gadanum, leader of the Arabs of the King of Saba and of Kindat ..."[88]

It is illogical to claim that an ancient Mecca existed for 2,400 years without any record in a region where every kingdom which existed in history has been attested to.

We see that the closest cities to Mecca, whether in the north, south or east, are very well-documented through archaeological findings which allow us to discover the history of the region and a majority of the names of the rulers. With such complete records from kingdoms located less than 500 miles from the location of Mecca, we see that no city could have possibly existed in that area without leaving at least some records behind to tell us its history. To claim that Mecca existed in the region for at least 2,400 years, from the time of Abraham until the 4th century A.D., without any record, would be inconsistent with everything that has been recorded by archaeologists. Not only do Greek and Roman geographers and historians fail to mention Mecca, but the archaeologists of ancient Arabia exclude its existence prior to the 4th century A.D. How, then, can we insert Abraham and monotheism into Mecca if it did not exist, not just in one period, but also in all periods of Arabia? Yet, Muslims around the world believe that Abraham and his son, Ishmael, founded a temple in Mecca. No one can rewrite history, trying to convince humanity of things which he claims happened over a land or region, whose history already has been written by historians and attested to by archaeologists.

THE ARCHAEOLOGY OF EASTERN ARABIA NEGATES THE IDEA OF AN ANCIENT MECCA

The history of ancient cities in eastern and western Arabia which existed for many millennia before Christ, and even date back to the time of Abraham, have abundant archaeological findings which unveil their history. Yet, they also prove that Mecca, without any such record, could not have existed during Abraham's lifetime.

Eastern Arabia has a well-documented history, and it is intimately tied to ancient Mesopotamia, which is present-day Iraq. The history of eastern Arabia, which includes the Persian Gulf coastal region, is totally independent of western Arabia, mainly because eastern and western Arabia are separated by two huge desert regions: Ar' Rub' al-khali in the south and An Nafud in the north. We find no communication in ancient history between eastern and western Arabia. We have many archaeological findings in the Persian Gulf region which help us understand the history of eastern Arabia and its relationship to Mesopotamian dynasties, which existed several millennia before Christ. We have also learned about eastern Arabia's golden periods of self-dominion. For help in dating the archaeological findings of eastern Arabia, we have the chronology of the events in Mesopotamia.

Dilmun

One of the most important ancient kingdoms of eastern Arabia was Dilmun, which ruled over the land in what is present-day Bahrain. In many epochs, Dilmun's control extended over most of the Persian Gulf region. Dilmun has flourished since 3000 B.C., due to its trade with the Indus valley (India and Pakistan) and Mesopotamia.

Archaeological findings, such as pottery and other wares, tell us that ancient eastern Arabian civilizations are as old as ancient Mesopotamian civilizations. Contacts between Dilmun and Mesopotamia are documented from the 4th millennium through the 3rd millennium B.C. Sumerian and Akkad inscriptions also mention Dilmun throughout early history.[89] The Dilmun Kingdom, especially in what is now Bahrain, has many archaeological sites abundant in findings which allow us, with help from the Mesopotamian inscriptions, to discover valuable information about the history of Dilmun. Scholars can attest to a line of Dilmun kings which began in 1800 B.C. Although the first king is unnamed, there are three kings documented in the line, with their names, between 1470-1320 B.C. Then the series appears again in 720 B.C. with King Uperi and continues with attested kings until the occupation of Dilmun by the Babylonian Nabonidus. Nabonidus appointed a governor over Dilmun between 550-540 B. C.

The occupation of the land of Dilmun by the Assyrians, Babylonians, Greek and Persians is attested to by the local archaeological findings, and by outside inscriptions.

Magan

Another important kingdom in eastern Arabia is Magan, the present location of Oman. From the Sumerian city of Ur we have inscriptions concerning Magan, dated somewhere between 2800-2500 B.C. We have additional Magan inscriptions from the Akkadic period which began with Sargon, the person who first conquered Sumerian states in Iraq. He established the Akkad Empire around 2340 B.C. Inscriptions of King Sargon mentioned that Sargon "caused ships from Meluhha (Pakistan), ships from Magan and ships from Dilmun to moor at quay of Agade."[90]

Magan extended from Oman, across the Straits of Hormuz, into part of Iran, and also extended north toward what is now the United Arab Emirates in the Persian Gulf. There are many archaeological sites in Oman and the United Arab Emirates which furnish much data about the kingdom of Magan. Internal archaeological data with external inscriptions have provided scholars with valuable information. For example, there were three kings in Magan. The first was King Manitan, who ruled around 2240 B.C., 150 years before Abraham. The second was an unnamed king who ruled around 2060 B.C., and the third was King Nadubeli, who ruled around 2043 B.C. I mention these three kings because they were contemporaries of the patriarchs, especially Abraham and his sons. This is a significant finding, proving that the ancient civilizations in Arabia, at the time of Abraham and prior to his time, are not just names, but actually existed. Their ruins have remained as testimony to their presence in eastern Arabia, just like the ruins of other civilizations in the region of Mesopotamia. The ruins of these civilizations are a testimony to their existence, not just since the time of Abraham, but for thousands of years before Abraham, as we saw in the case of the civilizations of Dilmun and Magan.

As we have seen, even the names of kings of these civilizations are documented as far back as the time of Abraham, and his sons and grandchildren. As for Mecca, which is claimed by Muslims to be present at the same time as these civilizations, there are no known archaeological or historical records to vindicate such a claim.

The archaeology of Mesopotamia and Eastern Arabia demonstrates that western Arabia was unknown to the inhabitants of Mesopotamia and Eastern Arabia. How could Abraham, the inhabitant of Ur in Iraq, go to a place unknown in his time?

In the case of Dilmun in eastern Arabia, we see clear archaeological records of kings and related events dating from as far back as the 3rd millennium B.C., until its Islamic occupation in the 7th century A.D. On the other hand, in central western Arabia, where Mecca was eventually built, there is no record of any civilization until several centuries after the time of Christ, as we have seen from our study of the classical geographers and writers. The fact is that nobody in the ancient world recorded the existence of any civilization at the time of Abraham in western Arabia. The huge deserts which separate eastern Arabia from western Arabia were not crossable by humans at the time of Abraham. This made western Arabia a complete mystery to the inhabitants of eastern Arabia and Mesopotamia at that time. This case is similar to the way Europeans thought about what lay beyond the Atlantic Ocean before the Columbus Expedition.

Not only was western Arabia unaware of eastern Arabia, but it was also unknown to the people of Mesopotamia at the time of Abraham. You may remember from the Bible that Mesopotamia is where Abraham lived before he was called by God to set out for the Promised Land.

We have many inscriptions in the history of Mesopotamia about the Persian Gulf region in the east, including the Sumerian and Akkadic periods and their control of Abraham's home, the city of Ur in Iraq. But we don't have any records coming from Mesopotamia about central western Arabia, where Mecca was eventually built. The first historical records to mention western Arabia were about Yemen, located in southwestern Arabia. Yemen records have been found in Egyptian inscriptions from around the 14th century B.C., which was seven centuries after Abraham. Archaeological inscriptions in Mesopotamia, including Ur, the city of Abraham, make no mention of Yemen until the 8th century B.C. Then Assyrian inscriptions mention the king of Saba-Yemen, presenting tribute to the Assyrian king, Sargon II. This demonstrates that even Yemen, the oldest civilization of southwestern Arabia, was unknown in Mesopotamia at the time of Abraham. No Mesopotamian records at any time in ancient history mention the central western region of Arabia along the coast of the Red Sea. Why is there a lack of information about central western Arabia, where Mecca was eventually built? Simply because this region was completely uninhabited until the 3rd century B.C., when the trade routes of Yemen along the Red Sea began to flourish. Western Arabia, during the time of Abraham, was an unexplored area, and no known expeditions were made into it.

In addition to the historical events which we have been examining, there is an interesting novel written during that period. *The Epic of Gilgamesh* was written in the city of Uruk, in Mesopotamia, around the year 2000 B.C., about 100 years after the time Abraham lived in Ur, one of the main cities in Mesopotamia. The setting for the *Epic of Gilgamesh* gives us some insight into life in Mesopotamia. Hommel, a scholar commenting on the ninth canto of the *Epic of Gilgamesh*, says:

> We are told how Gilgamesh set out for the land of Mashu in central Arabia, the gate of which was guarded by legendary scorpion-like men; hence, perhaps, the name "land of darkness" is applied to Arabia in early Hebrew annals.

> For 12 miles the hero had to make his way through dense darkness. At length he came to an enclosed space by the seashore where dwelt the virgin goddess, Sabitu, who tells him that "no one since eternal days has ever crossed the sea, save Shamash, the hero. Difficult is the crossing, and extremely dangerous the way, and closed are the waters of death which bolt its entrance. How then, Gilgamesh, wilt thou cross the sea?"[91]

We understand from this epic, which came from the time of Abraham and the civilization of Mesopotamia, that men were not able to go into central Arabia because of "the gate of which was guarded by legendary scorpion-like men," and nobody succeeded in crossing the waters that led to southwestern Arabia. So, western Arabia was an enigma to the inhabitants of Uruk and Ur (where Abraham lived), and no one had crossed to western Arabia before. If this were the case for Yemen, in southwestern Arabia, then it would be even more true in central western Arabia, the area where Mecca was built, which was not known in any Mesopotamian literature in any time.

TRUE HISTORY OF MECCA

If the area of Mashu, toward central Arabia, was an enigma for the Mesopotamians, and no one crossed this region, then west Arabia was non-existent for the inhabitants of Mesopotamia. How could a man like Abraham, who came from the city of Ur (which was one of the most civilized cities in the fertile land of Mesopotamia) leave Palestine to go into the deserts of Arabia to build a sanctuary in a place where no man in his time had ever gone to live? It's like imagining that Napoleon went to the North Pole to build a church before anyone had yet reached the North Pole. Or, like imagining Napoleon reaching the top of Mount Everest to build a resting place there, when we know that the top of Mount Everest wasn't even known to him. In the same way, claiming that a civilization in Yemen was in contact with kingdoms in Palestine at the time of Abraham is something we know could not have been true. The first kingdom in Yemen originated in the 14th century B.C., seven centuries after Abraham. Cities along the Yemeni trading route by the Red Sea, through central western Arabia, didn't exist in the time of Abraham. These cities came into existence after Yemen began trading with Israel and Syria. In addition, we learned previously that Mecca was one of the later cities to be built by tribes from Yemen, several centuries after Christ.

The life of Abraham, as recorded by Moses, showed the desire of the patriarch to go to Egypt at the time of a famine which occurred in Palestine, and not in deserted and unknown places in his time, such as western Arabia.

Let us look at the history of Abraham, as revealed in the Bible. Abraham was a citizen of Ur of South Mesopotamia, who lived in one of the most fertile and civilized lands of the 21st century B.C. When a famine came to Canaan, Abraham did what any civilized man might do. He didn't choose to travel to a land which was inferior to his homeland; instead he traveled to Egypt. Why? Because, at that time, Egypt was the only civilization which could compete with his homeland. Because of the Nile River, Egypt had an abundance of water and was known for its advanced civilization. After the famine ended, Abraham returned to Canaan, the beautiful land which God had promised to give to him and the descendants of Isaac as an inheritance. Abraham preferred the Egyptian civilization, even if it meant leaving Canaan. How, then, could he consider traveling to an unknown desert such as western Arabia, and the eventual location of Mecca?

The patriarchs who lived close to Abraham never mentioned a journey of Abraham to the unknown desert of western Arabia during his time. Neither any of the inspired prophets of the Bible, nor any literature of Abraham's descendants, mentioned such a journey.

For the sake of argument, let's assume Abraham would have chosen western Arabia. Why wouldn't his descendants mention this historic journey? They recorded the rest of Abraham's life in great detail, from the point when he began his journey to the Promised Land. Why would they omit something as important as this?

We know that Moses wrote about Abraham's life in great detail. How could Moses have missed such a significant journey and fail to mention the Muslim claim that Abraham built a temple in Mecca? How could all the other prophets of Israel also be silent about such a significant event if it had actually occurred? Why don't we find any clue to such a journey of Abraham anywhere in the ancient Hebrew writings? If Abraham had visited the desert, where Mecca was later built in the 4th century A.D., he would have been a pioneer. His descendants would have boasted of such an accomplishment through the prophets, historians and other writers. The temple at Mecca would have been a place of pilgrimage for the descendants of Isaac and Jacob because of the importance of Abraham as the father of their faith. Yet, we don't see anyone in Israel, from the time of Moses through the prophets, traveling in search of a religious temple in Arabia or making a pilgrimage to Mecca.

To illustrate my point, let's suppose the people of Alaska would claim that Shakespeare had lived among them and built a temple there. To prove such a claim, Alaskans would have to depend on historical evidence, not some claim made by a religious writer, or the testimony of someone who had lived many centuries after Shakespeare. The only authoritative source would be English history, since there are no documented writings of the Alaskan people at the time of Shakespeare which speak of a visit by Shakespeare to their land. As it is, English history has a complete account of the famous English poet, and it doesn't mention a visit to Alaska. Therefore, we would conclude that historical resources confirm that Shakespeare never visited Alaska. The same is true in establishing if Abraham ever visited western Arabia. With the absence of documented writings in Arabia at the time of Abraham, mentioning a visit by Abraham, then it is logical that we look at all the writings of his descendants in Israel since the time of Moses. Nowhere is there any mention about this claim of Islam that Abraham visited Mecca and built a temple there. Therefore, we can see that Islamic claims about Mecca existing in the 21st century B.C., and Abraham building its temple, are fanciful and mistaken notions inserted into history. After examining the evidence, no intelligent and honest person would accept these Islamic claims.

Basing their religion on a false historical assertion, which is contradictory to true world history, is something Muslims should renounce. Muslims should be encouraged to stop trusting their eternal destiny to a religion which depends upon such enormous mistakes.

4 _____

ABSENCE OF MECCA IN ARCHAEOLOGICAL RECORDS FOUND IN THE OTHER ANCIENT CITIES AND KINGDOMS OF ARABIA

Although kingdoms and civilizations at the time of Abraham were few, and their inscriptions prove that they were well-known to each other, none of them mentions Mecca.

Previously, we discussed an important argument refuting the Islamic claim that Mecca has existed in Arabia since the time of Abraham. We saw that each civilization which appeared in Arabia left significant archaeological findings, proving its presence. Yet no such evidence can be found for Mecca before the 5th century A.D. We will now discuss another important archaeological argument against the idea of an ancient Mecca – namely, the absence of Mecca in archaeological records found in the other ancient cities and kingdoms of Arabia.

Abraham lived during the 21st century B.C. If Mecca had existed at the time of Abraham, it definitely would have been represented in the detailed inscriptions of the civilizations of eastern Arabia, such as inscriptions which come from the kingdoms of Dilmun and Magan, also called Oman. Furthermore, if Mecca were present in the 21st century B.C., it would have been the only kingdom to exist in western Arabia at that time. For thousands of years, Magan was known for its trade with Mesopotamia and the Indus Valley, which is modern-day India and Pakistan. Dilmun was known to have rich commerce with Asia, bringing its products to Mesopotamia as far back as 1,000 years before the time of Abraham. If Mecca had existed when Abraham lived, it would have been an important market for Magan and Dilmun trade, but no mention is made of Mecca in their inscriptions.

We also know that southwestern Arabian civilizations began to appear in Yemen in the 13th century B.C., causing us to conclude that no civilizations existed for Magan and Dilmun to trade with in western Arabia at the time of Abraham. Kingdoms and civilizations in the region at the time of Abraham were few, and were all known to each other. The kingdoms which appeared in Mesopotamia were known to each other and to the rest of Middle Eastern civilizations as far back as 3,000 B.C. Many inscriptions of the eastern Arabian kingdoms, such as Magan (Oman) and Dilmun, have been found which prove the claim that they were aware of these other Middle Eastern civilizations, such as those in Mesopotamia.

If Mecca had existed in the time of Abraham, it would have been impossible for civilizations in Eastern Arabia, some of which continued more than 3,000 years, not to have been aware of another old city which would have existed parallel to them in the western part of Arabia during all these thousands of years.

It is difficult to justify such a long span of time, from 3,000 B.C. to the 3rd century A.D., without any of these eastern Arabian kingdoms mentioning a city like Mecca in their inscriptions. To continue to claim that Mecca existed in ancient times, in spite of the evidence shown, is like claiming that the royal dynasties of northern Egypt had never heard of the royal dynasties of southern Egypt during thousands of years of history. In reality, the inscriptions found in northern Egypt are full of information about southern Egypt, and vice versa. This supports our claim that Mecca was not built until after the 3rd century A.D. It's unreasonable to claim that two civilizations, existing in the same geographical region (e.g., India, Egypt, Mesopotamia, China) for several millennia, would never have heard of each other, and would never have made mention of each other in inscriptions or other archaeological records. How could Arabia be an exception? How could Mecca have existed in western Arabia and been totally unknown to eastern Arabia for at least 2,400 years?

169

THE ABSENCE OF MECCA IN THE INSCRIPTIONS OF OTHER ARABIAN REGIONS

Up till now, we have been looking at eastern Arabian civilizations. Now let's turn our attention to the civilizations of northern, southern and central Arabia.

It is significant that we find inscriptions from the various Arabian kingdoms and cities mentioned in the inscriptions of other Arabian kingdoms and cities co-existing at the same time.

The Absence of Mecca in the Yemeni Inscriptions

As I mentioned previously, the Yemeni archaeological inscriptions are among the richest discoveries in the Middle East. In them we discover much information about their kings, wars and historical events. In addition, we learn a great deal about the surrounding civilizations in Arabia, and beyond.

From Yemeni inscriptions, we find a significant amount of information about the various kingdoms of southern Arabia. For example, Kinda was a kingdom in central Arabia located about 500 miles from where Mecca was later built. It is well-represented in the Yemeni inscriptions. Likewise, the northern Arabian cities of Qedar and Dedan, which are north of today's Mecca, are also richly represented in the Yemeni inscriptions. They confirm the commercial relationships which existed between the Yemeni kingdoms, and the Arabian cities and kingdoms east and north of Mecca's eventual location.

Even the city of Yathrib, also called Medina, is represented in the Yemeni inscriptions. As an example, the Sabaean inscriptions report the dedication of female slaves in a Sabaean temple. According to the inscriptions, the slaves were from Gaza, Yathrib, Dedan and Egypt.[92] So, if Yathrib (also called Medina), which did not exist before the 6th century B.C., is represented in the Yemeni inscriptions, how could Mecca have been in existence during the time of Abraham and never be found in any Yemeni inscription, even though Mecca is closer to Yemen than Yathrib is to Yemen?

We also find significant mention of the kingdoms of Axum and Habashat in the Yemeni inscriptions. These kingdoms existed in the region of Ethiopia to the west of Mecca, across the Red Sea.[93] We find more information in the Yemeni inscriptions about kingdoms situated to the north, east and west of the location where Mecca was eventually built. Yet, with all this rich detail, we still don't find any Yemeni inscription mentioning Mecca. Once again, if Mecca were a major city in Arabia before the 4th century A.D., as Muslims claim, it would have been mentioned in the Yemeni inscriptions even more than any of the other Arabian and Ethiopian kingdoms to which I have referred.

Proximity is also important. If it existed at all, Mecca would have been closer to Yemen than any of the other kingdoms mentioned. For the Yemeni inscriptions to simply skip over Mecca is something that cannot be justified or explained logically. It would be like the Romans mentioning Spain and Britain in their chronicles, but failing to mention France, which is far closer to Rome than these two countries. It's illogical to claim, without any archaeological evidence or support, that Mecca, which would have bordered on Yemeni territory, was a dominant city in the ancient history of Arabia before the 4th century A.D.

Mecca is Absent in the Inscriptions of the Northern Cities of Arabia

When we look at the inscriptions found in northern Arabian cities, such as Dedan, we see the same phenomena. Their inscriptions reveal aspects of their own history and mention civilizations of western and southern Arabia. For example, we find mention of some of the kings of the Main Yemeni kingdom of southern Arabia in the inscriptions of the northern Arabian city of Dedan.[94]

There is plenty of information about the western and southwestern Arabian kingdoms found in the northern cities' inscriptions, yet we don't find Mecca mentioned at all – even though it would be closer to the northern cities than the southern and western Arabian kingdoms which I mentioned. In light of this evidence, the Islamic tradition to claim that Mecca has been a major Arabian city since the 21ˢᵗ century B.C. is like Rome existing in Italy for centuries, but seeing no mention of it in any Italian inscriptions. In reality, Rome is the most-mentioned city in the ancient Italian inscriptions. The same logic holds true with the city of Athens in Greece, and Babel in Mesopotamia. So it would also be with Mecca, if the claims about Mecca from the Islamic tradition were true.

We have seen previously that some Muslims claim that Ptolemy's mention of a city called Macoraba is actually a reference to Mecca. We have already proven, with Ptolemy's longitudinal and latitudinal system, that Macoraba is not Mecca but, instead, a small settlement in Yemen, south of the old Yemeni city of Carna in the 2ⁿᵈ century A.D. To cling to such a claim as proof of Mecca's existence as a major city since the time of Abraham is inadequate and illogical. So, to claim that Mecca has continually existed in Arabia since the time of Abraham, in spite of all the evidence to the contrary, is inconsistent and illogical. It is a ridiculous claim. The truth is that clear archaeological and historical facts cannot be reinterpreted or ignored in order to support a claim which is inconsistent with archaeology and history.

Once again, we see the witness of history confirming our research which shows that Mecca was built long after Muslims claim it was.

5 _____

THE ABSENCE OF MECCA THROUGH STUDYING THE RECORDS OF THE NATIONS WHO OCCUPIED THE REGION

The absence of Mecca prior to the 4th century A.D. is a verifiable conclusion based upon the documented history and ruins of the many ancient civilizations which inhabited northern and central western Arabia, the region where Mecca was eventually built. Northern and central western Arabia was occupied by many nations throughout history, but nowhere in their chronicles do we find inscriptions and archaeological findings with any mention of Mecca.

The Kingdom of Ma'in's Expansion

The Ma'in kingdom expanded to the north, colonizing regions and cities, but there is no mention of Mecca in their inscriptions, even though Mecca would have been the closest city to them.

Ma'in is among the kingdoms which colonized northern Arabia. It expanded from Yemen, in southwestern Arabia, to the north through their commercial colonies. These colonies facilitated their trade with Syria and Palestine. Ma'in's colonies in northern Arabia were in existence from the Achaemenid era, which began around 559 B.C. In their northward colonization, the Minaeans occupied the northern Arabian city of Dedan. Dedan had a Minaean dynasty of kings or rulers and left a great collection of inscriptions. Minaean inscriptions are scattered in many places across northern Arabia. Minaean inscriptions were found at the site of al-Jawf, near the border with Iraq. [95] Minaean inscriptions are also scattered in the commercial colonies which the Minaeans established in Tran-Jordan. Minaean inscriptions were found in Jabal Ramm, about twenty miles from Aqaba.[96] There was a very well-known colony in the city of Maan, bearing their Minaean name, which is located in the south of Jordan. Clearly, the Minaeans occupied Hijaz (north and central western Arabia) for a long period of time. As we think about it, we ask ourselves how those Minaean people who occupied Hijaz could neglect the city of Mecca, for they would have encountered it on the trip between Yemen and northern Arabia. If Mecca had existed at the time the Minaeans colonized the cities of the north, then it would have been important for them to subdue and colonize Mecca in order to protect their trade route through central Arabia. Mecca would have been a convenient city in which caravans could rest while traveling through the desert, and would have been located on the most direct route between Yemen and the cities of northern Arabia. But Minaean caravans encountered no such settlement of any kind in the region where Mecca was eventually built. Instead, caravans traveled a longer route toward the interior of Arabia, reaching the city of Yathrib, and then the city of Dedan.

Lihyan Occupied the Area Without Mentioning Mecca

Lihyan was another tribe which controlled northwestern Arabia. Their kings ruled from the city of Dedan and controlled the trade routes of northwestern Arabia. Lihyan also controlled Hegra, which is also called "Madain Salih," extending its control south toward the central western regions of Arabia. Yet, we don't find any inscriptions or other mentions of Mecca among the abundant Lihyanite literature.

Mas'udu, who ruled over Dedan from around 120-100 B.C., was the last king of Lihyan, according to the inscriptions of Dedan.

The Nabataean Domain

The Nabataeans colonized along the land route toward the south including the desert of central western Arabia where Mecca was eventually built.

The Nabataeans expanded toward the south and occupied the territory held by the Lihyan kingdom. Their inscriptions in north Arabia continued to be written till the beginning of the 4th century A.D. [97]

The Nabataeans played an important part in the history of the region. From the Roman Expedition into Arabia in 24 and 23 B.C., we know that the village of Leuce Come, on the Red Sea, was under the control of the Nabataeans at the time of the expedition. [98] Strabo, the Greek geographer who accompanied the expedition, recorded that the control of the Nabataeans extended south to Leuce Come. In fact, he mentioned another region governed by Aretas who was related to Obodas, the king of the Nabataeans. [99] The Nabataean influence didn't stop there. Strabo referred to "a village in the territory controlled by Obodas;" that village was Egra, close to the Red Sea, about 62 miles from Malathan. [100] Obodas was a Nabataean king, and Malathan, as we saw previously, was a port very close to where Mecca was later built. Strabo also reported on the size of the Nabataean caravans which came from Yemen, passing through Leuce Come on their way to Petra, the capital of the Nabataeans. Strabo wrote that these caravans traveled in such numbers that "men and camels differed in no respect from an army." [101] Strabo's comments reveal that the Nabataeans, who controlled northwestern Arabia and parts of central western Arabia at the time of the Roman Expedition, used to guard their caravans all the way to Yemen as they traveled the land route along the Red Sea.

Another ancient historian, Pliny, speaks about how the Nabataeans controlled the land route "through the Nabataean Troglodytae, a colony of the Nabataeans." [102] This deserted

175

segment of land in north and central Arabia lies opposite to the Troglodytic Land across the Red Sea on the African shore, confirming that the Nabataeans colonized along the land route toward the south. They controlled the central western Arabian desert, including the area where Mecca eventually was built.

Mecca was built on the heavily-traveled land route which was walked centuries before by the Nabataeans, yet the Nabataeans did not mention Mecca, even though they repeatedly mentioned the smaller cities under their control.

Considering the abundance of Nabataean inscriptions, and other archaeological findings, how could the Nabataeans have failed to mention a city like Mecca? Especially since it was claimed that Mecca was built along their heavily-traveled land routes in a territory which they controlled. Since the Nabataeans wrote in their inscriptions about even the smallest and most insignificant places under their control, how could they have missed Mecca? For a nation's long historical records to neglect one city, when it repeatedly mentions the few villages and smaller cities under its control, is something implausible.

Kinda controlled central western Arabia. The study of their inscriptions excludes that Mecca existed during the 2ⁿᵈ and 3ʳᵈ centuries A.D.

Not only did the Nabataeans control Hijaz, but there were other nations in Arabia who, at one time or another controlled the region located in northwestern and central Arabia, where Mecca was eventually built. One of these kingdoms was Kinda, which formed a confederacy in central Arabia. Kinda, at times, dominated Hijaz, including the deserts where Mecca was later built. Through its inscriptions, the documented history of Kinda dates as far back as the 2nd century A.D. Their capital, Qaryat al-Fau, was located just 500 miles east of Mecca, near the city of Yamama. There is no mention of Mecca in their inscriptions, further supporting our conclusion that Mecca did not exist in the 2nd and 3rd centuries A.D.

The inscriptions of the Himyarites, who occupied the area where Mecca was later built, confirm that Mecca did not exist during the 3rd century A.D.

Another kingdom to occupy Hijaz was the Himyar kingdom from Yemen, which started around 115 B.C. In 275 A.D., Himyar occupied Saba, and afterward it expanded northward toward the land of the Carnaites.[103] Himyar controlled the land route, then enforced its authority over most of Hijaz.

In spite of the abundance of Himyarite inscriptions, Mecca again is missing, suggesting that Mecca did not exist at the end of the 3rd century A.D. or at the beginning of the 4th century A.D.

It is illogical that all the nations who occupied central western Arabia would overlook Mecca, if it existed when these nations existed.

As we look at these facts, we come to the same conclusion which we reached as we examined the narrations of classical writers and others such as Ethiopians, Coptics and Christians. Mecca is missing in all the inscriptions and archaeological records of the Arabian nations who occupied Hijaz, or who controlled the land route where Mecca was eventually built. This means that Mecca did not exist prior to the 4th century A.D. It is an assertive fact. All nations which occupied central western Arabia were known for their numerous inscriptions. None of these nations failed to record a city in the area where they also mentioned smaller villages. So how can all of these nations have missed Mecca, which is closer to each of them than other small cities and villages which they recorded? It's as though all the kingdoms in a land like Mesopotamia would fail to record the city of Babel. No one would accept this, because an ancient city of importance would have been evident, and impossible to exclude in the inscriptions of the kingdoms which occupied its territory. It would appear in their inscriptions, not only once from one nation, but hundreds of times in the inscriptions of each nation which occupied its territory, or even nations with which it came in contact.

Therefore, our Muslim friends should learn from the archaeology of the nations surrounding Arabia, even the archaeology of all countries of the world. How much proof is required to support the claim that a specific city existed 2,000 years before Christ? What are the archaeological conditions needed to make that claim acceptable? Especially in conditions like Arabia, where the area of Mecca was surrounded by kingdoms who occupied Hijaz in various eras, and whose archaeology and history are documented as well as, or better than, the surrounding countries of the Middle East. Mecca, if it existed, should surely have had a prominent place in history. But it did not. It should be the apparent reference and the essential base of its archaeology in all ages and history.

THE RECORDS OF THE GREAT NATIONS WHO OCCUPIED CENTRAL WESTERN ARABIA, AND THE ISLAMIC CASE FOR THE EXISTENCE OF MECCA

The Assyrians, Babylonians, Persians and Romans all had ancient empires which occupied northern and central western Arabia. None of them mentioned the existence of Mecca.

Many great empires throughout history annexed parts of Arabia and, in particular, northwestern and central western Arabia. Interest in this desolate area was primarily due to its strategic location on the trading routes between the Far East and the Mediterranean regions. Trade from the Far East crossed the Indian Ocean to ports in southern Arabia. The trading routes then proceeded across western Arabia toward Middle Eastern countries which lay along the Mediterranean. From these, trade reached the rest of the Mediterranean region. This made control of the area essential to ancient empires.

A secondary reason empires wanted to annex northwestern and central western Arabia was for their own protection. Tribal confederations from northern and anterior Arabia were known for frequent attacks on their neighbors. Annexations provided a buffer between the great empires and the hostile tribes of Arabia.

A third reason for interest in northwestern and central Arabia was the presence of gold and other important minerals. The region of central Arabia called Yamama, about 500 miles east of where Mecca was later built, was famous for its gold and copper mines. Arabia was also known for copper mines in Oman.

The Assyrian Control

Glaser, an expert scholar of Arabian history, maintains that the Assyrians extended their control over Yamama in the 8th and 7th centuries B.C. He identified locations which are referenced in the Assyrian inscriptions which tell about Assyrian wars against Arabian tribes. Of particular interest was King Assurbanipal's campaign south of the cities of Teima and Khaybar.[104]

The Assyrian inscriptions are significant because many describe Arabian tribes, rulers and cities. These inscriptions are very important, for they are based on first-hand knowledge which the Assyrians gained during their occupation of the area during the 8th and 7th centuries B.C. It is assumed that the Assyrian control reached south to near the area where Mecca was built; yet, we don't see any mention in the Assyrian inscriptions about Mecca or the tribes, such as the Jurhum tribe, which Islamic tradition claims inhabited Mecca as far back as the time of Abraham.

Assyrian inscriptions mention more than one king of Saba who controlled Yemen. We are told that the kings of Saba gave tribute to Assyrian kings as a symbol of cooperation in the land trading route which reached the Fertile Crescent, including: Mesopotamia, Syria, Lebanon, Palestine and Trans-Jordan, extending from the borders of Iraq and Iran to the Mediterranean Sea.

Once again, since the Assyrian inscriptions fail to mention Mecca, we can only conclude that Mecca did not exist between the 9th and 7th centuries B.C., or it would have been mentioned in the records.

The Babylonian Occupation of Hijaz

Nabonidus occupied the cities of the region close to where Mecca was eventually built. Although he lived for ten years in Teima, he never mentioned Mecca.

Not only did the Assyrians occupy northern and central Arabia, but so did the Babylonians. They occupied these portions of Arabia during the reign of Nabonidus, the king of Babylon, who reigned from 556-539 B.C. Information about this king and his occupation is found in the Harran Inscriptions (known as H2), Nabonidus and the Royal Chronicles, and the so-called *Verse Account of Nabonidus*.

Nabonidus left the empire to the control of his son, Belshazzar, and Nabonidus traveled to the Arabian city of Teima. Once there, he killed its king, occupied the city, made Teima his residence, and built a palace.[105] From *The Harran Inscriptions of Nabonidus*, we know that during his sojourn in Teima, Nabonidus went further south to conquer the cities of Dedan, Fadak, Khaybar, Yadi and Yathrib (which is the Medina).[106] The city of Yathrib, about 200 miles from Mecca's eventual location, later played an important part in the rise of Islam.

Since Nabonidus controlled the whole region, he was assured of dominating all three land routes from Yathrib. Though he controlled the whole region, he does not mention Mecca in the inscriptions he left behind. If Mecca had existed in his time, it would have been an important target for his attacks, because it would have been the only city in the region around Yathrib which was not under his control (see Fig. 4).

If Mecca were the influential city Islamic tradition claims, it would have been an even more important target than the other

180

cities which Nabonidus conquered. So why would he conquer all the other cities in the region, many of which were less important than Mecca, and fail to even mention Mecca? There should have still been some mention of it, since he ruled in the area for ten years and reached the other cities nearest its location. This shows that Mecca did not exist in the area around the 6th century B.C.

The Persian Occupation

The Persians occupied many parts of Arabia and had alliances with tribes and states, but Mecca is absent in their records.

Following the Babylonians, the same area came under the control of the Persians. An examination of inscriptions found near Dedan show that they subjugated northern Arabia in the Achaemenid period at the end of the 6th century B.C. The Persians also appointed a governor to oversee Dedan. This occurred before the Lihyanite kings dominated the cities of Qedar and Dedan, and some other regions in northwestern Arabia.

In the 5th century B.C., Herodotus, the Greek historian, tells us that the Persians made alliances with the Arabians. Centuries later, the Persians occupied the region of Oman at the time of the writing of the *The Periplus of the Erythraean Sea.*[107] I previously mentioned that the date of the writing of *The Periplus of the Erythraean Sea* was about 62 A.D. In fact, in the 1st century A.D., the whole Persian Gulf area, including Oman, was under the Parthian empire, a ruling dynasty of old Iran (Persia).[108] The land of Jerra, near the Persian Gulf, became Persian territory around 320 A.D. Today, Jerra is known as al-Qatif.[109] The Persians made alliances with many Arabian tribes. Among them was the tribe of Kinda, which once extended its domain over central Arabia and part of Hadramaut, south of Yemen, in South Arabia.[110] The Persians held mines in Yamama, even up until the time of Mohammed. Yamama was the area where Kinda's capital was situated, about 500 miles from today's Mecca. This reflects just how far the Persians penetrated and influenced the region. The Persians used the Lakhmids, who were a tribe of al-Hira situated on their borders in Mesopotamia, to protect the borders. The Lakhmids became vassal governors during the Sasanian periods. Al-Tabari says that the Arabian tribes settled in the area of Hira at the time of Ardashir, son of Papak .[111] Ardashir was the founder of the Sassanian Kingdom. He is also known by the name "Artaxerxes." He reigned between 226-240 A.D. Through the Lakhmids, the Persians formed tight relationships with other tribes and cities in southern and southwestern Arabia. This was in addition to their continuing influence in central Arabia.

If Mecca had existed in the 3rd century A.D., Persian records would certainly have mentioned it. Although the Persians penetrated into many parts of Arabia, we don't find Mecca mentioned in any Persian record or literature. This is significant, because the Persians were interested in controlling all the land routes between southern Arabia and the Fertile Crescent, and Mecca was eventually built on one of the most important branches of these trading routes. Even more significant is the fact that the Persians were interested in extending their influence all over Arabia, whether through direct conquest or through alliances with existing states. We find that Mecca is absent in any official Persian records relating to the Persian plan of conquest over Arabia. This indicates that Mecca did not exist until at least the beginning of the 4th century A.D.

The Roman Expedition Into Western Arabia

During the Roman Expedition to western Arabian, they accurately documented all the villages and cities of the area. Their work demonstrates that Mecca was not in existence around the Christian era and the 1st century A.D.

We've written about the Assyrians, the Babylonians, and the Persians. Now we turn to the last ancient empire to occupy northern and central western Arabia, the Roman Empire. The Romans conquered this area of Arabia during their expedition under Gallus around 23 B.C. I have already discussed this expedition in detail, as to how Gallus first occupied northwestern Arabia, and then conquered all the cities in central western Arabia as far south as the city of Najran, on the border of Yemen. From there Gallus conquered cities in Yemen until he reached Ma'rib. We saw how this expedition was historically documented by Strabo, an important historian and geographer of the time. In detail, he recorded the contents of the regions of northwestern Arabia and central western Arabia, where Mecca was eventually built. But even though Strabo's survey mentioned tiny and seemingly insignificant villages in northwestern and central western Arabia, he never mentioned Mecca.

In addition to Strabo's writing, we have other Roman records which Pliny consulted in his survey of northwestern and central western Arabia. As in Strabo's work, Mecca was absent from Pliny's survey. The Romans have a reputation for great accuracy in reporting the places, cities and villages in any region which they conquered or even visited. Their work assures us that Mecca did not exist in the 1st century B.C. during the times of Strabo and Pliny.

Great empires who covered spans of thousands of years, or more, occupied central western Arabia, and mentioned the tiny villages without mentioning Mecca. How can Muslims disregard the records of these great empires?

We have examined the records of the great ancient empires who occupied portions of north and central western Arabia over the years. We've tried to find a case for the existence of Mecca in the writings and inscriptions of the Assyrians, Babylonians, Persians and Romans, but to no avail.

Although Mecca would have been situated at a strategic location between the northern cities of Arabia and Yemen in southern Arabia, we have no record of its existence. These regions were well known to these empires. Although controlling of the area around Mecca was strategic to controlling the trade routes and caravans traveling between Yemen, the Fertile Crescent and the rest of the Mediterranean region, we have no record of Mecca's existence. Yemen was a strategic point in the marine trade with the Far East, especially India. It is difficult to believe that all four of these empires would neglect to mention a city like Mecca in the area, considering all of their ambitions to control this trade. To not study the records of such great empires, who all occupied and penetrated this region, is to abandon the most important historical records we have. If we were to make our judgment without taking into consideration the records of these great empires, we would certainly be amiss. By what criteria then, do Muslims assert that Mecca existed during the reign of these empires which covered the thousands of years they dominated the Middle East? What support does the Islamic claim have that Mecca actually existed? The answer is simple: Muslims do not have any historical documents from this long period which show that Mecca existed when they claim it did, yet they tenaciously hold to their teachings.

6 _____

THE STUDY OF THE ASSYRIAN INSCRIPTIONS ALSO EXCLUDES AN ANCIENT MECCA

Although Muslims contend otherwise, the land along the Red Sea, containing the place where Mecca was eventually built, was uninhabited until land trading routes were established through that region in the 3rd century B.C. I mentioned previously about the absence of Mecca in the records of the nations and cities of Arabia that existed prior to the 4th century A.D. I also showed how four foreign empires occupied northwestern and central western Arabia and yet made no mention of Mecca within their records. I now will show how Mecca is absent from the records of the Mesopotamia civilizations, especially the Assyrians. I mentioned the Assyrians previously as one of the four empires which occupied northwestern and central western Arabia in the 8th and 7th centuries B.C.

Mecca is Excluded From the Reports of the Second Millennium B.C.

The civilizations of Mesopotamia were very aware of the cities and the respective kingdoms which dotted the Middle East, such as Egypt and Syria. They were equally aware of those which lined eastern Arabia, such as Dilmun and Magan. The ancient nations that existed in the region are represented in their inscriptions and records. Previously, I had mentioned the connections between the civilizations of Mesopotamia and those of eastern Arabia, connections which go as far back as 3,000 B.C. For example, Magan, also called Oman, as far back as 2800 B.C. is mentioned in Akkadic inscriptions.[112] Any western Arabian kingdom or city that existed at that time was sure to be mentioned in

Mesopotamian inscriptions. History confirms that kingdoms in southwestern Arabia, such as Yemen, were represented by the Saba Kingdom, which didn't exist before the 13th century B.C. Some scholars contend it was the 12th century B.C., and others say it was the 11th century B.C. In any case, in the 14th century B.C., the Egyptians mentioned Yemen before any kingdom or city was established and known in that region. So the silence of the Mesopotamian inscriptions pertaining to southwestern Arabia is because there were no kingdoms there to make themselves known in the area.

The cities of north Arabia began to appear after the 10th century B.C. That's when the kingdoms of Yemen began to communicate with the Fertile Crescent through the oases of northern Arabia, where cities like Dedan, Qedar, and other cities were built. It was only in the 6th century B.C., and later, that the city of Yathrib was built, in addition to other cities. Although Muslims contend otherwise, the land along the Red Sea, containing the place where Mecca was eventually built, was uninhabited until land-trading routes were established through that region, starting from the 3rd century B.C. These coastal trading routes, which ran parallel to pre-existing inland trading routes, connected Yemen with the oases of northern Arabia, which had been established in the 8th century B.C. During these ancient times, Mecca was not mentioned among the many cities known to lie along these Arabian trading routes. We already saw this when we studied the ancient Greek and Roman geographers, and other nations which occupied north and central western Arabia.

We have constructed a historically-accurate picture of southwestern Arabia, principally Yemen, and its expansion through north and central western Arabia as it traded with other Middle Eastern kingdoms such as Mesopotamia, Syria and Palestine. It's important to have a historically-accurate picture if we are to discount the Qur'an's claim that Hagar, the mother of Ishmael, traveled to Mecca, and that Abraham also visited Mecca and built a temple there. It's abundantly clear from the history of western Arabia that there were no cities in that region which would interest Abraham, nor were there any caravans traveling through that area at the time of Abraham, Ishmael and Hagar.

The study of the ancient Assyrian inscriptions is very important because Assyria had existed in northern Iraq since the 3rd millennium B.C., along with the other kingdoms of Mesopotamia. Yet, there is no mention of western Arabia in their records and inscriptions, since there were no kingdoms in existence in western Arabia at that time.

Let us look at the history of the region. Assyria grew powerful under King Adad-Nirari II, who reigned from 911-891 B.C. Under his rule, the Assyrians occupied Babylonia, Anatolia and part of Syria. Following Adad-Nirari II, King Tukulti-Ninurta II ruled from 890-884 B.C. Then King Ashurnasirpal II reigned from 883-859 B.C. He extended Assyrian domination as far as the Mediterranean Sea. What is of interest to us is that southern and northern Arabia are not mentioned at all during the reigns of these kings who ruled while Assyria's sphere of influence bordered on Arabia.

It is not until the reign of Shalmaneser III that we have inscriptions concerning Arabia in Assyrian records. Shalmaneser III reigned from 858-824 B.C. This is because only in the 9th century B.C. were the cities of northern Arabia constructed in the oases. Let's look at those inscriptions. Shalmaneser III, in the inscriptions called the Monolith Inscriptions from Kurkh, mentioned that the Assyrians engaged an alliance formed of many kings in battle at Qarqar. Among the kings he lists in the alliance are: Hadadezer, king of Damascus; Ahab, the king of Israel; and Gindibu', the Arab, whose army had 1,000 camels.[113] In the inscriptions of Tiglath-Pileser III, who reigned from 744-727 B.C., we also find a reference to the kingdoms of northern Arabia. In these inscriptions, particularly in the annals which were removed from the walls of the palace of Shalmaneser III at Nimrud – also called Calah, the old capital of the Assyrians – we see that tribute was paid by Queen Zabibe, "Queen of the Arabs" to Shalmaneser III, around 738 B.C. More information about Queen Zabibe's tribute is given in a stele found in Iran. (A stele is a carved stone monument, much like our grave markers.) The Qedarites are mentioned in the stele as being separated from the Arabs. By this, we assume that the Qedarites, an Ishmaelite tribe, preserved its ethnic identity as Ishmaelites until it was invaded by other Arabian tribes. As the Qedarites intermingled with other tribes, they lost their independence. However, in a short time, the invaders also took the name Qedarites. The inscriptions of Tiglath-Pileser III also mention the subduing of another Arabian queen named Samsi.

It is clear that the kingdom of Qedar in northern Arabia did not appear until the 8th century B.C. Although early inscriptions from Mesopotamia don't mention any kingdoms in northern Arabia, the 858-824 B.C. inscriptions of Shalmaneser III do mention "Gindibu, the Arab." Gindibu might be the chief of the Arabian tribe whose one thousand camels were rented by King Ahab of Israel and the King of Damascus, along with the other kings who were engaged in battle against the Assyrians.

That takes us to Sargon II, who reigned over Assyria from 721-705 B.C. Egypt was among the nations he captured. He also enforced Assyrian control over the Babylonians. From the time of Sargon II, information about Arabians increases in frequency. The inscriptions of Sargon II are famous because they contain information about tribute given to Assyria by several kings, including the King of Saba. Also, the inscriptions mention some tribes of northern Arabia.

Following Sargon II come the inscriptions of Sennacherib, who reigned from 704-681 B.C. Sennacherib is best remembered for destroying the city of Babylon. Prominent inscriptions from the time of Sennacherib were the Herper Letters, which date to the epochs of Sennacherib and Assurbanipal.

Following Sennacherib come the inscriptions of Esarhaddon, who reigned from 680-669. Then come the inscriptions of Assurbanipal, who reigned from 668- 627 B.C. Assurbanipal defeated Elam, Egypt and Lydia. The inscriptions of Assurbanipal, which concern the Arabs, date back to the year 649 B.C.[114]

There are also many letters which furnish information about Arabs. Among them are the Herper Letters, mentioned before, and the Nimrud Letters. Nimrud Letters can be dated back to the end of the 8th century B.C.[115] We also have other resources like the Babylonian Chronicles, which speak about the campaign of Esarhaddon in the land of Bazu in central Arabia. The Babylonian Chronicles also speak about a Babylonian attack in the Arabian desert at the time of Nebuchadnezzar. The Nabonidus Chronicle speaks about Nabonidus' campaign in Arabia and his sojourn in Teima.

We see that Assyrian and Babylonian records contain information about west, north and central Arabia from the end of the 9th century B.C. until the 6th century B.C. This is a long period of time that exposed the tribes and kingdoms, and reigning cities in that part of Arabia to the Assyrians and Babylonians. Yet no mention of Mecca, or the tribes which Islamic tradition claims to have lived in Mecca, are found in any of these Assyrian and Babylonian records. The Assyrian and Babylonian inscriptions give us five centuries of contact between this area of Arabia and these two Mesopotamian nations. Their records date from the 9th century B.C. Between the northern tribes and Saba, there is no city like Mecca mentioned in the Assyrian or Babylonian records. While in each century many records tell about nations and tribes in western and north Arabia, none mention a city like Mecca.

Mecca is absent from the Assyrian political, military and commercial scene, while other tribes of western Arabia are mentioned in the Assyrian records.

In the second part of the 8th century B.C., Assyria began to exert more influence over the Arabian tribes – tribes which attempted to avoid Assyrian occupation by paying tribute. Other Arabian tribes wanted to ensure that their trade would be protected along the spice route. This route connected Assyrian-controlled territory in Sinai and south Jordan with the regions of the Fertile Crescent, which were also under their control. All the kingdoms and cities in western Arabia were dependent upon trade for their wealth and livelihood. To maintain this trade, they paid tribute to the kings of Assyria. This was especially important for cities in this region because they had no rain to support agriculture, and they needed to trade for food. The region where Mecca was built is one of those regions with little rain. Therefore, Mecca began as a city of trade in the 4th century A.D. Its existence depended on the continuity of its trade, especially with the countries of the Fertile Crescent, such as Mesopotamia, Syria and Palestine. Thus, the main concerns of the commercial cities of Arabia was to build relationships with these countries where their trade was destined, and to find markets.

The Assyrians received tribute from the Qedarites, one of many historically-documented nations which presented tribute to Tiglath-Pileser III around 738 B.C.[116] The kings of Saba also paid tribute to the Assyrians to ensure their trade. To ensure their influence and protect their trade in the region, many Arabian tribes attempted to create alliances with each other. This often led to wars and campaigns.

We find that Mecca is absent in the trade-relation records between the people who dominated the Fertile Crescent from ancient times through the time of the Assyrians and Babylonians. Not only is Mecca absent from trading records, but it is also absent in any alliance which listed the tribes and cities of western Arabia through these same eras.

In the inscriptions of Tiglath-Pileser III, dated 744-727 B.C., we find information about the wars fought by him against many of the Arabian tribes. He mentions his campaign against Samsi, "Queen of the Arabs," in northern Arabia. Other inscriptions speak about campaigns in which the Assyrians fought against Arabian tribes. Tiglath-Pileser, in an early record, wrote :

10,000 warriors, I made bow down to my feet. The people of Massa, Teima, Saba, Hayappa, Badanu, Hatte, Idiba'ilu [I-di-ba'-il-a-a], On the border of the countries of the setting sun Of whom not one of my predecessors knew and whose place is remote, praise of my lordship.

....Camels, she camels, all kind of spices, their tribute as one, they brought before me and kissed my feet.

I appointed Idibi'ilu for the wardenship of the entrance of Egypt.[117]

In analyzing the list of people mentioned in the Tiglath-Pileser III inscriptions, we find they lead with the names Massa, Teima and Saba. Massa is known to be an Ishmaelite tribe which existed in the Syro-Arabian desert. Teima was a northern Arabian tribe and city. Saba is well known as a kingdom that dominated Yemen at the time of Tiglath-Pileser III in the 8th century B.C. Many scholars consider Badanu as the tribe of Bdn, which is found in Thamud and Safaitic inscriptions.[118] In my research, I found that Pliny mentions the city of Badanatha as located in the area of the Thamud tribe.[119] I conclude that Badanatha may have been named after the tribe of Badanu which united with, and then was integrated into the Thamud tribe in the 8th century B.C. I assume that they were located in the same area where the city, Badanatha, was eventually built.

The I-di-ba'-il-a-a tribe is identified by many scholars as the tribe of Adbeel. Adbeel was one of the sons of Ishmael. In the Tiglath-Pileser III inscriptions, we learn that he appointed this tribe as the warden of the entrance to Egypt. The inscription says: "I appointed Idibi'ilu for the wardenship of the entrance to Egypt." This inscription suggests that this Ishmaelite tribe was still living in the Sinai around the 8th century B.C.

A study of inscriptions confirms the accuracy of the Bible when it talks about the origin of the tribes and nations mentioned in the book of Genesis. It's logical that people like the Assyrians would write down tribal names as they pronounced them in their own language. Thus, we have Adbeel (written as I-di-ba'-il-a-a), and Saba (written as Saab'-a-a).

In the inscriptions of the 8th and 7th centuries B.C., we encounter many of the tribes about which Moses wrote in the Bible. However, we don't see any mention of Mecca or the other tribes, such as Jurhum, which Islamic tradition claims lived in Mecca as far back as the time of Abraham. Many of the tribes mentioned in the Bible since the 15th century B.C. are mentioned again later in other books of the Bible, shedding light on their existence, as well as their historical activities. One such tribe is

Ephah, which evolved from the sons of Abraham and Keturah, the wife Abraham took after Sarah died.

The scholars think that the tribe of Hayappa, mentioned in the inscriptions of Tiglath-Pileser III and Sargon II, was the tribe of Ephah. In the Septuagint, which is the Greek translation of the Hebrew Bible, the tribe is called Ghaiphah. The Bible helps us locate this tribe, since Genesis gives us the genealogy of the sons of Keturah. Ephah was the elder son of Midian, the father of the Midianites. Ephah became the strongest tribe of the Midianites, often representing all the Midianites. The Midianites lived in northwestern Arabia, near the Aqaba region. They united with the Ishmaelites at the time of Gideon, whose battle with the Midianites occurred around 1170 B.C. Midianite pottery has been found in Negev-Sinai, south of Jordan, and in many parts of north Arabia. It has been found as far south as Teima. The Midianite pottery in Teima is dated between the beginning of the 13th century B.C. and the middle of the 12th century B.C.[120] We don't find Midianite pottery south of Teima. This demonstrates that the Midianites and Ephah never reached central western Arabia, where Mecca was eventually built.

In the Bible, the book of Isaiah, we see Ephah and Midian as one group. We read in Isaiah, chapter 60, verse 6:

> The multitude of camels shall cover your land. The dromedaries of Midian and Ephah; all those from Sheba shall come; they shall bring gold and incense.

Ephah was located in northwestern Arabia around the Gulf of Aqaba. This verse shows Ephah had a role in the trade between Yemen's Saba, here called Sheba, and Palestine. Knowing that Isaiah began to prophesy in 739 B.C., the year that King Uzziah died, and that Tiglath-Pileser III began to reign as King of Assyria in 745 B.C., we can conclude that the Bible confirms the presence of Ephah as a trading people between Saba and Israel around the last quarter of the 8th century B.C. We read about Saba elsewhere in the Bible, as well. Some scholars think that there might have been a Sabaean tribe in the north of Arabia, toward Dedan. Those who support this idea base their hypothesis on Job 1:15, where it says that the Sabaeans raided the sons of Job and killed his servants. Other scholars think that Saba was a northern colony of the Saba of Yemen. Other Biblical verses show the existence of Saba of Yemen. The Lord Jesus Christ shows that the Queen of Sheba came from the uttermost region of the south (Matthew 12:42). Jeremiah 6:20 says:

> for what purpose to me comes frankincense from Sheba, and sweet cane from a far country?

Here we see a kind of poetic parallelism in which Jeremiah also speaks of Saba. First, he describes it as a place where frankincense comes from, which is historically true that Saba in Yemen was a great trader of frankincense. Then he describes it as a far off country. Even in the book of Job itself, Saba is mentioned again as a country from which travelers come, as we read in Job 6:19, "the caravans of Teima look, the travelers of Saba hope for them." It is known that Sabaeans of Yemen were merchants who accompanied the caravans across the desert toward Palestine and Syria, and other Mediterranean countries.

Job, chapter 1, records that the Sabaeans attacked the possessions of Job. These Sabaeans are thought to be a tribe of northern Bedouins, located in the Syro-Mesopotamian desert. They were descendants of Keturah, the second wife of Abraham. Other scholars believe that the Sabaeans mentioned in Job could have been a colony of Sabaeans from Yemen who tried to control the spice trade route. They reached the place where Job lived, as they are seen in the inscriptions of Tiglath-Pileser III, having connections with areas of northern Arabia and the Sinai. Inscriptions show that Tiglath-Pileser III forced 10,000 Sabaean warriors to bow at his feet. Then he demanded "all kind of spices" in tribute, confirming that he dealt with people on the spice route, especially Saba, Teima and Ephah. The three were known for controlling the spice land route. Tiglath-Pileser III says that their lands were remote, and none of his predecessors knew about these places. Tiglath-Pileser III said in one inscription, "I made bow down to my feet the people of Massa', Teima, and Saba" may indicate that the Assyrians were engaged in wars against these tribes. Just how much the Sabaeans were engaged is not clear from the inscriptions. Whether the Sabaeans were a colony of the Saba of Yemen, or Bedouins from the north, is not easy to establish. In either case, we know that in later times the kings of Saba offered tribute to the Assyrian kings, a sign that they recognized the supremacy of Assyrians in the region. They were also willing to allow their trade to pass through the lands under the Assyrian control.

With this historical picture at the time of Tiglath-Pileser III, who ruled from 744-727 B.C., we find historical documentation about the tribes that dominated the commercial, political and military scene in western Arabia. We saw Qedar paying tribute to the Assyrians. We also saw Ephah, the dominant Midianite tribe, paying tribute. In addition, the tribe of Badanu, which was associated with the Thamud, the tribe that appeared a decade after at the time of Sargon II (who reigned from 721-705 B.C.) paid tribute. Then we find Teima, and finally the tribe of Saba, which dominated Yemen. Also, after examining the important records of Sargon II, which I will discuss later, we find many other tribes, yet there is no mention of a city like Mecca between the northwestern tribes and Saba. Nor do we find any mention of any other tribe, like Jurhum, which Islamic tradition claims lived in Mecca and became the dominant tribe in western Arabia. Mecca is absent from the records of the nations in the beginning of the 1st millennium B.C., like it is absent from the classical records in the last half of the 1st millennium B.C. It is implausible to believe that less important tribes, like the Badanu and others in western Arabia, were recorded by the Assyrians while the city which Islamic tradition makes the center of faith and supremacy is forgotten. The Assyrian leaders recorded movements of armies and commerce in their ancient records, but they never mentioned Mecca. Muslims need to challenge their knowledge, and question the things on which they base their religious hope.

THE REIGN OF SARGON II AND ARABIA

Mecca, if existing at the time of Sargon II, would have been mentioned with the various Arabian tribes including Saba, which were all mentioned in the inscriptions of that period.

Sargon II was one of Assyria's greatest kings. As the successor to Shalmaneser V, he reigned from 722-705 B.C., and consolidated the conquests made by Tiglath-Pileser III. Philistia, Babylonia, Kurdistan and Israel were among the lands he conquered. In 717 B.C., he deposed the king of the Hittite city of Karkemish and made the city an Assyrian colony. He put down rebellions in many cities, such as Arpad, Damascus and Hamath, and he defeated the plans of the Egyptians who supported these rebellions. After conquering a nation, Sargon would deport some of the inhabitants and mix the remnant of the population with inhabitants from other regions. Samaria is one example of this. Sargon II deported Israelites living in Samaria to the north of Assyria and then brought some Arabian tribes that were threatening his border to live in Samaria.

Excavations in Sargon's palace and capital at Dur Sharrukin have uncovered his annals. Among the events recorded in these annals is his triumph over several Arabian tribes, such as Thamud, Marsimani, Ephah and Ibadidi. He deported part of their populations to Samaria. His annals also record tribute given to him by Pir'u, the King of Egypt; by Samsi, the Queen of northern Arabia and the desert between Arabia and Palestine; and by Ita'amra, King of Saba, who is known in the Saba inscriptions as Yathi' amar.[121] We also find this information about the defeat of the Arabian tribes in other Assyrian records, namely the Cylinder inscription. We also find the tributes of the kings in the Display inscription. We see that the historical events during this period are confirmed from more than one record.

The tribe of Marsimani is identified as the tribe of Mesamanes, mentioned by Ptolemy in the sixth book and seventh chapter of his work simply titled *Geography*.[122] Ptolemy placed the location of this tribe close to the area of the Thamud. Thamud is mentioned

195

in the inscriptions and is an Arabian tribe in northwestern Arabia. It's also mentioned by Greek and Roman classical writers, and richly documented in northern Arabian inscriptions. Thamud is located between Teima and the region where Mecca was eventually built.

Ephah, which we saw participating at the time of Tiglath-Pileser III with the other Arabian northwestern tribes in an alliance against the Assyrians, is seen again here in a new alliance.

Considering the events of the 8th century B.C., including the things already recorded in inscriptions by Tiglath-Pileser III and Sargon II, we have a clear picture of which nations and tribes dominated the scene in western Arabia. This picture contains both the military point of view and the trading activity point of view. Mecca is absent from all these records, even though it would have been near the location of tribes mentioned in the inscriptions of the 8th century B.C., like the tribes of Thamud and Mesamanes. Mecca, if it had existed at that time, would have been located between the aforementioned tribes and Saba.

THE REIGN OF SENNACHERIB

Mecca is absent from the military, trade and religious scene during Sennacherib's reign.

Sennacherib, who ruled from 705-681 B.C., fought to maintain the empire established by his father, Sargon II. Among Sennacherib's actions was a campaign against Babylonia. Later, he initiated campaigns against countries located on the Mediterranean coast, and supported by Egypt, two of which were Phoenicia and Philistia. Next, Sennacherib campaigned against Jerusalem. Then, he defeated the Egyptians around 701 B.C. Another important campaign that Sennacherib conducted targeted Elam around 691 B.C.

Sennacherib defeated the Arabs, who took sides with Merodach Baladan, the Babylonian king who rebelled against the Assyrians.

Another campaign was against the queen of northern Arabia named Te'lhunu. The queen was defeated and she was pursued to the city of Adummatu, identified with the Dumah. Classical authors mention Dumahas. Domatha, a city of north Arabia built on an oasis. Dumahis located between al-Medina and Syria. It was known also as Dumaht al-Jandal. Dumah was known to be an important religious center for Arabian tribes. A temple to the god, Wadd, was located in Dumah. We know that in later times, a temple in the Aqaba Gulf region replaced Dumah, an important religious center. The Greek geographer, Agatharchides, attests to this religious center. We know that Sennacherib's army captured images that the Arabians had veneered in Dumah and brought to Assyria. Later, Esarhaddon returned them to Dumah.

According to Assyrian inscriptions, around 689 B.C. the Assyrians conducted a campaign in northern Arabia against Adummatu. They fought against an alliance of two northern Arabian rulers: Telehunu, Queen of the Arabs; and Hazael, King of Qedar. The inscriptions tell us the alliance was defeated, and Hazael resumed sending tribute to Sennacherib. Through these wars, Sennacherib established himself in the lands that his father, Sargon II, had captured. Sennacherib gained notoriety beyond his borders by defeating the Egyptians, the Babylonians, the Arabian Queen Te'lhunu, and Dumah. Sennacherib was also known for gaining control of the spice land routes. His fame had spread to the point that Herodotus, the Greek historian, called him "king of the Arabs and Assyrians."[123]

Arabian cities like Teima regularly paid tribute to Sennacherib. There was an inscription at Nineveh which describes a gate in Nineveh as "the desert gate through which gifts from the people of Teima enter."[124] This indicates how much the trade cities, like Teima, were at the mercy of the Assyrians if they wanted their trade to continue. These cites needed to have the favor of the Assyrians to survive.

The Assyrian annals mention gifts or tributes paid by the King of Saba named Kariba'ilu. This king is Karib'il Water, well known in the Saba inscriptions. This is because of the Assyrian control of the land route boundaries of the Fertile Crescent. King Hazael of

Qedar paid tributes to the Assyrian king, Sennacherib. After the defeat of his alliance with Queen Telehunu, Hazael resumed paying tributes to Sennacherib.

Mecca, which depended for its survival upon its trade with markets controlled by Assyrians, could not have been silent in the trade relationships with the Assyrians if Mecca had existed in the 8th and 7th centuries B.C.

Many nations in western Arabia are mentioned by Sennacherib, especially kingdoms trading along the spice route. Among them were Dumah, Qedar, Teima, and Saba in Yemen. Sargon II also mentions spice route cities such as Saba, Teima and Ephah. Cities which depended on their relationships with other nations couldn't be silent in the history of empires like Assyria, when it dominated the routes that led to the markets.

Since the construction of Mecca in the 4th century A.D. in an arid area of Arabia, Mecca bought goods from Yemen and marketed them to Palestine, Syria and Mesopotamia in the Fertile Crescent. Assyria controlled that land beginning with the end of the 8th century B.C. and recorded tribes of secondary importance in its trading records. How, then, could the most important and ancient city in the region, according to the Islamic claim, be missed if it existed in the 8th century B.C. and in the beginning of the 7th century B.C.?

The Religious Center of Dumah

Mecca is absent from the religious scene, when a religious city of that time like Dumah was the place of attention for the Arabian tribes.

Another important observation we also see in the Assyrian inscriptions is about Dumah, the religious center for tribes of northern Arabia. The images and gods of Dumah were of such primary importance to the Arabians that they went to Assyria begging Esarhaddon for their return. This was many years after Esarhaddon's father had taken the images to Assyria. Dumah had religious preeminence during the Assyrian period before the

Arabians built another temple in the Aqaba Gulf region. Knowing that the Arabians of the desert are faithful to the religious center they revere, if Mecca had existed in Assyrian times, then it could not have been hidden. Mecca would have been the city where people went to worship and consult their gods before battle. Mecca would have been their refuge when they suffered military defeat. Kings would have fled there like they used to flee to Dumah. They would have gone to their holy city to invoke the protection of their gods.

Yet, we see once more that Mecca is absent from the trade, military and religious records of the Assyrian and Babylonian empires. To affirm a claim, like Mecca being the center of monotheism established by Abraham, and continuing to be the place where the Arabian tribes tried to have the prerogative and privilege to control through all history of Arabia, as it claimed by the Islamic tradition, is something that would make Mecca the center of interest and contentions for all Arabian tribes. It would consequently have been obvious in all epochs, and recorded historically in each of these eras. The fact of the matter is, if Mohammed had selected any city as his religious claim other than Mecca, he could have made connections to the old local pagan Arabian religious centers of the 7th century B.C., like Dumah. But Mecca has no history to support these ancient connections beyond the pagan star worship of Yemen in the 4th century A.D., for which, historically, the temple of Mecca was built.

THE REIGN OF ESARHADDON

As we continue our quest to understand the dating of the founding of the city of Mecca, we come to the reign of Esarhaddon, who followed his father Sennacherib. Esarhaddon reigned from 680-669 B.C. Among his campaigns, the most important were his invasions of Egypt, Ethiopia and the Arabian desert. Near the river Kalb, which is near Beirut, Lebanon today, one of his inscriptions was found. It records his campaigns into Egypt and Ethiopia. Egypt was under the rule of the Ethiopians when Esarhaddon invaded it. He eventually conquered all the kingdoms along the eastern shore of the Mediterranean, and he brought their kings to Nineveh.

The inscriptions of Esarhaddon provide us with a lot of information about his wars with the Arabs, reflecting just how much land the Assyrians controlled in some parts of Arabia at the beginning of the 7th century B.C. The annals of Nineveh reveal many such events. One event was the return of the images of the Arabian gods to Dumah. Dumah became a religious center for the Arabian tribes since the 9th century B.C.

Esarhaddon also rescued Tabua. She had been taken as a small girl from her own people, and she grew up in the court of the Assyrian kings. Then the Assyrians appointed her to be the queen of the Arabs in Dumah. For Assyrian kings to appoint rulers for some of the Arabian lands shows the influence they had over parts of Arabia at the time of Esarhaddon.

The Annals of Nineveh also report the tribute that Hazael, King of Qedar, paid to Assyria. Assyrian records describe Hazael as he came to Nineveh to express his submission to Esarhaddon:

> As for Hazael, king of Arabia, the splendor of my majesty overwhelmed him, and with gold, silver, and precious stones he came into my presence and also kissed my feet.[125]

The Annals of Nineveh also tell us about Hazael's son, Ia'-hi-u', who was also called Yauta'. He became king of Qedar after Hazael's death. The Assyrian army intervened to help Ia'-hi-u' defeat a revolt conducted by U-a-bu. U-a-bu led an Arabian alliance against Yauta', but the Alliance was defeated by the Assyrian army. Later IA'-hi-u' became disloyal to the Assyrians who, in turn, attacked IA'-hi-u', who was defeated and fled. He later returned and swore a loyalty oath to Assurbanipal, the next king of the Assyrians.

These, and other examples from the inscriptions of Esarhaddon show that northern Arabia, especially Qedar, was under Assyrian rule. The Assyrians appointed kings, took tributes, and suppressed any revolts directly against them, or against any Arabian rulers who were loyal to them. The aforementioned episodes are also found in other Assyrian inscriptional documents.[126] Also, there are other inscriptions in Nineveh and Assur reporting these same episodes. These examples testify as to how the historical events occurring during the reign of Esarhaddon are well-attested in the archaeological records. We find an interesting fact in the so-called "Fragment F" from Nineveh. When Esarhaddon's army crossed the Sinai desert to suppress a revolt in Egypt, they used Arabian camels to supply them with water.[127] This suggests that through the domain of Esarhaddon over the many Arabian lands, through the Arabs' experience in the deserts, and with their camels, the Assyrian army was capable of crossing huge deserts to attack distant lands. In fact, among the episodes recorded in Esarhaddon's inscriptions was his campaign into the land of Bazu.

The Land of Bazu

Another important argument (for the case against the existence of Mecca at the time of Esarhaddon) hinges on the fact that there were no more cities for Assyrian to conquer in northwestern Arabia, so they marched in profundity into central Arabia to the land of Bazu.

Ba'zu is considered by many scholars to have been located in central Arabia, or toward the Persian Gulf region. This supports the idea that the Assyrians controlled parts of northern and central Arabia. Details about this campaign are found in Esarhaddon's Inscriptions, his Chronicles and some Babylonian Chronicles. Ba'zu is described as:

> A distant country, beyond a salt desert, beyond sandy and thorny land, beyond the sphere of military activity of earlier Assyrian kings.[128]

The same records describe Ba'zu as: "An arid land, saline ground, a waterless region." Heidel Prism III speaks of a march of about 140 beru (which corresponds to 1,500 kilometers) through a region "covered with sand, thorny plants, snakes and scorpions cover the land like ants."[129]Another description of the land of Ba'zu says: "A district located afar off, a desert stretch of alkali, a thirsty region of sand, thorn brush and gazelle mouth, stones, 20 double hours of serpents and scorpions, with which the plain was covered as with ants."[130] Inscriptions name nine places the Assyrians conquered in the land of Ba'zu, and give the names of eight of their kings. Assyrian records tell us that the Assyrian army burned seven walled cities in Ba'zu. Then they appointed a local king by the name of Layale' to rule the country. He was the king of a land near Ba'zu under the name of Ia-di.[131]

These episodes reflect how deep the Assyrian influence was in Arabia at the time of Esarhaddon. They were able to march across a desert over a distance of 1,500 kilometers. Scholars suggest two places for the location of Ba'zu: One is in central Arabia, near the city of Khaybar and beyond,[132] and the other is west of the Persian Gulf.[133] The events involving Ba'zu reflect the depth of the Assyrian influence in Arabia at the time of Esarhaddon. It is significant that the Assyrian army conquered a distant and arid land like Ba'zu, instead of going west toward the area where Mecca was eventually built. This supports the fact that the classical writers found that the area in which Mecca was eventually built was uninhabitable at that time. The area divided northern Arabia from Yemen, to the point that the Assyrians possessed no more cities or kingdoms in that area. Instead, they proceeded into central and eastern Arabia to conquer new lands, such as the land of Ba'zu.

ASSURBANIPAL'S REIGN

Although Assurbanipal had many contacts with Arabian tribes, and had reached the area of Teima, Mecca is absent in the Assyrian records which talk about him.

Our argument doesn't stop with Esarhaddon. When he died, he divided the Mesopotamian territory between his two sons. He gave Babylonia to his eldest son, Shamash-shum-ukin, and he gave the throne of Assyria to his second son, Assurbanipal, who ruled Assyria from 669-626 B.C. Assurbanipal drove the Ethiopian king,

Taharka, out of Egypt and appointed Necho to replace him. Then, around 660 B.C., during Assurbanipal's campaign against Elam and the Chaldeans, Psamtik, son of Necho, rebelled and separated Egypt from Assyria. Then Shamash-shum-ukin, Assurbanipal's elder brother and King of Babylonia, formed an alliance with several nations to make war against his brother, Assurbanipal. Assyrian records list the Arabian tribes which joined Shamash-shum-ukin. The Assyrian record reads like this:

> In these days Shamash-shum-ukin, the faithless brother of mine, king of Babylon, stirred to revolt against me the people of Akkad, Chaldea, the Arameans... the Sealand from Akaba to Bab-Salimeti.[134](Akaba may be the actual name of Aqaba.)

He also mentioned tribes of Arabia which rebelled with Shamash-shum-ukin against Assurbanipal. Around 648 B.C., when Assurbanipal defeated the alliance and annexed Babylonia to his empire, his brother killed himself. Some years later, Nabopolassar, the leader of Chaldean dynasty, rebelled against Assurbanipal.

The inscriptions of Assurbanipal present information about the Arabs. The annals of Assurbanipal record a treaty that he made with the Qedarites prior to year 652 B.C.[135] The annals also provide us with information about the revolt of Yauta', the son of Hazael and King of Qedar. He attacked regions in Trans Jordan before the hostilities between Assurbanipal and his brother, Shamash-shum-ukin, King of Babylonia, began. Yauta' was defeated and fled to the land of Nebaioth to seek refuge under their king, Natnu. Assurbanipal replaced Yauta' with Abiyate', son of Te'ri, who submitted to Assurbanipal and paid tribute to him. Also Natnu, King of Nebaioth, did the same. The Assyrian inscriptions show that the Qedarites had more than one leader. One of them was called Ammuladi. Ammuladi attacked the western border of the Assyrian empire and was defeated.

According to Shamash-shum-ukin's Chronicles, the siege of the city of Babylon was in the year 650 B.C. Among the Arabians who helped Shamash-shum-ukin was Abiyate', son of Te'ri.[136] There was another Arabian called Uaita', son of Birdada, king of a tribe called Su-mu-An, who sent forces to help Shamash-shum-ukin. The Su-mu-An tribe is considered one of the Qedar tribal confederations.[137] The reason that Arabian tribes took sides with Shamash-shum-ukin against Assurbanipal was that Babylonia was closer to them, and they thought that Babylonia would win the conflict and control the land routes to the markets in the Fertile Crescent. They also thought the Babylonians would not impose heavy tributes like Assyria did.

Around the year 645 B.C., an Assyrian campaign took place against the tribes of Qedar, Su-mu-An and Nebaioth. This campaign came after the Assyrian victory against Elam. So Assurbanipal was now ready to punish the tribes who gave aid to his rebellious brother, Shamash-shum-ukin. Before Assurbanipal's Assyrian empire declined, and was superseded by the Babylonians, Assurbanipal waged many other campaigns against the Arabs. He fought them in the Syro-Arabian desert, starting from Tadmur and moving south. In the final stage of his campaigning, according to the historian Glaser (as we mentioned previously), Assurbanipal penetrated the Arabian desert as far as Teima.

Mecca was a city built on the spice route, and it depended on the markets of the Fertile Crescent which, before the 7th century B.C., was under the Assyrian occupation for centuries. To survive, Mecca would have made itself known to traders and other cities if it had existed during that long time span.

From the study of Assyrian inscriptions of the 7th century B.C., we see in all of this that Mecca is conspicuously absent, just as it is absent from all the other Assyrian inscriptions. This long period of time spans several centuries. Each king documented his conquests and kept meticulous records. Some events appear in not only one inscription, but in many. We have seen how each tribe in north and western Arabia, even as far away as Saba, was eager to please the Assyrians in order to protect their interests. Many paid tribute annually. Some Assyrian-controlled tribes and cities at times rebelled and were punished. Still others formed alliances, hoping to occupy new regions, or have more influence over the land trading routes which influenced their markets.

Yet, there's no explanation for the absence of Mecca in all the Assyrian records during this long period of history. The names of kingdoms and cities on the spice route appear many times, but the city of Mecca is never among them. If it had existed, as Muslims claim, Mecca would have had more reason than any other nation to build a strong relationship with the Assyrians. Mecca would need to gain Assyrian favor with tributes and gifts, because Mecca's location would require it to be dependent on trade in order to survive.

Much later in history, the city of Mecca does appear in central western Arabia, but that's not until the 4th century A.D. Like the nations before it, the historical record shows that Mecca was dependent on trade (after its appearance) because of its location on the spice-trading route. The silence of Mecca during the Assyrian domination of the Fertile Crescent, and its preeminence over the tribes of northern Arabia, points once again to the fact that Mecca could not have existed during the era of Assyrian control. This information would have importance only for historians who study this time period, if it were not for one thing: The followers of Islam claim that the city of Mecca began long before the time of Assurbanipal. They claim that it was founded by Abraham and Ishmael, his son by Hagar. They claim that these two men built a temple in Mecca as early as 2050 B.C. We have shown this cannot be true.

7 _____

CHALDEAN RECORDS ALSO EXCLUDE ANY RECORD OF MECCA DURING THE 7TH AND 6TH CENTURIES B.C.

The Chaldeans were people of Arabian origin who settled in the region of Babylonia. After the death of Assurbanipal, the Chaldean, Nabopolassar, the ruler of Babylonia, established his independence in 625 B.C. Nabopolassar occupied the Assyrian provinces and destroyed Nineveh in the year 605 B.C. with the help of Manda, a nomad tribe from Kurdistan, which many scholars identify with the Medes. The Assyrian dynasty of Harran asked for help from Pharaoh Necho II, the ruler of Egypt who controlled Syria at that time. Nabopolassar placed his son, Nebuchadnezzar, in command of the Babylonian army. They encountered and defeated the Egyptians in the old Hittite city of Carchemish in 604 B.C. When Nebuchadnezzar heard that his father had died, he returned to Babylonia and became the king of one of the most powerful empires in the Middle East. In 586 B.C., Nebuchadnezzar occupied and destroyed Jerusalem, forcing the Jews into exile.

When Nebuchadnezzar ruled the Chaldeans, he fought many wars with Arab countries. Information regarding the Chaldean period can be found in the Babylonian Chronicles, as well as other resources. According to the Babylonian Chronicles, Nebuchadnezzar raided the Arabs several times between 599-598 B.C. The echo of such raids was recorded in the Bible by the prophet Jeremiah. In Jeremiah 49: 28, he writes:

> Concerning Qedar, and concerning the kingdoms of Hazor which Nebuchadnezzar the King of Babylon shall smite, thus says the Lord: " Arise and go to Qedar..."

Another of Nebuchadnezzar's raids is confirmed in the apocryphal book of Judith, which was written in the 4th century B.C. In the second chapter of that book, Midian is mentioned among the tribes. It says:

> he compassed about all the children of Midian and set on fire their tents, and spoiled their sheepcotes.[138]

Some scholars think that Nebuchadnezzar reached further than Midian, all the way to Teima.[139]

The last king of Babylonia was Nabonidus. We already have dealt, in part, with the campaigns Nabonidus waged in Arabia. He reigned from 556-539 B.C., and occupied the Arabian city of Teima, to which he transferred his residency. Nabonidus was from Harran. His mother, Addagoppe, who was a priestess of the god-moon, Sin, had a special relationship with Nebuchadnezzar. It is thought that this is the reason Nabonidus ascended to the throne of Babylon after Nebuchadnezzar's grandson, Labasi-Marduk, had been killed in his palace as a result of a conspiracy.

Addagoppe was born in 649 B.C., lived for 102 years, and died around 547 B.C. From Nabonidus' Inscriptions, we learn that Addagoppe was mourned as a great queen. This incident, along with other details, supports the idea that she was married to Nebuchadnezzar.

The Inscriptions of Harran mention that Addagoppe was brought to the Babylonian court around 610 B.C., where she became very influential. When Labasi-Marduk was assassinated, and the throne became empty, she found herself in the position to name a successor, largely due to her status as the widow of Nebuchadnezzar. She replaced Labasi-Marduk with her son, Nabonidus. Some scholars believe that Nabonidus was married to the daughter of Nebuchadnezzar. If so, Nebuchad-nezzar would have been a stepfather to Nabonidus and step-grandfather to Nabonidus' son, Belshazzar; and, perhaps, the father-in-law of Nabonidus, as well. Belshazzar and his father would have been considered members of the family of the great King

Nebuchadnezzar. This justifies their ascensions to the throne of Babylonia.

Nabonidus, who controlled north and central western Arabia, including the area where Mecca was eventually built, mentioned all the cities there, but he did not mention Mecca.

Nabonidus left the affairs of the kingdom to his son, Belshazzar, and traveled in Arabia to control north and central western Arabia. He marched toward Edom in southern Jordan, and then to Teima. He killed the king of Teima, subdued the inhabitants, and built a royal palace for himself. After establishing himself in Teima, Nabonidus launched campaigns to ensure his control over all northern and central western Arabia. He eventually occupied the cities of Dedan, Fadak, Khaybar, Yadi, and Yathrib, which is also called al-Medina. (See Fig. 4.)

Inscriptions which date back to the 6th century B.C. were found in Teima. These inscriptions describe wars between Teima and Dedan.[140] This may suggest that people of Teima were used by Nabonidus in his campaigns against Dedan and other cities in the region. Historians believe cities like Khaybar and Yathrib were most probably built during the 6th century B.C. The city of Qedar, prior to the time of Nabonidus, had been subdued by Nebuchadnezzar. Thus, Nabonidus eventually controlled all the existing cities in the area. He controlled all the routes which branch from Medina to the north with the cities of Yathrib, Teima and Dedan; to the east with the city of Yathrib-Hail; and to the south of Yathrib, which is only 200 miles from where Mecca was built.[141]

Since Nabonidus wished to control the whole area, Mecca would have been one of his main goals, if it had existed then. Nabonidus was in the area a long time. His military activity was more than one campaign lasting a few days or months. Nabonidus traveled the area for ten years. All north and central western Arabia was his province. He was there so long that he couldn't have missed Mecca, if it were there at the time.

We see that Mecca is not mentioned at any time during the Chaldean period, even when Nabonidus made all of northern and central western Arabia, which included the area where Mecca was eventually built, into another province of his empire. This is significant, because cities that would have been less important than Mecca were mentioned as part of this province, but Mecca was not mentioned.

8 _____

THE MISSING MERCHANTS OF MECCA

While the merchants of the Arabian routes were discussed in many places, no merchant from Mecca is ever mentioned.

Not only is Mecca absent from all the military campaign records during the Chaldean period, but it is also missing from the records of trading activity. Trade was important to the Babylonians as early as the 6th century B.C. We know that there was an increase in trade along the Arabian land routes to the Fertile Crescent. Babylonian records reflect increased trade activity and Babylon's relationship with Arabian merchants, but these records don't mention Mecca. Arab merchants were known for their trade with the Babylonians. The records show Nabonidus sending a letter to one of his assistants, instructing him to give an Arabic merchant of the tribe of Thamud (Te-mu-da-a Ar-ba-a-a) several talents of silver.[142]

Some documents before Nabonidus show people arriving from Teima in Babylonia, mainly as merchants. Other documents also mention the Qedarites. Travelers from Teima also appear in the Assyrian and Babylonian records. One example is a letter mentioning Am-me-ni-ilu tamkaru Te-ma-a-a, and his journey to the King of Babylonia.[143] Yet, in all these records, we see no one coming from Mecca. If Mecca had existed during the Chaldean period, it indeed would be strange not to have been listed in the Chaldean trade records of the time, especially since other cities on the northern and central western Arabian spice route were recorded as a testimony to their trade activity. The fact of the matter is that, in all historical documents, we do not see a merchant of Mecca in any place in the Middle East, while the trace of merchants of cities of western Arabia are found even as far away as Sinai. In Sinai, for example, inscriptions have been found identifying merchants belonging to the Thamud tribe. We also find Minaean merchants in various epochs traveling to the Fertile Crescent. The Minaean merchants were also involved in trade with Egypt in the 3rd and 2nd centuries B.C. There has been a sarcophagus found of a Minaean merchant who supplied the Egyptian temples with incense.[144] Minaean inscriptions found in Memphis, Egypt and Delos give us more activities of Minaean merchants.[145] Minaean and Dedanite inscriptions in Jordan reflect the activity of their merchants in the Fertile Crescent.[146] Saba merchants are mentioned in the book of Job, around the 9th through 7th centuries B.C. These merchants were traveling in the area of Palestine. Inscriptions telling us about Sabaean merchants were found in northeastern Arabia.[147] Scholars confirm the presence of Sabaeans near Yathrib, also called Medina, in a place called Wady ash Sheba, which means the Valley of Saba. There is also a village named in a Greek inscription as "Pool of the Sabaeans." [148]

With all these trade records, it is unreasonable to suggest that Mecca had existed since the time of Abraham, and was located on an ancient trading route. No archaeological or documented testimony is found anywhere which refers to even one merchant from Mecca. Yet, each kingdom and city on the same land route has many well-documented testimonies of its trade, including in places where it used to trade, or in places the caravan used to pass through. All the historical facts we have tell us that Mecca could not have existed prior to the Christian era. We hold our Muslim friends in high regard, but it is time for them to see that they have been taught a serious mistruth.

THE BIBLE AND THE ANCIENT MECCA CLAIM

An important argument for rejecting the claim that Mecca is an ancient city: the Bible makes an excellent case.

The Bible is considered the most important resource for us to understand ancient history. Because it is a book inspired by God, it presents the origin of races, nations and tribes. At the beginning of this part, we want to look at the people born after the flood who descended from Noah. Narrations found in Genesis, as well as other books of the Bible, prove that the Bible could not be a compilation of human writings. The Bible accurately numbers the tribes in the genealogies of the book of Genesis. It gives the placement for each tribe, and an accurate chronology regarding their appearance in history, although some of the tribes and nations date back nearly to the time of the flood.

Moses: a Dependable Resource, Excludes the Existence of Mecca in his Time.

Moses, the prophet inspired to write the book of Genesis, wrote it in the beginning of the 15th century B.C. As many as 3-4,000 years elapsed between the origin of many of the ancient tribes and the time Moses wrote the chronology in Genesis. Oral tradition, itself, is unable to remain intact for that long a period of time. The only explanation for the accuracy and completeness of the ancient data is that God inspired the book which Moses wrote. God provided information above and beyond what Moses received through oral tradition.

In the book of Genesis, we can trace the origin of Arabian tribes from their beginnings to the time of Moses. He gives us an accurate chronology of those tribal generations, and the names of their ancestors. But more than that, the book of Genesis provides us with information on how Arabia was populated after the flood. Genesis names the tribes which populated Arabia. The records of these Arabian tribes began soon after the flood, and continued through the time of Abraham, up to Moses and his servant, Joshua, in the 15th century B.C. So the study of Genesis is not just inspired data covering tribal names, origins and chronologies from early times, but it is also an historical data bank of the nations living at the time of Moses. He received much of this historical information from the Egyptians when he studied in their institutions as the adopted son of Pharaoh's daughter. Years later, Luke wrote in Acts 7:22, "Moses was learned in all the wisdom of the Egyptians."

The Midianites never heard of Mecca.

Historians suppose that the tribes of Arabia were well-known to the Midianites, with whom Moses came in contact through his residency in Sinai. You may remember that Moses went to live in the Sinai desert, when he escaped from Egypt after killing the Egyptian who murdered the Israelite. This was before God sent Moses back to Egypt to convince Pharaoh to free Israel from their servitude in Egypt. We can assume that Jethro, Moses' father-in-law, knew the names of tribes of western Arabia, since he was also a priest of the Midianites, living partially in the Sinai and partially in northern Arabia. Jethro knew more about Arabian tribal names than did the contemporaries of Mohammed at the end of the 6th century A.D. It is analogous to my situation as originally a resident in the Middle East; I know about the names of the contemporary nations of Arabia, mainly because I lived in such close proximity to them. I believe the Midianites were in a position to know more about western Arabia because they were, at that time, the closest people to the location where Mecca was eventually built. We can be sure the Midianites would have known about Mecca, if it had existed when Moses lived in the 16th B.C. and part of the 15th century B.C.

We cannot ignore the historical statements made by an inspired man like Moses when he gives us the historical picture of his own times. Moses lived for 40 years in the Sinai desert with the Midianites, who were partially Arabian. He was educated in Egyptian institutions, which were the most-advanced centers of knowledge in his time. Not only was Moses a great prophet of God, but he was well-qualified as a reliable source for a historical narration.

Ibn Ishak, the unreliable resource, contradicted by Moses.

On the other hand, Ibn Ishak, who lived in the 8th century A.D., and rewrote history for Muslims, was not nearly as qualified as Moses for the task. It is evident that Ibn Ishak modified the genealogies which Moses had been inspired to write in the book of Genesis, creating for Muslims a so-called "Islamic tradition." Previously, I mentioned that the tribes and genealogies about which Ibn Ishak wrote were a product of his imagination, and never encountered in the writings of others before him. As I also stated earlier, Ibn Ishak was judged by the scholars of his time to be a man of forgery who invented false genealogies. How, then, can his narration be a competitor with the writings of Moses in the book of Genesis?

THE GENEALOGY OF HAM AND THE TRIBES OF ARABIA

Turning to what Moses wrote, the first genealogy we study is the account of Ham, the second son of Noah. Genesis 10:6-7 says, "The sons of Ham were Cush, Mizraim, Put and Canaan." Those are the fathers from which some of the ancient tribes came. For example, the nation of Cush was located in today's Ethiopia. Egypt came from Mizraim. Put was an old North African tribe, and Canaan was located in Palestine and Lebanon. From the first three came the rest of the African tribes. From the elder Cush came tribes in Ethiopia and Yemen. We see this from Cush's progeny presented in Genesis 10:7, "The sons of Cush were Seba, Havilah, Sabtah, Raamah and Sabtechah; and sons of Raamah were Sheba and Dedan." It is clear from the names of the sons of Cush that some of them represented places in Arabia. Cush is the father of the tribe of Cush, which dominated Ethiopia and Sudan in ancient times. The Bible presents other tribes which came from Cush. Some of these tribes traveled to Yemen through the Bab al-Mandeb Strait, a narrow channel of less than 20 miles. Since ancient times, this geographical location has affected historical connections between Ethiopia and Yemen.

The Bible identifies the origin of the Sabaeans of Yemen as Cushites who came from Ethiopia.

The fourth son of Cush, Raamah, is the father of Sheba, the tribe which inhabited Yemen. We don't know when the descendants of Sheba left Ethiopia and traveled to Yemen. Many scholars think that the Sabaeans of Yemen came from Ethiopia. One reason for their conclusion is the similarity between the languages of Saba of Yemen and the Mahri language of Ethiopia. This is in addition to the old connection between Yemen and Ethiopia through the straight. Migration from Ethiopia to the Arabian coast of Yemen, and vice versa, was quite extensive. This could be part of the reason Sheba dominated the Ethiopian coast, and established a line of kings in the 1st millennium B.C. The region became known as Di'amat, a nation which became independent around 350 - 320 B.C.

The name of Raamah, who was the father of Sheba, the fourth son of Cush, is found in Yemeni inscriptions.[149] This testifies to the accuracy of the Biblical accounts which state that Sheba was descended from the Cushites along the coast of Ethiopia. The Bible confirms the descendancy of the tribe of Sheba–Yemen from Sheba, the son of Raamah, the Cushite. This we find in Ezekiel 27:22. Ezekiel was given a word against Tyre, the Phoenician city. He described the trade of Tyre with other cities and nations:

215

> The merchants of Sheba and Raamah were your merchants. They traded for your wares the choicest spices, all kind of precious stones and gold.

We find Raamah, the father of Sheba, is mentioned with Sheba in this Biblical narrative. To identify a nation by the name of the father from whom the nation originated is a common Biblical style. We find this in many places in the Bible. The Lord refers to the nation of Israel by the name of Jacob, and also by the name of Isaac, the father of Jacob, after whom the nation of Israel was named. In the Ezekiel passage, Sheba and his father are mentioned to remind us that the Sheba, or Saba, kingdom came from Raamah, the Cushite. This passage in Ezekiel also reflects on the richness of commerce between Saba of Yemen and the Phoenician cities, such as Tyre, where spices, precious stones and gold were traded.

The brother of Raamah was named Seba. He is the first-born of Cush, which may explain the linguistic affinity between the Sheba of Yemen and the tribes of Ethiopia on the opposite shore of the Red Sea. It seems that there was a tribe named Seba which came from Seba, the son of Cush, in addition to the tribe of Sheba which came from the son of Raamah, the brother of Seba. We notice that the brother of Sheba, son of Raamah, was Dedan. This is not the father of Dedan, the tribe in northern Arabia which settled in the city of Dedan. We'll see that the northern tribe of Dedan came from Keturah, Abraham's second wife, whom he married after the death of Sarah. This Dedan, the son of Raamah, might have been a small tribe, which was integrated by other Cushite tribes over time.

So we see that the Biblical and historical facts point to the conclusion that ancient Yemeni populations have Cushite origins, and that the tribe of Saba is a Cushite tribe which migrated from Ethiopia.

The True Origin of Mohammed

The family of Mohammed, as Sabaean of Cushite origin descending from Ham, can't be connected with Ishmael and Abraham, who were of Semitic origin.

This Biblical and historical fact points to the true origin of the family of Mohammed. We know that the ancestors of Mohammed lived in Saba in Yemen. Around 150 A.D., when the dam of Ma'rib had a serious collapse, many Yemeni tribes left Yemen as a result of this devastation, before it was repaired.[150] The family of Mohammed was among those who emigrated to an area in central western Arabia, close to where the tribe of Khuzaa'h, also from Yemen, later built Mecca. They lived in the area surrounding Mecca before the city was constructed around the 4th century A.D. Therefore, the ancestors of Mohammed were from the tribe of Saba, which we saw is of Cushite origin, descending from Ham. And like all the Sabaeans from Yemen, they were not of Semitic origin. We know that the Quraish tribe of Mohammed learned its Arabic language when it emigrated and came in contact with the Bedouins of central western Arabia. How then can Mohammed be a descendant of Ishmael, as Islamic tradition claims?

The Ishmaelites lived in Sinai. From there they spread to the deserts of the Fertile Crescent. They never reached the area where Mecca was later built, nor did they ever reach Yemen.

Ishmaelite tribes are known to have lived south of Palestine, in the part of the Sinai desert which borders Canaan. From there they spread toward the Syro-Mesopotamian desert, and also to the north. Only the tribes of Qedar and Teima touched the northern portion of Arabia.

The locations of the Ishmaelite tribes are clearly revealed in the Bible, and confirmed through Assyrian inscriptions. We never find an Ishmaelite tribe south beyond Teima, which is about 180 miles from the border between Arabia and Jordan, nor do we find a historical record of an Ishmaelite tribe in the area where Mecca was later built.

Islamic tradition claims Mohammed descended from the Nabaioth tribe, which lived in southern Jordan and became extinct before the 7th century B.C. How could a Sabaean family, like the ancestors of Mohammed, be connected to a tribe that lived in southern Jordan, and disappeared more than 1,300 years before Mohammed was born? Islamic claims seem to be unaware of the historical facts concerning the Ishmaelites. They use fiction to connect Ishmael with Mecca, claiming that Ishmael's mother, Hagar, brought him through uninhabited desert. They also claim that Abraham visited Ishmael on the Baraq, a Persian mythological winged camel.

Islam further claims that the Ishmaelites lived in Mecca and established a great kingdom there. They claim the Ishmaelites even traveled to Yemen centuries before Mecca was actually built. Yet, history proves that Ishmael lived in southern Palestine, from which his descendants, the Ishmaelites, expanded their influence. Some tribes went north toward Damascus and Lebanon, while others went east toward Jordan and the desert between Jordan and Iraq. Still others went northeast toward the Syro-Mesopotamian desert, and a few went south toward the border of north Arabia. If the Ishmaelites had lived near Mecca, then their tribes would have extended their influence in all directions, with Mecca as the center. Apart from the fact that Mecca never appeared in history before the 4th century A.D., no Ishmaelite tribe was ever recorded to have lived in Yemen, Yamama (east of Mecca), or where Mecca was eventually built. For Islamic tradition to claim that Ishmaelite tribes lived in Yemen, and that they were the ancestors of Mohammed, and to claim that Ishmael built the temple at Mecca, is an illogical assertion. No one who studies the history of Ishmaelite tribes would accept this. I refer the reader to Part IV in this book, where I elaborate with more detail on the Ishmaelites.

The Unknown Family of Mohammed Compared to the Genealogy of Jesus

The family of Mohammed was from unknown Sabaean and Yemeni origin. There is no historical documentation of their family line, nor of any prophets of the faith of the God of Abraham. In contrast, the genealogy of Jesus has been recorded in each century since the time of Abraham.

We already studied the genealogy of Ham. We saw that Yemen was populated from the descendants of Sheba, son of Raamah, son of Cush. We also saw that, throughout history, tribes from Yemen have emigrated to the north. The language of the tribe of Saba, the main tribe of Yemen from which Mohammed is descended, differs significantly from the Arabic language, but the Saba language does have similarities to the Ethiopian language. We find this to be true, because the tribe of Saba is of Ethiopian Cushite origin, as we saw from our last study. Yet, the Saba language was not prevalent outside Yemen.

We saw that the ancestors of Mohammed lived in Saba as recently as 150 A.D., the date of the famous collapse of the Ma'rib Dam in Yemen. There is no documentation in history about this family prior to this famous collapse of the Dam of Ma'rib. Nothing supports the Islamic claim that Mohammed's family lived outside Yemen at any time in history. Since Mecca didn't exist prior to the 4th century A.D., the claim that this family was living in Mecca in ancient times is unhistorical. When we study the matter further, we discover that we are dealing with an unknown Sabaean family which never appeared in history with any religious claim, and is not documented by any inscriptions in the history of Yemen.

When we compare the genealogy of Jesus with Mohammed's claims, we find a much clearer genealogical path. We have written testimony in the Old Testament concerning each important member in the Messianic family. Remember that Jesus is one Person of the Trinity, and the one promised in the Old Testament to be incarnated as perfect man. We see promises, as well as prophecies, given to significant men in the genealogies of the Old Testament: men like Jacob, David, Solomon and Zerubbabel. These promises and prophecies describe the coming of the Messiah as the divine personality, born in the flesh, as the ultimate purpose of the genealogy of Jesus.

The record began with Abraham in the 21st century B.C., and was fulfilled in the miraculous virgin birth of Jesus, in 4 A.D., according to the prophecies of Isaiah. Micah 5:2 says,

> But you, Bethlehem Ephrathah, though you are little among the thousands of Judah, yet out of you shall come forth to Me the One that is to be ruler in Israel, whose goings forth have been from old, from everlasting.

The prophecy indicates that Jesus is from everlasting. But, for the ancestors of Mohammed, there is no historical document which indicates that they were more than an unknown Sabaean family. Islamic tradition wanted to create a story around this family to support Mohammed's claims. Ironically, Mohammed's ancestors, themselves, never supported any of his ancestral claims. No prophet was known to have come from this unknown Sabaean family. The statements on which Islamic claims are based lack historical evidence. For example, they claim that Mecca existed in ancient times, but we have already seen that Mecca never existed before the 4th century A.D.

Muslims contend that Ishmael was the foundation of Islam, and Mohammed carried a prophetic role.

Muslims also claim that the Ishmaelites lived in the area of Mecca, but we have documentation stating that this was not the case. The Ishmaelites originally resided in the desert of southern Palestine where their ancestor, Ishmael, lived. Later they migrated north and east. Only two tribes went a little toward the south, about 180 miles into the Arabian desert. They claim Mohammed is an Ishmaelite. This can't be true, because none of the Ishmaelite tribes ever lived in Yemen. Mohammed is Sabaean and, therefore, of Cushite origin.

Another fact is that Ishmael did not have a spiritual role, nor did any of his descendants. More specifically, the Ishmaelites never predicted that a prophet would come from Ishmael's descendants. On the other hand, the prophecy that the Messiah would come from the progeny of Isaac is documented in each generation. Of the twelve Ishmaelite tribes, no one ever expected or prophesied the coming of a prophet from their lineage. God never presents the world with a message of faith without building a solid historical foundation to establish credibility. In each era God sent His prophets, believing the same things He requires the world to believe. The prophets each supported the claims that His eternal Son would come, die on the cross as atonement for the sins of humanity, and be resurrected on the third day. God laid the foundation for this message in each generation through the messianic genealogy, and through the prophets whom He sent. Many religions present a man claiming to be a prophet, but without this unique historical foundation. Islam is one of these religions of the world that presents a claim of one man, Mohammed, who is a prophet from God, but without any sort of valid historical foundation. Then Islam unhistorically tries to connect to the heritage and the Biblical foundation, but without any historical elements of veracity.

THE GENEALOGY OF SHEM AND THE ARABIAN TRIBES WHICH DESCENDED FROM HIM

I would like you to look at another genealogy in the Bible which contributed significantly to the population of eastern Arabia. It is the genealogy of Shem, the first-born of Noah. We find this genealogy in the book of Genesis 10:22-30:

> The sons of Shem were Elam, Assur, Arphaxad, Lud and Aram. The sons of Aram were Uz, Hul Gether, and Mash. Arphaxad begot Salah, and Salah begot Eber. To Eber were born two sons: the name of the one was Peleg, for in his days the earth was divided; and his brother's name was Joktan.

> Joktan begot Almodad, Sheleph, Hazarmaveth, Jerah, Hadoram, Uzal, Diklah, Obal, Abimael, Sheba Ophir, Havilah and Jobab. All these were the sons of Joktan. And their dwelling place was from Mesha as you go toward Sephar, the mountain of the east.

Verse 22 lists the sons from which all the Semitic tribes are generated. Elam is the father of the Elamites. Asshur is the father of the Assyrians, at the very least. Lud is the father of other Semitic tribes. Aram is the father of the Arameans, and other Mesopotamian and Syrian tribes. Arphaxad is the father of many Semitic tribes, including the Hebrews, as well as some people in Mesopotamia, and eastern Arabia.

Of particular interest for our study is Joktan, from whom came many tribes, which are identified as some of the tribes of eastern Arabia. The Bible comments on the tribes that came from Joktan:

> And their dwelling place was from Mesha as you go toward Sephar, the mountain of the east.

In the Septuagint, which is the Greek translation of the Hebrew Old Testament, Mesha is rendered as Massae. This suggests that the location of the tribe of Massa, one of the Ishmaelite tribes which lived in the Syro-Mesoptomian desert, as between Syria, Jordan and Iraq. The same translation renders Separ as Sopher.

Mount Sephar of the east is identified by many scholars as Mount Seir in Edom,[151] located in what is now southern Jordan. In Numbers 23:7, Balaam speaks of himself by saying that Balak brought him from the "Mountains of the East." We know that Balaam lived in the Edom area, which suggest that the "Mountain of the East" was Mount Seir in Edom, today called "the Mountains of Sharah" in southern Jordan. We conclude that these tribes coming from Joktan lived in the Syro-Mesopotamian desert and southern Edom in Trans-Jordan. This is before some tribes moved toward the Persian Gulf, and before others went south and east to southeastern Arabia.

Among Joktan's sons, Hazarmaveth is identified with the nation of Hadhramot, which is located in eastern south Arabia.

Although its location was actually in the southeastern part of Arabia, throughout history this nation was known for its connection to the Persian Gulf.[152] This suggests that the original emigration of this tribe, along with other tribes which stemmed from Joktan, was through the Persian Gulf, toward the southeastern part of Arabia. Another tribe which descended from Joktan is Ophir, whose location is placed (by most scholars) in the Persian Gulf. Ophir was known for its rich commerce with India.[153] It was the intermediate trading center between India and Middle Eastern nations. Products from eastern Arabia, such as gold, and products from India, came through Ophir. The Bible says Solomon made ships to go to Ophir to benefit from her position in the gold trade. 1 Kings 9:26-28 says:

> King Solomon also built a fleet of ships at Ezion Geber, which is near Elath on the shore of the Red Sea, in the land of Edom. Hiram sent his servants with the fleet, seamen who knew the sea, to work with the servants of Solomon. They went to Ophir and acquired four hundred and twenty talents of gold from there.

I Kings 10:11 says:

> Also the ships of Hiram, which brought gold from Ophir, brought great quantities of almug wood and precious stones from Ophir.

The Phoenicians were known to be great traders between the Persian Gulf and the Mediterranean nations. One reason is because the Gulf region was their original homeland before they emigrated to Lebanon. History also tells us that the region of Carmania, in Iran, opposite to Arabian territory in the Persian Gulf, was rich in gold. Pliny testifies to this fact in his writings, calling the gold "apyron gold."[154] Also, Onesicritus, the commander of Alexander's fleet, spoke about the gold coming from Carmania.[155] This suggests that Ophir was close to Carmania, yet opposite it in the Arabian part of the Gulf region. This justifies the gold trade of Ophir throughout ancient history.

Jerah is identified by scholars with Jerakon Kome, which Ptolemy spoke about as north of Dhofar in southeastern Arabia.[156]

Diklah most probably is Dilmun, the tribe that inhabited Bahrain in the Persian Gulf. Dilmun is known to have existed since at least 3000 B.C. Generally, we see these tribes moving from the Syro-Mesopotamian desert and southern Jordan toward the Persian Gulf to eventually dwell in east and southeastern Arabia.

Another son, Sheba, is mentioned among the sons of Joktan. We assume this is not the Saba who dwelt in Yemen. As we saw from our study of the genealogy of Ham, Sheba of Yemen descended from Cush, which became the dominant tribe of Ethiopia. Sheba penetrated into Yemen through the strait of Bab al-Mandub.

Here, we are dealing with tribes that first inhabited the Syro-Mesopotamian desert. Some of them emigrated gradually toward the Gulf region, but others seemed to remain in the desert of Syro-Mesopotamia. Sheba - if it represents a tribe, and is not just the name of one of Joktan's sons - seems to have been a Nomadic tribe which lived in the Syro-Mesopotamian desert.

Although central western Arabia is closer to where Moses lived than other parts of Arabia, neither Mecca nor the tribes which the Islamic tradition claims to have lived at Mecca since the time of Abraham, are listed by Moses within the tribes of Arabia.

We have studied the Biblical revelation regarding how Arabia was first populated. It was partially populated from its southwestern part, that is Yemen, through one or more of the progeny of Cush, son of Ham. It was also partially populated in the eastern and southeastern parts through the sons of Joktan, from the genealogy of Shem. We have seen how the Bible mentions places and names of tribes and nations in Arabia, which came from the progeny of Ham and Shem, and which were present at the time of Moses in the 16th century B.C. Yet, in all this documentation, there is no mention of Mecca, or the tribes which Islamic tradition claims lived in Mecca at the time of Abraham. This is in spite of the fact that Mecca is located closer to Palestine than the other places, tribes and nations mentioned in the genealogies of two sons of Noah, Shem and Ham. We know that from Noah's third son,

Japheth, came the tribes that inhabited land as far away as Asia and Europe. If Mecca existed at the time of Moses, or if the tribe of Jurhum existed then, as claimed by Islamic tradition to have inhabited Mecca since the time of Abraham, then Mecca, because of its proximity to Canaan in respect to south Arabian and western Arabian tribes and nations mentioned in Genesis, would be the first to be genealogized in the book of Genesis. We know that the book of Genesis documented the genealogies of all the nations and tribes of the Middle East, from the least significant to the greatest. Genesis also genealogized the tribes of far-flung regions of the world, like Europe, Africa and Asia. We can surmise that Moses was less interested in accounting for tribes far from Israel, than he was from giving the genealogies of areas relatively close to him, like central western Arabia, where Mecca was eventually built. Yet, in all his genealogies, there is no mention of Mecca.

Because the Bible is a reliable resource for ancient history, especially as it represents tribes, nations and places as they descended from Noah, the Bible is further proof that Mecca didn't exist in the 2nd millennium B.C., nor in the 1st millennium B.C. This rather simple fact is significant to understanding Islam. If a religion is to be believable, it must be built on accurate information.

THE DESCENDANTS OF ABRAHAM AND KUTTARAH AND NORTH ARABIA

We already looked at passages in the Bible which showed us how southern and eastern Arabia were populated. Northern Arabia was uninhabited before, during and, for some time, after Abraham. The descendants of Abraham and Keturah, the wife Abraham married after Sarah died, eventually settled as the first inhabitants of northern Arabia. Historically, there is no mention of any people or tribe inhabiting northern Arabia before the descendants of Keturah. Just how the region was settled is told in

Genesis 25:1-6, which has become the third most important genealogy for the study of the tribes of Arabia. Genesis says:

> Abraham again took a wife, and her name was Keturah. And she bore him Zimran, Jokshan, Medan, Midian, Ishbak and Shuah. Jokshan begot Sheba and Dedan. And the sons of Dedan were Ashurim, Letushim, and Leummim. And the sons of Midian were Ephah, Epher, Hanoch, Abidah and Eldaah. All these were the children of Keturah.
> Abraham gave all that he had to Isaac. But Abraham gave gifts to the sons of the concubines which Abraham had; and while he was still living he sent them eastward, away from Isaac his son, to the country of the east.

What did the Bible mean when it said, "the country of the East?" Since the country to the east of Palestine is Edom, in southern Jordan, it is telling us that in the beginning, the descendants of Keturah lived in Edom. Afterward, they spread out in many directions. We know that two of the sons of Keturah, Jokshan and Midian, migrated south to northern Arabia. Jokshan, the second son of Abraham and Keturah, begot Sheba and Dedan. Dedan is the father of the tribes of Dedan, which dwelt in northern Arabia in the city of Dedan. From Dedan came the tribes of Ashurim, Letushim, and Leummim. Ashurim is documented in southern Arabian texts as lying in northwest Arabia.[157] This confirms the Biblical genealogy for the sons of Keturah. In particular, it confirms that the tribes of Dedan were derived from Keturah's progeny. It also confirms the true organization of Dedan and its main tribes in history. These confirmations agree exactly with the Biblical narrative.

There are other proofs that the Dedanites were descendants of Abraham and Keturah. Archaeologists discovered in the ruins of Dedan that the original language of the Dedanites is very close to the Hebrew language, rather than to the Arabic.[158] This is further proof that the city of Dedan was built by the descendants of Dedan, the son of Jokshan, son of Abraham and Keturah, and that the progeny of Abraham and Keturah were the first to inhabit northern Arabia, and build its cities. This happened only after the

10th century B.C. Therefore, to claim that Hagar crossed this uninhabited and deserted area with (the child) Ishmael in the 21st century B.C. is illogical.

The first-born son of Jokshan was Sheba. As the brother of Dedan, Sheba seems to have been the father of a tribe which lived in southern Jordan, in the desert between Jordan and Iraq. The book of Job, in the 15th verse of the first chapter, mentions the Sabaeans who attacked Job's servants, killing them and taking away the oxen and the donkeys. Job lived in the land of Uz. We understand from Genesis 22:20 that Uz was the son of Nahur, the brother of Abraham. Therefore, Job was from the same tribe of Uz, which came forth from Uz, the son of Nahur. His friend, Elihu, came from the land of Buz, as we see in Job 32:2. The land of Buz was also named after a tribe descended from the other son of Nahur, named Buz, as we see in Genesis 22:20, where the sons of Nahur, the brother of Abraham, are mentioned. Buz, as a tribe, is mentioned in Jeremiah 25:23. It seems that the land of Uz was located toward Mesopotamia, making it vulnerable to the raids of the Bedouins living in the desert between Jordan, Iraq and Syria. This suggests that the descendants of Sheba, the brother of Dedan, were the same people who attacked Job's servants. It also suggests the Sabaeans were living a nomadic lifestyle in the desert between Jordan and Iraq.

In addition to the Bible, Assyrian inscriptions record a tribe called the Sabaeans, who frequently attacked the Assyrian border from the desert. These attackers were most probably the Sabaeans, who were also Bedouins descended from Sheba, the brother of Dedan, in contrast to the Sabaeans of Yemen, who were great traders and the most civilized people of Arabia.

Shuah, the youngest son of Abraham and Keturah, was the father of a tribe by that name, and identified with the land of Suhi in the middle of the Euphrates. It appears in Cuneiform inscriptions dating back to the 18th century B.C.[159] Job 2:11 tells us that one of Job's friends was Bildad the Shuhite, who was also from the tribe of Shuah. The Cuneiform inscriptions confirm the Biblical narration and Job's location in Mesopotamia, which was probably close to where Bildad visited Job.

Ishbak, the fifth son of Abraham and Keturah, is identified with the country of Ia-as–bu-qa-a. The inscriptions of King Shalmaneser III of Assyria say it was allied with the Neo-Hittite kingdoms against Shalmaneser III around 858 B.C.[160]

Where did the Midianites Live During the 16th and 15th Centuries B.C.?

In addition to Dedan, the son of Jokshan, we have another son of Abraham and Keturah. This is Midian, their fourth son. His descendants controlled land which stretched toward northern Arabia. According to the Bible, the tribes of Midian were Ephah, Epher, Hanoch, Abidah and Eldaah. In history, the most important tribe of Midian was Ephah, written in the Greek of the Septuagint as Eypah. It is attested to in the Assyrian inscriptions under the name of Haiapa, which often attacked the Assyrian borders with other tribes.[161] Midian lived in southern Sinai and stretched toward the Gulf of Aqaba region in the area of northern Arabia bordering the south of Jordan. At the time of Moses, part of the tribe of Midian dwelt in the Sinai Desert, specifically around Mount Sinai. Exodus 2:15 says:

> Moses fled from the face of Pharaoh and dwelt in the land of Midian; and sat down by a well. Now the priest of Midian had seven daughters, and they came and drew water.

We know that the priest of Midian lived around Mount Sinai. The Exodus passage suggests that during the 16th century B.C. and the beginning of the 15th century B.C., the tribe of Midian was still living in the Sinai before part of the tribe migrated toward the Gulf of Aqaba, on the border between Jordan and northern Arabia.

Midian seems to be associated with Moab. When Moses guided Israel through the desert, we read in Numbers 22:7 that the elders of Midian and the elders of Moab sent for Balaam to curse Israel. This confirms that the location of Midian was in the southern

Sinai, extending to the eastern part of Sinai, close to Moab in southern Jordan. According to Numbers 25, when Israel reached the desert which borders Moab, many Israelites committed fornication with the women of Moab and Midian. This confirms that Midian dwelt in the Sinai desert between Mount Sinai and Moab in southern Jordan. In Numbers 31, the Israelites were engaged in a war against Midian, because the Midianites employed their women to sexually seduce the Israelites. Israel killed five of their kings. This is another confirmation that Midian dwelt in the southern Sinai in the 15th century B.C.

THE GENEALOGY OF HAGAR, AND THE DWELLING PLACE OF ISHMAEL AND HIS DESCENDANTS

The genealogy of Hagar, the servant who begot Ishmael to Abraham, contains three grandsons who extended their dwelling toward northern Arabia after the 10th century B.C. The grandsons of Hagar are mentioned in Genesis 25:12-18

> And these were the names of the sons of Ishmael, by their names according to their generations. The firstborn of Ishmael, Nabaioth, then Qedar, Adbeel, Mibsam, Mishma, Dumah, Massa, Hadar, Tema, Jetur, Naphish and Kedemah....These were the years of the life of Ishmael: one hundred and thirty seven years; and he breathed his last and died, and was gathered to his people.

> They dwelt from Havilah as far as Shur, which is east of Egypt as you go toward Assyria. He died in the presence of all his brethren.

I will discuss in detail the progeny of Hagar and their dwelling in Part IV. From verse 18, we understand that, at the time of Moses in the beginning of the 15th century B.C., Ishmaelite tribes were still living from the desert of Shur, part of Sinai, which is east of Egypt, with projection toward Havilah on the border between the eastern Sinai and southern Jordan. This means that, at the time of Moses, the descendants of Ishmael still dwelt in the Sinai. At that time no Ishmaelite tribe yet stretched toward north or eastern, or the border of, Arabia. This clearly demonstrates that Ishmael and his descendants did not go to Mecca to live, as the Islamic tradition and the Qur'an claim. Another thing that we understand from this verse is "he died in the presence of all his brethren." When Ishmael died, Isaac, and perhaps Esau, the son of Isaac, were there. By oriental custom, close brethren visit and stay a few days while the person is experiencing his last days on earth. This indicates that Ishmael lived in Paran, near southern Palestine, in his later days.

The tribes which stretched toward northern Arabia were Qedar and Teima. Dumah dwelt in the desert between Mesopotamia and Arabia.

How ironic it is to claim that Hagar and her child crossed a huge desert, which no caravan had ever crossed, to find an unknown place no one had ever lived in.

As tribes, the Midianites came after the death of Abraham and Keturah and, perhaps many generations after the death of their father, Midian. The Midianites first began to occupy only a portion of the Sinai Desert before stretching their land toward the Gulf of Aqaba.

We know Abraham sent Hagar and Ishmael away to the south of Palestine, which Scripture calls the desert of Paran. We saw previously that Paran borders Hebron, where Moses sent twelve men to spy on the land of Canaan. Midian was not yet born at that time, because Abraham didn't marry Keturah until Sarah, his first wife, had died. We know also that Dedan, another son of Keturah, dwelt in northern Arabia much later than did Midian. By this we can only conclude that northern Arabia was a virgin desert uninhabited by any tribe at the time of Hagar. How could Hagar go through north Arabia and its vast desert to reach Mecca, as Muslims claim? There were no cities in the desert during the time of Hagar. The city of Dedan appeared only after the 10th century B.C. The oases of Qedar and Teima were the dwelling places of two Ishmaelite tribes that inhabited north Arabia many centuries after Ishmael died. Qedar and Teima were about 150-180 miles distant from the border with Jordan. The cities of

Qedar, Teima and Dumah did not appear before the 10th century B.C. No trade caravans traveled between Yemen and Palestine before the 10th century B.C. Without the cities of northern Arabia, which appeared only in the 10th and 9th centuries B.C., it was impossible for caravans to travel the desert from Yemen to Palestine and Syria, and vice-versa. What made their movements possible were the cities which the descendants of Keturah, and some of the descendants of Hagar, built in the 10th and 9th centuries B.C.

One reason we draw this conclusion is that camels traveling in the desert require water about every sixty miles. Without water it is impossible for caravans to cross the desert toward a remote region in central western Arabia. In the 10th and 9th centuries B.C., cities were built in northern Arabia, initiating caravan travel between Syria and Yemen. These cities dug wells which provided water to their inhabitants and to the passing caravans.

In addition to a lack of water, before the construction of these cities, caravans also faced savage Bedouins who roamed such places from time to time. It was not practical to travel this route before the 10th century B.C. Travel along the Red Sea, through the area where Mecca was built, did not begin until the 3rd century B.C. How, then, could a woman with a small baby and a skin of water take the initiative to cross such a vast desert - a desert which no caravan in history before her had ever crossed, especially since caravan travel was unknown? No one during her lifetime inhabited the region, and no station existed for her to replenish water and food. Later, around the 6th century B.C., cities like Khaybar and Yathrib were built on the land route between Teima, Dedan and Qedar in north Arabia, and Yemen in the south. It's inconceivable that Mecca existed before Dedan, Qedar and Teima.

If Mecca had existed at the time of Moses, it would have been the only city in western Arabia. Yet Moses did not mention it in his inspired records.

Finally, the Bible mentions all the tribes which finally dwelt in northern Arabia. It talks about Saba and Ma'in, tribes of Yemen.

The Bible even mentions small tribes during the time of Moses, before any of them were known as nations, kingdoms or cities – tribes like Dedan, Qedar and Teima-even Saba, before it was known as a nation in Yemen. How then could the Bible fail to mention such an important city as Mecca which, according to the Islamic claim, would have been flourishing at the time of Abraham? Between the 21st and 15th centuries B.C., Mecca would have been the only city in all of western Arabia. Moses would have paid special attention to it, more than any of the other small tribes he mentions. But Moses never mentions Mecca. Is not this a clear sign that Mecca did not exist in Moses' time?

It's important for us to question the claims of Islam, because its followers are being deceived. For a religion to be credible, it must first be true. I invite you to examine the claims of the Bible, as well. You'll soon find that its claims are consistent with the records of history.

With all the records of the marine activity of Solomon, and the kings who came after him, there is no mention of Mecca.

In the Bible, we can trace the initiation of trade between Yemen and the Mediterranean countries, complete with the kingdoms and cities involved. No city located along land trading routes is missing from Biblical records. Some of the trading cities were mentioned many times; yet, Mecca, which was built eventually on the land route, is not mentioned at all in the Bible.

Two kingdoms existed in Yemen, beginning in the 12th century B.C. Those two kingdoms were the Saba and Ma'in kingdoms. Scholars are not in agreement about which kingdom came into existence first. Some think that the Minaean kingdom is the older of the two, dating back to the 13th century B.C. Others think that the Sabaeans were older and began around the 12th century B.C.

The Bible reports on the trade activity of the Minaeans of Yemen with the Fertile Crescent.

Verses in the Bible confirm the presence of Ma'in in the north, perhaps as colonies associated with civilizations in Trans-Jordan which made war against Israel. One of these verses is II Chronicles 20. In the first verse, we read about an alliance in Trans-Jordan against Jehoshaphat. The Greek Septuagint translation of the Hebrew Old Testament reads:

> It happened after this that the people of Moab, with the people of Ammon, and with them some of the Meunites, came to make war on Jehoshaphat.

According to Montgomery, the term "Meunites" in Hebrew is "Meinim," and identical to how the word "Minaeans" was pronounnced in South Arabia.[162]

Jehoshaphat reigned in Judah beginning in 873 B.C. It seems that the Minaeans, who tried to establish alliances in southern Jordan, participated in an attack initiated by Moab and Ammon against Judah. Moab and Ammon were the two nations which controlled the land routes where the Minaeans wanted to establish a presence. At the time of Uzziah, King of Judah, we encounter the Minaeans again in alliances with other Arabians, and with the Philistines. In II Chronicles 26:7, the Bible says:

> God helped him against the Arabians who lived in Gur Baal, and against the Meunites.

According to Montgomery, the word Meunites in Hebrew is "Meinim," again referring to the southern Arabian tribe in Yemen.[163] Uzziah began his reign in 790 B.C. We see the kingdom of Ma'in penetrating into Trans-Jordan and southern Palestine, making colonies along the land routes perhaps as early as the 8th century B.C.

In the book of Ezra 2:50, we find that some families of the Meunim were forced into slavery around 458 B.C. It seems the slave trade with southern Arabia was vigorous at the time of Ezra.

Again, we find the Meunites mentioned in the book of Nehemiah, chapter 7, verse 52. Around 445 B.C., they were again being used as servants. This may indicate the abundance of trade between Palestine and southern Arabia, and that among the variety of things traded by the Minaean merchants were slaves.

Although not discernable in the English version of the Bible, in Job 2:11, the Septuagint renders the last name of Zophar, a Naamathite and friend of Job, as "Minaean."[164] This may indicate that Zophar may have been an important merchant who was trading on the land route between southern Arabia and Mesopotamia, or he could have been a responsible leader in the Minaean colony in south Jordan. Because Job 1:17 mentions the Chaldean raids on Job's servants, we date the book between the 9th and 6th centuries B.C. Job's land was the land of Uz, which might have been on the southwestern border of Mesopotamia, where land routes from Arabia were used by people on their way to the heart of Babylonia. Therefore, Job might have been dwelling where merchants traveled. According to the book of Job, Job was one of the richest men of the east, and it's possible he hosted some of the merchants. The term "lands of the east" in the Bible referred to the land east of Palestine, extending from southern Jordan, through the desert, and reaching as far as Mesopotamia.

The Chaldeans appeared in the 11th century B.C. on the border of Mesopotamia. They ascended to power only in the 7th century B.C. After the death of Assurbanipal, the Chaldeans gained their independence from the Assyrians. The Chaldean, Nabopolassar, ruler of Babylonia, established his independence around 625 B.C. We assume the Chaldeans deployed military units on their borders, especially on the western and southern borders, to defend against attacks from the Bedouins. All this leads us to believe that the 7th century B.C. might be the date for the writing of the book of Job.

So we see that the Biblical narration confirms what we know about Minaean trade and traffic in its early stages. It couldn't have existed before the 10th century B.C. This means that the 10th century B.C. was also the earliest possible date for the construction of cities in northern Arabia, such as Qedar, Teima and Dedan, which made the land route for trade and traffic possible.

Saba of Yemen in the Bible

Trading relationships between Saba, called Sheba, in Yemen and the Mediterranean countries, such as Israel, are significant to our understanding of the founding of Mecca. In I Kings, chapter 10, we read about the visit of the Queen of Sheba to King Solomon. I already mentioned in Part I of this book how the Queen of Sheba could easily hear about the wisdom of Solomon. But we must also understand how Solomon wanted to trade gold with Ophir on the Persian Gulf, so he built a fleet of ships in Ezion Geber near Elath on the Red Sea. I Kings 9:26-28 says:

> King Solomon also built a fleet of ships at Ezion Geber, which is near Elath on the shore of the Red Sea, in the land of Edom. Then Hiram sent his servants with the fleet, seamen who knew the sea, to work with the servants of Solomon. And they went to Ophir and acquired four hundred and twenty talents of gold from there.

Perhaps Sabaean merchants were already traveling the land route through northern Arabia by the 10th century B.C. If so, the cities on the oases of northern Arabia, such as Teima, Dedan and Qedar, may have been only small villages which facilitated trade along the land route from Yemen to Israel. This is probably the reason the Queen of Sheba was convinced to travel by land to Jerusalem, rather than by sea. In the previous century (11th B.C.), it was impossible to make the trip by land. In part I of this book, I mentioned the assumption that Solomon's name was famous in Saba, many years before the visit of the Queen of Sheba, because of his ships, built many years before her visit. The fleet traveled across the Red Sea to Ophir on the Persian Gulf and made many stops along the way, many of which were to Saba ports, the most important ports on the Red Sea. The Saba ports were places where ships traded merchandise and re-supplied themselves with water and food.

Many years before Solomon's fleet was constructed, King Hiram, the Phoenician King of Tyre, began sailing his fleet on the Red Sea to the Persian Gulf. Hiram traveled to Ophir, passing through the Sabaean's ports. Hiram traded in the Mediterranean, and even provided Solomon, his son-in-law, with gold, special wood and precious stones. Mediterranean nations were connected to the Gulf region, where there were important kingdoms such as Dilmun, which is now Bahrain; and Magan, which is now Oman. There were also rich ports like Jerra, which traded with India and made far-away Asian products available to the Phoenicians. All the marine traffic from India to the Persian Gulf passed through the ports of Saba.

Although the area where Mecca was eventually built was only 30 miles from the shore, the marine traffic through the Red Sea never attested to the existence of a city called Mecca.

As we've already discussed Solomon's ships, we need to emphasize that marine-trading traffic through the Red Sea existed for some time before Solomon. The fleet of the Phoenician city of Tyre had already been sailing the trade routes before Solomon built his own fleet of ships. If Mecca, being only 30 miles from shore, had existed, then it would have been known to the Israelites. Since there were no cities on the Red Sea before ships would reach the far Saba ports, Mecca would have been a very long journey, because it would have been the only city close to the shore. The Israelites, as well the Phoenicians, would have stopped there on their long journeys to Saba and on to the Persian Gulf. But neither the Hebrews nor the Phoenicians recorded a city called Mecca. With all the marine activity of Solomon, and the kings who came after him, there is no mention of Mecca.

TRADE AND THE FERTILE CRESCENT

The Bible gives us a clear picture of the cities and nations located on the land route from Yemen to north Arabia in the 9th and 8th centuries B.C., but nowhere does it mention Mecca.

We will proceed in the next pages to study the trade through Arabia to the Fertile Crescent as it is seen through many Biblical references. Mecca is conspicuous by its absence.

In our study of the Biblical passages which mention Arabia, we look at the time of Solomon as documented in the book of II Chronicles. It shows the relationships between Solomon and the kings of Arabia. 2 Chronicles 9:13, 14 says:

> The weight of gold that came to Solomon yearly was six hundred and sixty-six talents of gold, besides what the traveling merchants and traders brought. And all the kings of Arabia and the governors of the country brought gold and silver to Solomon.

We have discussed previously the marine trading routes which Israel established in the time of Solomon. These routes provided a connection between Israel and the kingdoms of Arabia, including Saba. Because of the trade routes, the kingdoms and cities of Arabia became well-known to Israel. Merchants brought gold to Palestine during the time of Solomon. The verses from II Chronicles refer to all the kingdoms in north and western Arabia. All of these kingdoms are mentioned throughout the prophetical books of the Bible, such as Isaiah and Ezekiel. Yet, there is no mention of Mecca at all in these prophetic books.

Trade Traffic Between Yemen and the Countries of the Fertile Crescent During the 9th Century B.C. as Seen in the Book of Joel.

The trade traffic between Yemen, Palestine, Syria and Lebanon (Phoenicians) is attested to in the Bible as early as the time of the prophet Joel, who prophesied around 830 B.C. We read in the book of Joel 3:8 an oracle against Tyre and Sidon. The prophecy announces that calamities will come upon the two Phoenician cities, resulting in some of their sons being sold to the Sabaeans. Sabaean inscriptions confirm this Biblical statement. They say the Sabaeans were involved in the slave trade, buying slaves from far countries. Female slaves were bought from countries like Egypt, Gaza, Yathrib and Dedan for consecrated service in a Sabaean temple.[165]

Land Routes From Saba and Teima as Seen in the Book of Job

In addition to II Chronicles and Joel, the book of Job gives us information on Arabian countries. Job knew about the land routes from Saba and Teima. Job 6:19 says:

> With high hopes, the caravans from Teima and from Sheba stop for water, but finding none, their hopes are dashed.

Job lived in the land of Uz which was on the western border of Mesopotamia, at the end of the trading route. Since Job probably lived between the 9th and 7th centuries B.C., the Bible helps us date the early beginnings of Sheba's trading and its caravans which traveled the land route.

Trade Routes From Yemen as Seen in the Book of Isaiah

In the Bible, a book written by the prophet Isaiah provides more information about the trade routes coming from Yemen. Isaiah lists the important cities and tribes involved in commerce on the spice route. Isaiah began to prophesy in 739 B.C. when King Uzziah of Judah died. Isaiah also prophesied during the reigns of several other kings, such as: Jothan, who became king of Judah in 739 B.C.; Ahaz, who became king of Judah in 735 B.C.; Hoshea, who became king of Israel in 732 B.C.; Shalmaneser IV, who became king of Assyria in 727 B.C.; Sargon II, who became king of Assyria in 722 B.C.; King Hezekiah, who ascended to the throne of Judah in 715 B.C.; and Sennacherib, who ascended to the throne of Assyria in 704 B.C. So we can see that Isaiah prophesied up to the beginning of the 7th century B.C.

In the 60th chapter of Isaiah, probably written during King Hezekiah's reign, Isaiah confirms that the spice route had flourished by the end of the 8th century B.C., and that some tribes were known in Palestine for their trade with the region. Isaiah 60:6-7 says:

> The multitude of camels shall cover your land, the dromedaries of Midian and Ephah. All those from Sheba shall come, they shall bring gold and incense. All the flocks of Qedar shall be gathered together to you, the rams of Nabaioth shall minister to you.

From these verses, we see that by the end of the 8th century B.C. there was trading between Yemen and the Fertile Crescent, especially in Palestine and Syria. Significantly, the most important merchants who traveled to Saba and traded with Israel and the surrounding nations were the Midianites and Ephahites. You may remember that the Midianites descended from the firstborn of Midian, the descendant of Keturah. Ephah was subdued, along with other tribes in the region, such as Thamud, under the Assyrian King, Sargon II, who reigned from 722-705 B.C. The Bible says that their caravans came from Saba, and specified that gold and incense were the main goods which they brought from Saba. The Sabaeans had brought incense from Hadraumout, south of Saba; gold from Ophir on the Persian Gulf; and minerals from Yamama and other places in western Arabia.

Nebaioth Trading Partner With Israel in the Fertile Crescent

The Nabaioth tribe inhabited the deserts of the Fertile Crescent. Contrary to Islamic tradition, the family of Mohammed, who lived in Yemen as Sabaeans, could not be connected with this tribe.

Nebaioth furnished rams to Judah. Isaiah says "the rams of Nabaioth shall minister to you." The Jewish people may have depended upon trade with Nabaioth for a constant supply of animals for their sacrificial rites, especially in the temple at Jerusalem.

Nabaioth was an Ishmaelite tribe. Genesis 28:9 mentioned their father, Nabaioth, as living in Edom. The tribe spread into Sinai at the time of Moses. During the reign of Assurbanipal, the people of Nabaioth settled in the northeastern part of Palmyrena.[166] The Assyrian inscription, ABL 260, dated around the middle of the 7th century B.C., shows them on the border of Babylonia, in the Syro-Mesopotamian desert near the tribe of Massa,[167] implying that the tribe emigrated from south Jordan toward the north and east, seeking better pastures for their flocks. They lived like Bedouins, roaming from place to place in the Fertile Crescent.

If these records are true, and we have no reason to believe otherwise, how then can Islamic tradition make Mohammed a descendant of the tribe of Nabaioth which lived in the deserts of Syria, Iraq and South Jordan, when we know his family was Sabaean and resided in Yemen?

Other lands and cities on the spice routes and their trade mentioned by Isaiah.

We notice that Qedar sent flocks to Judah, as Isaiah 60:7 says: "All the flocks of Qedar shall be gathered together to you." Because the Qedarites exercised influence in southern Jordan, it seems the sheep they transported to Palestine were one of their main commodities. In Isaiah 42:11, we find Qedar mentioned with Sela, the old city of Petra in south Jordan. The text speaks about the "villages that Qedar inhabited." It says, "let the inhabitants of Sela sing," suggesting that the Qedarites penetrated into some of the villages in South Jordan toward the end of the 8th century B.C. This is something the Assyrian inscriptions had attested to.

Isaiah also prophesied concerning the defeat of Arabian tribes by the Assyrian army. We find it in chapter 21, verse 13, "The burden against Arabia." Assyria's intended target was the land and cities in north and central western Arabia, including Dumah, the Dedanites, the land of Teima and Qedar. All these tribes were actively trading on the land route from Yemen. Verse 14 mentions the caravans of the Dedanites, which were from the city of Dedan in north Arabia. Verse 16 predicts that, "the glory of Qedar will fail," reflecting how rich Qedar became because of its trade.

The book of Isaiah shows how the land routes from Saba were flourishing around the end of the 8th century B.C. The book also shows that all the cities which were along branches of this trade route were already present at the end of the 8th century B.C. This refers to the route which passes from Teima to Dumah, Mesopotamia, Trans-Jordan and Syria. This also refers to the route that passes from Dedan and Qedar going to Palestine, Syria and Egypt. The book of Isaiah also mentions the tribes of Midian and Ephah, which traded with Saba. This trade certainly followed the route which passes by Dedan, and was closer to them.

Even though the Bible gives us a clear picture of the cities and nations located on the land route from Yemen in the 8th century B.C., nowhere does it mention Mecca. If Mecca had existed, as Muslim tradition claims, then there is no reason for it not to be mentioned along with the rest of the cities in the book of Isaiah.

Jeremiah Prophesied About Arabia and Trade on the Spice Routes Over Long Periods of Time

We know that the prophet Jeremiah was a youth when the Lord commissioned him to prophesy, and we know he lived many years after the destruction of Jerusalem. He began to prophesy around 627 B.C., near the end of the reign of the Assyrian king, Assurbanipal. He prophesied during the reigns of several other rulers, too. There was Nabopolassar, who became King of Babylonia around 626 B.C. Next was Jehoahaz, King of Judah in 609 B.C. Then came Nebuchadnezzar, King of Babylon in 605 B.C. He was followed by Jehoachin, King of Judah in 597 B.C., and Zedekiah, King of Judah in 597 B.C. Jeremiah also prophesied during the destruction of the Temple by the Babylonians in 586 B.C. We read in Jeremiah, chapter 2, verse 10, about the gods the tribe of Qedar worshipped through the ages. In Jeremiah, chapter 49, verse 28, we read about a prophecy against other tribes, including Qedar. It states that Nebuchad-nezzar, King of Babylon, would attack them.

Jeremiah prophesied about campaigns conducted by the Chaldeans in northern Arabia. We find in Jeremiah 25:23 that Dedan and Teima were among the nations which the Chaldeans were to conquer. The oracle against Dedan is repeated in Jeremiah 48:8. The frankincense trade from Sheba to Israel is expressed in Jeremiah 6:20:

> For what purpose to Me comes frankincense from Sheba, and sweet cane from a far country ?

This shows that the trade of frankincense from Saba to the Mediterranean region continued in Jeremiah's time.

Ezekiel and the Nations Which Traded With Mediterranean Countries

In the 6th century B.C., Ezekiel mentions the merchandise which was traded with Mediterranean countries through the Arabian routes, and the cities which were involved in those trades, but Mecca is not among them.

Ezekiel began to prophesy around 593 B.C. We know his prophecies reflect events of the first third of the 6th century B.C. In Ezekiel 25:13, the prophet mentions the Chaldean occupation of Dedan, and other nations, such as Edom and Philistia. Ezekiel also sheds light on trade routes from Arabia in the beginning of the 6th century B.C. He elaborates on the kind of goods, traded by Mediterranean cities along these routes, especially the Phoenician cities of Tyre and Sidon. In Ezekiel, chapter 27, the prophet speaks a prophecy, or an oracle against Tyre. He describes Tyre's wealth, and the commerce it had with other nations of the world at that time. Ezekiel mentions several cities and nations on the land route from southern Arabia. In verse 15 he says:

The men of Dedan were your traders; many isles were the market of your hand. They brought you ivory tusks and ebony as payment.

This verse reflects the commerce of ivory and ebony wood which Dedanite merchants brought to Tyre on the Mediterranean. These goods originated in India. They were transported to southern Arabia, and the Dedanites brought them to the Mediterranean region. The Phoenicians from Tyre would then distribute their wares to various nations along the Mediterranean. Ezekiel 27:20 speaks about another product which Tyre imported from Dedan, when he says, "Dedan was your merchant in saddlecloths for riding." In verse 21, he mentions the imports Tyre received from Qedar: "Arabia and all the princes of Qedar were your regular merchants. They traded with you in lambs, rams and goats."

These are the same commodities which Qedar traded with Israel, as we saw in the book of Isaiah. This verse also confirms that Qedar was governed by many kings or princes which, historically, we know to be true, because Assyrian inscriptions showed many kings governed in Qedar at the same time.

Ezekiel 27:22 speaks about the trade with Sheba (Saba):

The merchants of Sheba and Raamah were your merchants. They traded for your wares the choicest spices, all kind of precious stones and gold.

We already have discussed that, according to Genesis 10:6,7, Raamah was the father of Sheba, from whom came the Saba tribe of Yemen. Raamah was the fourth son of Cush, and a grandson of Ham. Raamah was mentioned in the inscriptions of Saba. The Bible connects Raamah with Sheba, which is called Saba. In the Bible, a nation is often named after the father of the founder: for example, Israel is also called Jacob, or Isaac. According to the last verse we read in Ezekiel, the imports Tyre received from Yemen consisted "of choicest spices, precious stones and gold." We know this is true from other historical evidence, as well.

Ezekiel 27:23, 24 lists other nations and cities which traded their goods with Tyre:

> Haran, Canneh, Eden, the merchants of Sheba, Assyria and
> Chilmad were your merchants. Those were your merchants in
> choice items; purple clothes, embroidered garments, chests of
> multicolored apparel, and sturdy woven cords, which were in your
> marketplace.

We recognize among the aforementioned cities and nations some southern Arabian cities; namely, Canneh and Eden, in addition to the merchants of Sheba. Canneh is mentioned in the historical book "*Periplus of the Erythraean Sea,*" which is dated around 60 A.D. It's identified with Hisn Ghorab, a port of southern Arabia located 14 degrees and 10 minutes north, by 48 degrees and 20 minutes east. Canneh was an important place, importing Asian wares and clothes. From Canneh, the items were brought to Phoenician ports, such as Tyre. That's why Ezekiel mentioned that through Canneh came precious bolts of cloth, clothes of purple, woven cords and embroidered garments. These goods were known to have originated in China and India.[168]

The text tells us that, in addition to the Sabaeans, the city of Eden, in south Yemen, also traded these items. These records document the beginning of the 6th century B.C., when marine trade was flourishing between Asian countries and the Mediterranean region, through southern Yemen. This description of the richness of the city of Tyre, the purple in Tyre's homes, and the other items which the book of Ezekiel mentions, are confirmed by classical historians, such as Strabo in his seventeenth book.[169] The ebony wood trade from India and far islands is also confirmed historically.[170]

During the period between the 8th and 6th centuries B.C., the Bible mentioned many of the cities and nations on the Arabian trade routes, but it does not mention Mecca.

The major prophets of the Bible: Isaiah, Jeremiah and Ezekiel, reflected the trade with western Arabian kingdoms and cities, from the 8th century B.C. until the beginning of the 6th century B.C. – a period in which the trade between southern Arabia, the cities on the land trading routes, the Mediterranean countries and the Fertile Crescent countries flourished. There's not a single city along these western and northern Arabian trading routes that was not mentioned by the inspired prophets of the Bible. Not only does the Bible mention the cities, but it also mentions the kinds of items and wares which were traded. In spite of the fact that the prophets mentioned all the cities on these trading routes, such as Dumah, Qedar, Teima and Dedan, it never mentions Mecca. The Bible even mentions many tribes involved in trading, such as Midian, Ephah, Saba and Ma'in, but Mecca is absent in all this!

As we have discussed many times before, Mecca was built around the 4th century A.D. on the caravan route between Yemen, Teima and Dedan. If Mecca had existed during the times of these major prophets, then there would be no reason for not mentioning it. This is especially true when we consider that inspired authors, like the prophet Ezekiel, talked about all the cities on the route, even those which were in remote places such as Canneh and Eden. If only because of its strategic place on the trading route, Mecca should have been mentioned – not one time, but many times, if it had existed then. Many times, the Bible mentions the primary cities and nations which traded along these routes and ran through western and northern Arabia. For example, Midian is mentioned 20 times, Qedar eight times, Dedan six times, and Teima three times. Mecca was built in the most strategic location on the land route. It's a place where the route split in two. One route went to Teima, and the other to Dedan. Yet, Mecca is not mentioned even once, although its location is closer to Palestine than to Sheba and Ma'in in Yemen.

These cities, which were mentioned many times, all appeared after the 10th century B.C. Kingdoms like Sheba and Main started their trade activity with the Mediterranean countries after the 10th century B.C. Ma'in started its trade many centuries later. Yet, Sheba and Ma'in are mentioned many times in their relationship with the region. But Mecca, the city which Islamic tradition claims existed since the time of Abraham in the 21st century B.C., is not mentioned, even once, in any book of the Bible.

The Bible is a reliable source of ancient history. Not mentioning Mecca during the period it covers, from the time of Abraham to the 5th century B.C., is significant proof that Mecca was not in existence during that period.

We also see that Mecca does not exist in the Biblical narration of the old nations of Arabia, and how they originated from the children of Noah. Nor does it exist in other genealogies, such as the sons of Keturah, who was the wife Abraham took after Sarah died. Mecca is not mentioned in any Biblical genealogy of how Arabia was populated in ancient history. However, all the actual ancient tribes and cites of western and northern Arabia are mentioned.

The Biblical narration is the only source of ancient history for many regions of the Middle East. Therefore, it is of fundamental importance in understanding the region. The Bible mentions nations and cities, even when no other resource confirms its narration. Tribes mentioned in the Bible, such as the Hittites, and cities, such as Ur, were questioned by historians in the past. Some wondered if they even existed in history. But then we discovered their ruins, and the same historians discovered that the rich and extended coverage of the Bible is perfectly true and correct. This means that, when the Bible mentions the cities of northwestern Arabia and the two nations of Saba and Main of Yemen, without even mentioning Mecca, it's a definitive affirmation that Mecca failed to exist through the long history which the Bible covers in this region, from the time of Abraham until Malachi, the last inspired author of the Old Testament who began prophesying around 436 B.C. This is a rather simple fact, yet it is significant to the understanding of Islam. If a religion is to be followed, it must be credible, and it must be built on accurate information.

10 _____

THE TRUE STORY OF THE CONSTRUCTION OF THE TEMPLE OF MECCA

The True Dates for the Construction of the Temple of Mecca, the Digging of the Well of Zamzam, and the Transfer of the Black Stone to Mecca.

Islamic claims that Abraham and Ishmael founded the temple in the city of Mecca are recognized as false, when we study the Black Stone, which was the heart of the temple.

Abraham never went to where Mecca was eventually built, nor did his son, Ishmael, or Ishmael's son, Nabaioth. Despite these facts, Ibn Ishak, Mohammed's biographer, claimed that Abraham was responsible for building the temple at Mecca, and that it was then run by Ishmael, and eventually Nabaioth. The story, created by Ibn Ishak and his companions, goes on to say that after Nabaioth, the tribe of Jurhum, which they claim inhabited Mecca at the time of Abraham, took the responsibility to serve the Temple at Mecca. According to the story, they served until the tribe of Khuzaa'h came from Yemen. This was after the dam at Ma'rib began to show signs of damage and drove them away. The story continues that, when the tribe of Khuzaa'h came to Mecca, they defeated Jurhum. Jurhum then left Mecca to hide the Black Stone of the temple and two golden gazelles. They hid them in the water spring called Zamzam, then covered the spring, the stone and the gazelles with dust so they would escape detection.[171] The date these things supposedly happened is critical. According to the stories, Jurhum lived in Mecca until the Ma'rib dam was damaged, and the tribe of Khuzaa'h left Yemen. We know these things occurred around the year 150 A.D.

Islamic tradition is illogical when it talks about Jurhum and the hiding of a spring of water and the Black Stone.

If Jurhum's story were true, why did the classical authors, who visited and wrote about western Arabia, mention all the tribes who were living there, even the tiny ones, but never once mention Mecca or the tribe of Jurhum?

Second, after being defeated, how could Jurhum bury two precious golden gazelles and a huge stone belonging to Mecca's temple without any of the inhabitants noticing? Any tribe leaving Mecca would surely take its golden treasure and not bury it in a public place, well-known to all. And this spring of water was the only spring in Mecca.

Third, the black Stone is a huge stone. It is not easy to move it from its location in the temple. According to Islamic claims, the war erupted over who should be responsible for the temple. How could a defeated Jurhum tribe succeed in moving the stone without the winning Khuzaa'h tribe intervening, or at least noticing where the stone had been hidden?

The fourth argument concerns the spring of water itself. If it existed in western Arabia, its location would be important to remember. After all, water was especially important for the Arabians living in the desert. Islamic tradition claims that this spring existed since the time of Abraham. If it were miraculously brought into existence when the angel Gabriel gave water to Hagar and her child, Ishmael, then its existence would have been known, not just in Mecca, but in many other cities around Mecca. Bedouins would have come to the spring to water their sheep. Area inhabitants would have come to refresh themselves. No one could hide the spring, even if it were possible to cover it with dust.

The story of Jurhum hiding items in the spring during the 2nd century A.D. continues by claiming that Abdel Mutaleb, the grandfather of Mohammed, rediscovered the spring near the end of the 5th century A.D. We can only conclude that the spring never existed before the time of Abdel Mutaleb, and that by digging finally the Meccans found underground water, which eventually became a spring. This phenomenon of digging to find water which comes in the form of a spring is common in the Middle East. To claim that a spring existed in a city for 2,500 years before Jurhum succeeded in covering it for another three centuries is an impossible assertion, since the springs of Arabia were significantly more important to the Bedouins than the Red Sea. You may hide the sea from the eyes of thirsty tribes, but you cannot hide a spring and its location for that amount of time.

It is also impossible to believe that the Black Stone was hidden for three or four centuries. The stone was considered the main shrine, or sacred element, in each temple, called Kaabah in Arabic. This big stone, which represented the moon, was considered to be divine. The worship of the Arabian Star Family with Allah, who was the moon as its head, revolved around the Black stone. Ellat, Allah's wife, was the sun, and al-'Uzza and Manat, his daughters, represented two planets. The Muslims believe the Black Stone divinely came from Allah, who was the moon before the planet Venus replaced it in Allah's title. How could a huge black stone, greatly worshipped and revered by the people, be hidden while they were fighting to preserve the prestige they found in serving it? It is implausible to suggest that they could hide their greatly-worshipped stone, without any of the people who chased the defeated Jurhum noticing where it was hidden, especially when the place where it was claimed to be hidden was the spring of water from which they drank every day of the battle. Hiding the worshipped huge stone in such a way is more implausible than hiding the spring of water itself.

The story of the Black Stone has some important implications. The Black Stone was not in existence near Mecca until, perhaps, the end of the 5th century A.D. That's why Islamic tradition tried to justify the absence of the stone by inventing implausible stories. Therefore, we can estimate that the Black stone, which was the main element of worship in all Kaabahs of Arabia, was brought by chariot from another area – most probably Yemen – toward the end of the 5th century A.D.

Asa'd Abu Karb was the True Builder of Kaabah in the Beginning of the 5th century A.D.

It is said that, prior to the construction of the Kaabah, a tent existed on the spot where it was built.[172] The tribe of Khuzaa'h came from Yemen around the 2nd century A.D. In the 4th century A.D., they moved toward the area where Mecca was eventually built. Since they didn't find a temple there in which to worship, they pitched their tent in a field.

Information from the writers of the 8th century A.D., who depended on information from the time of Mohammed, indicates that the Kaabah was built at the beginning of the 5th century A.D. by a Himyarite pagan Yemeni leader named Asa'd Abu Karb. He is also called Abu Karb Asa'd, and he reigned in Yemen from 410-435 A.D.[173]

The fact that the Islamic historians admit that Asa'd Abu Karb was the first ruler in history to dress the Kaabah is a significant indicator that he was the true builder of the Kaabah.[174] Dressing a temple in Arabia was the second stage of its construction. It included decoratively finishing the inside walls, putting carpets on the walls and the floor, and adding textured and crocheted items on various parts of the interior building. (Arabians will not pray in a temple which is not dressed.) Asa'd Abu Karb used Amer from Azed to build the inside walls of the Kaabah.[175] (Azed is a tribe which came from Yemen at the same time that Khuzaah's tribe came.) So Asa'd Abu Karb, the first to build and dress the Kaabah, must have first built it when there was just a tent where the Yemeni tribe of Khuzaa'h worshipped.

Asa'd Abu Karb, also called Tubb'a, occupied the city of Yathrib before coming to Mecca.[176] It seems he found many temples in Yathrib, but when he came to Mecca, he didn't find any temple there. Because the inhabitants were recent emigrants from Yemen, Asa'd Abu Karb built them a modest temple in the Yemeni style. He did this to connect the people with himself. He also wrote a poem in which he described the sun setting in a spring of black mud, something Mohammed included in the Qur'an.

Additions by Quraish to the Building Which Asa'd Abu Karb Built

Quraish, the tribe which Mohammed came from, later occupied the city. They acquired a black stone from Yemen so that their temple would be like all the other Kaabahs which, according to the worship of the Star Family of Arabia, were built around a black stone. Family Star worship started in Yemen, the place from which the Quraish emigrated. The first Kaabah built by Asa'd Abu Karb had a wood roof. That roof burned, so next they used wood carried by a Byzantine ship, which stopped on the coast of the Red Sea at a place called "al-Shaebieth." The owner of the ship was a Coptic Egyptian named Bachum. He sold the wood to them and made the roofing for the Kaabah.[177] Later, when Mohammed was still young, further elements were added to the simple building.[178]

These facts about the construction of the temple at Mecca should cause Muslims to question all that Ibn Ishak and his companions said about the city, in their attempt to back Mohammed's claim in the Qur'an that the temple was built by Abraham and Ishmael.

YEMENI RESPONSIBILITY IN BUILDING THE TEMPLE OF MECCA

The Yemeni tribe of Khuzaa'h built the city of Mecca in the 4th century A.D. Yemeni pagan religious worship has left its fingerprints all over the temple, showing that Abraham and Ishmael could not have built it.

We will discuss why the marks of Yemeni worship characterized the temple of Mecca. The sayings and customs of Mohammed are called Hadith. "Sahih Muslim" and "Sahih Buchari" are considered the main authoritative books which contain the words or Hadith of Mohammed. In those books, we read about Mohammed's custom to embrace and kiss two stones, "the Yemenite Rukun" and "the Black Stone." Ibn Abbas, the cousin of Mohammed and the reporter of his authoritative

Hadith, says that Mohammed customarily embraced the two Yemeni Rukuns. By "Yemeni Rukuns," he meant the Black Stone and the other stone, also called Rukun.[179] From this we know that Kaabeh had two main elements, also called Rukuns, which were considered sacred. Those were the stones around which the Kaabeh was built. These were the true elements revered by the inhabitants of Mecca and by Mohammed. Both stones were called "Yemeni," which indicates that they were brought to the temple from Yemen, confirming that the Kaabeh was built by the Yemeni leader, Asa'd Abu Karb, whom I previously mentioned. This also confirms that the Kaabeh was built according to Yemeni pagan worship, specifically the worship of the Star Family of Arabia. Allah was the head, and Ellat, the sun, was his wife. His daughters, al-'Uzza and Manat, were given names of planets.

It seems that the Black Stone was brought from Yemen at the time of Abdel Mutaleb, the grandfather of Mohammed. Islamic tradition claimed it was hidden along with the spring of Zamzam for centuries prior to Mohammed. I demonstrated previously that such a claim could not be true. The fact is that Mohammed and Islamic tradition endeavor to connect the pagan Yemeni worship of the ancestors of Mohammed, which transferred from Yemen to the Temple of Mecca, with Ishmael and Abraham, even though there are historical evidences that point to the contrary. We will look at some of them.

First, the confirmed date of the construction of the city of Mecca is sometime after the 4th century A.D. Abu Karb Asa'd was the first to consecrate the Kaabah, which reveals that he was the builder of the Kaabah. He did this during his reign in Yemen, which was between 410-435 A.D. The two Rukuns, or stones, which were the main elements of worship in the temple, were of Yemeni origin. The date on which the Black Stone first appeared in Mecca was at the time of Mohammed's grandfather, sometime between 495-520 A.D. Though Islamic tradition was aware of these facts, people invented unreliable stories to fill the historical gaps. I've already proved such stories are not logical, and are easily refutable.

An important factor in tracing Yemeni responsibility for constructing the Temple at Mecca, and in establishing the true date of construction for such temple, is found in the Himyarite kingdom of Yemen. Abu Karb Asa'd, the reigning monarch of Himyarite kingdom, tried to extend his empire over central western Arabia in order to control the spice route from Yemen to North Arabia, and then to the Fertile Crescent. Abu Karb Asa'd, also called Tubb'a, occupied the cities of central western Arabia at the beginning of the 5th century A.D. Among those cities were Mecca and Yathrib, also called al-Medina. The occupier's strategy was to bind these cities to his kingdom by reinforcing the Yemeni religious system which the inhabitants of Mecca and Yathrib were already embracing. The inhabitants of Mecca had emigrated from Yemen, so they were of Yemeni origin. Yathrib was formed by two Yemeni tribes, Oas and Khazraj. They, too, emigrated to Yathrib after the dam at Yemen was damaged around 150 A.D. These tribes were living with two Jewish tribes, Beni Kharithah and Beni Nathir, which were already established. Abu Karb Asa'd was of Yemeni origin. He built the Kaabeh at Mecca to reinforce his rule over the city, and to show favor to the citizens of Mecca who were without a temple of worship. They, like him, shared the same pagan beliefs.

Tubb'a's ideas of Jewish and Yemeni pagan myths and their influence on the Arabians of central western Arabia, and consequently on Mohammed.

Tubb'a also tried to build bridges with the Jewish community in Yathrib. He learned their religious thoughts and rites. He learned the Jewish myths, such as the legend of the hoopoe bird that announced the kingdom of Saba to Solomon. This myth came from the Jewish mythological book called the *Second Targum of Esther*. Mohammed incorporated the same myth into the Qur'an.

To accomplish his ends, Tubb'a brought two Jewish rabbis to Yemen.[180] They added to his knowledge by teaching him many Judaic religious rites and myths, enabling him to mix various items in his own Yemeni pagan background with Jewish mythology and

253

religious tradition. For example, he combined Arabian Star worship with Jewish myths. With mixed knowledge like this, he thought he could control the regions in central western Arabia, where people of Jewish and Arabian origin lived. He then claimed himself to be a prophet, expounding many thoughts which the Yemeni people considered indisputable about the sun, the earth and the cosmos. At Mecca, in an attempt to convince his listeners that he was a prophet, Tubba' taught that the sun sets in a spring of black mud.[181] This myth, too, was incorporated by Mohammed in the Qur'an.

After his death, Tubb'a's claim left an impression on many groups, even on groups that lived until the time of Mohammed. Mohammed considered him as a Muslim and almost as a prophet.[182] There have been myths about Tubb'a among the Arabians. Al-Taberi attributed victories to him in China and Tibet. This is unhistorical, but it shows how great an impact Tubb'a left on the Arabians at the time of Mohammed, to the point that many considered him to be a prophet.[183]

The Kaabah of Mecca was built for the Arabian Star worship, and it shares all the characteristics of the Kaabahs that were built for their worship.

The fact that the temple at Mecca was built as a Kaabah for Arabian Star worship is shown in many ways. First, it was built in the same architectural style as other Kaabahs in Arabia. They were all temples for the same Arabian Family Star religion, in which Allah is considered the head and Ellat is his wife. All the Kaabahs had a Black Stone as the most-revered element. It represented the Star deity in Arabia. Many of the black stones were meteorites which the Arabs saw descending to earth. They thought the meteorites were envoys from the moon, which was considered to be Allah himself. This is before that title was given to Venus, who replaced the moon as head of the Star Family.

Another thing which shows that the Kaabah of Mecca was built as a temple for Arabian Star worship is that the Kaabah of Mecca reflects members of the Star family in many of its elements. The main door of the Kaabah was called "the door of worshippers of the sun,"[184] the wife of Allah.

Mohammed confirmed that the origin of the Kaabah's faith was Yemeni.

The role of Yemeni religious paganism in building the temple at Mecca, and its religious nature, cannot be hidden. Even Mohammed recognized the origin of the religious system of Mecca as Yemeni. Mohammed uttered many Hadiths about the Yemeni origin of the Kaabah faith. Such teachings are reported in the authoritative Hadith, the book of al-Bukhari, in which Mohammed says: "the faith is Yemeni and the wisdom is Yemeni." In another Hadith, he says: "the doctrine and jurisprudence is Yemeni."[185] Therefore, not just the Rukuns, the sacred stones in the Kaabah, were from Yemen, but also religious laws, doctrine and faith are Yemeni. It is undeniable proof that the Temple of Mecca was constructed by a Yemeni leader according to a Yemeni pagan style and specification. He established Yemeni religiosity at Mecca, and it was known in other parts of Arabia. How, then, could Abraham have built the Kaabeh, if what we have learned about its construction is true? How did the Black Stone come from heaven, and how did Abraham sacrifice on it, and build the Kaabah around it, if the stone was not in Mecca before the 5th century A.D.? How could Mohammed's teaching come from Allah through the angel Gabriel and still be of Yemeni origin?

The important Egyptian scholar, Tah Hussein, has criticized Islamic tradition for linking the construction of Mecca's temple to Abraham and Ishmael.[186] Tah said: "The case for this episode is very obvious because it is of recent date and came into vogue just before the rise of Islam. Islam exploited it for religious reasons."[187]

If Muslims search diligently in history, like this great Egyptian scholar did, they will reach the same conclusion.

Establishing the Date the Tribe of Khuzaa'h Built Mecca

Many historical elements help us determine the true date Mecca was built. One major factor is the damage which occurred to the dam of Ma'rib in Yemen around the year 150 A.D. It caused the emigration of many families and tribes from Yemen to the north. One of these families was the family of Amru bin Amer, a Yemeni individual whose progeny fostered many tribes. Among them was Khuzaa'h, which settled in central western Arabia. Later, they built the city of Mecca.

Other tribes which came from Amru bin Amer were Oas and Khazraj. They settled in Yathrib, also called al-Medina, where the Jewish tribes of Beni Kharithah and Beni Nathir were already located.

From the writings of Tabari, the famous Arabic historian, we understand that this happened at approximately the same time the Lakhmids moved from Yemen to Mesopotamia. It is also the same time Amru bin Amer, the father of Khuzaa'h, moved from Yemen.[188] The Lakhmids came from Yemen in the 2nd century A.D. They lived in a region of Mesopotamia later known to be the city of Hira. Later, the Persians used them to protect Persian borders with the Byzantine Empire, which was dominating Syria. The first Lakhmid king was Amr I bin Adi, who ruled from 265-295 A.D.[189] The serious collapse of the dam of Ma'rib precipitated the emigration of tribes such as Ghassan, which settled in the Byzantine border; Shammar, which inhabited the Syrian Desert; and other tribes which emigrated to the north of Arabia and the Fertile Crescent.[190] Some of these tribes were related to each other because they were progeny of Amru bin Amer.[191] Other tribes who came out of Yemen at the time the dam collapsed were Oas and Khazraj. They went to live in al-Medina. Ozd al-Sarat went to al-Sarat, a location near Orfeh, which is near where Mecca was built. The tribe of Khuzaa'h inhabited a place called Mur, also called Mur al-Thahran,[192] another place near where Mecca was built.[193]

Mecca was Built by Khuzaa'h as a Desolate Station on the Spice Route

There was no city named Mecca in that area; otherwise, Khuzaa'h and Ozd would have inhabited it, as Oas and Khazraj inhabited the city of Yathrib. For more than a century and a half, Khuzaa'h remained in the area near where Mecca was later built. They then decided to build a station on the caravan route where traders could rest and conduct business. If Mecca had existed before Khuzaah's emigration from Yemen, Mecca would have been the city to which they would go to search out a living, even as their sister tribes, Oas and Khazraj, went to Yathrib to benefit from commerce and agricultural activities of the Jewish tribes there. But neither Khuzaa'h nor Ozd, as new emigrants in semi-deserted areas around the area where Mecca eventually built, found a city to host them when they left Yemen. They waited more than 170-200 years before building a city on the caravan route, which became a station for the caravans competing with Yathrib, which was about 200 miles away. The station they built was called Mecca.

It is important to note that none of the tribes who came from Yemen inhabited Mecca. If Mecca was in existence at the time the dam was seriously damaged, around the year 150 A.D., we would find many tribes locating in Mecca, because it is closer to Yemen than Yathrib is to Yemen. But, because the area where Mecca was eventually built was desolate and had no cities, it induced the tribes of Ozd and Khuzaa'h to live there. They did so, although they previously lived in a civilized city in Yemen which was Ma'rib, the capital of Saba. This is an important argument which points out that Mecca could not have existed before Khuzaa'h built the city in the 4th century A.D.

Let's review these historical facts. I've shown that the Yemeni tribe of Khuzaa'h built the city of Mecca in the 4th century A.D. We've seen the connection between the Temple of Mecca and Yemeni pagan religious worship. All this shows that the claim of Islam about Abraham and Ishmael building the Temple of Mecca contradicts the true historical facts. Building faith on the sand is unwise. I pray that our Muslim friends will return to true faith as found in history and announced in the Bible. In the Bible they can find a solid foundation, documented in the writings of the prophetic books, and considered by historians to be the accurate resource for ancient history.

REFERENCES AND NOTES TO PART II

[1] *Dinkard*-Book IX, Chapter XVIII, 2-7 , *Pahlavi Texts*, Part IV, Translated by E.W. West, *The Sacred Books of the East*, Volume 37, Published by Motilal Banarsidass, Delhi, 1969, pages 224-225

[2] K.A. Kitchen, *Documentation For Ancient Arabia*, Part I, Liverpool University Press, 1994, page 110

[3] Strabo, *Geography*, xv.1:4

[4] Stanley Burstein, *Agatharchides of Cnidus, on the Erythraean Sea*, The Hakluyt Society London, 1989, page 1

[5] Stanley Burstein, *Agatharchides of Cnidus, on the Erythraean Sea*, The Hakluyt Society London, 1989, page 30

[6] Stanley Burstein, *Agatharchides of Cnidus, on the Erythraean Sea*, The Hakluyt Society London, 1989 , page 3

[7] *The Geography of Strabo*, Book XVI .4:4
The Geography of Strabo, Volume VII, Harvard University Press, 1966, page 313

[8] See C. Muller, *Geographi Graeci Minores*, Paris, 1855-1861, I,LIV-L,VIII; quoted by Burstein, page 13

[9] Fraser, P.M., *Ptolemaic Alexandria*, Oxford, 1972, I, 549; cf. Peremans, W., *Diodore de Sicile et Agatharchide de Cnide'*, Historia xvi, 1967, pp. 443-4; cited by Burstein, page 30

[10] From Book 5 of *Agatharchides of Cnidus, on the Erythraean Sea*, excerption from Photius, *Bibliotheca*, cited by Burstein, page 147-fragment 87

[11] From book 5 of *Agatharchides of Cnidus, on the Erythraean Sea*, excerption from Diodorus, *Library of History*, cited by Burstein, page 79-fragment 40b

[12] Peremans, W., *Diodore de Sicile et Agatharchide de Cnide'*, pp. 447-55, cited by Burstein, page 32

[13] Burstein, *Agatharchides of Cnidus, on the Erythraean Sea*, The Hakluyt Society London, 1989, page 160

[14] There are fragments of the book of Pythagoras, kept by Aelian, NA 17.8-9 and Athenaeus, Deipnosophists 4 .183-4; citation of Burstein

[15] Strabo wrote: "Eratosthenes takes all these as matters actually established by the testimony of the men who had been in the regions, for he has read many historical treatises - with which he was supplied if he had a library as large as Hipparchus says it was – he means the Library of Alexandria" Strabo, *Geography*, book 2. 1:5

[16] Burstein, *Agatharchides of Cnidus, on the Erythraean Sea*, The Hakluyt Society London, 1989 , page 36

[17] From book 5 of *Agatharchides of Cnidus, on the Erythraean Sea*, excerption from Photius, *Bibliotheca*, cited by Burstein, page 169-fragment 105a

[18] See Burstein's study, footnotes, page 33

[19] From book 5 of *Agatharchides of Cnidus, on the Erythraean Sea*, excerption from Photius, *Bibliotheca*, cited by Burstein, page 148-fragment 87a

[20] From book 5 of *Agatharchides of Cnidus, on the Erythraean Sea*, excerption from Diodorus, *Library of History*, cited by Burstein, page 153-fragment 92b

[21] Musil, page 303

[22] Wilfred Schoff, *The Periplus of the Erythraean Sea*, Munshiram Manoharial Publishers Pvt Ltd., 1995, page 54

[23] From book 5 of *Agatharchides of Cnidus, on the Erythraean Sea*, excerption from Photius, *Bibliotheca*, cited by Burstein, page 150-155-fragment 90 a- 95a ; from book 5 of *Agatharchides of Cnidus, on the Erythraean Sea*, excerption from Diodorus, *Library of History*, cited by Burstein, page 150-155 –fragment 91b-93b

[24] From book 5 of *Agatharchides of Cnidus, on the Erythraean Sea,,* excerption from Photius, *Bibliotheca*, cited by Burstein, page 155-fragment 95a

[25] cf.Woelk, p. 223; cited by Burstein, page 155

[26] Nonnosus cited by Photius, *Bibliotheca*, 1,5

[27] Crone, page 197

[28] Noted by Wellhausen, *Reste*, p.92, cited by Crone, page 197

[29] Ibn Abbas in Tabari, Jami', xxx,171, cited by Crone, page 205

[30] Nonnosus cited by Photius, *Bibliotheque*, 1,5

[31] Sidney Smith, *Babylonian Historical Texts*, London 1924, Chapter III, page 27-97; Dougherty, Nab. And Bel., pages 105-11; cited by F.V.Winnett and W.L.Reed, *Ancient Records from North Arabia*, University of Toronto Press, 1970, page 89

[32] C.J.Gadd, The Harran Inscriptions of Nabonidus, (*Anatolian Studies*, 8 (1958), page 59 ; cited by F.V.Winnett and W.L.Reed, *Ancient Records from North Arabia*, University of Toronto Press, 1970, page 91

[33] From book 5 of *Agatharchides of Cnidus, on the Erythraean Sea*, excerption from Photius, *Bibliotheca*, cited by Burstein, page 152-fragment 92a

[34] cf Woelk, p.223; quoted by Stanley Burstein, *Agatharchides of Cnidus, on the Erythraean Sea,* The Hakluyt Society London, 1989, page 155

[35] H.Von Wissmann, Zaabram', *Pauly's Realencyclopadie der Klassischen Altertumswissenschaft* (Stuttgart, 1894-1980) supp., XI (1968) col.1310 ; cited by Stanley Burstein, *Agatharchides of Cnidus, on the Erythraean Sea*, The Hakluyt Society London, 1989 , page 155

[36] *Western Arabia and the Red Sea*, 1946, Naval Intelligence Division, page 585.

[37] See Stanley Burstein on his introduction to "*Agatharchides of Cnidus, on the Erythraean Sea*," The Hakluyt Society, London, 1989, page 13

[38] Leopoldi, Helmuthus, *De Agatharchide Cnidio* (Diss.Rostow, 1892) pp.13-17 ; cited by Burstein, page 39.
Strabo made abridgement of Agatharchides's book, adding material from the lost book of Artemidorus. The work which Artemidorus developed, especially about Arabia, is contained in Strabo's chapters, especially 16.4.5-20. See Bunbury, E.H. *A History of Ancient Geography*, 2nd ed. (London 1883), pages 61-69; Burstein, page 38
[39] *The Geography of Strabo*, Book XVI .4.18
The Geography of Strabo, Volume VII, Harvard University Press, (London, 1966), page 343
[40] *The Geography of Strabo*, Book XVI .4.18
The Geography of Strabo, Volume VII, Harvard University Press, (London, 1966), page 345
[41] Wilfred Schoff on his comment on *The Periplus of the Erythraean Sea*, Munshiram Manoharial Publishers Pvt Ltd. (New Delhi, 1995), page 101
[42] *The Geography of Strabo*, Book XVI. 4 . 24
[43] Dio Cassius: *History of Rome*, Book LIII. xxix.3-8.
[44] *The Geography of Strabo*, Book XVI .4.20
The Geography of Strabo, Volume VII, Harvard University Press (London, 1966), page 349
[45] *The Geography of Strabo*, Book XVI .4.2
[46] *The Geography of Strabo*, Book XVI .4.22
[47] *The Geography of Strabo*, Book XVI .4.22
[48] Wilfred Schoff on his introduction to *The Periplus of the Erythraean Sea*, Munshiram Manoharial Publishers Pvt Ltd.(New Delhi, 1995), pages 14,15
[49] Among the places where Josephus mentions Malchus are in *"The Wars of the Jews,"* Book 1, chapter 14 and *"The Antiquities of the Jews,"* Book 14, chapter 14.
[50] *The Periplus of the Erythraean Sea,* section 27
[51] *The Periplus of the Erythraean Sea*, section 23
[52] Inscription No. 1619 by Glaser, cited by Wilfred Schoff, page 11
[53] *The Periplus of the Erythraean Sea*, section 4
[54] H.Rackham, Introduction to Pliny, *Natural History*, Cambridge, Massachusetts, Harvard University Press, William Heinemann Ltd. (London, 1979), page vii
[55] *Tarikh al-Tabari*, first volume, Dar al-Kutub al-Ilmiyeh (Beirut –Lebanon 1991), page 142
[56] *Tarikh al-Tabari*, first volume, page 355
[57] *Tarikh al-Tabari*, I, 421
[58] Josephi Fischer S.J., Commentatio de *CL. Ptolemaci vita*, operibus, influxu sacculari, pages 65-79 (in his introduction to Vatican publication of Ptolemy: Claudii Ptolemaci Geographiac Urbinas Codex graccus 82 phototypice depictus); the same mentioned by Josephi Fischer in his introduction to

Claudius Ptolemy The Geography, translated by Edward Luther Stevenson, Dover Publications, INC, (New York, 1991, page 7

[59] Josephi Fischer in his introduction to *Claudius Ptolemy, The Geography*, translated by Edward Luther Stevenson, Dover Publications , INC, (New York, 1991), page 5

[60] Claudius Ptolemy, *The Geography*, Book II, *Claudius Ptolemy, The Geography*, translated by Edward Luther Stevenson, Dover Publications , New York, 1991, page 47

[61] Claudius Ptolemy, *The Geography*, book VI chapter VI, *Claudius Ptolemy, The Geography*, translated by Edward Luther Stevenson, Dover Publications , New York, 1991, page 137-138

[62] Yaqut al-Hamawi, *Mujam al-Buldan*, iv, 587; quoted by Patricia Crone, *Meccan Trade*, Princeton University Press, 1987, page 136

[63]) *The Geography of Strabo*, Book 16, chapter iv, 2 (The Geogrophy of Strabo, volume vii, translated by Horace L. Jones , 1966, page 311)

[64] *Natural History* of Pliny; Book VI, chapter 32

[65] Patricia Crone, *Meccan Trade*, Princeton University Press, 1987, pages 134,135

[66] Nallino Carlo Alfonso , *Raccolta di Scritti editti E ineditti*, Roma, Istituto per l'Oriente, 1939-48 , Vol.III, page 122 ; Caetani, Annali Dell' Islam, I, (1907), page 125

[67] James Montgomery, *Arabia and the Bible*, University of Pennsylvania Press, Philadelphia, 1934, page 131

[68] K.A. Kitchen, *Documentation For Ancient Arabia*, Part I, Liverpool University Press, 1994, page 135

[69] Rabinowitz, *Journal of Near Eastern Studies* 15 (1956),1-9, pls.6-7, quoted by K.A. Kitchen, *Documentation For Ancient Arabia*, Part I, Liverpool University Press, 1994, page 169

[70] Reed, *Ancient Records from North Arabia*, Toronto, 1970, 50 f., 115-117 quoted by K.A. Kitchen, *Documentation For Ancient Arabia*, Part I, Liverpool University Press, 1994), page 169

[71] K.A. Kitchen, *Documentation For Ancient Arabia*, Part I, Liverpool University Press, 1994, page 237

[72] James Montgomery, *Arabia and the Bible*, University of Pennsylvania Press, Philadelphia, 1934, page 138

[73] F.V. Winnett and W.L. Reed, *Ancient Records from North Arabia*, University of Toronto Press, 1970, page 104

[74] F.V. Winnett and W.L. Reed, *Ancient Records from North Arabia*, page 103

[75] K.A. Kitchen, *Documentation For Ancient Arabia*, Part I, Liverpool University Press, 1994, page 237

[76] K.A. Kitchen, *Documentation For Ancient Arabia*, Part I, pages 170-175;238

[77] K.A. Kitchen, *Documentation For Ancient Arabia*, Part I, pages 175-180; 238

[78] C.Robin, *Inventair des Inscriptions Sudarabiques*, 1ff. Paris/Rome, 1992 ff.1, 67-68, Haram 3 & 4; *Repertoire d'Epigraphie Semitique*, esp.V-VIII, Paris, 1929-1968, 2751/M.15; quoted by K.A. Kitchen, page 180

[79] K.A. Kitchen, *Documentation For Ancient Arabia*, Part I, pages 181; 239

[80] C.Robin, *Inventair des Inscriptions Sudarabiques*, 1ff. Paris/Rome, 1992 ff.,1, 5-6, pls.2b,3a; Inabba; quoted by K.A. Kitchen, *Documentation For Ancient Arabia*, Part I, page 181; see also K.A. Kitchen, page 239

[81] Private building-dedication, al-Harashif 3 (C.Robin, *Inventair des Inscriptions Sudarabiques,* 1ff. Paris/Rome, 1992 ff., 1, 200-201, pl.59b); quoted by K.A. Kitchen, page 182

[82] K.A. Kitchen, *Documentation For Ancient Arabia*, Part I, Liverpool University Press, 1994, pages 181, 182; see also K.A. Kitchen, page 239

[83] Comptes-rendus de l'académie des Inscriptions et Belleslettres, 1992, 68; cf.C.Robin in Robin(ed.), *L'Arabie Antique de Karib'il à Mahomet*, Aix-en-Provence, 1993,55,128, fig.20; quoted by K.A. Kitchen, page 183

[84] K.A. Kitchen, *Documentation For Ancient Arabia*, Part I, pages 181, 182; see also K.A. Kitchen, page 240

[85] K.A. Kitchen, *Documentation For Ancient Arabia*, Part I, pages 181, 182; see also K.A. Kitchen, pages 183-188

[86] See K.A. Kitchen, *Documentation For Ancient Arabia*, Part I, pages 181, 182; see also K.A. Kitchen, pages 90-222

[87] A.Jamme, W.F., *Sabaean Inscriptions from Mahram Bilqis* (Ma'rib), the Johns Hopkins Press,Baltimore, 1962, Volume III, page 137

[88] A.Jamme, W.F., *Sabaean Inscriptions from Mahram Bilqis (Ma'rib),* the Johns Hopkins Press, Baltimore, 1962, Volume III, page 169

[89] R.W. Ehrich, *Chronologies in Old World Archaeology*, 3rd Edition, I-II, Chicago, 1992, I, pages 67-68; see also D.T. Potts, *Dilmun, New Studies in the Archaeology and Early History of Bahrain*, (BBVO2), Berlin, 1983, quoted by K.A. Kitchen, *Documentation For Ancient Arabia*, Part I, page 145

[90] J.B. Pritchard, *Ancient Near Eastern Texts Relating to the Old Testament*, Princeton, 268

[91] Hommel, *Ancient Hebrew Tradition*, pages 35-39, cited by Wilfred Schoff on his comment on *The Periplus of the Erythraean Sea,* Munshiram Manoharial Publishers Pvt Ltd., 1995, page 134

[92] Halevy, nos.190, 231-234 ; Hommel, *Chrestomathie*, page 117; Hartmann, *Die arabische Frage*, pp. 206: cited by James Montgomery, *Arabia and the Bible*, University of Pennsylvania Press, Philadelphia, 1934, page 182

[93] A. Irvine, *Journal of Semitic Studies* 10, (1965), pages 178-196; A.F.L.Beeston, *Proceedings of the Seminar for Arabian Studies*, 17 (1987), pages 5-12; quoted by K.A. Kitchen, *Documentation For Ancient Arabia*, Part I, Liverpool University Press, 1994, page 39

[94] James Montgomery, *Arabia and the Bible*, University of Pennsylvania Press, Philadelphia, 1934, page 138

[95] F.V. Winnett and W.L. Reed, *Ancient Records from North Arabia*, University of Toronto Press, 1970, page 75

[96] *Revue Biblique*, 43(1934) pp.578-9 and 590-1; quoted by F.V. Winnett and W.L. Reed, *Ancient Records from North Arabia*, University of Toronto Press, 1970, page 75

[97] F.V. Winnett and W.L. Reed, *Ancient Records from North Arabia*, page 130

[98] *The Geography of Strabo*, Book XVI .4.23 *The Geography of Strabo*, Volume V, Harvard University Press, 1966, page 357

[99] *The Geography of Strabo*, Book XVI .4.24 *The Geography of Strabo*, Volume V, page 359

[100] *The Geography of Strabo*, Book XVI. 4 . 24 *The Geography of Strabo*, Volume V, page 363

[101] *The Geography of Strabo*, Book XVI .4.23 *The Geography of Strabo*, Volume VII, page 357

[102] Pliny XII, 44

[103] D. H. Mullar in his article *Yemen*, *Encyclopaedia Brittanic*, 9th edition; Weber, *Arabien vor dem Islam in Der alte Orient*, III, Leipzig, 1901; cited by Wilfred Schoff, *The Periplus of the Erythraean Sea*, Munshiram Manoharial Publishers Pvt Ltd., 1995, page 109

[104] See I. Eph'al, E.J.Brill, *The Ancient Arabs*, Leiden, 1982, page 161, note 161

[105] For "Verse Account of Nabonidus," see *Ancient Near Eastern Texts Relating to the Old Testament*, ed. J.B. Pritchard, 2nd edition, Princeton, 1955, page 313; Sidney Smith, *Babylonian Historical Texts*, London, 1924, Chapter III, pp. 27-97 ;quoted by F.V. Winnett and W.L. Reed, *Ancient Records from North Arabia*, University of Toronto Press, 1970, page 89

[106] See C.J. Gadd "The Harran Inscriptions of Nabonidus," *Anatolian Studies*, 8 (1958) page 59; cited by F.V. Winnett and W.L. Reed, *Ancient Records from North Arabia*, University of Toronto Press, 1970, page 91; The exact part in the Harran Inscriptions is (Nab. H2 I 26; ii 11) see I. Eph'al, *The Ancient Arabs*, 180

[107] *The Periplus of the Erythraean Sea*, 33;*The Periplus of the Erythraean Sea*, Translated by Wilfred Schoff, Munshiram Manoharial Publishers Pvt Ltd, 1995, page 35

[108] Wilfred Schoff, in his introduction to *The Periplus of the Erythraean Sea*, page 16

[109] Hirschfeld, *New Researches*, 6. Frankel, *Aramaisch. Fremdworter*; quoted by De Lacy O'Leary, *Arabia before Muhammed*, D.D., London, New York: Dutton & CO., 1927, page 181

[110] De Lacy O'Leary, *Arabia Before Muhammed*, page 19

[111] *Tarikh al-Tabari*, I, page 360

[112] P. Michalowski, *Journal of Cuneiform Studies*, 40 (1988), pages 156-164; citation, p. 163; cited by K.A. Kitchen, *Documentation For Ancient Arabia*, Part I, Liverpool University Press, 1994, page 159

[113] Luckenbill, *Ancient Records of Assyria and Babylonia*, I, Chicago, page 223 ; Rogers, *Cuneiform Parallels to the Old Testaments*, page 296; Barton, *Archaeology and the Bible*, edition 6, 1933, page 457; cited by *Arabia and the Bible*, James Montgomery, University of Pennsylvania Press, Philadelphia, 1934, page 58

[114] A.C. Piepkorn, *Historical Prism of Assurbanipal*, Chicago-USA, 1933, pages 19-20

[115] Saggs, *Iraq* 17, (1955), pages 142-143; Von Soden, *Orientalia* 35, (1966), page 20; cited by I. Eph'al, *The Ancient Arabs*, E.J. Brill, Leiden, 1982, page 94

[116] P. Rost, *Die Keilschrifttexte Tiglat-Pilesers III*, Leipzig, 1893, pages 150-170; quoted by I. Eph'al, *The Ancient Arabs*, page 82

[117] *The Ancient Arabs*, I. Eph'al, page 36

[118] Winnett, *Safaitic Inscriptions from Jordan*, 1957, Nos. 87, 237

[119] Pliny, *Natural History*, book VI, Chapter 32

[120] Sawyer John and Clines David, *Midian, Moab and Edom*, JSOT Press , Department of Biblical Studies, University of Sheffield, 1984, page 101

[121] Luckenbil, op. cit., vol. II, 7; Rogers, op. cit., page 331; Barton, op. cit., page 463; quoted by James Montgomery, *Arabia and the Bible*, page 59

[122] Claudius Ptolemy, *The Geography*, Book vi, chapter VII, translated by Stevenson, Dover Publications, 1991, page 139

[123] Herodotus II, page 141

[124] Tablet of the British Museum, 103,000 vn 96-viii 1(Luckenbill, *Sennacherib*, 113); quoted by I. Eph'al, E.J. Brill, *The Ancient Arabs*, page 41

[125] Luckenbill, *Records of Assyria II.* 551.

[126] One such example is the Cylinder inscriptions found in the city of Nimrud, the most important of which is called Klch. A; there is also an inscription called "Trb.A- a," cylinder inscription from Tarisu (see E. Nassouhi, *Mitteilungen der altorientalischen Gesellschaft*, III, 1-2, (1927), pages 22-28; quoted by , I. Eph'al, page 45

[127] Inscriptions from Nineveh (K 3082+ K 3086+ Sm 2027); see R. Borger, *Die Inschriften Asarhaddons, Konigs von Assyrien*, Graz 1956, pages 112-113, quoted by I. Eph'al, *The Ancient Arabs*, page 46

[128] Heidel Prism iii, 9-18, quoted by Eph'al, page 130

[129] *The Ancient Arabs*, I. Eph'al, E.J. Brill, Leiden, 1982, page 132

[130] Luckenbill, *Ancient Records of Assyria and Babylonia*, Vol. II, page 214

[131] Nin. A.; Heidel Prism iii 21;quoted by Eph'al page 131

[132] Hommel, *Ethnologie und Geographie des alten Orients*, Munchen, 1926, pages 558-559; quoted by Eph'al.

[133] Eph'al, *The Ancient Arabs*, E.J. Brill, Leiden, 1982, page 137

[134] Luckenbill, op. cit., page 301; Doughty, *Arabia Deserta*, Volume I, page 51; quoted by *Arabia and the Bible*, James Montgomery, University of Pennsylvania Press, Philadelphia, 1934, page 62

[135] Annals of Assurbanipal; R.F. Harper, Assyrian and Babylonian Letters, I XIV,(London-Chicago, 19140), 350; cited by Eph'al, page 55

[136] A.R. Millard, *Iraq* (1964), cit. 28 ; quoted by Eph'al, *The Ancient Arabs*, page 154

[137] *The Ancient Arabs*, I. Eph'al, E.J. Brill, Leiden, 1982, page 168

[138] *Judith* 2:26

[139] *Arabia and the Bible*, James Montgomery, University of Pennsylvania Press, Philadelphia, 1934, page 64

[140] Inscriptions found on Jabal Ghunaym, about 10 miles from Teima. See F.V. Winnett and W.L. Reed, *Ancient Records from North Arabia*, University of Toronto Press, 1970, page 29

[141] Harran Inscriptions Nab. H2 I 26 and Nab. H2 I 24-25; quoted by Eph'al, pages 180 and 181

[142] E. Ebeling, *Neubabylonnische Briefe*, Munchen 1949, No. 276; E.W. Moore, *Neo-Babylonian Documents in the University of Michigan Collection*, Ann Arbor, 1939, No. 67; cited by I. Eph'al, *The Ancient Arabs*, page 189

[143] R. F. Harper, *Assyrian and Babylonian Letters*, I, XIV, (London – Chicago 1892-1914) quoted by Eph'al , page 190

[144] Abdel Monem Sayed, "Reconsideration of the Minaean Inscription of Zayd 'il bin Zayd," *Proceedings of the Seminar for Arabian Studies*, XIV, (1984), pp.93-99; qouted by Stanley Burstein on his comment on *Agatharchides of Cnidus, on the Erythraean Sea,* The Hakluyt Society London, 1989, page 149

[145] Memphis text was published by Rhodokanakis in *Zeitschr.f.Semitistik*, II, (1924), 113 ff; cited by James Montgomery, *Arabia and the Bible*, University of Pennsylvania Press, Philadelphia, 1934, page 135; there is a dedication by two merchants of Main to the god Wadd on Delos, see Felix Durrbach, ed., *Choix d'Inscriptions de Delos*, (Paris, 1921-1922), page 129; cited by Stanley Burstein on his comment on *Agatharchides of Cnidus, on the Erythraean Sea*, page 150;

[146] See David Graf, Dedanite and Minaean (South Arabia) Inscriptions from the Hisma', *Annual of the Department of Antiqueties*, XXVII (Amman-Jordan, 1983,) pp. 563-5; cited by Stanley Burstein on his comment on *Agatharchides of Cnidus, on the Erythraean Sea*, page 149

[147] Two inscriptions were found at Taj in Kuweit, *Geog. Journal*, 1922, page 59; cited by James Montgomery, *Arabia and the Bible*, page 166

[148] A village named in a Greek inscription as " Pool of the Sabaeans " of Leja, Dussaud, *Les Arabes en Syrie*, page 10; quoted by James Montgomery, *Arabia and the Bible*, University of Pennsylvania Press, Philadelphia, 1934, page 181

[149] James Montgomery, *Arabia and the Bible*, page 42

[150] Caussin de Perceval, I, 84 ff ; cited by James Montgomery, *Arabia and the Bible*, page 125

[151] James Montgomery, page 41

[152] See Van den Berg, *Le Hadhramout et les colonies arabes dans l'Archipel indien,* (Batavia, 1886); quoted by James Montgomery, page 81

[153] Wilfred Schoff on his comments on *The Periplus of the Erythraean Sea,* Munshiram Manoharial Publishers Pvt Ltd., 1995, page 175

[154] Pliny 11:11

[155] Wilfred Schoff on his comments on *The Periplus of the Erythraean Sea,* page 161

[156] Quoted by Wilfred, page 107

[157] Halevy, no. 525; quoted by James Montgomery, *Arabia and the Bible,* page 44

[158] F.V. Winnett and W.L. Reed, *Ancient Records from North Arabia,* University of Toronto Press, 1970, page 115

[159] *Archives Royales de Mari* (Paris), xv 133; J.A. Brinkman, *Post-Kassite Babyloniam,* page 183, note 1127; quoted by I. Eph'al, *The Ancient Arabs,* page 232

[160] Delitzsch, *Zeitschrift Für Keilschriftforschung,* 2 (1885), 92; quoted by I. Eph'al, *The Ancient Arabs,* page 232; see also Shiffer, *Die Aramäer,* page 89; quoted by James Montgomery, *Arabia and the Bible,* page 44

[161] James Montgomery, *Arabia and the Bible,* page 43

[162] James Montgomery, *Arabia and the Bible,* page 183

[163] James Montgomery, *Arabia and the Bible,* University of Pennsylvania Press, (Philadelphia, 1934), page 183

[164] James Montgomery, *Arabia and the Bible,* page 184

[165] Halevy, nos.190, 231-234; Hommel, *Chrestomathie,* page 117; Hartmann, *Die arabische Frage,* pp. 206: cited by James Montgomery, page 182

[166] Tablet Signature of Kouyunjik Collection in the British Museum, 2802 vi 17-37; Quoted by I. Eph'al, page 221

[167] R.F. Harper, *Assyrian and Babylonian Le*tters, I XIV, (London-Chicago, 1892-1914), 1117

[168] See *The Periplus of the Erythraean Sea,* 27, 33, 36 and specially 57

[169] *The Geography of Strabo,* Book XVI. II. 23
The Geography of Strabo, Volume V, Harvard University Press, 1966, page 269

[170] *The Periplus of the Erythraean Sea,* 36

[171] *Tarikh al-Tabari,* I, page 524

[172] Al-Azruqi, *Akhbar Mecca,* 1, page 6

[173] A. Jamme, W.F., *Sabaean Inscriptions from Mahram Bilqis (Ma'rib),* the Johns Hopkins Press, Baltimore, 1962, Volume III, page 387; there are also texts numbered by G. Ryckmans after himself, G. Ryckmans, *Le Museon* 66 (1953), pages 363-7, pl.V; quoted by K.A. Kitchen, *Documentation For Ancient Arabia,* Part I, Liverpool University Press, 1994, page 219

[174] Al-Azruqi, *Akhbar Mecca,* 1:173; Yaqut al-Hamawi, *Mujam al-Buldan,* 4:463

[175] Ibn Saad, *Tabakat,* 1, page 64

[176] Ibn Hisham 1, page 20

[177] *Halabieh* 1, page 235; *Ibn Hisham* I, page 157; al-Azruqi, *Akhbar Mecca* I, page 104

[178] *Tarikh al-Tabari*, I, page 526

[179] *Sahih Muslim* 9, page 15

[180] *Tarikh al-Tabari*, I, page 426-428; al-Ya'akubi I, page 226

[181] *Tarikh al-Tabari*, I, page 429

[182] *Halabieh* I, page 280

[183] *Tarikh al-Tabari*, I, pages 331, 332, 360

[184] *Halabieh* I, page 236

[185] *Al-Bukhari* 5, page 122; Halabieh I, page 259

[186] Quotation by Alessandro Bausani, *L'Islam,* Garzanti Milano, 1980, page 208

[187] Quoted in *Mizan al-Islam* by Anwar al-Jundi, page 170 ; *Behind the Veil*, page 184

[188] *Tarikh al-Tabari*, I, pages 431 and 360 also mentioned the emigration to the area of Hira in Mesopotamia of tribes descended from Maad bin Adnan from Yemen.

[189] K.A. Kitchen, *Documentation For Ancient Arabia*, Part I , Liverpool University Press, 1994, page 251

[190] James Montgomery, *Arabia and the Bible*, University of Pennsylvania Press, Philadelphia, 1934, page 126; Montgomery also quotes Philby, *The Heart of Arabia*, II, page 97

[191] *Ibn Hisham* I, page 12

[192] *Ibn Hisham* I, page 13

[193] The commentators on *Ibn Hisham* I, page 13

Part III

The Kaabah and Allah as Expressions of the Arabian Star Family Worship

1 _____

THE KAABAH AS TEMPLE OF THE ARABIAN STAR FAMILY WORSHIP

The Kaabah of Mecca was one of many Kaabahs that were branches of the Kaabah of Taif; It was of the same building style and had the same religious pagan functions.

Islam is a form of the Arabian Star Family Worship of Mohammed's time. The veil which tries to hide this reality falls when we study the roots of the Islamic religion.

Ibn Abbas, the cousin of Mohammed, and one of the reporters of the tradition of Mohammed called Hadith, speaks of two pilgrimages of the Quraish tribe. One of the journeys was to the city of Taif.[1]

At Taif there was also a temple called Kaabah of Ellat, or Kaabah of the Sun. This Kaabah was more significant and much older than the Kaabah of Mecca. All Arabs, including the tribe of Quraish from which Mohammed came, venerated this Kaabah. The Kaabah of Taif was identical to the Kaabah of Mecca, and it had the same religious functions. Like the Kaabah at Mecca, it had a sacred valley where no animals or humans were allowed to be killed. The Kaabah of Taif had the same Sidaneh, or religious rituals, adopted by the Kaabah at Mecca. The Kaabah of Taif also had the Istar استار, a kind of dress to cover the sacred stones like we find at the Kaabah of Mecca. Both the Kaabah of Taif and the Kaabah of Mecca had a yard, or an area, which was inviolable. No one could cut its trees or hunt its animals. Anyone who entered there for refuge was protected. Both Kaabahs also had a well in which to put gifts.[2]

In Hijaz, the region of western and central western Arabia where Mecca was built, there were many Kaabahs which were dependent on this main Kaabah.[3] Was the Kaabah of Mecca just one branch of this famous Arabian Kaabah? It's probable, for many factors point to that. First, the tribe of Tamim, which inhabited the city of Taif where this Kaabah was built, was of Yemeni origin. Second, the tribe of Tamim had preeminence over other tribes in the region, including the tribe of Quraish. We have already seen that the tribe of Tamim were judges for disputes among the Arabian tribes of the region.[4] Third, the main door to the Kaabah at Mecca was called the "door of the sun worshippers," which indicates that the Kaabah of Mecca was, in particular, dedicated to the worship of the sun, just as was the Kaabah of Taif. However, this doesn't mean that Allah was not worshipped as the Star, along with his daughters, al-'Uzza and Manat.

The tribe of Quraish, in particular, worshipped Ellat, the Sun. They had an idol dedicated to Ellat in a place called Nekhlah, which was part of a larger area called Suk Ukkath (or Ukkaz), or the market or fair of Ukkath.[5] Ukkath is a place where many came, not just to trade, but also to conduct a Hajj, or pilgrimage. Since Ukkath housed the idol Ellat, and Ukkath was close to Mecca, people would visit Mecca after visiting Ukkath. There was also an idol of Ellat in the Kaabah of Mecca,[6] but it was less impressive than the idol of Ellat at Ukkath.

All this suggests that there were connections between some of the Kaabahs of Hijaz, even though they were built by Yemeni tribes and leaders at various times in history. We assume the Kaabah of Taif was the leading Kaabah of the ones dedicated to the worship of Ellat, the sun. This could explain why the Quraish neglected the Kaabah of Mecca and participated in an annual religious trip with other worshippers of Ellat to the main Kaabah at Taif. Members of Arabian Star Family Worship were venerated in all the Kaabahs, such as Allah and his daughters, al-'Uzza and Manat. But it seems each Kaabah had a particular emphasis on the worship of one of the members of the Arabian Star Family.

As in the Kaabah of Mecca, the Kaabbah of Taif had a large Black Stone around which the people circled.[7] The stone was the main element in Arabian Star Family Worship.

The Kaabah of Mecca was insignificant, even to the tribe of Quraish, until Mohammed imposed it as the exclusive place of worship for Muslims.

The tribe of Quraish continued to make two religious trips, or pilgrimages. One was to the northern Kaabah, which I discussed before, and the other was to the Kaabah of Taif. When Mohammed occupied Mecca, he came with a verse from the Qur'an, prohibiting his followers to make such trips. The Qur'an compelled them to worship only in the Kaabah of Mecca. The verse I'm referring to is found in Surah Quraish 106:1-3,

> For the covenants by the Quraish, their covenant journeys by winter and summer, let them adore the lord of this house.

It is clear that the tribe of Quraish was to have two religious journeys, one in winter and one in summer. We understand from old Islamic resources that the journey of Quraish in summer was to Taif.[8] But the Qur'an prohibited Mohammed's followers from worshipping other lords in other Kaabahs. Worshippers were to express their adoration only in the Kaabbah of Mecca. All this demonstrates that, among the Kaabahs dedicated to Star Family Worship in Arabia, the Kaabah of Mecca was not an important Kaabah until Mohammed made his ruling. Instead, it was almost insignificant, even to the tribe of Quraish, which occupied Mecca after evicting the tribe of Khuzaa'h, the builders of the city and its Kaabah. The Kaabah at Mecca was important to the tribe of Khuzaa'h and to the tribe of Sufa, seemingly a branch of Khuzaa'h. Sufa was responsible for pagan ceremonies held in the mountains around Mecca. Such ceremonies were later incorporated into Islam by Mohammed, and became part of its pilgrimage.

Even the tribe of Quraish considered the Kaabah of Mecca as irrelevant. They preferred to go to Ukkath to worship Ellat, the sun, rather than restricting their worship to the Kaabah at Mecca. They considered the northern temple and the main temple dedicated to the worship of Ellat – that is the Kaabah of Taif – as the more important temples.

The Kaabah at Mecca was not Important to Other Arabian Tribes

Not only did the tribe of Quraish fail to hold the Kaabah at Mecca in esteem above the other Kaabahs, but many Arabian tribes felt the same way. We see that Thaqif, the main tribe of Taif, was not interested in preserving the Kaabah of Mecca. This was shown when Abraha, the Ethiopian, who controlled Yemen around 570 A.D., passed through Thaqif. They asked Abraha not to destroy their Kaabah, but instead to destroy the Kaabah in Mecca, because they knew his plans were to go there after occupying their city.[9] This shows that the Kaabah of Mecca was not important to the Arabian tribes because it was originally the Kaabah belonging to one tribe, the tribe of Khuzaa'h, which built Mecca.

Hubol was a shrine of the Kaabah representing the moon. Hubol was called "Allah" before Venus took the title of "Allah" from the moon.

Quraish worshipped an idol belonging to another tribe, the tribe of Kinaneh. The idol was called "a companion or friend of Kinaneh." Kinaneh then worshipped an idol called "companion of Quraish."[10] This deity was Hubol. Hubol was worshipped as the main shrine in the Kaabah at Mecca. Scholars think this shrine represented Allah, the head of Arabian Star Family Worship, whose wife was Ellat, the sun. This god, Hubol, was found in the Nabataean inscriptions as the god of the moon,[11] and he was formed in the image of a man.[12]

Scholars agree that Hubol, as the god of the moon, was the god of the Kaabah. For a certain period, he was also "Allah" for the inhabitants of Mecca.[13] This was before Venus gained the title of Allah as the "great star."

2_____

WHO WAS ALLAH IN THE WORSHIP OF ARABIA?

The Origin of "Allah" and How the Name was Developed from the god of the Moon in Arabia, as it is Attested in Various Arabian Inscriptions

We know that the term "Allah," as the god of the moon, was derived from the Thamud god of the moon. His name was Hilal, or Hlal, which means "crescent." Later, the name "Hilal" became Hilah, as we see in many inscriptions which were found in Arabia. In the Thamud inscriptions he is found as H-ilah, Ha-ilah and H-alah.[14] We see the same development for "Hilah," the moon deity in Yemen, where Almaqah is called "Halal," or "Hilal, the Crescent."[15]

Safaitic tribes were nomads wandering in many parts of Arabia, especially in the north. The god of the moon was found in their inscriptions as "H-lah." In the Safaitic inscriptions, the letter "H" pronounced as "Ha" is the definite article, "the." It corresponds to the Arabic, "Al."[16] This led the Arabians to call him "Al-lah."

The Big Star Athtar– Venus – Replaces the Moon for the Title of "Allah"

From the Thamudic inscriptions, we know that Venus worship endeavored to overshadow the worship of other deities of Arabia, willing to impose itself as the monotheistic worship of northern Arabia. The worshippers of "the big star" even underestimated the worship of the other members of the Star Family, such as the worship of the wife of the head, Ellat, which represented the sun, or the worship of the moon itself. Over time, Venus stole the title

273

of "Allah" from the moon. Both the moon and the sun became subjects to Allah, the biggest star. We encounter this concept in the Qur'an, where it says:

> He subjected the sun and the moon till they say Allah. (Sura 29 : 61)

This was because competition grew between the different members of the Star Family. The worshippers of Allah, the biggest star, considered other deities of the Star Family as subordinate to Allah, and maintained that he was the most important in the Star Family. They taught that the other stars became servants to Allah and worshipped him before his throne. The followers of Allah, the head of Arabian Star Family Worship, professed and fought against the followers and worshippers of the other members of the Star Family. This concept of the supremacy of the head of the Star Family over the rest of the members of the family is encountered very clearly in the Qur'an. In the Sura 36:38, we read, "the sun goes to an abiding place." Mohammed then explained this verse in his Hadith saying:

> The sun goes to the throne of Allah where it worships with the moon.

There are many Hadith of Mohammed in which he claimed that the setting sun goes to the throne of Allah. We quote a Hadith reported in Bukhari, the authoritative book containing the most-confirmed Hadith of Mohammed:

> From Abi al-Thur. "I asked the prophet, peace upon him from Allah, about the verse of Allah in the Qur'an which states that 'the sun goes to an abiding place,' the prophet answered: "the sun's abiding place is under the throne."[17]

Another Hadith also reported in Bukhari:

> I was with the prophet in the mosque when the sun was setting. He asked me: "Do you know where the sun goes after the sunset?" I

answered: "Allah and his prophet better know." The prophet said: "The sun goes under the throne in order to worship, this is the interpretation of Allah's saying 'the sun goes to an abiding place.'"[18]

Al-Tabari also reported a Hadith of Mohammed, in which he describes the sun and the moon going to the throne of Allah to worship.[19]

The concept of the robe of light given to the sun in order to enable it to shine: a myth copied by Mohammed from the Sabian Mandaeans, along with other rituals he took from them and incorporated into Islam.

Mohammed claimed that the sun and the moon, after worshipping Allah before his throne, were dismissed by the angel Gabriel, who put robes of light on them, which were taken from the throne of Allah.[20] This myth of Mohammed is derived from Babylonian mythology. In fact, the Babylonians believed that there was a door in heaven through which the sun god, also called Samas, or Utu, passed. Then the sun reached a room where it stayed to worship.[21]

In the Babylonian mythology, the gods wear a melam – a robe of light.[22] The idea of robes of light was transferred to the Mandaeans, also called Sabians, a Gnostic sect which appeared in northern Mesopotamia in the 2nd century A.D. In their main sacred book, called Ginza Rba, we read about one of their personalities of light called Pthahil, how he was provided with robes of light that enabled him to enlighten the worlds.[23] (It may be interesting to know that Pthahil was also called Gabriel.) The Mandaeans believed that Pthahil-Gabriel gave light to the sun and the moon.[24] The sun in the Mandaean sacred books, such as in "The Canonical Prayerbook of the Mandaeans," wears robes of light.[25] Those robes are given to the sun by Pthahil-Gabriel, who is the Creator of the universe in the Mandaean Mythology.

The Sabians had a great influence in Mecca at the time of Mohammed. In fact, Mohammed was called "Sabian" by his fellow citizens,[26] because he adopted many of their rites – including washing the hands, legs and face before every prayer, and the practice of praying five times a day. The community of the Sabians used to call itself Mushulmana,[27] that is, Muslim, from where Mohammed took the name of Muslim. In fact, till today the Mandaeans recite in their prayers "O Muslims, do not go away from your covenant in which you pledged to God."[28] ; " every one who does ablution Yaslem – meaning become a Muslim –"coming from the Aramaic "Ansh Sabi .. Shalmi." [29]

Mohammed's childhood also influenced what he taught. He fostered the idea that every night the sun and the moon go to the throne of Allah to worship. This seems to be an idea which he learned in his childhood, taught to him by his family. In one of his Hadiths he mentions that, when he was a child, the moon used to look at him and entertain him, and that he used to hear the noise of the moon when it prostrated itself before the throne of Allah to worship.[30]

Arabian Monotheism, Which is Based on the Star Venus-Athtar, is the Root of Mohammed's Monotheism

In later times, Athtar, which was the planet Venus, and called the son of the moon, was venerated by the Yemeni tribes. Athtar's worship spread to the north and replaced the moon as Allah. Athtar became the chief deity for monotheism in Arabia. His worshippers rejected the other gods who were worshipped in Arabia and insisted that Athtar, who became Allah, must be worshipped alone. This worship was at the root of Mohammed's monotheistic ideas.

The Qur'an copied the attributes given to Athtar and attributed them to Allah. In Yemeni inscriptions, we find Athtar Khaham, which corresponds in the Arabic of the Qur'an to "al-Khadir" القدير, which means "the potent," a term used to refer to Allah. We also find in the inscriptions attributed to Athtar the title: "Athtar al-kaher," عثتر القاهر, which means "Athtar the conqueror," which we find also attributed to Allah in the Qur'an. We also find another term, "Athtar Yaglin" which is translated in the Qur'an as "al-montakim," which means "the revenger" or "revengeful." Still another term referring to Athtar was "Athtar Samum" عتثر سمعم , corresponding to the Arabic of the Qur'an as "Samie" السميع , or "hearer." All these titles were attributed to Allah in the Qur'an.[31]

We see, also, that Athtar, in some Thamudic inscriptions, is given the title of "Rami," which, in the Arabic language of Mecca and the Qur'an, means "Akbar," translated "the biggest." This is the same title given to Allah in the Qur'an. The intention of the worshippers of Venus was to say that the Venus deity star was the biggest of all stars. Both Allah in the Qur'an, and Athtar in the Thamudic inscriptions are called "Rahim," which means merciful.[32] In the inscriptions from the area of Teima, there is a mention of a star called "Lame'h," which means "bright." This is most likely a reference to Venus, which is given in the inscriptions the title of "Rahim."[33]

The Qur'an has copied many attributes of Arabian gods and given them to Allah. For example, the Thamud gods are described with the inscription:

> He was not conceived nor generated nor born.[34]

This expression often was used in the Jahiliyah period; in fact, Kes Bin Saideh mentioned it in his sayings.[35] Mohammed used to listen to Kes Bin Saideh when he was young. The same idea was copied in the Qur'an and used about Allah, such as Surah al-khlas 112:3, "he begetteth not, nor is he begotten." This became a verse in the Qur'an.

Azizos, as Another Title of Venus-Athtar, Became a Synonym for Allah in the Qur'an

Athtar was also called "al-Aziz" العزيز,[36] the main title for Allah in the Qur'an. Mohammed emigrated to the city of Yathrib, or al-Medina, after his message was refused in Mecca. The city is known better by its name, Medina. The inhabitants of Medina were worshipping the sun, and another deity which rises before the sun. They called the early riser "Azizos." They also worshipped a deity which rises after the sun under the name of "Monimos."

Scholars identified Azizos with Aziz, or al-Aziz, which is Venus.[37] Athtar, as Venus, was described in the Thamud inscriptions as the one who appeared before the sun in the last part of each night.[38] Azizos and Monimos were venerated at Edessa, a city of northern Mesopotamia. We find this mentioned by Emperor Julian in his speech delivered at Antioch in 362 A.D. Azizos and Monimos were venerated also at Palmyra, an Arabic city in the Syrian desert.

Connections of Mecca with Athtar-Venus's worship, and with other Kaabahs that were built for the same kind of pagan worship.

The Athtar-Venus worship was in places like the Kaabah of Mecca. Al-Shahrastani, one Islamic historian, says that in Yemen there was a Kaabah for the worship of Venus similar to the Kaabah of Mecca.[39] Al-Masudi, another Islamic historian, says that the Kaabah of Mecca is furnished in the same style as a Kaabah in Yemen, which is dedicated to the worship of Venus.[40] This helps us see that the Kabbah in Mecca relates to the same worship of Venus (and others) in the Star Family.

Al-Masudi also reveals that, for each region in Arabia, there was a special star which was considered the main deity venerated by the inhabitants of the region. He goes on to say that Venus was the star of Mecca, Yathrib and Yemen.[41]

*Athtar-**Venus** became Allah, who appears at Mecca in the third part of each night. Mohammed shared the same concepts of this star deity.*

No wonder Venus snatched the title "Allah" from the moon. Later, the same Athtar-Venus was called "Allah" in Mecca and in other parts of Northern Arabia. Allah became a great and high star which descended every third part of the night to appear to his worshippers. We can see this from many authors who wrote about the life of Mohammed, and who wrote about the life and creeds of Jahiliyah, the period before Islam. Among the authors was Ali Bin Burhan al-Din al-Halabi, known as the author of Halabieh. He wrote that Allah descends to the heaven of this world when it is the last part of the night.[42] It is clear that, by the word "Allah,"

278

they meant the morning star which they saw in the third portion of each night.

From these sources we learn that Allah was understood at the time of Mohammed to be a big star appearing each night. It is clear that they meant the morning star which appears in Arabia in the third part of the night. This morning star is the same Aziz who appeared to the inhabitants of the al-Medina early before the sunrise. Ideas attributed to Athtar-Venus, the old monotheistic deity of Arabia who appeared in the last part of every night to his worshippers, became the foundation of Arabian monotheism. The northern Arabians replaced the title of Athtar with Allah, but kept the identity of Venus.

We find that Mohammed explained his concept of deity in the same terms adopted by the ancient Arabians. Mohammed's concept of deity is not different from his fellow citizens. We understand from many verses in the Qur'an, and from his documented Hadith, that his concept of deity is consistent with the pagan roots of the star deity revered by his family and tribe. The Hadith contains Mohammed's words, and is considered by Muslims as inspired. In the book of Sahih al-Bukhari, the book which contains the authoritative Hadith of Mohammed, we find the words of Mohammed:

> Allah, our Lord, his name is blessed and high, descends to the heaven of this world every night when it remains in the last third of the night.[43]

We see that the deity for Mohammed is the same old monotheistic Arabian concept shared by his contemporaries, and based on a planet which appears in the last third of every night. That is surely Venus, whom Arabians in the past called Athtar, and to whom they attributed monotheistic concepts which Mohammed copied into the Qur'an and attributed to Allah. Mohammed's concept of Allah is identical to what his tribe believed. The connection between Mohammed's religion and the roots of the Arabian Star religion is too great to be ignored. His religion has the face and features of the paganism of his

279

contemporary Arabians, even though he attempted to make a connection with the God of the Bible.

Islam is a form of the Arabian religion of the Star Family Worship of Mohammed's time. The veil that tries to hide this reality falls when we study the roots of the Islamic religion. The face of the old Arabian religion is easily recognized and identified.

Sura Najm (star) in the Qur'an in which Mohammed recognized the daughters of Allah, representing two planets, and Ellat – Allah's wife – representing the sun, as intercessors to Allah.

The claims of Mohammed regarding monotheism reflect the old claims of the Athtar star worship. That is, the head of the Star Family should have preeminence over the worship of the rest of the Star Family. Thus, Mohammed's contention with his tribe is the old Arabian claim that the Allah star should be more revered than his wife, Ellat, representing the sun, or his daughters, al-'Uzza and Manat, representing two planets. The worshippers of the sects of the Allah star, before Mohammed, wanted to impose their worship over the worship of the rest of the family, reckoning the rest of the Star Family as intercessors to Allah, the biggest star. We find Mohammed having the same concern. In fact, he wrote a verse of the Qur'an in the Chapter known as Najm, that is, the star chapter, in which he discusses the roles of al-'Uzza and Manat and Ellat, who are the daughters and wife of Allah according to the tribe of Mohammed. He recognizes that they are like important birds of the high, and that their intercession role with Allah is important and should be respected.[44] As a result, the pagan Arabians of Mecca worshipped together with him, because he recognized their deities and their deities' role as intercessors with Allah.[45]

This shows us that Mohammed was spreading the star monotheism doctrine of old Arabia which claimed the preeminence of the worship of the Allah star over the worship given to his wife and daughters. Some of these verses are not in the Qur'an today. The reason is that, under Judaic influence, some of Mohammed's followers were disappointed with these verses, so Mohammed took the verses from the Qur'an took the verses out, claiming that the devil put them in his mouth. But the study of the entire chapter of Najm, the star chapter, shows that Mohammed intended to clarify that Allah is the head of the Star Family and that he has preeminence over his daughters and wife; they should be given the role of intercession before his throne, and nothing else. Thus, he expressed the ideas of the star monotheism of Arabia. Yet, these verses are in the same poetic form as the rest of the chapter. This should cause Muslims to wonder how Mohammed can consider the Qur'an language a miracle that no one can imitate, and also claim that verses of the same poetical level are from the devil. This implies that the devil is also capable of repeating the miracle Arabic language of the Qur'an. If the devil could inspire Mohammed to write this portion of the Qur'an, why couldn't he inspire Mohammed to write other portions, also?

Mohammed, to justify himself, claimed that, in like manner, the prophets of the Old Testament were sometimes inspired by the devil to say and write what they did. But, the fact of the matter is that no prophet of the Old Testament, or author of the New Testament, was suggested to be subjected to this satanic inspiration phenomenon which Mohammed attributed to himself. According to the Bible, men receiving inspiration from the devil are the mediums of the same devil. The Bible orders that such mediums should be stoned. We read this in the book of Leviticus of the Old Testament: "A man or a woman who is a medium, or who has familiar spirits, shall surely be put to death; they shall stone them with stones. Their blood shall be upon them." (Leviticus 20:27).

Comparing Islam to the religions which preceded it, and its reliance on star mythology, points out its inconsistencies, and paves the way for Muslims everywhere to turn to the God of the Bible, in Whom we have forgiveness of sins and the hope of eternal life.

REFERENCES AND NOTES TO PART III

[1] Ibn Abbas in Tabari, Jami', xxx, 171. cited by Patricia Crone, *Meccan Trade*, Princeton University Press, 1987, page, 205

[2] Ibn al-Kathir 4:253 quoted by Jawad Ali, vi, 228

[3] Jawad Ali, vi, 228

[4] *"Mecca and Tamim,"* Kister, page 145 ff, quoted by Patricia Crone, *Meccan Trade*, Princeton University Press, 1987, page 156

[5] *Tafsir al-Tabari* 27; page 35; Al-Allusi, *Ruh' al-Maani* 27:47

[6] Al-Allusi, *Ruh' al-Maani* 27: 47 ; Al-Khazen 4: 194, quoted by Jawad Ali vi, page 232

[7] Yaqut al-Hamawi, *Mujam al-Buldan* 7, page 310; Taj al-Aruss 1, page 580; *Tafsir al-Beithawi* 1:199 ; al-Kalbi, *al-Asnam*, Dar al-Kutub al-Masriyah, Cairo-Egypt, 1925; Al-Lusi, *Ruh' al-Maani*, 27, page 47; Azruqi, *Akhbar Mecca*, page 79

[8] Crone cited Ibn Abbas in Tabari, Jami', xxx, 171; Patricia Crone, *Meccan Trade*, Princeton University Press, 1987, page 205

[9] *Tarikh al-Tabari*, I, page 441

[10] Ibn Habib, *al-Mahbar*, page 318

[11] Jawad Ali,vi, 328; Rino' Disu, *al-Arab Fi Suryia Khabel al-Islam*, page 116

[12] Al-Tabarsi al-Fadl ibn al-Hasan, *Majma' al-Bayan fi tafsir al-Qur'an*, (Beirut, 1954) 29, page 68

[13] Wellhausen, *Reste Arabischen Heidentums*, Berlin, 1927, S.73,221 ; Grohmann, S.87 cited by Jawad Ali, vi, page 252

[14] James Montgomery, *Arabia and the Bible*, University of Pennsylvania Press, Philadelphia, 1934, page 154; Wellhausen, *Reste, Arabischen Heidentums*, Berlin, 1927, S.209; cited by Jawad Ali, vi, page 117

[15] *Repertoire Dépigraphie Semitique*, Tome VI, Paris, Imprimerie Nationale 3945, 4067, 4228, 4991, 4992, 4993; A. Grohmann, *Arabien*; S. 244; cited by Jawad Ali, vi, page 299

[16] *Ency.Religi.* Volume 6, page 248; cited by Jawad Ali, vi, page 24

[17] *Al-Bukhari* 8 page 179

[18] *Al-Bukhari* 6 page 30

[19] *Tarikh al-Tabari*, I, pages 46, 47

[20] *Tarikh al-Tabari*, I, pages 46, 47

[21] Jeremy Black and Anthony Green, *Gods Demons and Symbols of Ancient Mesopotamia*, University of Texas Press, 1995, page 137

[22] Jeremy Black and Anthony Green, *Gods Demons and Symbols of Ancient Mesopotamia,* pages 130,131

[23] *Ginza Rba*, book 17, hymn 7, translated by Yousef Matta Khuzi and Sabih Madlul al-Suheiri (Bagdad, year 2001), page 290

[24] *Ginza Rba*, book 1, hymn 2, translated by Yousef Matta Khuzi and Sabih Madlul al-Suheiri (Bagdad, year 2001), page 9

[25] *The Canonical Prayerbook of the Mandaeans*, translated by Drower, Leiden1959, page 178

[26] *Taj al-Aruss* 1, page 306 ; Al-Fayruz-Abadi, *al-Qamus al-Muheet* 1, page 20

[27] Sabih Al Suheiri, *Al Nushu' and Khalek Fi Al Nussus Al Mandaeah*, University of Bagdad, 1994, page 127; translating a work of Kort Rudolph on the subject.

[28] Quoted by Mohammed Abed Al Hamid Al Hamed, *Saebet Harran Wa Ikhwan Al Safa*, (Al Ahali, Damascus, Syria, 1998), page 37

[29] Mohammed Abed Al Hamid Al Hamed, *Saebet Harran Wa Ikhwan Al Safa*, (Al Ahali, Damascus, Syria, 1998), page 30

[30] *Halabieh* I, page 128

[31] A. Grohmann, *Arabien*, S, 245 quoted by Jawad Ali

[32] A. Grohmann, *Arabien*, 246; H. Grimme, S.66; quoted by Jawad Ali, 6, page 178

[33] F.V.Winnett and W.L.Reed, *Ancient Records from North Arabia*, University of Toronto Press, 1970, page 103

[34] Grimme, S. 66 as cited by Jawad Ali 6:178

[35] Al-Shahrastani, page 583

[36] Pfannmüller, *Handbuch der Islam-Literatur*, Berlin und Leipzig 1923, I, S, 229; quoted by Jawad Ali, vi, page 171

[37] Pfannmüller, *Handbuch der Islam-Literatur*, Berlin und Leipzig 1923, I, S, 229

[38] *Repertoire Dépigraphie Semitique*, Tome VI, Paris, Imprimerie Nationale, 4194; Pfannmüller, *Handbuch der Islam-Literatur*, Berlin und Leipzig 1923, I, S, 229; Jawad Ali, *al-Mufassal*, vi, pages 170, 171

[39] Al-Shahrastani, *Milal Wal Nah'l*, page 575

[40] Al-Masudi, *Murj al-Thahab*, II, page 250

[41] Masudi, *Murj al-Thahab*, I, page 96

[42] *Halabieh* I, page 129

[43] *Bukhari*, II, page 47

[44] *Halabieh*, Volume II, page 6; Look to *Ibn Hisham,* II, page 5; al-Suheili cited by Mustapha al-Sakkah in his comments on *Ibn Hisham*, footnote, page 5

[45] *Al-Bukhari* 2, page 32; 4: page 239; *Halabieh* Volume II, page 6

Part IV

The Case of the Ishmaelites and Islam

1

THE ISHMAELITES AND THEIR EXISTENCE THROUGHOUT HISTORY

To claim that Ishmael, along with his sons and their descendants, lived in Mecca, built a temple there and dominated Arabia is unhistorical. When we examine history for ourselves, we avoid the menace of being distracted from the revelation of God provided in the Bible.

Islamic tradition claims that Ishmael and his Egyptian mother left Palestine and settled in Mecca. The same tradition claims that Ishmael and his father, Abraham, built a temple in Mecca, which is called Kaabah. Abraham was to have traveled there by riding on a winged camel. Tradition further states that Ishmael's sons lived at Mecca and in Yemen, and his descendants, the Ishmaelites, also lived there. All this is written in Islamic tradition so that Muslims can connect Mohammed with Ishmael, even though we know that Mohammed was from the tribe of Quraish, originally a Sabaean family, and never linked to Ishmael.

We have seen previously that Mecca didn't exist prior to the 4th century A.D. This shows us that Islamic claims about Abraham and Ishmael living in Mecca are historically false. We also saw that communication between Palestine and central, western and southern Arabia was impossible, until cities were constructed at the oases of northern Arabia around the 10th and 9th centuries B.C.

The Ishmaelites make a fascinating historical study. We learn that they never lived in the area where Mecca was eventually built. We saw through our past studies that the area around Mecca was uninhabited throughout the Assyrian and Chaldean periods of the 10th through the 6th centuries B.C., and through the epochs covered by the Greek and Roman writers (from the 5th century B.C. through the Christian era).

Ishmael lived all his life in Paran, a wilderness in the northeastern part of the Sinai, and not at Mecca.

Both history and the Bible tell us that Ishmael lived with his mother, Hagar, in the Paran Desert, which is in the northeastern part of the Sinai, and not far from the border with South Palestine. Paran is also the land from which Moses sent the twelve spies to gather information on the promised land of Canaan. Ishmael remained in the Sinai region his entire life. One of the facts I gave previously as proof of this is that Ishmael and Isaac attended the funeral of their father, Abraham. If Ishmael had lived in central western Arabia, he couldn't have attended the funeral. The distance between Mecca's eventual location and Hebron, the place where Abraham died, is about 1,000 miles. At that time, to make the 1,000-mile journey would have taken more than five months. Weather conditions required that the dead should be buried on the same day of death. Since Ishmael lived in Paran, which is close to Hebron, he could have easily traveled to Hebron in a single day.

Ishmael's Residency was Established Before he was Born

The first time Hagar left the household, she fled to the Wilderness of Shur. The Wilderness of Shur is on the border between Sinai and Egypt, and it appears that Hagar was trying to return to her homeland in Egypt. We read about this in Genesis 16:7-12:

> Now the angel of the Lord found her by a spring of water in the wilderness, by the spring on the way to Shur. And he said: "Hagar, Sarah's maid, where have you come from, and where are you going?" She said, "I am fleeing from the presence of my mistress, Sarah." The angel of the Lord said to her, "return to your mistress, and submit yourself under her hand." And the angel of the Lord said to her: "...and he shall dwell in the presence of all his brethren."

So the angel specified that Ishmael was destined to live "in the presence of all his brethren," which means, "in the same area where the descendants of his brother, Isaac, were going to live." You may remember that Isaac's descendants were Jacob and Esau. Jacob lived in the land of Canaan, also known as Palestine, while Esau lived in southern Jordan. Ishmael lived in-between the two regions in the desert of Paran, exactly as the angel announced before Ishmael was born. Historically, we will see that Ishmael's descendants continued to live in the same area. Ishmael's descendants migrated into southern Jordan, into the rest of the Sinai, and even to the north toward Gilead and other areas in the Syro-Mesopotamian deserts, but they never migrated anywhere that was even near the area of Mecca.

Other Proofs that Ishmael Lived all his Life in Northeastern Sinai

As we follow the history of Ishmael, we see that he continued to live in southern Palestine. He socialized with his nephew, Esau, the son of Isaac. Eventually Esau married Ishmael's daughters and moved to the south of Trans-Jordan, not far from Paran where Ishmael lived.

The first daughter of Ishmael whom Esau married was Mahalath, about whom we read in Genesis 28: 9. It says:

> So Esau went to Ishmael and took Mahalath the daughter of Ishmael, Abraham's son, the sister of Nabaioth, to be his wife, in addition to the wives he had.

This occurred while Ishmael was still alive. The Bible doesn't mention any offspring coming from the union of Esau and Mahalath. There is, however, a mention of another of Ishmael's daughters, Basmath, in Genesis 36:3. Esau also took her as a wife, and she bore sons to Esau. After he married Basmath, we read:

> Esau took his wives, his sons, his daughters, and all the persons of his household, his cattle and his animals, and all his goods which he had gained in the land of Canaan, and went to a country away from

the presence of his brother Jacob-so Esau dwelt in Mount Seir. Esau is Edom.

When Esau was in Canaan, he could socialize with Ishmael, because Ishmael was living in Paran, not far from the border of Canaan.

Another thing specified clearly in the Bible is that Ishmael lived "in front of his brethren" all his life. This is clearly specified in Genesis 25:18, where we read, "He died in the presence of all his brethren." That phrase commonly meant that he lived all his life in the same area. That's where the sons of his brother, Isaac, lived. Jacob lived in Palestine, and Esau lived in Edom in South Jordan.

The Ishmaelites Continued to Live in the Sinai Throughout the 19th Century B.C.

The Ishmaelites are depicted at the time of Joseph as merchants trading between Gilead (north of Jordan, on the border with Syrian) and Egypt. Joseph was brought to Egypt around 1863-1860 B.C.

We read about this in Genesis 37 where the sons of Jacob sold Joseph, their brother, to a company of Ishmaelites who were coming from Gilead, carrying from there balm and other things to bring down to Egypt. We present the text of Genesis 37:25-28:

> And they – meaning the brothers of Joseph – sat down to eat a meal. Then they lifted their eyes and looked and there was a company of Ishmaelites, coming from Gilead with their camels, bearing spices, balm, and myrrh, on their way to carry them down to Egypt ... then Midianite traders passed by, so the brothers pulled Joseph up and lifted him out of the pit, and sold him to the Ishmaelites for twenty shekels of silver. And they took Joseph to Egypt.

Notice that, in verse 28, the Scripture called the company of traders both Midianites and Ishmaelites. In Genesis 39:1, the people who took Joseph to Egypt are again called Ishmaelites. This interchangeability between the terms "Ishmaelites" and "Midianites" grew from a later alliance between the Ishmaelites and the Midianites, who also inhabited the territory south of the Sinai. We find this in the book of Judges, which I'll discuss later.

The verses in Genesis, chapters 37 and 39, show us that, in the 19th century B.C., the Ishmaelites were living in South Palestine, and perhaps one tribe or more of them settled toward Trans-Jordan and Gilead. Their location enabled them to use the products of their nearest neighbor, Gilead, which produced spices and vegetable products, such as balms, balsam and myrrh. They, in turn, traded with other nearby countries, such as Egypt, in the western border of Sinai. If those Ishmaelites were living in the area where Mecca was later built, then why would they travel as far away as Gilead on the border with Syria? If they had lived near Mecca, it would have been much easier to obtain better quality spices from Yemen. It would also have been much closer for them. In addition, since Mecca was built in the land route from Yemen to Palestine, the Ishmaelites would not have needed to travel anywhere for the best spices of Yemen because the caravans carrying the best spices would pass daily by their country. Yemeni products were known to be the best in the world at that time.

Another thing to mention is that the desert of Mecca and its valleys were known to have the plant of balsam. This plant of Mecca – short tree of the desert – enjoyed special popularity in the Medieval Muslim world, and it was a source of resin.[1] Trading the balsam of Mecca started only after the rise of Islam in the beginning of the 7th century A.D.[2] Since the balsam tree is local to the area around Mecca, anyone living there at the time of Joseph would have found it available to them near home. Why go up to Gilead to get balsam? Why pay high prices for something they could get from the desert of Mecca without money? They went to Gilead because it was much closer to their home than the deserts of Mecca.

All this confirms the Biblical narration that the Ishmaelites lived where their father, Ishmael, had lived: in the Paran Desert, on the border of south Trans-Jordan. Because of the trade route between Palestine and Egypt, they were in contact with east and south Palestine from the north and with the Desert of Shur in the northwest. The strategic location of the Ishmaelites in Paran - between North Jordan and the trade route to Egypt - allowed them, as local merchants, to buy products from their neighbors and sell them to Egypt, their most important consumer at the time. To claim that Ishmael, and his sons and their descendants, lived in Mecca, built a temple there and dominated Arabia is not historical. Muslims should not hold tightly to what they have been taught. They should examine history for themselves. This will help them understand the revelation of God provided in the Bible so that they can know the truth which will lead them to salvation. It is not difficult to discover the right path, because the false path is littered with enormous historical mistakes, obvious to any honest and inquiring mind. The Bible, on the other hand, is proven to be a consistent and unerring historical document true to the ancient historical facts contained in it. The Bible is also proven to be the true word of God by accurately providing hundreds of prophecies about the coming of Christ, His death on the Cross for our sins, and His resurrection from the dead to reconcile us to God.

The Ishmaelites' Location at the Time of Moses

We continue our study of the Ishmaelites, who descended from Ishmael, the son of Abraham, by Hagar. We'll look at the lands they inhabited throughout history and, specifically, where they lived during Moses' time.

Moses was born around 1525 B.C. He spent 40 years in South Sinai near Mount Sinai, a region which was inhabited by the Midianites at that time. This was after he fled from Egypt when Pharaoh learned that he had killed an Egyptian who had murdered an Israelite. In the Sinai, he lived with Jethro, a Midian priest, and married one of his daughters. Moses became resident of that part of Sinai, pasturing the flocks of his father-in-law. This is before the Lord appeared to him and ordered him to return to Egypt to bring the Israelites out of Egypt. Not only did Moses live in Sinai at Midian for 40 years, but he spent another 40 years wandering in the Sinai desert before God allowed the Israelites to enter Canaan. The second 40 years was because of God's punishment for the generation of Israelites who saw the miracles God performed in Egypt, yet rebelled against Him when He told them to conquer the Promised Land.

Shortly after the Israelites left Egypt, God instructed Moses to send twelve spies into Canaan in preparation for conquering the land. When the spies returned with reports about how strong and tall the men in Canaan were, the Israelites were afraid. They did not have faith that God would provide, so they rebelled. They wanted to kill Moses and return to Egypt. That is why God was angry and swore that Moses' generation would not enter the Promised Land, but their children would. So he made them wander in the Sinai desert until the older generation perished in the desert.

Since Moses lived in Sinai for 80 years, the five books written by Moses under the inspiration of God, known as the Pentateuch, is a highly reliable source regarding the location of the Ishmaelites. In those 80 years, Moses had contact with the Midianites, and certainly with the Ishmaelites and Amalekites, the peoples that the books of the Pentateuch reveal to have inhabited Sinai at the time of Moses.

The Habitation of the Sinai by the Amalekites, Midianites and the Ishmaelites

The Amalekites, a tribe descended from Edom, were the descendants of Esau, Isaac's first child. The Edomites lived in the southern region of Trans-Jordan, but the Amalekites lived in the eastern part of Sinai in contact with Edom. The Midianites lived in the south around Mount Sinai, beside the Gulf of Aqaba, also called Elath. The Ishmaelites were nomads who occupied both the north and central parts of Sinai as far as the border with Palestine. The Ishmaelites were not militarily organized as were tribes like the Amalekites and the Midianites. Not until the time of Gideon were the Ishmaelites organized as a military force under an alliance led by the Midianites and Amalekites.

The Report of Moses (a Resident of Sinai for 80 Years) About the Location of the Ishmaelites in his Time

Moses, a resident of Sinai during these 80 years, is like a scholar who describes the main ethnic people living in his vicinity. Moses' words in the book of Genesis form an important document regarding the history of the Ishmaelites in ancient times. In Genesis 25:12-18, he describes how he observed the Ishmaelite tribes living:

> Now this is the genealogy of Ishmael, Abraham's son, whom Hagar the Egyptian, Sarah's maidservant, bore to Abraham. And these were the names of the sons of Ishmael, by their names, according to their generations: the first-born of Ishmael, Nabaioth, then Qedar, Adbeel, Mibsam, Mishma, Dumah, Massa, Hadar, Tema, Jetur, Naphish, and Kedemah.
>
> These were the sons of Ishmael and these were their names, by their towns and their settlements, twelve princes according to their nations. They dwelt from Havilah as far as Shur, which is east of Egypt as you go toward Assyria.

We understand from these verses that the offspring of Ishmael were already organized into twelve tribes at the time of Moses. Each tribe was ruled by a prince. Moses also defined the area where their settlements were located; that is, between Havilah and Shur. Moses wrote, "they dwelt from Havilah as far as Shur, which is east of Egypt as you go toward Assyria." We can identify in Sinai where those two locations were.

Locating the Area Referred to as "From Havilah as far as Shur" Which Moses Revealed as the Ishmaelites' Location in his Time

The phrase "from Havilah to Shur" is used in the Bible to designate the farthest distance across the northern part of Sinai. On the east is "Havilah," and on the west is "Shur." We encounter this terminology again in 1 Samuel 15:7, where the Bible records Saul's attack against the Amalekites (you may remember that Saul was the first king of Israel):

> Saul attacked the Amalekites, from Havilah all the way to Shur, which is east of Egypt.

The Amalekites were descended from Eliphaz, the first-born of Esau, the son of Isaac. This we read in Genesis 36:12:

> Now Timna was the concubine of Eliphaz, Esau's son, and she bore Amalek to Eliphaz.

In verse 16 of that passage, we find that three tribes came from Eliphaz. They were Korah, Gatam and Amalek. The Amalekites tribe originally dwelt with the rest of the Edomite tribes in southern Jordan, but later they migrated to the western part of Sinai and southern Palestine. The spies sent by Moses to scout out the Promised Land attested that Amalek lived with the Canaanites, who also dwelt in southern Palestine. We read about this in Numbers 13:29 and in Numbers 14:25.

Exodus 17:8 tells us that, during the migration of the Israelites through the Sinai desert, the Amalekites came and fought against them in the desert of Rephidim, which is located in southern Sinai. It appears that the Amalekites fought Israel there to prevent them from moving into the eastern part of Sinai and into southern Canaan. In the 12th century B.C., during the time of Gideon, the Amalekites formed an alliance with the Midianites, the Ishmaelites, and with "the people of the East," who were thought to be the tribes of Edom and others living east of Israel. They fought against Israel. In Judges 3:13, we find that the Amalekites also allied with Moab and Ammon against Israel, occupying the "city of palms," which is Jericho.

By about 1040 B.C., the time of King Saul of Israel, the Amalekites had extended their residency into western Sinai, reaching the Shur desert at the border with Egypt. Saul asked the Kenites to "depart from among the Amalekites, lest I destroy you with them." Jethro, the priest of Midian, whose daughter Moses took for his wife, was from the tribe of the Kenites.

The Kenites accompanied the Israelites in their journey to Jericho and settled between southern Palestine and the mountains of Sinai. The tribe of Amalek still lived in northeastern Sinai, south of Judah, which is the same place where they lived at the time of Moses. The Amalekites also penetrated into northern Sinai and toward the west. We read, "And Saul attacked the Amalekites from Havilah all the way to Shur, which is east of Egypt." This is the same area where the Ishmaelites lived at the time of Moses. It is clear that Havilah is the farthest place east in the Sinai. Saul had destroyed the people of Amalek; then David had attacked the remainder of the tribe when he attacked other people in the same area.

The Amalekites, after David's reign, were no longer an organized tribe, nor were they mentioned again in the Bible. With the tribe's destruction, the people living in Sinai absorbed the few survivors. Yet, Islamic tradition would have the Amalekites inhabiting Mecca from ancient times. We know that this Islamic claim is unhistorical because the Amalekites were known as local people of northeastern Sinai before their extinction around the 10th century B.C.

We have just examined the eastern border of the Ishmaelites, which is Havilah. Havilah was located on the border of eastern Sinai and southern Jordan.

Shur, the Northwestern Part of the Sinai

Now we turn our attention to their western border, which is Shur. Shur was the most northwestern part of Sinai. In fact, when Moses brought the Israelites out of Egypt, they departed from the region of Goshen, a fertile area situated in northern Egypt between the old Egyptian cities of Raamses and Heliopolis. Moses brought the Israelites to the Red Sea, which God parted, and the Israelites passed through unhindered. Then they came to the Shur desert. We read in Exodus 15:22,

> So Moses brought Israel from the Red Sea; then they went out into the Wilderness of Shur:

We see that the southern part of the Shur desert extended from the border of Sinai with Egypt to the beginning of the Gulf of

Suez. The northern part of Shur reached close to the part of the Sinai near the Mediterranean.

At the time of Moses, the Ishmaelites inhabited the northern and central parts of the Sinai. How, then, can Islam claim that they lived in Mecca since the time of Ishmael?

From this we can conclude that in the 16th and 15th centuries B.C., at the time of Moses, the Ishmaelites inhabited the northern and central parts of Sinai. They continued to live in the desert of Paran where Ishmael lived, and they extended their domain further to the east, toward Havilah at the border with south Jordan. This included the northern part of Sinai called the Desert of Zin. In the west they extended their domain to the Desert of Shur until they reached the border of Sinai with Egypt. It is clear that, for 400 hundred years after the death of Ishmael, his descendants continued to live in the same place. They lived in Sinai and extended around Paran, which is in the same area of Sinai. How, then, could Ishmael and his sons be living in Mecca? How could they build a temple there and establish a monotheistic religion in Arabia?

The Bible, the most reliable resource for ancient history, shows them living in the Sinai. It's absurd to teach that Ishmael and his descendants were the founders of a religion in Arabia designed around a city that wasn't even built until the 4th century A.D. This ignores the true history of the Ishmaelites and their true dwelling place throughout ancient history in the northern and central Sinai.

What would cause people to believe such a lie? Muslims believe it, in part, because of the writings of people like Ibn Ishak, who lived in the 8th century A.D. He invented a new history to fit the narration of Mohammed in the Qur'an. Though Ibn Ishak was considered, even by Islamic scholars of his time, to be inventing forgery and unhistorical stories without foundation, he has attracted many followers. By examining history and the Bible, we see that such claims are accepted only by individuals who fail to study the true, documented history, and instead rely on writings of Ibn Ishak.

The Ishmaelites in the 12th Century B.C. Still Lived in the Sinai

In the 12th century B.C., the Midianites became the dominant and leading power in the Sinai when the tribes of the Sinai region united. The north was populated by Ishmaelites, and the south was populated by Midianites. The union was so strong that all the tribes in the region were simply referred to as Midianites.

We see this generalization in Judges, chapters 6 through 8, where the Bible describes the inhabitants of Sinai in 1162 B.C. as resisting Israel for seven years. Judges 6:1-3 says:

> The hand of Midian prevailed against Israel. Because of the Midianites, the children of Israel made for themselves the dens, the caves, and the strongholds, which are in the mountains.

Judges 8:24 calls this same people group Ishmaelites. The resistance ended when the Midianites-Ishmaelites were defeated in a final battle, in which Gideon led the Israelites against them around 1169 B.C.

At the end of the 11th century B.C., the Ishmaelites were still living in the area surrounding Palestine, mainly in the Sinai. Two tribes, Jetur and Naphish, moved north toward Gilead.

We find the Ishmaelites mentioned again in Psalm 83, a psalm of Asaph. Asaph, son of Berachiah, was considered one of the leaders in David's choir, according to 1 Chronicles 6:39. David reigned from 1004-971 B.C. In Psalm 83:5-8, we learn that a confederacy formed against Israel. The psalm reads:

> They formed a confederacy against you: the tents of Edom and the Ishmaelites; Moab and the Hagrites; Gebal, Ammon, and Amalek; Philistia with the inhabitants of Tyre. Assyria also has joined with them. They have helped the children of Lot.

Here we find the Ishmaelites forming alliances with nations and tribes such as Edom, Moab, Ammon, Philistia, Amalek, Tyre and the Hagrites, nations which were known to surround Israel.

The Hagrites were a group of people descended from the relatives of Hagar, the Egyptian mother of Ishmael. Because of kinship with the Ishmaelites, the Hagrites lived with them in Sinai before moving east toward Gilead. We read in I Chronicles 5:10 that at the time of Saul, the first king of Israel, the Israelite tribe of Reuben made war with the Hagrites. The Bible says, "they dwelt in their tents throughout the entire area east of Gilead." The Hagrites lived in tents, were nomadic, and pastured flocks like the Ishmaelites. Two Ishmaelite tribes, Jetur and Naphish, also traveled with the Hagrites to Gilead and were defeated by the Reubenites, according to I Chronicles 5:19.

Assyria wanted influence in the region, and it later succeeded under Adad-Nirari II, who reigned from 911-891 B.C. Adad-Nirari II was responsible for the conquest of Babylonia, Anatolia, and the Syrian plain. This involvement among the people surrounding Israel meant that the Ishmaelites continued to live in Sinai, partially in Trans-Jordan - especially in Gilead toward the last half of the 11th century B.C. During the last half of the 11th century B.C., the Ishmaelites continued to be seen as one united group. Later, however, the different Ishmaelite tribes became independent from each other, and many of them spread from Sinai to the surrounding regions, as we'll discuss later.

During his reign, King David subjugated the Ishmaelites. David was a strong king who dominated southern Palestine and made constant raids into northern and central Sinai. He conquered all the area tribes, including Amalek. David then used the Ishmaelites in his service, especially using their camels in his army. In IChronicles 27:30 we read that "David placed Obil, the Ishmaelite, over the camels." This suggests that David employed cavalry mounted on camels, and these troops were Ishmaelites who were experts in using the camels. This use of the Ishmaelites was even at the point where David places Ishmaelite leader, Obil, over these cavalry.

The camel was an effective military aid, especially in the desert, since a camel can walk 62 miles before requiring more water. I Chronicles 27:31 tells us that David also employed the Hagrites to pasture his flocks, and appointed Jaziz, the Hagrite, over them. This fact shows that David subjugated the inhabitants of the north and central Sinai, who were mainly Ishmaelites and Hagrites. It also shows that, in David's time, most of the Ishmaelites were still living in the Sinai.

After David subjugated the Ishmaelites, there were close ties between them and the Israelites. The Ishmaelites continued to live in southern Palestine, northern Sinai, and parts of Trans-Jordan. These close ties can be seen in the marriages which took place between the Israelites and Ishmaelites. The sister of David married an Ishmaelite. We read about the marriage of Abigail, the daughter of Jesse (who was the father of David) in I Chronicles 2:17. Abigail gave birth to Amasa, "and the father of Amasa was Jether, the Ishmaelite."

THE ISHMAELITES AFTER THE 10TH CENTURY B.C.

The Ishmaelites are not mentioned in the Bible as a coherent group, or a united nation, after the 10th century B.C. This is because some of the Ishmaelite tribes migrated from their homeland in Sinai. Some of their tribes, like Adbeel, did remain in Sinai, as attested by Assyrian inscriptions. Others mingled with the Midianites and the other populations of Sinai. Some tribes did move to other areas in search of better pasturing fields for their flocks. By the 10th century B.C., there was little connection between the various Ishmaelite tribes.

Ethnic changes took place in some tribes because of their contact with non-Ishmaelites. The intermingling reached a point where some tribes were completely integrated into the tribes which invaded their settlements. This is particularly true for the two tribes which went to live in Qedar and Teima in northern Arabia. These regions were dominated by Arabian tribes, so Arabian culture and ethnicity prevailed.

I would like us to look briefly at the Ishmaelite tribes after the 10th century B.C. In I Chronicles 5:19, we already saw that Jetur and Naphish lived in east Gilead, north of Trans-Jordan, at the time of King Saul. The Biblical text shows that they lived in tents and followed a Bedouin lifestyle. They moved to the vicinity of Gilead from their original homeland in Sinai because of Gilead's fertile grassy fields and hills, which provided good pasture for their flocks. No mention of the remaining Ishmaelite tribes is found in external evidence or on inscriptions before the 9th century B.C. We can only conclude that the remaining tribes emigrated from Sinai after the 9th century B.C., except for Qedar and, perhaps, Teima. We assume that those tribes emigrated from Sinai around the the end of the 11th century B.C., or at the beginning of the 10th century B.C.

The Tribe of Qedar After its Emigration From the Sinai

The first reference to Qedar in the Bible as a place independent from the other Ishmaelites is in the Song of Solomon (written around 940 B.C.). Song of Solomon 1:5 mentions "tents of Qedar," showing that the tribe and their tents were well known to the author of the book. There is no mention in the Bible of Qedar as an actual city before the time of the prophet Isaiah, who began to prophesy in the year 739 B.C. We have records about Qedar in the Assyrian inscriptions dated 738 B.C., the same time that the prophet Isaiah started to prophesy. We can read about Qedar on a stele, or monument, belonging to King Tiglath-Pileser III, which was found in Iran. It records a list of people whom Tiglath Pileser III supplanted.[3] The list mentions "Aribi" as distinguished from "Qidri," meaning the Qedarites. This indicates that, during the 8th century B.C., the Qedarites had not yet mingled with Arabs and, consequently, their city or settlements had not yet been invaded by Arabs.

It was not until the time of Sargon II, who reigned from 721-705 B.C., that we have evidence of the first extensive and conspicuous penetration of Arabian tribes into the regions of Qedar and Teima. This signaled the beginning of Arabic ethnicity, replacing Ishmaelite ethnicity, a process which other tribes and nations in the Fertile Crescent were to become subjected to in the Middle East.

The Tribe of Nabaioth After its Emigration From the Sinai, as Attested by Biblical References and Assyrian Inscriptions

As we continue, let us look at the tribe of Nabaioth, which came from Ishmael's first-born son. This tribe moved to southern Jordan and was known for providing Israel with sheep. This fact is alluded to in Isaiah 60:7 where the Bible says: "All the flocks of Qedar shall be gathered together unto thee. The rams of Nabaioth shall minister unto thee."

Through an Assyrian Inscription called ABL 260, which is dated around the middle of the 7th century B.C., Nabaioth is recorded as living on the western border of Babylon, close to where the tribe of Massa lived. King Natnu of Nabaioth and his people were found in the northeastern part of Palmyrena at the time of Assurbanipal. Palmyrena is located in south central Syria about 140 miles from Damascus, toward the desert.[4] These various locations in which the tribe was found indicate that the tribe had a nomadic lifestyle, moving from place to place, seeking refuge in many desert places. They were attested to in the Assyrian inscriptions as attacking the border of the Assyrians, along with other tribes. This is in addition to the need to move to new places where they pastured their flocks.

History shows that Nabaioth was a tribe which roamed the deserts of the Fertile Crescent. This does not allow for someone to claim that a connection existed between them and the Yemeni family of Mohammed. Furthermore, the tribe did not have a spiritual heritage upon which Mohammed could build a monotheistic religion.

Islamic tradition, unaware of the history of the tribe of Nabaioth, wanted to connect Mohammed with Ishmael. They chose to make this connection through Ishmael's first-born son, Nabaioth, and his descendants. They say Nabaioth lived most of the time at Mecca, then moved to Yemen, and then returned to Mecca, dominating the Ishmaelite tribes which, according to Islamic claims, were living at Mecca.

300

It is a violation of history to connect the Nabaioth tribe with the family of Mohammed, for Mohammed's family actually came from Ma'rib, the capital of the Sabaeans in Yemen. As we have seen through the Bible and the Assyrian inscriptions, the tribe of Nabaioth lived in Sinai with the rest of the Ishmaelites for centuries before it wandered in the deserts of Syro-Mesopotamia and Trans-Jordan. Because the Qur'an made serious mistakes when it claimed that Ishmael lived at Mecca and built the temple there, Islamic tradition had to fabricate stories to support the Qur'an. Any person who studies history, and the Assyrian inscriptions and chronicles, is aware of the absurdity of such claims.

The nomadic Ishmaelite tribe of Nabaioth was never known as a tribe which claimed prophecy that someone in a later time, like Mohammed, would build a monotheistic religion on them. Further, no prophet or religious leader was known to have come from the tribe of Nabaioth, nor was it known to have any religious heritage to transmit to consequent generations. It would have been less embarrassing for Muslims if Mohammed would have chosen to direct his religious allegations to any other ancient nation of the Middle East, but he chose these poor nomads who were roaming on the Sinai deserts.

Muslims need to return to the true foundation of monotheism in history, as it is shown in the Bible, and documented through the prophets of Israel. The true prophets of Israel told about the true Savior of the world, Jesus Christ. They prophesied about His incarnation, His death on the Cross for the salvation of mankind from sin, His resurrection from the dead, and the abundant spiritual life He bestows to all who believe in Him and accept Him as personal Savior. Our Muslim friends need to understand the enormous historical mistakes of the Qur'an, and the Islamic tradition, so that they won't be driven away from the truth of eternal life through Jesus Christ.

Finding the Location of the Tribe of Adbeel in Western Sinai and the Various Locations of the Tribe of Massa in the Fertile Crescent

We will now look at the Ishmaelite tribe of Massa. The tribe of Massa originated in the Sinai, but later migrated out of the Sinai and became an independent tribe.

The first mention of Massa in the Bible as an independent tribe is found in the book of Proverbs. Chapter 31, verse 1, mentions the name of King Lemuel whom, I believe, was a tribal chief in Massa. In that time period, tribal chiefs were often called kings. We see this custom in the book of Judges where three chiefs in Midian tribes were engaged in battle with Gideon, and the Bible refers to them as kings.

In addition to the verse from Proverbs, Assyrian inscriptions also tell us about Massa, but we only find them mentioned after the 9th century B.C., suggesting that they migrated out of the Sinai some time after the 9th century B.C. Other documents tell us that the tribe of Massa lived in many places in the deserts of Sinai and Syro-Mesopotamia. Tiglath-Pileser III, King of Assyria, mentioned in his Inscriptions that he subdued the tribes of Adbeel and Massa, along with others, and received tribute from them. His campaign was around 738 B.C. He described their location in these words:

> On the border of the western lands, or the countries of the setting sun, of whom no one of my predecessors knew and whose place is remote. I appointed Idibi'ilu for the wardenship of the entrance to Egypt.

Tiglath-Pileser's quotation refers to the western Sinai, west of Assyria, as the place which none of his predecessors had occupied. "Idiba'il," or "Idibi'ilu" in Akkadian, the language the inscription was written in, is Adbeel.[5] The appointment of the tribe of Adbeel as "the warden of the entrance to Egypt" indicates that this Ishmaelite tribe lived in Sinai, on the western part of the Shur desert, on the border with Egypt. The fact that Massa was subdued, along with other Sinai tribes, leads us to assume that

Massa was a nomadic tribe which maintained contact with the Sinai into the second half of the 8th century B.C. Massa may have lived with the tribe of Adbeel in Sinai during the attack of Tiglath Pileser III on that region.

The Nimrud Letters, which were written during the third part of the 8th century B.C., also contain important documentation regarding the location of the tribe of Massa. A letter was specifically sent by an individual named Belliqbi to the King of Assyria.[6] By studying the locations he mentioned in his letter, scholars have concluded that Belliqbi was to monitor certain areas in the Valley of Lebanon between the cities of Damascus and Lebanon. Belliqbi had appointed people to oversee road stations in those areas. Among the overseers he appointed, according to the letter, was "The son of Asapi who had been taken to the land of Massa."[7] We conclude that the land of Massa existed in south and central Syria at the time this letter was delivered.

The Harper Letters, specifically ABL 260, contain a letter sent to the King of Assyria by a certain individual called Nabu'-sum-lisir. It tells about a man called Aakaba/maru, son of Amme'ta of Massa, who attacked a caravan which left the territory of the Nabayateans. This is, perhaps, a reference to a tribal chief from Massa. The report goes on to say that only one person escaped and reached a fortified settlement of the Assyrians.[8] The same letters show that Nabu'-sum-lisir served in Assurbanipal's time along the southwestern border of Babylonia close to many nomadic groups. Scholars pinpoint the tribe of Massa, and its leader, Aakaba/maru, in this region.[9] So we can conclude that, during the reign of Assurbanipal, which was from 668-627 B.C., the tribe of Massa lived in the desert of Mesopotamia on the border of Babylonia.

The many documented locations of the tribe of Massa indicates its nomadic lifestyle. The tribe roamed in the Syro-Mesopotamian and Sinai deserts, searching for grazing land for its flocks, just as the other Ishmaelite tribes did.

The Tribe of Teima

Teima is another Ishmaelite tribe which migrated out of the Sinai. In the Bible, the first mention of Teima as a city is in the book of Isaiah around the end of the 8th century B.C. The first mention of Teima in Assyrian records is found in the Inscriptions of Tiglath-Pileser III, who reigned from 744-727 B.C., suggesting that the tribe of Teima may have emigrated out of the Sinai around the 10th or 9th century B.C. It appears that the tribe roamed in the desert south of Trans-Jordan, and eventually traveled about 180 miles into the area of northern Arabia, bordering south Jordan, to where the oasis of Teima is located. The region then experienced a large immigration of Arabian tribes. One of the tribes which appeared in the region of Teima, and other northern Arabian regions, was Thamud. Around the end of the 8th century B.C., Thamud attacked the border of the Assyrian empire.

This immigration and dominance of the Arabian tribes in the area where Teima settled transformed Teima's ethnicity until it became known as Arabic. The extensive Thamud inscriptions at Teima confirm this.

The Tribe of Dumah and its Emigration to the Oasis Between Mesopotamia and Southern Jordan

Dumah is another tribe which emigrated from the Sinai. It traveled into southern Trans-Jordan, and from there went to the desert between South Jordan and Mesopotamia on the border with northern Arabia. There, the tribe of Dumah established a settlement in an oasis, which is the first major oasis to be encountered by anyone coming east from Edom.[10]

The first time Dumah is mentioned in the Bible is in Isaiah 21:11. Here we find an oracle against Edom, including Dumah. Isaiah tells us that Dumah is connected with Edom – specifically South Jordan. Later in Isaiah 42:11, Qedar is mentioned with Sila, the Edomite city. Geographical and historical ties connect these Ishmaelite tribes and Edom. The tribes which left the Sinai around the 10th century B.C. seem to have spent time in the land of Edom, in southern Jordan, during their migration to the oases of the desert.

Dumah, on the border of northern Arabia, was on the migration path for Arabian tribes since the 8th century B.C. By this time, like the tribe of Teima, the ethnicity of the city became substantially Arabian. From Assyrian inscriptions, the city was known to be a religious center for various tribes in the Syro-Arabian desert. Even Edomites were consulting the shrines of Dumah.[11] Later, with Arabian penetration in the area, Dumah became an important religious center for Arabian tribes. This fact is documented in Assyrian inscriptions, which I discussed previously.

The Religious Center for the Ishmaelite Tribes was Beer-Lahai-roi in the Sinai, and not in Mecca

At the same time, Ishmaelite tribes had their religious center in Beer-Lahai-roi, which was between the Wilderness of Paran and the Wilderness of Zin in northern Sinai.[12] Beer-Lahai-roi is identified with a place in the northern Sinai called Ain Isaac, also known as Ain Muwileh. It was southwest of the city of Beersheba, about thirteen miles from Kadesh-Barnea. We are told in Genesis 24:62 that Isaac lived there when Rebecca arrived from Mesopotamia to be his wife.

Because Ishmaelite tribes were known to have their religious center in Beer-Lahai-roi in Sinai, it is further proof that these tribes lived in Sinai. We see that Ishmaelite tribes used to make pilgrimages to this place, very near Paran, which was where their father, Ishmael, lived all his life. They continued to live there, and from there they migrated into the western part of Sinai. Then they went to the wilderness of southern Jordan. Finally, some of them migrated still further to the Syrian-Mesopotamian and Arabian-Mesopotamian deserts, and to the north toward Gilead and south-central Syria. What all this means for us today is that Mecca was not the religious city of the Ishmaelite tribes, as Islamic tradition claims. Ishmaelite tribes never migrated as far away as Mecca.

The Assyrian inscriptions confirm perfectly the Biblical narration about the Ishmaelites' location in the Sinai and their projection into the surrounding deserts of the Fertile Crescent.

Previously, we mentioned that the Ishmaelite tribe, Adbeel, is documented in several inscriptions of Tiglath-Pileser III as being appointed the warden on the Egyptian border. This means that at the time of Tiglath-Pileser III, around 738 B.C., the tribe of Adbeel was in the western part of the Sinai, on the border of Egypt known as the Wilderness of Shur. It appears that the tribe was strong enough for the Assyrians to trust as the guard of its border with the kingdom of Egypt. Other Ishmaelite tribes, such as Mishma, Mibsam, Hadad and Kedemah, either seem to have been absorbed by the Adbeel tribe, or by another population in the Sinai, such as the Midianites. We saw previously that, even in the time of Gideon, there was unity among the main populations of the Sinai.

By examining the inscriptions of the Assyrians, we conclude that the original homeland of the Ishmaelites was Sinai. Their inscriptions show that Ishmaelite tribes, such as the tribe of Adbeel, inhabited Sinai as far as the Wilderness of Shur, which is the western border with Egypt. This confirms the Bible's claim that, at the time of Moses, the Ishmaelites lived between Havilah and Shur. Furthermore, we see that the migration of the other Ishmaelite tribes was toward the east and north of the Sinai, in harmony with the Biblical narration stating that the homeland of the Ishmaelites was in the Sinai during the whole 2nd millennium B.C. The migrations toward southern Jordan and Gilead (in northern Trans-Jordan) began near the end of the 2nd millennium B.C.

The Qur'an, and Islamic tradition, blatantly attempt to change the homelands of nations when they claim that the Ishmaelites moved to Mecca several centuries before Mecca was even built.

Islamic tradition blatantly contradicts the documented evidence by claiming that the Ishmaelites lived in Mecca and dominated all of Arabia from there. Islamic tradition also claims that the

Ishmaelites later migrated to Yemen, and then back to Mecca. All of these fabrications were created to attempt to connect Mohammed's Sabaean family, who lived in Yemen, with the descendants of Ishmael. It's as though we were trying to make Turkey the homeland of the old Egyptians, and claiming that they built their pyramids there, and that they reigned from there. One can't play these games with history, as the Qur'an, and Islamic traditions, do. They blatantly attempt to change the homelands of nations when they move the Ishmaelites to Mecca several centuries before Mecca was even built. If our Muslim friends are not aware of this serious mistake, they could be eternally misled.

2 _____

A DISCUSSION OF THE CLAIMS THAT THE ARABS WERE DESCENDANTS OF ISHMAEL, AND THAT ISHMAEL WAS THE FOUNDATION FOR A MONOTHEISTIC FAITH.

The Arabian Penetration into the Oases of Qedar, Teima and Dumah

We already saw that Ishmaelite tribes lived in Sinai until the 10th century B.C. As we saw from the Assyrian inscriptions, part of the Ishmaelites who were living as nomads searched for grazing lands in the deserts of the Fertile Crescent. The tribes of Qedar and Teima penetrated about 180 miles into north Arabia. They were the only tribes which moved that far into Arabia. The Dumah settled in an oasis on the border of Mesopotamia and Arabia in a place named after them.

Old Assyrian inscriptions distinguish the tribe of the Qedarites from the Arabs. We find the Qedarites and the Arabs listed separately in the annals of Tiglath-Pileser III, which were written around the year 738 B.C.[13] This suggests that, in that period, Qedar continued to maintain its Ishmaelite ethnicity separate from that of the Arabs. The Arabs either migrated into, or invaded the territory around, Teima and Qedar near the end of the 8th century B.C. The migration of Arabian tribes eventually reached as far as the eastern part of the lands which Babylonia controlled. In the second half of the 8th century B.C., in eastern Babylonian lands, there are attested Arab walled towns with Arab names.[14]

I doubt that the Ishmaelites, themselves, constructed the cities of Qedar, Teima and Dumah. Although these three tribes were the first to live near these oases, later the area became heavily populated by Arabian tribes. The Arab migration and invasion was due in part because the oases were located on the land routes between Mesopotamia, Arabia and Syria.

From the Inscriptions of Tiglath-Pileser III and Sargon II, we know that the regions around Teima, Qedar and Dumah were extensively populated by several different Arabian tribes, such as the Badanaa, Hattiaya, Marsimani, Isaamme and Thamuds. Extensive Thamud inscriptions indicate that the population of the oases became Arab, and took the names of the three Ishmaelite tribes. The ethnicity of the Ishmaelites was either absorbed by the invaders, or more probably, the Ishmaelites were expelled to the southern Jordanian, Mesopotamian and Sinai deserts. In other words, the Ishmaelites were expelled back to where they had originally lived as nomads before migrating into northern Arabia. Thus, we can't find semblances of Ishmaelite ethnicity in either the two northern Arabian oases or in Dumah, the city built on an oasis between Arabia and Mesopotamia.

Another fact that supports the idea that Arabs preserved the Ishmaelite tribe names, is that it is doubtful that these three Ishmaelite tribes had ever constructed cities in the oases. The Ishmaelite tribes were nomadic by nature, and had been roaming the Sinai desert since before the 10th century B.C. Even after some of them migrated from the Sinai to other deserts along the Fertile Crescent, they continued to retain their nomadic lifestyle. They wandered in the deserts of southern Jordan and Syro-Mesopotamia. For example, Nabaioth's tribe, Massa, was one of many tribes which came out of Sinai. We assume that Qedar, Teima and Dumah did the same, even though they were known to dwell around these oases after the 10th century B.C. They gave their names to the oases in later times, but they, themselves, continued to roam the other deserts of the Fertile Crescent, just like the other tribes.

The Bible Never Refers to the Ishmaelites as Arabs

The Bible never refers to the Ishmaelites as Arabs. They were not considered Arabs, just as other nations from the progeny of Abraham, like the nation of Edom, were not considered Arabs. Edom descended from the offspring of Esau, the elder son of

Isaac, who was the son of Abraham. In the same manner, the offspring of Lot, the nephew of Abraham, were not considered Arabs. Lot's descendants became the nations of Ammon and Moab in Trans-Jordan.

The continuing penetration of Arabian tribes into the southern part of the Fertile Crescent. The assimilation and extinction of the original peoples of the area, such as Moabites, Ammonites and Ishmaelites.

The Fertile Crescent, however, experienced radical changes in its populations and ethnicity. These changes began to appear before the Chaldeans controlled the region. After Nebuchadnezzar occupied southern Jordan and southern Palestine, there was a total change in the structure of the populations of the region. We find, for example, that Moab and Edom were no longer mentioned as sovereign political entities. We also find an increase in the penetration of Arabian tribes into these regions, and a corresponding increase in their ability to intermingle with the original population.[15] The same thing happened to the Ammonites. The book of Ezekiel prophesied that the land of the Ammonites would become desolate, deprived of its original inhabitants. Ezekiel 25:4, 5 says:

> Indeed, therefore, I will deliver you as a possession to the men of the East and they shall set their encampments among you and make their dwellings among you. I will make Rabbah a stable for camels and Ammon a resting place for the flocks.

This prophesy was fulfilled after the year 586 B.C., when Nebuchadnezzar occupied Ammon, Moab and Edom. Consequently, at that time, many Arabian tribes came to live in Trans-Jordan. By the 5th and 4th centuries B.C., its inhabitants included the sedentary state of Edom and several nomadic Arab tribes.[16]

A Change of Ethnicity Also Occurred in the Sinai

Ethnicity changes also occurred in the Sinai where the Ishmaelites, Amalekites and Midianites were living. During the 5th and 4th centuries B.C., the Edomites, along with other Arabian tribes, penetrated into southern Palestine and into the Negev, and completely changed the ethnic picture of that region.[17] Therefore, the Ishmaelites suffered like the Ammonites, Moabites and the other original inhabitants of the region, because of the penetration phenomenon.

The Ishmaelites were absorbed by other tribes, not only in the Sinai, but also in other deserts, such as Syro-Mesopotamia. Therefore, we conclude that the Ishmaelites became extinct, like other ancient peoples of the Fertile Crescent, such as the Ammonites, the Moabites, and the Philistines. They were simply absorbed by the wave of new ethnic populations which came to inhabit their lands. None of the people who originally lived in the Fertile Crescent, including the Ishmaelites, were Arabs.

The penetration of other populations continued in the Fertile Crescent. People, both from Arabia and outside Arabia, came to live in that region. One example is the tribe of Ghassan, which came from Yemen to live in southern Syria. Later, they became the dominant ethnic group in southern Syria, defending their border with the Byzantine Empire against attack from the Persians, who lived in Mesopotamia. The Lakhmids, another Yemeni tribe, immigrated to Mesopotamia and established themselves in the city of Hira on Mesopotamia's southwestern border. In the 3rd century A.D., the Lakhmids, then under the control of the Persians, were responsible for guarding the border against the Byzantine Empire. Another example of ethnic penetration is the Nabataeans who, since the 5th or 4th century B.C., dominated southern Jordan, and extended their domain toward the Mesopotamian desert, southern Syria and southern Palestine.

There is no Mention of any Ishmaelite Tribe in the Bible After the 7th Century B.C.

Activities of the Ishmaelite tribes were reported in the 8th and 7th centuries B.C., when Assyria controlled the Fertile Crescent. The Bible talks about them during the same period, but there is no further mention of any Ishmaelite tribe after the 6th century B.C., either in the Bible, or in the inscriptions of any other nation. This leads us to believe that they were absorbed into the other tribes which came to live in the Sinai and Syro-Mesopotamian deserts.

The 92 Nations and Tribes in Arabia Reported by Pliny in the 1st Century A.D. as the Origin of the Tribes Which Penetrated or Invaded the Middle East in Later Times.

To say that the Arabs are descendants of Ishmael is an unhistorical assertion. The historian, Pliny, in his work *Natural History*, written during the 1st century A.D., reported that there were 92 separate nations and tribes in Arabia. In subsequent centuries, they became part of what is now known as the Arab nations. Many of these tribes penetrated into the Fertile Crescent before the Islamic conquest of the Middle East. After Islam's conquest, most of the Middle Eastern nations were "Arabized," losing their own original ethnic values and languages, and assuming Arab values and the language of the Qur'an, which is in the Arabic language. Egypt, which was not an Arab nation, became "Arabized" after the Islamic conquest of Egypt. The same can be said for North Africa, Lebanon, Northern Syria, Sudan and Mesopotamia.

The Ishmaelites were nomads in the Sinai and part of the Syro-Mesopotamian desert. They became integrated into other nomadic tribes before the 6th century B.C. So, where are the descendants of the Ishmaelites with respect to the Arab nations and other nations of the Middle East that were "Arabized?" If we are to make a true analysis, we must say today that the Bedouins of the Sinai and Syro-Mesopotamian deserts may have a small mixture of Ishmaelite blood, along with that of hundreds of other nomadic tribes which were absorbed through history.

The extinct Ishmaelite tribes cannot be claimed as ancestors of the Arabs. Also, the Yemeni family of Mohammed cannot be connected with the Nabaioth tribe, a tribe which roamed the deserts of the Fertile Crescent and became extinct in the 7th century B.C.

Certainly, this doesn't support the claim that Arab nations were descendants of extinct Ishmaelite tribes. Neither can we say that ancient Arabian nations, such as Saba, which contained the family of Mohammed, were descendants of the nomadic tribes we've been talking about. As we saw in an earlier study, Saba was originally a Cushite tribe which descended from Raamah, son of Cush, son of Ham.

Assyrian records show that the tribe of Nabaioth roamed the deserts of Syro-Mesopotamian and southern Jordan until they became extinct after the 7th century B.C. We see how ridiculous it is for Islamic tradition to claim that Mohammed is descended from the ancient nomadic Ishmaelite tribe of Nabaioth. This claim not only lacks historical evidence, but it actually contradicts historical evidence.

The Arabs are one nation among many who claim to date back to Abraham, either through Ishmael or Isaac. But many of the claims are unfounded.

Previously, we saw that the Ishmaelites began as nomads living in the Sinai. Later, some of them migrated from the Sinai to the Syro-Mesopotamian desert. Like other nations in the region, such as Ammon, Moab and Philistia, eventually the Ishmaelites became extinct in about the 7th century B.C. We also saw that today's Arab nations descended from 92 ancient Arabian nations and tribes mentioned by Pliny in his work, which was written in 77 A.D. Other nations were "Arabized" with the conquest of the Middle East by the Muslims during, and after, the 7th century A.D., but the Ishmaelites had become extinct 14 centuries before this Arabization process began. Therefore, as we concluded

313

previously, the Muslim claim that Arab nations were descendants of Ishmael is unhistorical, and without any factual basis.

The names of Abraham and Ishmael never appeared in Arabia before the introduction of Judaism and Christianity to the Arabian tribes.

But, there is more to consider. The Israelites are the offspring of Abraham, a fact attested to in every Israelite generation. You will find the names of Abraham and his sons expressed clearly in Hebrew literature in each and every era. The fact that Abraham was the father of the Hebrews has influenced the spiritual, cultural and sociological life of the Israelites throughout history, causing them to follow in the faith of Abraham.

Within the Arab history there is no mention of Abraham – even in the Jahiliyah period, the time period prior to Islam's appearance in Arabia. The use of Biblical names among the Arabs occurred because many Arabic tribes embraced Judaism or Christianity. However, al-Kalbi, an ancient famous historian, mentioned two names, which were derived from the name of Abraham. He wrote:

> Ibrahim (that is Abraham), grandfather of Adi, son of Zayed, son of Hamad, son of Zayed, son of Ayuob (that is Job) from the sons of Emrea' al-kais (who is a famous Christian Arabian poet), son of Zayed Manat, son of Tamim. The other was Mukatil, son of Hassan, son of Thaalabeh, son of Aus, son of Ibrahim (that is Abraham), son of Ayuob. Ibn al-Kalbi said, "I don't know in the Jahiliyah period any other person from the Arabs, other than these two who called themselves with such Biblical names. And these two were called so because they were Christians."[18]

When we study the period before Judaism and Christianity penetrated Arabia, we do not find any Biblical names, including Abraham and Ishmael, in any Arabian inscriptions. Historically, the ancient names of a nation's founding fathers, and other great national figures, are always recorded and repeatedly mentioned as their stories pass from generation to generation. Thus, it would be most unusual if the Arabs were actually descendants of Abraham through Ishmael, and failed to ever mention them. For example, we see the name, Israel, which God gave to Jacob, the father of the Israelites. We see his name mentioned in Hebrew literature down through the generations. The Israelites also mention Ishmael, who is not the father of the Israelites, many places in their history. The names of Abraham, Isaac and Jacob are common names attesting to the lineage of the Israelites.

When we consider other people, such as those in Mesopotamia, we find the important figures in their history are listed by each succeeding generation. For example, in Genesis 10:8-11, we learn that Nimrod is the father of the Babylonians and the Assyrians. Nimrod is common to both Assyrian and Babylonian literature. Many people, and even locations, were named after Nimrod. The ancient capital of the Assyrians was called Nimrod. This attests to the fact that the important figures, such as the father of a nation, can't be forgotten by the following generations in those nations.

In contrast to this, we find that Arabian inscriptions never mention Abraham or Ishmael. Instead, they record the names of men and deities of a separate and distinct Arabian culture. How could Ishmael be the father of the Arabs when we don't find his name mentioned in any of the old Arabian inscriptions? The answer is simple: Ishmael could not be the father of the Arabs.

Many people in other nations claimed to be descendants of Abraham. Many Arabians also believed that the Romans and Greeks descended from Abraham.

Here's another fact to consider: At the time of Mohammed, it was customary for many people groups in many nations to claim to be descendants of Abraham. Al-Masudi, an Arab historian of the 9th century A.D., says that there were groups of Greeks who claimed that they were the descendants of Abraham through his son Isaac. Al-Masudi wrote, "the Greeks, like the Romans, were descendants of Isaac."[19] The Romans are mentioned because some Arabs claimed that the father of the Romans was a man named Rum, and they created a lineage dating back to Isaac, son of Abraham.

The Arabs also supported this claim that the Greeks were descendants of Isaac. In fact, the Arabs constructed a genealogy for Alexander the Great, which made him a descendant of Isaac, the son of Abraham.[20] The idea of the Greeks coming from Isaac was also prevalent at the time of Mohammed. It was not only supported by al-Masudi, but by the famous Arabic Muslim historian, al-Tabari, who was born in 844 A.D. Al-Tabari embraced the idea, which was spread among the Arabs, that Alexander the Great was descended from the offspring of Isaac. Al-Tabari also claimed that Alexander had reached beyond the places where, according to Arabian mythology and the Qur'an, the sun sets and rises from locations on earth, because Alexander was looking for the spring which gives immortality.[21] In Sumerian legends we find a story about Gilgamesh, who seeking immortality. The legend tells us that he located the place where the sun rises in the east so that he could consult the sun about his immortality. Such myths fueled the Qur'an's teaching that Alexander the Great visited the sunset and sunrise locations on earth.

Claims that the Greeks descended from Isaac, and that Alexander the Great was also among his descendants, were behind the idea of the Qur'an that Alexander the Great was a Muslim prophet and leader, making "Jihad" or "Holy War," to spread Islam into the world. In Surah al-Kahf, we find a narration concerning the wars of Alexander the Great. He is pictured as a Muslim reaching the "western edge of the earth and finding the sun having its sunset in a muddy spring." (Surah 18:86.)

Tubb'a's claims, and the myths he embraced, influenced Mohammed, who incorporated some of them in the Qur'an.

The idea of sunset in a muddy spring was first a Yemeni myth. We find it in the poetry of Tubb'a, a leader in Yemen. (Tubb'a reigned over the Himyarite kingdom of Yemen between 410-435 A.D.) Tubb'a, considered by Mohammed to be a prophet, said the sun has its sunset in a spring of mud. Mohammed considered Tubb'a's words inspired, and Tubb'a considered Alexander the Great to be a prophet of Allah.

Tubb'a's real name was Tuban Asa'd Abu Karb. As a military leader, he occupied Yathrib, also called al-Medina. There, Tubb'a captured two Jewish rabbis from the tribe of Beni Kharithah, which inhabited al-Medina at the time. The rabbis taught Tubb'a many things, especially the Jewish myths, such as the myth of the bird, Hoopoe. Hoopoe was said to have revealed to Solomon the existence of the Saba kingdom and its famous Queen. This myth is taken from a Jewish book called II Targum of Esther. Tubb'a mentioned it in his poetry,[22] and Mohammed included this myth in the Qur'an.

Mohammed included in the Qur'an what he considered to be the inspired words and thoughts of Tubb'a. Mohammed thought that this would make the Qur'an a more reliable book by including the thoughts about the cosmos and history believed by other sects in Arabia.

Many groups and poets at the time of Mohammed claimed that the Persians, Romans and the Kurds were descendants of Abraham.

There were also Persians and Arabs who claimed that the Persians came from the offspring of Abraham. According to Masudi, they created a genealogy of Persian mythological figures, such as Manoshehr. They made Manoshehr the son of Mashjer, son of Werik. They further identified Werik with Isaac, son of Abraham. They claimed that Mashjer went to the land of Persia and met a woman reigning under the name of Kork. Mashjer supposedly married her and she gave birth to Manoshehr, the king. From Manoshehr, they claimed, were born sons who multiplied and eventually became the race of the Persians.[23]

Al-Tabari also relates a genealogy through which the Arabs connect Manoshehr with Isaac, son of Abraham. Perhaps the Arabs took this genealogy from a group of Persians. The genealogy shows that the line of kings in Persia came from Manoshehr who, according to those who claim such a genealogy, came from the progeny of Isaac. Al-Tabari quotes a poem from the Arab poet, Jarir bin Atieh, in which he proclaims that the Persians came from Isaac, son of Abraham. The poet stated that the Persians had their own true prophets, and a book which he considered written by divine inspiration. To justify the claim of a divine book and prophets in their lineage, a group of Persians connected themselves to the descendants of Abraham through one of his sons.[24] Mohammed, himself, did the same thing. Al-Masudi quotes many Persian poems in which the poets boast that Persians were the descendants of Isaac, son of Abraham.[25] In addition to Persian poets, we find Arabic poets who wrote poems in which they said both the Persians and the Romans were descendants of Isaac, son of Abraham. One of these Arab poets is Jarir, son of al-khatfi al-Tamimi.[26]

Also many Arabic and Kurdish groups considered the Kurds to be descendants of Abraham. According to al-Masudi, some said the Kurds came from Ishmael, and others claimed they were from King Solomon through one of his concubines.[27]

As I mentioned earlier, the Arabs claimed that the Romans came from the offspring of Isaac. The Arabs claimed that the father of the Romans was a man named Rum, and they create a lineage from Rum back to Isaac, son of Abraham.[28]

The Reason why People in Many Nations Wanted to Associate Themselves with Abraham

We understand from all this that not only groups of Arabs at the time of Mohammed claimed to be the progeny of Abraham through Ishmael, but most of the nations at that time were made to be the progeny of Abraham. That is because so many of these unhistorical claims hinges on the monotheistic faith of the Old Testament, as presented by Jews and Christians. Their faith attracted many thinkers and religious people from many nations. At the same time that these thinkers were attracted to the Jews and Christians, they rejected the truth of God's Word as proclaimed in the Bible, and they held to their pagan beliefs. In the process, they tried to impart some legitimacy by claiming to be descended from Abraham, either through Isaac or Ishmael. It became a trend for many people groups to claim ancestry through Abraham, either for themselves, or for others – just as the Arabs claimed that the Romans, Greeks and Persians were descended from Isaac, son of Abraham.

To the Arabs, ancestry is very important. Arabic tribes glorified themselves if they could trace their lineage back through important historical figures. If a tribe could not trace their lineage back through an important historical figure, then they would feel a sense of shame. This is why some Arabic individuals claimed Ishmael, son of Abraham, as an ancestor. These individuals believed that the Romans, Greeks and Persians were descended from Abraham, and the Arabs did not want to feel inferior to them; thus, they created false genealogies of their own.

The claim that the Arabs were descended from Ishmael first appeared at the time of Mohammed and was embraced by Ahnaf, an occultic group.

This claim that the Arabs came from the progeny of Ishmael is not attested before the advent of Islam. If it was claimed by some individuals at the time of Mohammed, then they should have been a very small number who wanted to elevate their ethnicity to compete with other ethnicities who claimed to be from Abraham, such as the Persians. They also wanted to compete with the Jews who distinguished themselves from the Arabs, among whom they dwelt in Arabia, as believing in the true God. This small group was called "Ahnaf" and was living in Mecca. Mohammed lived among them, and he was influenced by their ideas. Mainly, Arabian Christian cults mixed with other Gnostic cults, and Sabian sects formed this small group. Many of them were from the Kuhhan, the priests of the religion of Jinn in Arabia. The Jinn were also identified with devils.

The False Genealogy Created by Ibn Ishak Upon Which the Muslims Base Their Claim of Connecting the Arabs with Ishmael

Around 773 A.D., centuries after Islam began, Ibn Ishak created a genealogy connecting Mohammed with Ishmael. Today, the idea that the Arabs came from the offspring of Ishmael has been accepted by all Muslims. However, when Ibn Ishak created the genealogy, he was attacked by the scholars of his time as "creating false genealogies." It's not only interesting for us to see these early nations flocking under the umbrella of Abraham, either through Isaac or Ishmael, but it demonstrates how far from the truth Islam finds itself today.

Arabic scholars confess the absence of any reference in pre-Islamic Arabia to genealogies that would connect the Arabians with Shem, the son of Noah. How, then, could Ibn Ishak come up with a genealogy connecting Mohammed with Ishmael? I quote al-Husseini, who citing Saad Zaglul and Ibn Khaldun, says:

> In reality, there is nothing left by the inhabitants of Arabia, whether of archaeological findings or poetry, which indicates that the Arabians believed in their ancestry to Shem, son of Noah. Furthermore, the attempts of Islamic writers to genealogize such a thing made them fall into great embarrassment and contradictions, when they tried to invent genealogies, and create a history to fill the gap between the Arabs and other nations who might have been "Arabized."[29]

ISHMAEL HAD NO SPIRITUAL ROLE TO BUILD UPON A RELIGION

The Word of God was fulfilled regarding Ishmael and his descendants, the Ishmaelites, that they would live near Israel and live as a savage nation.

Although Ishmael was never a prophet, Mohammed sought to connect himself with Abraham through Ishmael. We read about Ishmael in the Bible, but the Bible never attributes anything of a spiritual nature to him. His life was described by an angel of the Lord who appeared to Hagar in the wilderness while she was pregnant with Ishmael, and was fleeing from Sarah, Abraham's wife. These are the words the angel announced concerning Ishmael and his future, in Genesis 16:11,12:

> Behold, you are with child, and you shall bear a son. You shall call his name Ishmael, because the Lord has heard your affliction. He shall be a wild man; his hand shall be against every man, and every man's hand against him. And he shall dwell in the presence of all his brethren.

When the angel announced that Ishmael would "dwell in the presence of all his brethren," he was speaking of location. Ishmael was to dwell in the same geographical area as the sons of Isaac, Abraham's son with Sarah. We've come to know these people as Jacob's descendants, the Israelites. The land in which they lived was Palestine. The descendants of Jacob's brother, Esau, were the Edomites who dwelt in south Jordan. Ishmael and his descendants settled between the descendants of Isaac, and the descendants of Esau, in the northeastern part of the Sinai, fulfilling the word of God regarding where Ishmael would live. History also confirms this prophecy, as I demonstrated when I mentioned earlier about the Ishmaelites. In fact, Ishmael and his descendants dwelt between them; that is, in the northeastern part of Sinai, fulfilling the word of God regarding Ishmael's dwelling. The Ishmaelites dwelling in Sinai was attested to in history, as we proved through the study on the Ishmaelites.

However, we don't see any promise or spiritual role for Ishmael in the Bible. Rather, we see his descendants living a savage life, just as God's Word prophesied they would. They were constantly in conflict with the descendants of Jacob and Esau. The prophecy about Ishmael was fulfilled. They were known throughout history as nomads attacking and being attacked by every nation in the area. We see this throughout their history in Sinai until the 10th century B.C., and also after the 10th century B.C., when most of them left Sinai. They continued their savage character prophesied by the Word of God, attacking the borders of nations, such as the Assyrians and Chaldeans. These nations, in turn, retaliated, as prophesied in Genesis. This continued until these Ishmaelite nomad tribes were absorbed and became extinct after the 7th century B.C.

God made a covenant with the descendants of Isaac because He intended to be incarnated in that lineage. All the Biblical prophets came from that lineage.

The angelic announcement at the time of Ishmael was not the only time an angel had appeared in the Bible to announce the birth of a child. Usually, such an announcement contained a prophetical declaration of the child's future role, and whether or not he was to have such a role. We see this, also, in the case of Isaac. God promised Abraham that in his seed all the nations of the earth would be blessed, referring to Christ, who was one of Abraham's descendants. God told Abraham that the promise would pass through Isaac, Abraham's son with Sarah. Christ was descended through Isaac.

God's purpose in history is expressed in the Bible. It's called a "covenant," through which God obligates Himself to fulfill His promise regarding His coming in the flesh to redeem humanity from sin. God reconfirmed His promise and covenant each time an important person was born in the genealogy, which ultimately would lead to His own appearance in the flesh in the form of the Messiah. God also implied that spiritual blessings will accompany those in the Messianic line. Thus, God marked the line from which He intended to be incarnated.

There were others in the family of Abraham who were outside God's covenant. They were given material promises and were told that they would prosper as nations. One example was the nation which descended from Esau, the son of Isaac. Esau was not chosen to be in the line of God's promise and covenant, but his brother, Jacob, was chosen. We know that all the prophets came from Jacob's descendants until Christ was born, and He, of course, is the culmination and the essence of God's promise.

God appointed the sons and the grandsons of Abraham and Lot as the founders of nations, yet he established his covenant with Isaac and his son Jacob.

Like many of the other sons of Abraham, Ishmael was not chosen to be in the genealogy which eventually produced Christ. But Ishmael, like Abraham's other sons and grandsons, was blessed to father his own nation.

Although nations like these existed for centuries, no eternal or spiritual covenant was given to them. God blessed Abraham in such a way that He allowed the progeny of Lot, Abraham's nephew, to form two nations, Ammon and Moab, which continued until the 6th century B.C. God allowed Abraham's grandson, Esau, to be the head of the nation of Edom. God allowed another one of Abraham's grandsons, from his marriage with Keturah, to head the nation of Midian. With this in mind, we can clearly understand God's words to Abraham, telling him that Ishmael will become a nation, also. History confirmed what God promised, and we saw the Ishmaelites form a nation and live in Sinai near the other nations who descended from Abraham and his nephew, Lot.

Ishmael was not included in being part of the covenant which God established with Abraham. This promised covenant was done in order to produce all of the Biblical prophets and the Messiah.

We see the difference between the covenant which God made with those whom He chose for the Messianic genealogy, and those who were not chosen, but were still blessed to become heads of nations. Genesis 17:15-22 tells us:

> Then God said to Abraham, "as for Sarai your wife, you shall not call her name Sarai, but Sarah shall be her name. And I will bless her and also give you a son by her; then I will bless her, and she shall be a mother of nations; kings of peoples shall be from her." Then Abraham fell on his face and laughed, and said in his heart, "Shall a child be born to a man who is hundred years old? and shall Sarah, who is ninety years old, bear a child?"

And Abraham said to God, "Oh, that Ishmael might live before you."

Then God said: "No, Sarah your wife shall bear you a son, and you shall call his name Isaac; I will establish my covenant with him for an everlasting covenant, and with his descendants after him. And as for Ishmael, I have heard you, behold, I have blessed him, and will make him fruitful, and will multiply him exceedingly. He shall beget twelve princes, and I will make him a great nation. But my covenant I will establish with Isaac, whom Sarah shall bear to you at this set time next year."

It was difficult for Abraham to believe that, when he was 100 years old and his wife was 90 years old, they could have a son. So when God made a promise that a child would be born from Sarah, Abraham thought, "it's impossible." That's why he asked God that "Ishmael might live before God." Abraham wanted God to choose Ishmael to be Abraham's progeny with whom God's purposes would continue, and with whom God's promises to Abraham would come to pass. But the answer of God was prompt, "No, Sarah your wife shall bear you a son, and you shall call his name Isaac; I will establish my covenant with him for an everlasting covenant, and with his descendants after him." It was a clear "no." Ishmael would not be part of God's purpose or plan for the salvation of mankind. As difficult as it was for Abraham, God had said that Sarah was to bear a son by which the everlasting covenant was to be established.

The everlasting covenant implies that the prophecy is to come through Abraham's son, Isaac; through Isaac's son, Jacob, and then continue until the coming of Christ. After Christ was born, the eternal covenant flowed from Him to each one who believes in Him. This covenant means there will be no condemnation for those who trust in the redemptive death of Christ on the cross. They have an eternal relationship with God which their soul enjoys because they believe in Christ as their Savior.

The Promise that Twelve Princes Will Come From the Line of Ishmael Cannot be Linked With the Arab Nations

Ishmael was like many of the sons and grandsons of Abraham, and the sons of Lot, Abraham's nephew. God spoke of a nation coming from Ishmael's offspring. Many people think when God said, "I will make him a great nation" that He was talking about the Arabs. However, it is clear that the Arabs did not come from the Ishmaelites, for the Ishmaelites were integrated into other nomadic tribes in Sinai, and the surrounding deserts in the Fertile Crescent. Most of these were extinct after the 7th century B.C.

To understand this nation that came from Ishmael, we must look to the whole promise: "I will multiply him exceedingly. He shall beget twelve princes, and I will make him a great nation." From Ishmael had to come twelve princes, meaning twelve tribes. This was fulfilled historically. Twelve tribes dwelt in Sinai, some of them after the 10th century B.C. They spread into the Fertile Crescent, mostly in the deserts between Syria, Jordan and Iraq. The Arabs cannot be the twelve tribes identified with the Ishmaelites, for there are 19 Arab nations. We also saw how the Ishmaelites as nomads became extinct, yet the tribes who came from Arabia dominated the whole Middle East. So we can't imagine that the twelve nomadic Ishmaelite tribes, who wandered in the Sinai and Syro-Mesopotamia deserts, represented the Arab world.

The use of the term "a great nation" in the Bible can be used to refer to a few tribes. This substantiates the fact that the prophecy about Ishmael becoming a great nation was fulfilled by the twelve *Ishmaelite tribes in the Sinai.*

To understand the use of the word "nation" in the Bible, we have to look at how it was understood at the time of Abraham. Many verses in the Bible apply the term "nation" to the inhabitants of a medium size or small city. For example, in Genesis, chapter 20, we see Abraham emigrating south of Palestine to the northern Sinai to a city situated between the Wilderness of Shur and Kadesh, called Gerar. Gerar was later referred to as a nation.

Look at what happened in Gerar. Abraham said that his wife, Sarah, was his sister. Because she was beautiful, he was afraid that he would have been killed because others desired her. We read in Genesis 20:4 that Abimelech, King of Gerar, sent for Sarah. However, God came to Abimelech in a dream one night, and warned him that he would be killed if he took Sarah. Since Abimelech had not come near her, he said:

> Lord, will you slay a righteous nation also? Did Abraham not say to me, "She is my sister?"

Then God said to him in a dream,

> "Yes, I know that you did this in the integrity of your heart. So I withheld you from sinning against me; therefore I did not let you touch her."

Did you notice that Abimelech called his city a "nation" when he said, "Lord will you slay a righteous nation also?" The Bible, in the book of Genesis, uses the term "great nation" to refer to tribes with just a few people, or to tribes which had between one and two million inhabitants. One example of this term referring to a large group is found in Genesis 46:3,4. God ordered Jacob to go to Egypt:

> "I am the God of your father," God told him. "Do not fear to go down to Egypt, for I will make of you a great nation there."

According to the 27th verse of that chapter, only 70 people of the house of Jacob went to Egypt. They stayed there about 400 years, and the number of Israelites multiplied. By the time we get to Exodus 13, verse 37, we read that the number of those who were able to walk in the exodus from Egypt were 600 thousand people, not counting the children. Scholars estimate that nearly a million Israelites came out of Egypt. The Bible speaks about Israel as " a great nation," as we saw from Genesis 12:2, "for I will make of you a great nation there." That specific wording, "a great nation," as used at the time of Abraham and Jacob, was intended to refer to only a few tribes numbering about one or two million people. So, how could the word of the Lord concerning Ishmael becoming a great nation not be fulfilled in the twelve tribes of Ishmaelites who lived in Sinai? We have an idea about the large number of Ishmaelites when they fought Israel at the time of Gideon. The book of Judges, in chapter 7, verse 12, mentions that the inhabitants of Sinai formed an alliance with the Ishmaelites, the Midianites and the Amalekites. We read that:

> They were lying in the valley as numerous as locusts. Their camels were without number, as the sand by the seashore.

In the Bible, the term " nation" is also applied to a tribe. We see this when God spoke to Jacob in Genesis 35:11, "a company of nations shall proceed from you." He meant the twelve tribes of Israel. A "great nation" is a company of a few tribes, like the Israelites in Egypt, or the Ishmaelites in Sinai.

All the nations who came from the progeny of Abraham became extinct with the exception of the Israelites. The Israelites survived through the millennia as a sign for the first coming of the Messiah, and they will be a sign for His Second Coming.

Except for the Israelites, all the nations who came from Abraham and his nephew, Lot, were eventually absorbed and became extinct in history. That includes the Ishmaelites. The Bible, in Genesis 49, prophesied that the Jews will continue with a limited authority in Canaan until the coming of the Messiah. This prophecy was fulfilled, as we have seen.

The Bible also prophesied that Israel will be in Palestine again when Christ returns for the Second Coming. Zechariah, who began to prophesy around 520 B.C., said that when Jesus returns again to the earth, He will return to Jerusalem, where the Jews will look at the wounds in His body which He received during the crucifixion. In Zechariah, chapter 12, we see that, when God spoke to the prophets, He spoke about his return to

Jerusalem, proving for us that the pre-incarnate Christ is the God who spoke to the prophets. We read in verse 10:

> Then they will look on me whom they have pierced, and they shall mourn for him, as one mourns for his only son, and grieve for him, as one grieves for his firstborn.

It is evident that Israel will be convicted of sin, because they did not believe God when He came in the flesh, and when He was wounded and pierced on the Cross for the salvation of humanity.

The 11th chapter of the book of Zechariah contains many prophecies about the first coming of Christ, and about His Second Coming as well. One of the prophecies concerns His days on earth, and the amount of money His betrayer received for yielding Him to the Romans:

> They weighed out for my wages thirty pieces of silver. And the Lord said to me, "throw it to the potter, that princely price they set on me."

In the New Testament, we again pick up the thread of Zechariah in chapter 11, verse 12. Thirty pieces of silver is the same amount of money which Judas, Jesus' betrayer, took. He threw the money down in the Temple, showing he regretted his actions. With the money, the chief priest bought a potter's field to be used as a cemetery for foreigners.

Remember God's covenant for Abraham and his descendants? The nation which God made through the descendants of Abraham and Isaac would bring God in the flesh. He would die on the cross for the salvation of mankind. Though promised in the Old Testament, the promise was fulfilled in the New Testament, when Jesus died, rose again and ascended to His throne. From all nations, people believed in Christ and received salvation through His work on the cross. The time will come when the remnant of the Jews will see the importance of the Cross in bringing them salvation. This will occur when Christ returns to earth. Today, Christ's salvation is still open to every one who believes in Him.

Although Ishmael was still considered a great nation, and existed until the 7th century B.C., nothing was left by Ishmael and his descendants that was of significant spiritual benefit upon which Mohammed could build a religion.

Creating a Spiritual Legacy for Ishmael is Without Historical Foundation

Ishmael cannot be the foundation for a future true religion, because God cannot put his final inspiration and purpose where he never laid true foundation in history.

We already studied Ishmael, only to find that he never had a spiritual call from God. He was never chosen by God to be part of God's covenant, as Isaac and his descendants were. Ishmael never exhibited any worthy spiritual traits. The Bible fails to record a single word used by Ishmael to express that he was in fellowship with God. Not a single prophecy is known to come through him. Rather, it was prophesied that he would live a savage life, and history tells us he did just that.

In view of this, how can Ishmael be the foundation for a monotheistic faith, as Islam claims? If God intended to build a monotheistic faith on Ishmael, why did He not raise up prophets from among his offspring, as He did with the descendants of Isaac and his son, Jacob? Strong foundations are important to any builder. No one digs deep in the ground, fills the hole with cement and iron bars for a skyscraper's foundation, then moves away from that solid foundation only to build on a foundation of sand. How, then, could God, who laid the foundation in the Old Testament through many prophets descended from Isaac, neglect the solid foundation which He constructed throughout 2,000 years? To do so would contradict all He promised. The prophecies of the prophets who descended from Isaac laid the foundation for God to come in the flesh and to die on the Cross for mankind, providing salvation and redemption. Throughout ancient history, the prophets came from Isaac's line. None of

Ishmael's descendants ever claimed a spiritual role coming from Ishmael, nor did they speak of a prophetic role coming from any of his descendants. As I mentioned previously, it seems as though the Ishmaelites actually forgot they were descended from Ishmael. In various Assyrian inscriptions, such as those found in Qedar, Teima, and Dumah, they never mention Ishmael, nor did people name their sons after him.

On the other hand, the name of Isaac and his son, Jacob, were passed on to succeeding generations in almost every Judaic family. The remembrance of Isaac and Jacob as heads of the Israelites is commonplace throughout history.

The Area Where Mecca was Later Built had Never Been a Place of Interest or Pilgrimage for the Ishmaelites

We know that Mecca was not in existence before the 4th century A.D. However, putting this fact aside, let's assume Ishmael had gone to Mecca to build a temple. That temple, then, would have been a most important aspect of the Ishmaelites' existence. The Ishmaelites would have been sure to mention the temple in their written documents. But their temple was first built in Kadesh, in Sinai, and then moved to Dumah when some of the tribes left the Sinai to settle in other deserts of the Fertile Crescent.

Why didn't we see any one of them making a pilgrimage to Mecca? If the temple in Mecca was built by their father, Ishmael, then this temple would have been a constant topic of conversation. Thousands of Ishmaelites would have gone there and built cities around it. Military campaigns would have protected it, and each of their tribes would have tried to exercise control over it. Yet, a study of the history of Ishmaelite tribes shows that no one ever heard of Mecca. No tribe migrated south beyond the city of Teima; instead, they went to the north. No city was built by Ishmael's descendants in the area surrounding Mecca. There's not a hint of a pilgrimage to the area where Mecca was later built.

The Ishmaelites never exhibited the philosophy of monotheism, nor were they corrected by God for their continuing paganism; this is contrary to the experience of the Israelites.

In studying the religious life of the Ishmaelites, we never discover that they believed in a monotheistic God. They never mentioned the God of Abraham. They were known to be polytheistic worshippers of primitive idols. Conversely, the people who descended from Jacob were known to worship the God whom Abraham worshipped. Although a few of the kings of Israel worshipped polytheistic gods, the nation quickly rose to oppose these threats each time they did, demonstrating their deep legacy, and supporting the faith which they received from their fathers who were called by God to true monotheistic worship. If Ishmael had been chosen by God to create a monotheistic faith, as Islam claims, God never would have permitted Ishmael's descendants to be immersed in paganism throughout their history, until their extinction in the 7th century B.C. Muslims need to reflect on these facts. Trying to build a faith without foundation is against the way God acted in history. Not only do we fail to see prophets coming from the line of Ishmael, we don't even see Biblical prophets alluding to Ishmael. Nowhere does the Bible attribute any spiritual role or prophecy to Ishmael.

Though Ishmael married an Egyptian, Ibn Ishak claimed that he married a woman of Mecca. This claim is without any substantiation in fact. Ibn Ishak invented Arabic style names for her and her father, consistent with the naming traditions of his time.

The Bible tells us in Genesis 21:20:

> Ishmael dwelt in Paran — a wilderness northeast of Sinai — and his mother took a wife for him from the land of Egypt.

Because Hagar, Ishmael's mother, was an Egyptian, she made her son marry a woman from her own land. Paran was less than 200 miles from the border with Egypt. This allowed her to remain in contact with her own Egyptian family.

Ibn Ishak, Mohammed's biographer, claimed that Ishmael married a woman he called the daughter of Mathath, son of Amru al-Jurhami بنت مضاض بن عمرو الجرهمي.[30] We ask ourselves where Ibn Ishak got this information, since it never appeared in any other document, and no one mentioned it before. It's also unusual, because the style for these names is not found in any ancient Arabian inscription, but the style is characteristic of the 8th century A.D., the period in which Ibn Ishak lived. Ibn Ishak also created an Arabic poem which he attributed to Mathath, son of Amru al-Jurhami. The poem was written in a style similar to Ibn Ishak's time.[31]

The Arabic language is the language of the Qur'an. It's the language which Quraish, the tribe of Mohammed, spoke after they came in contact with the Bedouins of central western Arabia. This form of Arabic was unknown in Arabia before the Christian era, and it is considered one of the most recent Arabic forms, especially when compared to Thamud Arabic, which is carved on inscriptions dating back to the 7th century B.C. Although you can find Arabic Lihyanite before the Christian era, the Arabic of the Qur'an is the latest form of Arabic writing known in Arabia. We find Ibn-Ishak contradicting history when he attributes poems of his time to the 21st century B.C. The Arabic of Quraish, and of the Qur'an, became the official language in the Middle East, so Ibn-Ishak attributed his poems to the time of Ishmael, even though they were written in the Arabic language of his own time.

If Muslims would analyze what they were taught in light of history, they would see that creating a spiritual legacy for Ishmael is without historical foundation, and no credible historian ever advanced this idea. All those who depend upon these fabrications to back the claims of Mohammed were born in Ibn Ishak's generation, or later. It's easy to recognize it as unoriginal, a forgery and a fake. These claims stand in stark contrast to the historically accurate statements found about Isaac in the Bible. As we compare the claims of Islam and Christianity, we see how superior the Bible is. It behooves all men to learn the truth, for it is the truth which sets men free.

3

REFUTING THE ISLAMIC CLAIM ABOUT MOHAMMED AS DESCENDANT OF ISHMAEL

One Islamic Writer has Influenced the History Viewed by Muslims in his Attempt to Link Mohammed to Ishmael

We already saw that Muslims believe that Mohammed is a descendant of Ishmael. As proof of their position, Muslims refer to genealogies written by Ibn Ishak around 770-775 A.D.

What he has written is simply not true. Ishmaelite tribes, especially the tribe of Nabaioth from which, according to Ibn Ishak, Mohammed is said to have come, were nomadic tribes who lived in the Sinai and Fertile Crescent deserts. These tribes disappeared after the 7th century B.C.

Mohammed's family was a Sabaean Yemeni family, while the Ishmaelites, who lived in the deserts of the Fertile Crescent, became extinct many centuries before Mohammed's family left Yemen.

Historians say that the family of Mohammed was a family which lived in Saba-Yemen. In the 5th century A.D., Qusayy Bin Kilab, the 8th ancestor of Mohammed, gathered an alliance of many Yemeni families forming Quraish, the tribe from which Mohammed later came. These families only came to occupy Mecca in the 5th century A.D. The city of Mecca was built by the tribe of Khuzaa'h in the 4th century A.D.

Mohammed's family is not connected to any Ishmaelite tribe because Mohammed's family didn't leave Yemen until the 5th century A.D., and that's about 1,100 years after the Ishmaelites disappeared. Mohammed's tribe could not have lived in the same locations as the Ishmaelite tribes at any time throughout history.

The genealogy fabricated by Ibn-Ishak contradicts the sayings of Mohammed, who expressed his ignorance about his ancestors prior to his 17th ancestor.

We also saw that Ibn Ishak was considered by the Muslim scholars of his time as being guilty of forgery and fabricating false genealogies.[32]

Long before Ibn Ishak, Muslims who lived in Mohammed's own time also fabricated genealogies in an attempt to connect Mohammed to the descendants of Ishmael. Mohammed, himself, rejected all of these false genealogies, and he put limits regarding the genealogy of his ancestors. Regarding Mohammed's own rejection of the false genealogies, Amru bin al-As wrote:

> Mohammed genealogized himself regarding his ancestors until he reached al-Nather bin Kinaneh, then he said, "anyone who claimed otherwise or added further ancestors, has lied."[33]

By this, Mohammed confessed that neither he, nor anyone else, knew about his ancestors beyond al-Nather bin Kinaneh. Nather bin Kinaneh is the 17th ancestor in the genealogy which Mohammed recognized as true. Other narrations of the customs, or sayings, of Mohammed, called Hadiths, show Mohammed refused to be genealogized prior to Maad معد, who some suggested, was the 4th ancestor prior to al-Nather bin Kinaneh.[34]

When we look at the ancestors of Mohammed, it's reasonable to estimate 30 years for each generation of the 17 ancestors of Mohammed. Therefore, we can conclude that Mohammed knew about the genealogy of his tribe as far back as approximately 510 years. If we want to add the other four ancestors that Mohammed listed, we would go back 630 years. The truth is, nobody knew beyond such date. How, then, could Ibn Ishak and his followers reliably document a genealogy back to Ishmael, who lived in 2050 B.C.? This gives approximately 2,000 years between the 21st ancestor of Mohammed and Ishmael. How could Ibn Ishak claim the Ishmaelites lived in Mecca during this period and give details about their history when Mohammed, himself, said that nobody knew about his relatives prior to his 17th or 21st ancestor? Mecca was not even in existence during this period, as we have clearly demonstrated. Ibn Ishak's genealogy contradicts Mohammed's own claims that he did not know his ancestors farther back than al-Nather bin Kinaneh, the 17th ancestor before himself.

All the genealogies which appeared at the time of Mohammed were considered by Mohammed and his close followers to be false.

Many versions of Hadith of Mohammed coming from the followers of Mohammed all report that Mohammed opposed to be genelogized until Ishmael. All his closest contemporaries and followers considered the genealogies appearing at his time to be false. Among the people who reported Mohammed's opposition to such genealogies were his wife, Aisheh, and his cousin, Ibn Abbas, one of the most important reporters of Mohammed's Hadith.[35] Ibn Ishak went against what all these people had said by creating genealogies which connect the ancestors of Mohammed with Ishmael.

Ibn Ishak altered the genealogies listed by Moses in Genesis; he inserted Arabic names from his time and contradicted the history regarding Amalek.

The fabrication went beyond this. The genealogies created by Ibn Ishak and others who came after him inserted Arabic names into the genealogies which we find in Genesis. For example, Ibn Ishak inserted the Arabic name "Ya'rab," which comes from the word "Arab," listing him as the son of "Khahtan." Ibn Ishak then replaced Khahtan for Joktan, mentioned in the book of Genesis as the son of Eber, the son of Arphaxad, and the third son of Shem, the son of Noah.[36] We know that the term "Arab" didn't exist until the 10th century B.C. How, then, could it be inserted into history shortly following Noah, perhaps around 5500 B.C.?

Ibn Ishak went still farther. He changed the name of Lud, the fourth son of Shem, to Luth. He then made Luth the father of Amalek, who fathered the Amalekites. He also claimed that Amalek and his tribe lived in Mecca, and he claimed that the ancient Egyptians were also descendants of Amalek. He then made Amalek's original name "Arib," just to connect him with the Arabs.[37] Indirectly, through these false genealogies, Ibn Ishak claimed that Mecca existed at the time of Noah and his grandson, Lud. This directly contradicts the historical facts we examined before, showing that Mecca didn't exist until the 4th century A.D.

Previously, we also saw that Amalek is a descendant of Esau, the son of Isaac. Genesis 36:12 states that Timma was a concubine of Eliphaz, the first-born of Esau, and that she bore Amalek to Eliphaz. Amalek became the father of the Amalekites, which was an Edomite tribe that originally lived in southern Jordan, but moved to the eastern part of the Sinai, as was attested at the time of Moses. The Amalekites became extinct after the 10th century B.C. There's no mention of Amalek in any inscription, or in the writings of any Greek historian, which would indicate that the tribe lived in central, western or northern Arabia.

Refuting the Claim About Jurhum

Ibn Ishak claimed that the tribe of Jurhum lived in Mecca as far back as the time of Abraham. He also claimed that Jurhum was the grandson of Joktan, the son of Eber. He further claimed that Jurhum's original name was "Hathrem."[38] The significance of the name "Hathrem" is that it is characteristic of Arabic-style names used at the time of Ibn Ishak, which was in the 8th century A.D. The names given in the inscriptions of Yemen and northern Arabia are totally different from the style of the names given in Ibn Ishak's genealogies, which reflect the names of his generation. We already saw that no inscription, no Greek or Roman historian, and no geographer who visited Arabia, ever mentioned a tribe called Jurhum. The first mention of Jurhum is found in a poem of Ummyya bin Abi al-Salet, the maternal cousin of

Mohammed, who also claimed to be a prophet. The poem attributed to Ummyya says: "the Lord of Ad and Jurhum." [39] First of all, the poem most likely was composed after the event of Islam, because we do not have in Jahiliyah pre-Islam any mention about Jurhum. The idea that many of the so called "Jahiliyah poets" were added after Islam is embraced by great scholars, such as Tah Hussein, the famous Egyptian scholar. Secondly, for the case of argument, if we wanted to admit the originality of that verse, we could not build upon it a history that a nation called Jurhum existed in Arabia since the time of Abraham. The reason for this was because Ummyya was a contemporary of Mohammed, and he can't be a source of documentation about a nation which would have existed 2,700 years prior to his own time. As we discussed in the first part of this book, because there were no archiving methods nor any printing methods like we have today. It is commonly accepted that tradition can be considered accurate only if it was written within four centuries of the writers' lifetimes. If Jurhum existed as a tribe in Arabia, it could have been a small tribe that appeared some time after the Christian era. Since no classical writer mentioned this tribe, if it existed, it must have been insignificant. Ummyyia's poems are full of myths, such as his claim that the Queen of Saba, who visited king Solomon, was his aunt; he said this to justify his claim to the role of prophet. In addition, Ummyyia had a relationship with a Jinn-devil, who used to instruct him, which proves that he was a part of the occult religion of Arabia. If we wanted to accept that this poem was composed by him, then we would be relying on poems recited by an occultic and mythical personality to establish history dating back to 2,700 years before his time.

Enormous historical mistakes exist in the Qur'an, and the genealogies created after the rise of Islam, to support the Qur'an. Some examples are the genealogies regarding Thamud and Nimrod.

There are other serious historical mistakes in the Islamic genealogies regarding the tribe of Thamud. Thamud is an Arabic tribe which appeared in the 8th century B.C., as was attested at the time of the Assyrian King Sargon II through his inscriptions. Thamud later lost its political power about the 5th century A.D. The Islamic genealogies attempted to back statements made in the Qur'an which placed Thamud and Ad – another Arabian tribe which appeared after Thamud – as tribes which came right after Noah. So they created a father for the tribe of Thamud and named him "Thamud." Then they claimed he was the grandson of Shem, the son of Noah.[40] All this was created just to fit the narration of the Qur'an.

The Qur'an claims that the tribe of Thamud was the third generation after Noah,[1] and it was condemned by Allah to be punished by a wind. (The wind was the god who brought judgment in Zoroastrianism.[2]) We know that this is also an

---

[1] The Qur'an made the Arabian tribe of Ad to be second generation after Noah's generation; then Thamud as the third generation, See Surah 7:69; 23:31,32;14:8,9.

[2] **The Judgment Through Wind in Zoroastrianism**

The Qur'an makes the judgment to the tribe come through the wind. The judgment in the Qur'an is always either through the wind, or through a shout or blast from the mouth of the angel Gabriel.

I mentioned previously about Mohammed's Persian counselor by the name of Suliaman Al- farisi; his name means Solomon the Persian. This man was a priest in Zoroastrianism before becoming Muslim. When he met Mohammed and became Muslim, Mohammed gave him a golden egg, which was considered a great fortune at that time. Evidently, Mohammed saw in Soluiman Al-Farsi a great resource which would give him access and knowledge to Zoroastrianism. This explains the great data of Zoroastrianism in the Qur'an. In fact, the Qur'an as Cosmology and Eschatology depends in the major part on Zoroastrianism.

The judgment through wind is the way to execute judgments on peoples like we encounter in Zoroastrianism. In Ram Yast I, 2 and 3 (Ram Yast is part of the sacred Zoroastrian literature), Ahura Mazda, the god in Zoroastrianism, presents offerings to Vayu, the god of the air or wind, asking him to judge the creation of wickedness. The god of air or wind has great potency, with the ability to evacuate the whole earth from its inhabitants. In Ram Yast (V, 20), Azi Dahaka, a mythological potency as enemy of the Iranian nation, presented a request to the god of the air, Vayu, to evacuate the earth from its inhabitants, but Vayu refused to grant him this request.

All judgments in Zoroastrianism are done by the god of air, or by a blast shouted by the god of the air as an angel. We find the Qur'an also giving the

enormous historical mistake. Not only did Thamud not appear until the 8th century B.C., but the official history, as shown by Assyrian inscriptions, demonstrates that Thamud continued to exist during the 7th century B.C. Also, writings by various Greek and Roman geographers who wrote about Arabia, said Thamud continued until the 5th century A.D. as a politically-organized tribe which occupied a large part of northern Arabia. No wind destroyed the tribe, as the Qur'an claims.

This should be enough to convince us, but there's yet another enormous historical mistake in the Islamic genealogies. This one

---

judgment to the wind or to Gabriel shouting a blast. Gabriel has replaced the angel of wind in Zoroastrianism in this role of judging through blast.

The Qur'an has copied the style of judgment from Zoroastrianism. There is a good wind which executes judgment toward the creation of Ahriman, the god of evil. In the other part, there is wind as a devil appertaining to Ahriman, who carries out works of destruction toward the good creation of Ahura Mazda, the god of goodness. Zoroastrianism is known for such dualism. The wind devil, or the storm devil, destroyed the city where Zoroaster was born. With just one blast, part of the city was elevated up to the sky, and then made to go up side down.(This we find, for example, in Dinkard,VII, chapter II, 44-46.) The same concept is borrowed by the Qur'an, where Gabriel with his blast elevated the cities of Sodom and Gomorrah; then he turned them upside down.

The god of wind or air in Zoroastrianism is portrayed as a judge who executes judgments against persons or peoples who do not believe in Zoroaster's message. We find him carrying two kings who refuse to believe, carrying them too high and keeping them in that state as judgment (see Al Shahrastani, al Milal and Nahel, page 259).

The same concept we encounter in the Qur'an as judgment toward the tribe of Ad who refused to believe in "Hud," created by Mohammed for the tribe as prophet. Ibn Abbas, the cousin of Mohammed and the narrator of his important Hadith, says that the wind which came to Ad used to carry the men and livestock and fly in them in the sky, then strike them against the earth (quoted by Al Sabuni,III, page 199).

concerns Nimrod. According to Genesis 10:8-11, Nimrod was the first builder of the old cities of Mesopotamia. He was the son of Cush, the son of Ham, the son of Noah. We can date him to between 5000 and 4500 B.C. Islamic genealogies correctly state that Nimrod was the son of Cush, but incorrectly state that he lived around the time of Abraham.[41] This false claim about Nimrod was made to conform to a mistake in the Qur'an, which made Nimrod reign at the time of Abraham. The Qur'an says Nimrod persecuted Abraham and cast him into a fire which did not harm him. We read this in Surah al-Anbiya' 21:51-70 and Surah al-Safat 37:95. We already mentioned in Part I of this book that the narration of the Qur'an is taken from the Jewish book called Midrash Rabbah, chapter 17.

We urge Muslims to study history, and to compare the facts to what they have been told in the Qur'an and in Islamic tradition. The claims of Mohammed, the Qur'an and Islam are clearly unfounded. Even if such historical errors were accepted by the followers in Mohammed's time, we now have so much more evidence which proves them in error. How can anyone embrace these enormous mistakes, when a simple study of history demonstrates how wrong they are.

No one has the right to claim he descended from a specific man who lived 2,000 years before him, unless he has written documents which testify to his claim. In Mohammed's case, those documents simply do not exist. We have no proof that the ancestors of Mohammed were the descendants of Ishmael.

I will continue to analyze the Islamic genealogies which began to appear in the 8th century A.D., and which endeavor to connect Mohammed with Ishmael. I already quoted the Hadith of Mohammed, in which he prohibited any genealogy which described him any further back than Nather bin Kinaneh, who lived 17 generations before him. Other Hadith of Mohammed state that he didn't want to be genealogized prior to Maad معد , which some suggested to be the fourth person prior to Nather bin Kinaneh. The many genealogies which appeared since the 8th century A.D. confirm the same information, that the genealogy of Mohammed is limited to probably 17 generations before him, but certainly not more than 21 ancestors.

Why is this significant in our search for Mohammed's genealogy? In the first place, Mohammed himself confessed that he didn't know of any ancestor before his 17th ancestor. Secondly, after the 17th generation, we begin to notice the differences in these genealogies. After Maad bin Adnan, number 21, the genealogies begin to contradict themselves with big differences, reflecting the fact that the authors of such genealogies couldn't find resources on which to build their genealogies. That's because Mohammed prohibited his contemporaries from going any further back than his 17th ancestor. Thus, every one fabricated Mohammed's genealogy differently from the other.

Another interesting feature of their work is that all of the biographers used Arabic-style names of the 8th and 9th centuries A.D., but they applied the names to the generation in which Ishmael lived. As an example, we find a genealogy mentioned by Tabari, in which the author of the genealogy said Nabaioth, the first-born of Ishmael, begot a son under the name of al-Awam العوام, and al-Awam to beget al-Saboh الصابوح. Notice the Arabic names. In the genealogy, designations of al-Awam, and al-Saboh, respectively, follow the names.[42] We don't find this style even in the inscriptions of North Arabia before the Christian era. Instead, we see these names are of the same style as the Umayyad and Abassid periods, after the 8th and 9th centuries A.D.(the Abassid period began in the year 750 A.D.).

When we return to the genealogy fabricated by Ibn Ishak, on which other Muslim writers built in more recent times, we notice his Arabization of the genealogy. As I stated previously, he listed the son of Nabaioth, first-born of Ishmael, as Yashjub يشجب, his son is Yarob يعرب. Yarob is, in itself, a word derived from the word Arab. Ibn Ishak did this in order to make Ishmael appear to be an Arab. Though we know that the word "Arab" was not known before the 10th century B.C. This style for names like Yarob and Yashjub is characteristic of the 8th century A.D., in which Ibn Ishak lived. A common characteristic to all these

341

genealogies is that they claim Mohammed was descended from Ishmael, and they all give a limited number of ancestors between Mohammed and Ishmael.

There are 2,670 years between Ishmael and Mohammed – a large span of time which cannot be covered with only 40 generations.

Ibn Ishak listed 40 ancestors. When he fabricated his genealogy, he wasn't aware that 40 ancestors are not sufficient to cover the great time span between Ishmael and Mohammed. Ishmael lived around 2050 B.C., while Mohammed emigrated to Medina around 620 A.D. Therefore, there are about 2,670 years between Ishmael and Mohammed. How can this great period be covered by only 40 ancestors?

By contrast, the Gospel of Matthew reports the genealogy of Jesus Christ as far back as Abraham. We find 42 ancestors between Abraham and Jesus, though it's a period of only 1,950 years. The genealogy of Mohammed must account for another 720 years.

Another thing to consider is that a Jewish generation is longer than an Arabian generation. Consider the ancestors of Isaac from Abraham to King David. Many of these men fathered their first-born when they were 40 or 50 years old. We see that between the captivity in Babylon in 586 B.C., and the birth of Jesus, there are 14 generations. This shows that the Jewish generation in that period was around 41 years. But when we come to the Arabian generations, we can't allow 41 years for each generation. Scholars consider an Arabian generation to have been about 20 years, because Arabs married when they were about 17-20 years old, due to weather and their cultural environment.

The Archaeology of Arabia Confirmed the Relative Brevity of an Arabian Generation

Archaeology confirms the lower figures for the generations in Arabia. If we study the series of kings in Arabia, both in northern Arabia and Yemen, we come to verify the shortness of Arabian generations when compared to generations in other places, such as Israel. For example, the series of rulers in Saba and Himyar of Yemen begin with the Karibil A. in the 9th century B.C., and run through Maadikarib III, King of Himyar, who was number 102, the last one in the series. He reigned between 575-577 A.D.[43] We see 102 generations of kings in a span of about 1,400 years. Remembering that a few of these rulers were brothers of other kings in the same generation, we find between 75-80 generations, and we conclude that the average Arabian generation was about 17-20 years.

Considering the shortness of the Arabian generation, let's suppose that each generation in Mohammed's genealogy is 20 years. Since Mohammed is separated from Abraham and Ishmael by 2,670 years, there must have been a little over 133 generations between them. When we do the math, we have 2,670 years divided by 20 years, which equals 133 1/2 generations, not 35 or 40, as claimed by Ibn Ishak and the others who fabricated genealogies for the ancestors of Mohammed. We see how unprepared and unwise they were to claim Mohammed is descended from Abraham and his son, Ishmael.

Except for the lineage of Jesus, which was documented by written books of the Bible through the centuries, no other family in history has ever accounted for their ancestors over a period of 2,000 years.

Let's look at this another way. If we assume that the 21st ancestor of Mohammed is known, and if we make a generation 25 years rather than 20 years, then ancestor number 21 would still be 525 years distant from Mohammed. This means that the 21st ancestor of Mohammed lived between 50-70 A.D. This would make the gap between him and Ishmael about 2,000 years.

Except for the lineage of Jesus, no family in history had ever verified their ancestors over a period of 2,000 years. The family of Joseph, who was from the royal lineage of Judah, and the family of Mary, who was from the same tribe, could account for their ancestors as far back as Abraham. Because there have been documented, written books of the Bible in each generation, the facts are verified again and again. They give testimony to the promise God made to Abraham and to Isaac, son of Abraham, which God then confirmed to almost every member of the Messianic genealogy. God's divine promise accompanied others in the Messianic line, such as Isaac, Isaac's son, Jacob, and Jacob's son, Judah, as it was recorded by Moses in the book of Genesis, the first book of the Bible.

The genealogy continued to be recorded in many other books of th Bible. For example, we see God confirming the continuity of the Messianic line in the book of Ruth through Boaz, one of the ancestors of King David. The promise of God concerning the birth of a divine child as Savior was confirmed to David and his son, Solomon; then to many other kings, until we reach the last king who governed Judah at the time of Babylon's captivity, around 586 B.C. The confirmation of God's promise continued after the captivity of Babylon. In fact, God renewed His promise to another ruler in David's royal line, Zerubbabel, who became governor of Judah around 538 B.C.

Many prophets prophesied God's incarnation in human form after Zerubbabel was governor. The series of prophesies continue until we reach the prophet Malachi, who wrote the last book of the Old Testament around 436 B.C. The first chapter of Malachi begins with these words:

> Behold I send my messenger, and he will prepare the way before me. And the Lord, whom you seek, will suddenly come to His temple.

It is clear that the God of the Old Testament, who spoke to Malachi and to all the prophets, was the One who promised to come, announcing the sending of a messenger to prepare the way for Him as a sign of His coming. This messenger was John the Baptist, whom God called in the same generation in which Christ was incarnated, and who testified in John 1:26, 27 concerning Jesus. He said:

I baptize with water, but there stands one among you whom you do not know. It is he who, coming after me, is preferred before me, whose sandal strap I am not worthy to untie.

Later, when John was asked by the Jews if he was the Messiah, he said in Matthew 3:2 that he was "the voice of one crying in the wilderness." He was the one who came to prepare the way before the Lord, fulfilling the prophecy of Isaiah 40:3. John the Baptist pointed to Jesus as the Messiah, the Son of God, and the Lamb of God who takes away the sin of the world.

There is a complete continuity of documented records and historical testimonies regarding the Messianic genealogy of Jesus.

The royal lineage continued to be well-known between the time of Malachi and Jesus. In fact, rulers in Judah continued their rule in Jerusalem at the time of the Maccabees during the 2nd century B.C. This means that the period, which was covered only by oral tradition until we reach Mary and Joseph, doesn't exceed 120-140 years. That was a short time in which families would know about the father of their grandfather who lived 140 years earlier.

When we consider John the Baptist, of whom there is a written testimony, not just in the New Testament, but also in historical literature, such as the writings of Josephus Flavius, the Jewish-Roman historian, we have a complete continuity of documented records and historical testimonies regarding the Messianic genealogy of Jesus.

There is an absence of any record between Mohammed and Ishmael which would support the Islamic claim that Mohammed is descended from Ishmael.

On the other hand, when we come to the family of Mohammed, whose oldest disputable ancestor was 21 people distant from him, and who lived in Yemen in the first century A.D., how can we connect Mohammed's 21st ancestor with Ishmael who lived in Sinai 2,000 years before him? No Arabian documents written before Mohammed even allude to such a claim.

345

Islam also claims that Abraham and Ishmael founded the city of Mecca, but we saw that Mecca was not in existence prior to the 4th century A.D. There's no historical document written during the 2,000 years between Mohammed's 21st ancestor and the time of Ishmael, which claims that the 21st ancestor of Mohammed was a descendant of Ishmael. And there is no credible document written between the time of Mohammed's 21st ancestor and his own time.

As if this were not enough evidence that Mohammed couldn't have descended from Ishmael, we have the testimony of thousands of inscriptions, annals and archaeological records which speak about hundreds of rulers in Arabia who belonged to many different tribes, but no inscription or record includes material on any of the ancestors of Mohammed. This can only confirm that Mohammed's family was an ordinary and unknown family like any other family in Yemen, and that it never ruled in any city in western Arabia, even though Islamic tradition claims it ruled in Mecca.

The Impossibility of the 21st Ancestor of Mohammed Claiming to be Descended from Ishmael

Because Mohammed came from an average Yemeni family, how can his 21st ancestor possess information about ancestors who lived at the time of Abraham? Although printing was invented in the 15th century, and archiving and documentation has since become more organized, and easier, than in previous centuries, none of the families in our generation know the names of their ancestors who lived 1,000 years ago. How, then, could an ordinary man, such as the 21st ancestor of Mohammed, who lived around the 1st century A.D., know anything about an ancestor who lived 2,000 years before him?

From Assyrian records dated between the 9th and 7th centuries B.C., we know that Ishmaelite tribes lived as nomads in Sinai and the Fertile Crescent. But none of these records include the name Ishmael. No inscription shows that they called any person by that name. This demonstrates to us that they didn't know their lineage from Ishmael. Otherwise, they would certainly have been proud to be his descendants, and they would have recorded Ishmael in each subsequent generation, just as the Israelites recorded Isaac as part of their Israelite religious heritage in every ancient book they wrote.

Because Ishmael received no spiritual call from God, his only historical descendants were the twelve tribes which descended from his sons. In consequent generations, even his sons' descendants forgot about him, including his name, even though the time between Ishmael and these tribes was only about 1,200 years (between the 7th and 9th centuries B.C.). Since this is the case for the true descendants of Ishmael, how can a man who lived in Yemen, far from where Ishmael lived, conclude he descended from Ishmael who lived 2,000 years before him? If the Ishmaelites, themselves, were not aware of their ancestry from Ishmael, who would have told the 21st ancestor of Mohammed that he was descended from Ishmael?

There is no proof that Mohammed's ancestors, number 17 or number 21, ever claimed to be descendants from Ishmael. There's no written document before Mohammed that make such a claim. Even if such document were to have existed, still this ancestor would have no right to claim descendancy from a man who lived 2,000 years before him, without written documents in each generation to prove his case.

It is clear that the claim of Islam about Mohammed coming from Ishmael progeny is farther from the truth than if I claimed that I came from the line of Julius Caesar who lived 2,000 years before my time. Though I would claim that my 21st ancestor was from Julius Caesar, I have nothing to confirm my claim. Such a claim is impossible to verify by anyone living in our generation. That's why no one today, even in Rome itself, claims descendancy from Julius Caesar, nor did any Italian who lived 1,000 years ago dare to make such a claim. It's understood that even 1,000 years without any documented testimony renders the claim ridiculous.

It was a common custom in Arabia at the time of Mohammed for many who claimed to be prophets to claim that they were descended from Biblical figures.

Such claim, if anyone would embrace it, would be considered as transgressing honesty and logic. Yet, there were those people in Arabia, specifically at the time of Mohammed, who knowingly held to the claim that they were descendants of Biblical figures. Men who claimed to be prophets often claimed to descend from known figures in history, or from people mentioned in the Bible. Umayya bin abi al-Salt, a maternal cousin of Mohammed, claimed to be a prophet. He said that the Queen of Sheba, who visited Solomon, was his aunt.[44] He said this to establish that he was from the line of her brother. Also Tubb'a (the Yemeni leader who ruled between 410-435 A.D. and occupied Mecca) claimed to be a prophet, and claimed that the Queen of Sheba was his aunt.[45] Throughout history we have had people like Umayya bin Abi al-Salt, who wanted to be prophets over their people. They made their claims because knew that many around them were naive and ignorant and wouldn't refute their claims.

Although false prophets in Arabia had the audacity to claim that they were offspring from a man who lived 1,000 years before them, Mohammed claimed to descend from Ishmael who lived 2,700 years before him, yet without any historical written document. My heart goes out to our Muslims friends who continue to trust their eternal destiny to a claim which is against logic and history.

Mohammed claimed to have ascended to heaven, met Abraham, and learned that he was a true copy of Abraham, so as to convince his followers that he was descended from Abraham.

We saw how Mohammed claimed that Ishmael was his ancestor. He claimed this, even though the time between Mohammed and Ishmael was about 2,700 years, and there were no written documents at any time to support this claim.

But there is more involved than supporting an unhistorical claim. Mohammed connected himself to Abraham by saying he was a physically-true copy of Abraham, because he had ascended to heaven where he encountered many Biblical figures – and among them was Abraham.

He also claimed that heaven has seven layers, copying the idea embraced by many religions and sects of his time, such as Gnosticism, Manicheism and Zoroastrianism. Gnostic literature makes man responsible for each of the sky's seven layers. Mohammed claimed the same. Mohammed placed Abraham in the sky's seventh layer,[46] where he ruled over believers who did more works, and performed more religious rites, than the inhabitants of the lower layers.

The resources of Mohammed about Adam in the first layer of heaven, and about the idea that all the angels worshipped Adam, with the exception of Satan.

Mohammed described the overseers of each layer. He made Adam responsible for the first layer, deciding the destiny of those who desire to enter heaven. Adam smiles on some, sending them to one of the seven layers, depending on the works and religious rites they have done. He frowns in the face of others, sending them to hell.[47]   Adam looks to the right and laughs when he sees one entering heaven, and he looks to the left and weeps as he sees those who go into hell.[48]   This idea originates in a non-Biblical book called the Testament of Abraham. We read about Adam in the first chapter and the 11th verse.

Adam appears in many Gnostic writings, in which he declares the destinies of men. He also appears in Sabian Mandaean sacred books, where he is identified with one of their deities called Adkas Ziwa. Eve is identified with Adkas' wife, Anana Denhura, who is known as "a cloud of light" in Mandaean mythology.[49] Therefore, Adam is highly venerated in Mandaean mythology and has angels who worship him.[50]   In the sacred books of the Mandaeans, all the worlds and the angels worship Adam, except Satan.[51]

Mohammed copied the deception into the Qur'an, telling his followers that the reason Satan was expelled from heaven was because God ordered Satan to worship Adam, and Satan refused.

We see this claim in many Suras of the Qur'an. I quote one that is Surah 2nd, called Al Baqarah:

> Behold, we said to the angels, "worship Adam;" they worshipped him, except Satan; he refused and was haughty, and he became one of the infidels.

Therefore, the devil in Mandaean scriptures is portrayed as someone who refuses to worship anyone other than God, even when God, Himself, orders Satan to worship a creature like Adam. This is a serious deception showing the fault of the devil as if it were virtue, in that he was standing with the idea that creatures should worship only God.

The Qur'an Copied the Mandaean Idea About the Devils Serving King Solomon

The devils in Mandaean literature are elevated to envied positions. Like angels, they serve the prophets and kings. They are capable of doing miraculous works, and they participated in the creation of the universe. They dug the rivers and helped to build fancy palaces. In the Mandaeans' main sacred book, Ginza Rba, the devils serve King Solomon.[52]

Mohammed copied the idea of devils working for Solomon. In the Qur'an, Surah 21, al- Anbiya' 82, we read:

> And of the devils were some who dived for Solomon, and did for him other work besides, and we were keeping them.

Muslims, when translating the Qur'an into English, are embarrassed to translate the word "Shayatin" شياطين, the Arabic word for devils, into its true meaning; they try to translate it as "evil ones." Many words of the Qur'an are intentionally translated to not represent their true meanings; this is a way to alleviate the true occult and mythological nature of the Qur'an.

Mohammed wrote in the Qur'an that Allah protected the devils, but the Bible tells us that the devils are expelled from the presence of God because they refused to worship Him, and they revolted against Him. The Bible warns not to have any relationship with devils.

Mohammed's Negative Description of Moses, and his Indignation About the Black community

Let's look again at how Mohammed describes those responsible to govern the layers of heaven. We see Moses, whom Mohammed put in the fifth layer. He pictures Moses as a black, or dark, person with white hands, contrasting to the dark color of his body.[53] Mohammed describes Moses as if he were African; yet we know the Hebrew description from the Bible doesn't match the description given by Mohammed. We see nothing negative about being African because all members of the human race are beautiful, whether they are African, European or Asian. But Mohammed assigned little value to Africans. He, himself, owned black slaves, and he stated that slaves can't give testimony in a court of law unless they are scourged or whipped beforehand.[54] When any of Mohammed's followers wanted to free one of their slaves, Mohammed would refuse to allow it, and he would order the slave to be sold, rather than to be freed.[55] For example, we find Mohammed selling a slave boy whom his lord had freed.[56] He considered the freeing of slaves not to be a wise move.[57] When the Qur'an speaks of freeing a slave, it does not mean a true freedom. Mohammed explained in his Hadith that:

> The allegiance, or obedience, or loyalty of the slave is to be to the one who freed him, even though the parents of the slaves may put a hundred conditions.[58]

He means that the one who freed the slave always remains in authority over, and in ownership of, the slave, regardless of what the parents of the slave claimed. He often sold slaves or traded them for other slaves. For example, he traded two black slaves for one white slave.[59] He once bought a female slave by the name of Barbareh. Barbareh was married, but Mohammed refused any obedience of Barbareh to, or relationship with, her husband or her parents, under the excuse that the slave should be owned only by the one who enslaved him.[60] All this reflects his indignation and lack of esteem for slaves in general, and for the black people, in particular.

By describing Moses as he did, Mohammed intended to draw a negative picture of Moses. Mohammed wanted to be seen by his followers as superior to Moses. History also tells us that when Mohammed saw one of his followers reading the Torah, also called the Pentateuch (the first five books of the Bible which Moses wrote), Mohammed was furious and full of wrath.[61]

In his intent to discredit Moses, Mohammed called Moses "gloomy,"[62] a negative report indeed. There are no gloomy people in heaven, since it's a place of placid and eternal joy as described in the Bible. We know that in heaven prophets, like Moses, and all who love the Lord, are with Him, and are living in continuous joy and consolation.

Under the influence of Gnostic sects, Jesus is devalued by Mohammed and claimed to be inferior to John the Baptist.

Where does Jesus fit into Mohammed's descriptions? Mohammed put Jesus in the second layer of heaven. The idea of placing Jesus into one of the sky's layers is also found in Gnostic and Manichean literature. Manicheism is a religion founded by Mani in the 3rd century A.D. In the Manichean Psalm Book, written by a disciple of Mani around the end of the 3rd century A.D., we read that Jesus is placed in one of the layers.[63]

Manicheism spread to Mecca at the time of Mohammed, and Mohammed copied many of their claims. Like Mohammed, Mani also claimed he ascended into heaven.

Mohammed put Jesus in the second layer to make Him appear inferior to Moses, whom Mohammed placed in the sixth layer; and to Aaron; whom Mohammed placed in the fifth layer; and to Abraham, whom Mohammed put in the seventh layer; and to Enoch, whom he placed in the fourth layer; and to Joseph, whom he put in the third layer.[64] Mohammed made John the Baptist responsible over the second layer. It is clear that Mohammed followed the Gnostic order of seven layers, where

Enoch is elevated over many of the prophets. In the Mandaean sacred scriptures, John the Baptist is also a deified mythological figure, elevated over many of their gods. The reason the Mandaeans elevated John the Baptist was to de-emphasize Jesus in their war against Christianity. Remember, John the Baptist said that Jesus is the Lord for Whom he came to prepare the way. This was a fulfillment of Isaiah's prophecy concerning the incarnation of God, and the sending of a prophet who would come before Him to prepare His way and testify about Him. John declared that he was the one who came to prepare the way before the incarnated God, and that he was not worthy to untie His sandal strap.

Gnostic cults at the time of Mohammed were fighting to keep Christ from being preeminent over the prophets. They ignored the prophecies which spoke about Jesus and failed to consider Him to be divine. All these Gnostic and Sabian Mandaean false doctrines influenced Mohammed.

Mohammed Described Jesus in a Very Disdainful Manner.

You get a feel for the intentions of Mohammed. He wanted to devalue Jesus and create negative pictures about His appearance. After Mohammed's claimed ascension to heaven, he described Jesus: "About Jesus, the son of Mary: He was a red man, between short and long, full of black grain moles or spots, as if he came out of Dimas. You think his head is full of water." Another version translates Mohammed's words, "as if the sweating comes down abundantly from his beard."[65]

Some books narrating the life of Mohammed explain the meaning of the term "Dimas," from which Mohammed claimed Jesus came. Dimas was a negative expression for a bathroom or washroom. The book of Halabieh, another book describing the life of Mohammed, describes "Dimas" in these words:

It is originally the place where one comes out sweating, and its origin is the darkness, and it is called " Night Dames." The first to invent or create Dimas were the Jinn. They created and applied the concept to Solomon. They said when Solomon entered the Dimas, or bathroom, and encountered its heat and anguish, Solomon said it was the torment of God, because the entrance to the bathroom, called ruff, reminded him of hell. The ruff is the thing most similar to hell because the fire is in the lower part of it, and darkness and blackness cover it.[66]

This was the Dimas for the people of Mecca at the time of Mohammed, who was against bathrooms, and he prohibited his followers to enter them[67] because, in Zoroastrian law, bathrooms are considered to come from devils. The Magi are said to have overthrown a king, King Balash or Kavat, for having built bath-houses, and because they worshipped the water and cared for its cleanliness more than for the cleanliness of their bodies.[68] The baths were opposed by Aryans. We find in the Gautama, the sacred laws of the Aryans, a prohibition of bathing.[69] It seems the Dimas was seen as the most wicked of all bathrooms in the mind of the Arabians, who were under Zoroastrian influences.

Mohammed described Jesus in the lower part of the "layers of heaven" as if He were a personality coming out from a dark place, where there is anguish and sweating. His body is pictured as full of dark spots. It is, indeed, a very negative picture of Christ, very different from His real glory. We easily contrast Mohammed's picture to the teaching of the Bible concerning Jesus and heaven. After Jesus ascended into heaven following His resurrection, He sat on His heavenly throne, the very throne from which He had descended to become incarnated in human form and to provide the sacrifice for our sin.

But the enemy can never hide his animosity toward Christ, because Jesus is the human identity of God. In His humanity, Jesus lived on earth as morally and spiritually perfect. He defeated the devil through the Cross. The devil argues that God could never accept men and women to be heavenly inhabitants because they are sinners who have disobeyed God. But God reconciled humanity when, through the humanity He took upon Himself, He died on the Cross and paid the penalty for sins committed by humanity. That's why the devil, the enemy of God, tries to attack Jesus. Jesus is the humanity which God took upon Himself, through which He defeated the devil.

Mohammed intended to devalue Jesus and Moses because they represented the Old and New covenants; he wanted to hide them in heaven to make his own religion superior.

Certainly, when you consider the Dimas at the time of Mohammed, and you see its origin as a dark place likened to hell, and how Mohammed applies that place to Jesus, you can't help but see Mohammed's disdain for Jesus. In like manner, Mohammed treated Moses in the same insulting way. While treating Jesus and Moses so disdainfully, Mohammed painted a beautiful description of Joseph, whom he placed in the third level of heaven, saying his face was as beautiful as the moon. Mohammed also gave a beautiful description to Enoch, reflecting the position given Enoch in Gnostic and Mandaean literature as a divine figure. We also see the elevation of Aaron, Abraham and Adam.

When we see how Mohammed treats Jesus and Moses with disdain, while favoring lesser historical figures, we realize that Mohammed intended to devalue Moses and Jesus because they represented two covenants – the old covenant of the law, which Moses typifies, and the new covenant, which Jesus typifies. Consistent with ideas existing during the time he lived in Arabia, Mohammed believed that Moses represented the Old Testament of the Bible. Moses was viewed as the head of the Judaic religion, and was its major prophet. Jesus was seen as the prophet of the Christian religion. Mohammed wanted to hide them in the shadows of heaven and present them as lesser persons, ugly in comparison to the other prophets. Mohammed wanted to keep his followers from reading the Old and New Testaments because he wanted to make his religion superior to Judaism and Christianity. In the Qur'an Surah 98:6, he portrayed Christians and Jews as the worst of God's creatures.

In order to persuade his followers that he was the offspring of Abraham, Mohammed claimed that he was a true copy of Abraham.

When his followers asked Mohammed what Abraham looked like, he told them that Abraham was a copy of Mohammed himself. He told them:

> I did not see a man similar to him like your friend, nor is your friend likened to any person like him.[70] (By "friend," Mohammed meant himself.)

Al-Bukhari, the authoritative book of Mohammed's Hadith, quotes Mohammed as saying, "I am the most likened son to Abraham."[71] Mohammed wanted to persuade his followers that he was the offspring of Abraham, so he claimed that physically he was a copy of Abraham. Isaac did not dare to make such a claim, though he was Abraham's son, and his mother was Abraham's stepsister. Neither did Jacob, or any of his descendants who were close to Abraham's time, claim that they were a physical copy of Abraham. How could a man who lived 2,700 years after Abraham make such a claim?

4

THE HISTORY OF QURAISH DOES NOT INCLUDE A LINKAGE TO ISHMAEL IN ITS LINEAGE.

Who is the tribe of Quraish, from which Mohammed came, and when did Quraish occupy Mecca? The answers to these questions are critical to our understanding of Islam and its claims.

Another argument in our quest to discover the truth about Mecca concerns the identity of Quraish, the tribe from which Mohammed came, and when the Quraish occupied the city of Mecca.

Quraish is a gathering of many Yemeni families with no prior family connections between them. They were gathered by Qusayy, the 8ᵗʰ ancestor of Mohammed.

Ibn al-Kalbi, one of the most important Arabic historians, said:

> The tribe of Quraish was a gathering of different families, all related to each other through matriarchal lines, but it is not a tribe which began from one father or one mother or nursemaid.[72]

According to al-Tabari, another of the biographers of Mohammed, as well as other narrators of Islamic tradition, the term "Quraish" means "gathering."[73] This supports what Ibn al- Kalbi said. The one who had gathered these families was Qusayy bin Kilab[74] قصي بن كلاب. He was helped by his half brother on his mother's side, named Razeh bin Rabieh bin Haram رازح بن ربيعة بن حرام. Razeh belonged to the tribe of Kuthaah قضاعة , which was in Yemen.[75]

Armed with these historical facts, we conclude that the tribe to which Mohammed belonged did not exist prior to Qusayy bin

Kilab, the 8th ancestor of Mohammed,[76] who was a Yemeni. Since his half brother was living in Yemen, we assume Qusayy came from Yemen recently and nothing is known about his ancestors. We only know he was not part of a known tribe. We can also conclude that, when he wanted to occupy the city, he was not backed by a tribe, something Arabians were careful to do when they planned a raid. Instead, Qusayy bin Kilab gathered several Yemeni families with no tribal connections among them. This gathering later became known as Quraish.

No Marked Descendancy for the Ancestors of Mohammed in History

This refutes the Islamic claim that Mohammed's ancestors formed a clearly-delineated and well-known line in Arabia, extending back to Ishmael. If this were so, the ancestors of Mohammed would have been a large tribe, well-marked in Arabia for 2,600 years before Mohammed. If the Islamic claim were true, the tribe of Quraish would have been like the tribe of Judah, from which King David descended. Judah continued to be a well-organized and well-recognized tribe after the death of King Solomon. It continued throughout history until the Christian era. Its branch, which was the tribe of David, was well-marked in the history of Israel until the birth of Jesus, who drew His humanity from it. But when we study the history of the ancestors of Mohammed, we find no tribe before his 8th ancestor. No Yemeni inscription speaks about such a family or tribe, and individual families were never known as tribes. This is contrary to the idea that Mohammed's family had an old and well-marked descendancy, as Islamic tradition claims.

Ibn al-Kalbi's idea that Quraish was a gathering of various families of different backgrounds which formed the tribe is substantiated by the fact that no classical writer who wrote about the tribes of Arabia ever mentioned the tribe of Quraish. Like Pliny in the year 67 A.D., these writers mentioned the smallest tribes which were in existence in Arabia, but they never mentioned Quraish. Nor did the other classical writers who came after Pliny ever mention this tribe. This proves that, at least until the end of the 3rd century A.D., the tribe of Quraish did not exist.

Qusayy Formed Quraish and Occupied Mecca in the Middle of the 5th Century A.D.

If writers cannot document Quraish's existence before the end of the 3rd century A.D., just when was the tribe formed, and when did it occupy Mecca? We can determine this by estimating the time between Mohammed and his 8th ancestor, Qusayy bin Kilab.

Mohammed was born around 569 or 570 A.D., in the year known as the "year of al-feil," or the "year of the elephant." It was the year that Abraha, the Ethiopian who dominated Yemen, marched into Mecca, using elephants. Considering an Arabian generation to be about 20 years, as we discussed previously, we can estimate the time between Mohammed and his 8th ancestor, Qusayy, to be about 160 years. If we estimate that Qusayy was born around 410 A.D., then it was about 450-460 A.D. when he gathered and organized the various families, later known as Quraish, and occupied Mecca. This logic agrees with the findings of other scholars that Quraish had occupied Mecca sometime in the 5th century A.D.[77]

Islamic tradition's illogical attempts to connect the ancestors of Mohammed with Ishmael.

Islamic tradition created a genealogy for Mohammed's ancestors. The 14th ancestor they called "Faher bin al-Nather" فهر بن النضر, later named Quraish.[78] We saw that this did not match the historical evidence. Ibn Ishak also created a mother for Faher bin al-Nather. He called her Jindalah, daughter of Amer, son of Hareth, son of Mathath al-Jurhami, whom he said was living in Mecca at the time of Ishmael. Ibn Ishak claimed that Mathath al-Jurhami's daughter married Ishmael, and that Mathath was the king of Mecca when Ishmael came to Mecca with his mother, Hagar.[79]

In other words, Ibn Ishak allotted three generations between Faher and Ishmael. If an Arabian generation was 20 years, there would be 280 years between Faher and Mohammed, and the year would have been about 290 A.D. Ishmael would have lived 60 years before Faher in approximately 230 A.D. However, we know that Ishmael lived around 2050 B.C. – a huge difference – which should cause our Muslim friends to be concerned about Islamic tradition. It's foolish to depend on Ibn Ishak and Islamic tradition for historical information.

Quraish Never had Preeminence in Western Arabia Before the Advent of Islam

Islamic tradition gives preeminence to the tribe of Quraish over other Arabians, but this claim has no historical backing. We need only to look at Najran. It is well-known that the inhabitants of Najran, a city on the border of Yemen, were nobility, and had superior standing in western Arabia. As a city of great wealth, Najran gained the respect of the Arabians. Najran was also where Christianity spread and where a bishop was appointed.

Arabian poets before Mohammed recognized the preeminence of Najran and its people over the rest of the Arabs.[80] Only in the mind of the Muslims did Quraish have preeminence, and then only after Islam began, because it was the tribe from which Mohammed came. In Arabia, the tribe which judges has preeminence over the others. Tamim had preeminence because it judged the disputes of other tribes.[81]

Quraish had no religious preeminence, neither did the temple in Mecca. Instead, Quraish went to worship in temples outside of Mecca.

Quraish never had religious preeminence in western Arabia because the tribesmen were traders with no religious privileges. Islamic tradition claims that Quraish had inviolability before Islam arrived, but there is no testimony to this effect, not even from the Arabic poetry written before Islam started.[82]

The people of Quraish used to worship at other temples in other Arabian cities. They would make two trips each year. Later, after Mohammed occupied Mecca, the Qur'an prohibited them from doing this. Scholars think the Quraish trips were to a sanctuary in northern Arabia near Aqaba. The same idea is mentioned by classical writers. Nonnosus tells us that there was a temple on the Gulf of Aqaba which hosted various Arabian tribes. He says:

> Those of the Saracens, those of the Phoinikon and those beyond it and beyond the Taurenian mountains, consider as sacred a place dedicated to I do not know what god, and assemble there twice a year, of these gatherings, the first lasts a whole month and goes on until the middle of spring ... the other lasts two months ... while these gatherings last, they live, says Nonnosus, in complete peace, not only with each other, but also with all the people who live in the country.[83]

So we see that this temple in northern Arabia attracted many Arabian tribes as they made pilgrimages in both seasons, one of which was in the same month as Ramadan. Quraish used to make two religious trips each year, and one of them was to this temple.[84]

We assume that this temple was associated with another famous temple in the Nabataean territory. This one was in the city of Petra, in the same Nabataean territory, close to the sanctuary in northern Arabia near Aqaba. The temple at Petra was dedicated to Dushare ذو الشرى , the god of the Nabataeans. Dushare was called "the lord of the house," and we know that the Temple of Mecca was also called "the lord of the house." Because they copied its title, this indicates that the tribe of Quraish knew about the temple at Petra, which was used by many Arabian tribes who made a pilgrimage to it.[85]

The Qur'an Copied the Concept About the Day and Night Which the Arabian Mythology Attributed to the god, Dushare

According to Arabian mythology, Dushare, the god of the temple at Petra, was the god who separated the day deity from the night deity as they struggled each day with one another.[86]

Many nations of the Middle East, including the Arabians, thought that combat took place each day between the deities of the day and of the night. Usually the night would begin the combat by attacking the day. When the night enters into combat, the earth is under darkness. A major deity intervened, separating the night and the day. Then it was light on earth. Usually both the deities of the day and of the night would swim with the sun and moon. The night was a male deity while the day was female. The night chased the day, endeavoring to apprehend it.

The Qur'an copied this concept about the day and night swimming with the sun and moon upon a celestial sea. Day or night comes when one of them prevails in their struggle. Allah, rather than the Arabian god, Dushare, separates the day and night during their fight, making one or the other come to the earth.

In Arabian mythology, the morning is a son to the sun. The Arabians called the sun "Thuka' " ذكاء, and they called the morning Ibn al Thuka', which means "the son of Thuka'." They also portrayed the morning, or the day, swimming behind his mother, the sun.[87] We find the idea of personifying the day, the morning, or the light of the day, as swimming behind the sun in the sacred Zoroastrian literature. In the Dina-I Mainog-I Khirad, part of the Pahlavi Texts, we see Mitro, the angel of the sun light, swimming behind the sun.[88]

The Arabian mythology especially influenced the Qur'an in claiming that the day and night swim with the sun and the moon. In fact, we find the Qur'an expressing the swimming of the sun, moon, day and night over the "celestial sea." The Persians, Sabian Mandaeans and other sects in the Middle East at the time of Mohammed believed that a celestial sea existed between the sky and the earth. In Surah 21, called Al Anbiya', and verse 33, we read:

It is He who created the night and the day and the sun and the moon, all swim in a Falak.

Mohammed explained in his Hadith that this Falak is the celestial sea.[89]

The Qur'an expresses the Arabian myth about the night asking to wrestle and fight the day. We see this in Surah al-A'raf 7: 54:

He draweth the night as a veil over the day, seeking the day in power and velocity – to wrestle with.

Al-Bukhari, which contains the authoritative Hadith of Mohammed, explains the preceding verse of how the day and night continually fight each other until Allah comes and separates them.[90] In Surah al-Zumar 39:5, the Qur'an uses the term "Yukawer" يكوّر for this encounter between the night and the day, which means "wrestle and pin him down." This meaning is confirmed by the Munjid, the most authoritative Arabic dictionary.[91] Here, I present the verse in Surah al-Zumar:

He – Allah – makes the night wrestle and pin down the day, and the day wrestle and pin down the night.

In other words, the struggle between the day and the night is caused by Allah, whom Mohammed made to replace the Arabian gods in causing the fight between the day and night so as to secure the coming of light or darkness.

The Arabians thought that the night, as deity, is male, while the day is female.[92] It is believed that it is the day when the night is holding the day in front of him. This is because the night is dressed by the "day" so that the beautiful face of the day is covering the darkness. But when a deity separates the night from embracing the day, then the night remains alone without the beautiful color of the day, and the darkness is spread over the land.

As in the Arabian mythology, a deity separates the night from his attack and his hold on the day; we find in the Qur'an that when Allah separates the night from his attack and his hold on the day, then the darkness comes. This we find in Surah 36:37:

> And a sign for them is the night. We disengage (the night) from the day, and behold, they are plunged in darkness.

Mohammed also speaks of an angel who takes the "night" in his hand, and puts it again to swim on the celestial sea.[93] This myth is taken from Persian mythology.

REFERENCES AND NOTES TO PART IV

[1] Cf.Lane, *Lexicon*, S.V.Balsan; Grohmann, *Südarabien*, 1, 156; cf Jacob, *Beduinenleben*, p. 15.; quoted by Patricia Crone, *Meccan Trade*, Princeton University Press, 1987, page 65

[2] Patricia Crone, *Meccan Trade*, Princeton University Press, 1987, page 66

[3] Levine, *Two Neo –Assyrian Stelae From Iran*, (Toronto 1972), 18-20; quoted by I. Eph'al, *The Ancient Arabs*, E.J. Brill, Leiden, 1982, pages 23-24

[4] Tablet signature of Kouyunjik Collection in the British Museum, 2802 vi 17-37; Quoted by I. Eph'al, page 221

[5] H.Tadmor, *The Inscriptions of Tiglath – Pileser III King of Assyria*, Jerusalem, Summ.13

[6] A letter labeled Rm. 77, or R.F. Harper, *Assyrian and Babylonian Letters* I XIV, (London – Chicago, 1892-1914), 414; Quoted by Eph'al, page 95; R.H.Pfeiffer, *State Letters of Assyria*, New Haven 1935, pages 76-77

[7] Rm. 77, or R.F. Harper, *Assyrian and Babylonian Letters* I XIV, (London – Chicago, 1892-1914), page 414; R.H.Pfeiffer, *State Letters of Assyria*, New Haven 1935, pages 76-77 ; L.Waterman, *Royal Correspondence of the Assyrian Empire*, (Ann Arbor, 1930 -1936), I, 288-289; quoted by I. Eph'al, *The Ancient Arabs*, page 95

[8] See L.Waterman, *Royal Correspondence of the Assyrian Empire*, (Ann Arbor, 1930 -1936), I, No.260; R.H.P feiffer, *State Letters of Assyria*, New Haven 1935, No.91; A.L. Oppenheim, *letters from Mesopotamia*, (Chicago 1967), No.118

[9] Eph'al, *Journal of the American Oriental Society*, 94 (1974), 108 ff., 114-115

[10] *Studi sull'Oriente e la Bibbia*, chapter by Chaim Rabin, Genova 1967, page 305

[11] Ibn al-Kalbi, *Kitab al-Asnam*, says that there is a temple of the god, Wadd, at Dumah; see Wellhausen, *Reste Arabischen Heidentums*, Berlin 1897, p.16 ; quoted by Chaim Rabin, in *Studi sull'Oriente e la Bibbia*, Genova 1967, page 306

[12] I. Eph'al, *The Ancient Arabs*, E.J.Brill, Leiden, 1982, page 239

[13] Levine, *Two New-Assyrian Stelae from Iran*, (Toronto, 1972), 18-19

[14] Tablet signature of the British Museum, No: 113203; quoted by I. Eph'al, *The Ancient Arabs*, E.J.Brill, Leiden, 1982, page 115.

[15] Van Zyl, *The Moabites*, 157-158

[16] I. Eph'al, *The Ancient Arabs*, E.J.Brill, Leiden, 1982, page 200.

[17] This is seen by Edomite signs and the numerous Arabic names found in many sites and inscriptions in Negev and south Palestine. See I. Eph'al, *The Ancient Arabs*, page 200.

[18] *Taj al-Aruss* I, page 151

[19] Al-Masudi, *Muruj al-Thahab*, Beirut-Lebanon, 1991, I, page 294

[20] Al-Masudi, *Muruj al-Thahab*, Beirut-Lebanon, 1991, I, page 297

[21] *Tarikh al-Tabari*, Abi Jaafar Bin Jarir al-Tabari, Dar al-Kutub al-Ilmiyeh, (Beirut-Lebanon, 1991), I, page 339

[22] *Tarikh al-Tabari*, I, page 426- 429; al-Ya'akubi I, page 226

[23] Al-Masudi, *Muruj al-Thahab*, Beirut-Lebanon, 1991, I, page 247

[24] *Tarikh al-Tabari*, I, page 227

[25] Masudi, *Muruj al-Thahab*, Beirut-Lebanon, 1991, I, pages 245, 248

[26] Masudi, *Muruj al-Thahab*, I, page 246

[27] Masudi, *Muruj al-Thahab*, II, page 130

[28] Masudi, *Muruj al-Thahab*, I, page 316

[29] Lutfi Abdel Wahab al-Husseini, *Al-Arab Fi al-'Usur al-Khadimah*, Dar al-Nahthah al-Arabiah, Beirut-1978, pages 84-85; citing Saad Zaglul Abel Hamid, *Fi Tarikh al-Arab Khabl al-Islam*, Beirut, 1975, page 84; citing Ibn Khaldun, 2, page 47 and footnote 3 of the same page.

[30] *Tarikh al-Tabari*, I, page 189

[31] *Tarikh al-Tabari*, I, page 524

[32] *Halabieh*, I, page 93 ; comments on Ibn Hisham, page m

[33] *Halabieh* I, page 36

[34] Masudi, *Muruj al-Thahab*, Beirut-Lebanon, 1991, II, pages 280-282

[35] *Halabieh*, I, pages 35, 36

[36] *Tarikh al-Tabari*, I , page 127

[37] *Tarikh al-Tabari*, I, page 127

[38] *Tarikh al-Tabari*, I, page 127

[39] *Diwan Ummiah bin Abi al-Salt*, (Beirut-1938), page 58

[40] *Tarikh al-Tabari*, I, page 128

[41] *Tarikh al-Tabari*, I, page 128

[42] *Tarikh al-Tabari*, I, page 516

[43] K.A. Kitchen, *Documentation For Ancient Arabia*, Part I, pages 90-222

[44] *Diwan Ummiah*, page 26

[45] *Tarikh al-Tabari*, I, page 429

[46] *Sahih al-Bukhari*, I, page 92

[47] *Ibn Hisham*, 2, page 36; *al- Bukhari*, I, page 92; *Halabieh*, II, page 111

[48] *Halabieh*, II, page 112

[49] *The Secret Adam*, E.S. Drower, Oxford at the Clarendon Press, 1960, page 36

[50] *The Canonical Prayerbook of the Mandaeans*, translated by Drower, Leiden 1959 page 278; *The Secret Adam*, E.S. Drower, Oxford at the Clarendon Press 1960, page 25; *The Great First World (Alma Risaia RBA)*, *A Pair of Nasoraean Commentaries*, translated by Drower, Leiden Brill, 1963, page 5

[51] The angels, except Satan, worshipping Adam we find it in *Ginza Rba*, first book, second hymn, pages 9 and 10 ; The angels of fire serve Adam: see *The Secret Adam*, E.S. Drower, Oxford at the Clarendon Press, 1960, page 35. Adam having angels: *The Canonical Prayerbook of the Mandaeans*, translated by Drower, Leiden, 1959 page 278. The world worshipping Adam : see - *The Secret Adam*, E.S. Drower, Oxford at the Clarendon Press 1960, page 25

[52] *Ginza Rba*, second book, first hymn, page 28

[53] *Sahih Al- Bukhari* 4:125; *Ibn Hisham* 2: 32

[54] *Sahih al-Bukhari*, 3, page 150

[55] *Sahih al-Bukhari*, 3, page 135; 3, page 86; 8, page 117

[56] *Sahih Muslim* 11: 141, 142

[57] *Sahih al-Bukhari*, 3, page 135

[58] *Sahih al-Bukhari*, 3, page 128

[59] *Sahih Muslim* 11, page 39

[60] *Sahih al-Bukhari*, 3, page 29; 7, page 238; 8, page 9

[61] *Halabieh*, 1, page 372

[62] *Halabieh*, 2, page 91

[63] *A Manichaean Psalm-Book*, Manichaean Manuscripts in the Chester Beatty Collection, Part II, edited by C.R.C. Alleberry, W.Kohlhammer, Stuttgart, 1938, page 52

[64] *Halabieh*, 2, page 117

[65] *Ibn Hisham*, 2, page 32; Halabieh, 2, page 88

[66] *Halabieh*, 2, page 88

[67] *Halabieh*, 2, page 90

[68] Josue' Le Stylite, traduction Martin, xx; quoted by James Darmesteter in his Introduction to Vendidad, *The Zenda –Avesta* Part I, *The Sacred Books of the East*, Volume IV, page xc

[69] *Gautama*, Chapter IX, 61, *Sacred Laws of the Aryas*, Part I, Translated by Georg Buhler, *The Sacred Books of the East*, Volume 2, Published by Motilal Banarsidass, Delhi, page 225

[70] *Ibn Hisham*, 2, page 32; Halabieh, 2, page 91

[71] *Sahih al-Bukhari*, 4, page 125

[72] *Tarikh al-Tabari*, I, page 511

[73] *Tarikh al-Tabari*; I, page 511

[74] *Tarikh al-Tabari*, I, page 511

[75] *Tarikh al-Tabari,* I, page 506

[76] *Ibn Hisham* I, page 3

[77] Patricia Crone, *Meccan Trade*, Princeton University Press, 1987, page 169

[78] *Ibn Hisham* I, page 3

[79] Al-Masudi, *Muruj al-Thahab*, II, page 52; Tabari I, page 510

[80] *Al-Agani*, Abi Faraj Al-Asbahani, 10, page 145; 17, page 105

[81] " Mecca and Tamim," Kister, pages 145 ff, quoted by Patricia Crone, *Meccan Trade*, Princeton University Press, 1987, page 156

[82] Jahiz, *Tria Opuscula*, page 63 ; Cf. R.B. Serjeant, "Haram and Hawtah , the Sacred Enclave in Arabia" ; quoted by Patricia Crone, page 181

[83] Nonnosus cited by Photius, *Bibliotheque* ,1, 5

[84] *Tarikh al-Tabari*, I, page 504

[85] *Ency. Relig.*, 9 page 122; cited by Jawad Ali, vi, pages 415 and 416

[86] *Ency. Relig.*, 9 page 122; cited by Jawad Ali, VI, page 415

[87] *Taj al-Aruss* 10, page 137

[88] *The Dina-I Mainog-I Khirad*, Chapter LIII, 4, *Pahlavi Texts*, Part III, Translated by E.W. West, *The Sacred Books of the East*, Volume 24, page 96

[89] *Tarikh al-Tabari*, I, page 49
[90] *Sahih al-Bukhari*, 4, page 75
[91] *Al-Munjid*, page 702
[92] Halabieh 2, page 332
[93] *Tarikh al-Tabari*, I, page 50

Part V

The Hajj, the Occult Umra', and Ramadan

THE GREAT PILGRIMAGE OF ISLAM

Historical Facts Exclude Mecca as a Station in the Pilgrimage of Pre-Islamic Times

Making a pilgrimage, or Hajj, to Mecca and to its hills is one of the five pillars of Islam. Every Muslim has an obligation to make this pilgrimage at least once in his lifetime.[1]

Mohammed bestowed the Hajj with magical consequences for those who perform it. Mohammed said this in his Hadith, which is considered second in importance only to the Qur'an. He said:

> He who makes the pilgrimage, returns to how he was when his mother begot him.[2]

By this, Mohammed meant those who go on the Hajj become sinless. So many things in Islam hinge on the Islamic Hajj, that now I'm going to discuss the Hajj and its pagan roots.

There are some groups which make their pilgrimages to pagan places seem important by claiming that Biblical figures made pilgrimages to these spots.

Historically, the Hajj was known as a pagan rite to certain sects in the Middle East. One of the sects which practiced pilgrimages were the Harranians. Harran is a city on the border between Syria, Iraq and Asia Minor – today's Turkey. The main deity of the Harranians was the moon, but they also worshiped the sun, other planets, and other deities, such as the Jinn. They conducted their pilgrimages to the mountains around Harran. Al-Hashimi, an Arabic historian, mentions one of their feasts, "the feast of the

THE HAJJ AND RAMADAN

lords of the coming forth of the New Moons."[3] Harran became a famous city and a place of pilgrimage because of the worship of Sin, the god of the moon. Ibn al-Nadim, another Arabic historian, mentioned the pilgrimage of the Harranians to different places where they worshipped several gods, including Sin, god of the moon. They also worshipped planets, and other gods, such as Hermes and the Jinn.[4]

The Harranians exercised great influence over Mohammed. Mohammed joined a group at Mecca called "al-Ahnaf," which had connections to the Harranians. Many members of the group went to visit to the al-Jazirah area which lay on the border between Northeastern Syria, Iraq and Turkey. Historians tell us that members of these groups, such as Zayd Bin Amru, went there to search for religious knowledge.[5] Through these contacts, many rituals passed from the Harranians to Islam. Zayd Bin Amru was one of the founders of Ahnaf. He was related to Mohammed, and Mohammed was known to meet Zayd in the caves of Harra', where the members of Ahnaf often met[6] (see Introduction).

Because of Harran's effect on Mohammed, Harran became an important place in the Qur'an. The Qur'an intimates that Solomon subdued the wind, then mounted it to travel to a distant land. The Qur'an says in Surah 21:81:

> To Solomon the violent wind flows under his command to the land we had blessed.

Many writers in Islamic tradition interpret this verse to claim that Solomon mounted the wind to make a pilgrimage to Harran. Harran was considered a city of pilgrimage,[7] especially for the Harranians, who worshipped the moon. Many groups were influenced by Harranians, who made Harran a place where people went to worship heathen gods like Sin, the moon god. These groups wanted to think of Harran as an old city to which people had been making pilgrimages for many years. They wanted to look to important personalities of history, such as Solomon, and claim that they went to Harran on pilgrimages. It would add importance to their religion, if the prophets of the Old Testament recognized it.

The same is true concerning Mecca. Islamic tradition sought to make Mecca an ancient center for pilgrimages. They connected Abraham with Mecca when they said Abraham mounted a Baraq, which was a winged camel, and flew to Mecca. It was a habit for religious groups to make their pagan cities important places of worship in history, and they did so by connecting it with Biblical figures.

The Qur'an and Islamic writers claimed that Abraham called the people of the earth to make a pilgrimage to Mecca.

The Qur'an, in Surah al-Hajj 22, verse 27, claims that Allah ordered Abraham to present himself at a minaret, which is the tower from which faithful Muslims are called to prayer. Abraham was to call the people to perform the rite of the Hajj, which is a pilgrimage to Mecca. Then people from all over the world would respond to Abraham's call in Abraham's generation. Ibn Abbas claimed that when Abraham called for a Hajj to Mecca, all the stones, the hills and the trees that heard him, even the dust, went in Hajj to Mecca.[8]

Qur'anic verses claim that Abraham used the Athan آذان, or loud voice, to call the people to prayer. Crying in a loud voice from over a minaret is still the way Muslims call people to prayer. This method was known and practiced throughout the history of Arabia. The worshippers of various sects of Jinn at the time of Mohammed used to cry out from a minaret to call people to pray. This was adopted mainly by people who claimed to be prophets in Arabia, and they were known to have connections with the Jinn. Before Mohammed, Musaylimeh Bin Habib claimed to be a prophet in the city of Yamama. He had a person cry out to the people from minaret, calling them to pray, or to go on Hajj to a certain temple. This kind of rite was not known outside Arabia, nor was it used in the centuries prior to Mohammed.

The verse which shows Abraham crying out from the minaret also says that the voice of Abraham was heard by every human

THE HAJJ AND RAMADAN

being on the earth. This is a myth that cannot possibly be true. Historically, no one on earth has ever heard the voice of Abraham calling him to make a Hajj to Mecca. Further, we saw historically that Mecca was not in existence until the 4th century A.D. So, how can people in every part of the earth come to an unknown place in the desert of central western Arabia where no one in history had ever walked before?

Mecca's poverty of pasturing fields, and its scarcity of water, exclude it as a place of Hajj prior to Islam.

Mecca could not possibly have been a place to which pilgrims made the Hajj before Islam. Mecca was a city in poverty, with few places to pasture livestock. How could it provide grazing for the tens of thousands of camels that would carry the people on the Hajj? There were already other places with more conducive pasturing fields in Arabia. The Kaabahs of these cities were prepared to host pilgrimages.

Another important factor which excludes Mecca as a place of Hajj is the scarcity of water. Mecca was without water until Abdel Mutaleb, the grandfather of Mohammed, dug the well of Zamzam, 50-75 years before Mohammed. Mecca was unable to provide enough water for even the small tribe of Khuzaa'h, who first built and inhabited the city during the 4th century A.D. How, then, could Mecca provide enough water for the thousands of pilgrims who would have needed it? How would they water their camels, and the other animals they brought with them, to sacrifice as part of the Hajj ceremonies?

Before the well of Zamzam was dug just 50-70 years before Mohammed's times, it was impossible that Mecca could have been a place of Hajj for the Arabians, because of the reasons I just mentioned.

There was a Hajj in the region around Mecca in pre-Islamic times, but Mecca was not among the stations of the Hajj.

Years before Islam, a kind of pagan Hajj existed in the hills outside of Mecca, but it was revered by a limited number of pagan

Arabians. With the advent of Islam, Mecca was included in this pagan Hajj. Under Mohammed, the pilgrimage to Mecca later became a main pillar of the Islamic religion.

In pre-Islamic times, Mecca was known to be part of what is called "the small Hajj," but it was purely occult, and part of the rites of the Arabian religion of Jinn. I will discuss this in detail when I will next treat the subject of "the small Hajj."

It is well-known that the Arabians used to conduct trade while on the Hajj, or religious pilgrimage. In pre-Islamic times, the people who came to the area for a Hajj didn't trade in Mecca, but traded in Ukkaz and other nearby places, such as Majanna and Dhul-Majaz. Arabian writings tell us that Ukkaz was a city of "Haram," which means no one could kill, or do certain other things there, during the month of Hajj. We find that when Quraish, the tribe from which Mohammed came, visited these places, they ought to visit them in a state of Ihram, or a state of consecration. Ibn Habib tells us that the tribe of Quraish never visited Dhul-Majaz except in a state of consecration or Ihram[9]. We see that the tribe of Quraish was in state of Ihram, or consecration, when it was in Ukkaz, when the war of Fujjar started.[10] Fujjar means "miscreant, villain or malefactor." In the war of Fujjar, an alliance was formed by the tribes of Quraish and Kinaneh. Toward the end of the 6th century A.D., they fought against other Arabian tribes who were their enemies. The war was called Fujjar because it happened in the months of Haram, during which Arabians were prohibited to fight. Al-Azruqi, an old Islamic author who wrote about Mecca, also said that no one could visit Ukkaz or Dhul-Majaz or Majanna except in a state of Ihrah, or consecration.[11]

These historical witnesses show that the pre-Islamic Hajj started in centers other than Mecca. Pilgrims gathered in these places to visit temples there, conduct trade, and prepare themselves to make the pilgrimage to the sacred places which were in the hills of Mina', Arafa and Muzdalifah. These places were the true objects of the Hajj, as we will see later. Mecca is excluded from the Hajj, because its official rites began at the hill called Arafa and ended in Mina', where the state of Ihram concludes. It is clear that the Hajj was made to those hills where the Arabians worshipped their gods, and they did not include Mecca. These facts show us that Mecca was excluded from the Hajj, but the evidence does not end here. We notice that the officials at the city of Arafa were people from the tribe of Tamim not from Quraish.[12] This also tells us that Mecca and Quraish, the tribe who lived there, had nothing to do with the Hajj.

Crone, a scholar, in her work, Mecca's *Trade and the Rise of Islam*, also noticed that discussions concerning trade during the pilgrimage are focused on Arafa and Mina', to the exclusion of Mecca. People would trade during the pilgrimage, but not at Arafa and Mina'. When, according to their religious rites, they were eventually allowed to trade during the pilgrimage, they began to trade at Arafa and Mina', but there is no reference to Mecca in the discussions.[13] It is clear that Arafa and Mina' are the original places for the Arabian pilgrimage, and that pre-Islamic Mecca was not considered a pilgrimage station.

After Mohammed failed to convince people to become proselytes to Islam, he changed his strategy, and searched for a tribe he could deal with, and who would recognize him as a "prophet of Allah." He would lead the tribe to war against the Arabian tribes, kill the men, and give them the women and daughters of the Arabians and Jews they conquered. The women would become their concubines, the sons would be sold as slaves, and the houses and personal properties would become booty for the conquerors. For many years, Mohammed went to Ukkaz, Majanna, Mina' and Dhul-Majaz, stations of the Hajj, to display his program. However, he never met anyone like the tribes at Mecca.[14] But in these places he did meet representatives of Aos and Khazraj, the two tribes who accepted his offer.[15]

Although Islamic tradition endeavors to connect the pagan Arabian ceremonies of the pilgrimage with Abraham, the historical facts clearly contradict their claims. We can see that it is in vain for Muslims to rely on pagan Arabian ceremonies to try to obtain the remission of their sins. The remission of sins was never connected with religious rituals; otherwise, only rich people could afford to receive remission because, in ancient times, one encountered great expense to travel such long distances in the Hajj. For example, traveling from Bangladesh before the invention of motorized transportation was very troublesome and arduous. Taking this trip meant spending seven months in the journey to reach Mecca, and another seven months for the return. There was also a good chance the pilgrim would never survive the journey. Through the deserts of Asia and Arabia he would encounter many dangers, such as thieves, pirates, ferocious animals and snakes, not to mention the lack of food and water. The risk of epidemics spread among the huge numbers of pilgrims who gathered for the long trip. The time needed for a pilgrimage from a distant region could take as much as 12 to 16 months, a long time to separate the pilgrim from his family and his work. It also cost the man a large amount of money for his own expenses during this period, considering he was not working or living with his family. The Hajj was an extra-costly, illogical ritual that could destroy the family, and the social and economic life of the one who undertook it, and endanger his own health and, perhaps, require his life.

Mohammed and his tribe who lived at Mecca were the only people who benefited from the ritual of the pilgrimage to Mecca. Because pilgrims brought their animals to sacrifice, all the meat was left to the inhabitants of Mecca. Many goats and lambs were left behind, not to mention the money pilgrims brought with them, or the trade which they conducted. In reality, the pilgrimage each Muslim was to perform at least once in his lifetime was instituted by Mohammed in order to bring the riches of other Muslims to his own tribe of Quraish. Given the arduous and costly journey each pilgrim had to endure, the poor would be deprived from such presumptuous privileges.

The Hajj is an unnecessary sacrifice for men to perform when, in fact, the price for the remission of sins was paid on the Cross by Jesus, the only person who never sinned. He paid for our sins by His atoning death on the Cross in order that we would be liberated from our sin and considered righteous before a holy God. The salvation of God, through Christ, is accessible to any person, whatever his culture, social or economic condition. No one is required to make a pilgrimage to any place in order to receive the free gift of God's salvation and the remission of sins. The gift of God can't be bought through religious activities. Salvation was purchased with a costly price – the blood of the incarnate Son of God. We can only receive it by faith, not by creating religious rituals and works to earn it.

Mecca was Part of an Occultic Hajj, Which Took the Name Umra'

We already saw that pre-Islamic Mecca was never one of the cities served by the great pilgrimage called Hajj, although Muslims claim it was the key city.

We'll see that Mecca was part of Umra', a small occultic Hajj, which could be performed at any time during the year. In pre-Islamic times, this Hajj was connected to occult worship in Arabia. The pilgrimage began at the site of two Kuhhan statues named Asaf and Naelah. The Kuhhan were priests in Arabian Jinn worship. Their statues were placed on the main sacred stones at the temple in Mecca. Other pilgrims began the Hajj from similar statues of Asaf and Naelah located on the seashore near Mecca. The Hajj then proceeded to the hills of Safa and Marwa, where there were other statues of Asaf and Marwa. Historically, Safa and Marwa were the center for the occult Jinn religion. Mohammed incorporated the idea of the Hajj into Islam.

THE STAGES OF THE GREAT HAJJ AND THEIR PAGAN MEANINGS AND ORIGINS.

The Hajj Toward the Hill of Arafa

The Hajj, also called "the great pilgrimage," begins on the 7th of Du al-Hijjah, the month of the pilgrimage. At Mecca, pilgrims listen to preaching about the pilgrimage, but there are no rituals performed there which prove Mecca was originally part of that pilgrimage.

377

On the second day, the 8th of Du al-Hijjah, the pilgrims depart for the hill Arafa, located east of Mecca. It takes more than four hours to reach this hill by camel. In the middle of the journey to Arafa, there is a place called Muna, currently known as Mina', where they pray the prayer of noontime. Muna is an important place in the Hajj. Both the words Muna and Manat have the same Arabic meaning, "to wish or aspire." Manat was the daughter of Allah. This indicates Muna was dedicated to the worship of Manat. Later, I'll discuss the rituals of Hajj which were performed at Muna on their way back to Mecca.

On the third day, the 9th of Du al-Hajj, pilgrims continue to the hill called Arafa. They all wear white, showing they are in a state of consecration, according to tradition. They stand in a plain near a mount called the "Jabal Al-Rahmah," which means the "mountain of mercy," and they cry in loud voices from afternoon until sunset, "Labeik Allahumma Labeik." Allahumma means "Allah, are them," so their cry is translated, "Allah are them, I am here."

The Cry "Allah are Them, I am Here," and its Use in the Pagan Worship in Arabia

The meaning of this cry has special significance, because the worshippers of the Arabian Star Family would recite this sentence before each member in the Star Family to confirm their belief that all members of the Star Family are worthy of honor. Mohammed incorporated this cry into Islam, just like he incorporated the pilgrimage, itself, into Islam.

We also find that the worshippers at Hubol, the main shrine of the temple at Mecca, would recite this sentence.[16] "Hubol" was a symbol for the moon god.[17] Many scholars think Hubol was Allah, before the planet, Venus, replaced him with the title of Allah.

The same cry was spoken by Arabians before Manat. They said:

Allah are them, I am here. Without the prayerful who come early before you, people will fail and abandon you, but they will still come to you in one pilgrimage after another.[18]

This cry before Manat, the daughter of Allah, teaches us that it was a ritualistic formula which the worshippers of the Arabian Star Family presented when they conducted a Hajj to any sacred place dedicated to any member of the Star Family. Manat has places where her worshippers went to perform the same cry and conduct other rituals, like cutting their hair.[19] The same rituals of cry and cutting the hair at Muna were incorporated by Mohammed in the Islamic Hajj. Quraish and Khuzaa'h, the tribe who built Mecca, were among those who worshipped Manat and went there on pilgrimages.[20]

All these historical incidents reveal the reason why pilgrims used to cry the same cry on the hill of Arafa until the sun set, "Allah are them, I am here." Arafa was a place to worship Ellat, the sun, until it set. Ellat, like her husband, Allah, the moon, and her daughters Manat and al-'Uzza, was treated with the same honor and the same cry.

Mohammed has prohibited his followers to pray on the hill of Arafa after sunset,[21] which reminds us of the pagan Arabians when they went on a Hajj to the hill of Arafa. They continued their worship and cried before the sun until it set.

The term, "Allah are them," was adopted by the tribe of Quraish, from which Mohammed came, before he claimed to be a prophet. Quraish used to begin their letters or treaties "in the name of Allah are them."[22] Mohammed was from the clan of Beni Hashem, of the tribe of Quraish. Quraish wrote a document against Beni Hashem which started with the same term, "In your name Allah are them." The Quraish document prohibited their members from having any relationship with the Beni Hashem, because Beni Hashem refused to yield Mohammed to Quraish in order to be judged. The paper they wrote began with the phrase, "In your name Allah are them."[23] This pagan tribe used this formula because it honored each member of the Arabian Star Family.

379

Suhail Bin Amru, one of the leaders of the Quraish tribe, negotiated a treaty between the tribe of Quraish and Mohammed. In writing the terms of the treaty, Mohammed wanted to begin with the words, "In the name of Allah the Rahman al-Rahim." This formula was initiated before Mohammed by Musaylimeh Bin Habib, a man who claimed to be a prophet, with ties to a Jin-devil. Quraish was opposed to Musaylimeh. The tribe's spokesman, Suhail, objected to beginning the treaty with the words, "In the name of Allah, the Rahman al-Rahim." Suhail told Mohammed:

> "I do not know who is the 'Rahman.' Instead, write it this way, 'In your name Allah are them,' as you were accustomed to write."[24]

This shows that when Mohammed initiated a treaty, or wrote an important document, he used the same words his tribe used in honoring the members of the Arabian Star Family.

The religion of the Jinn-devils in Arabia spread their form of paganism through a theology which said that many gods were to be worshipped. That was contrary to the Biblical announcement that people are to worship only the one true God.

Umayya bin abi al-Salt was a cousin of Mohammed, from his mother. Umayya was also involved with a Jin-devil who taught him many things, among which was the phrase, "In your name, Allah are them."[25] Umayya claimed that two birds opened his chest and took "the black al-a'laka'" away from his heart. According to a Gnostic concept, "the black al-a'laka'" is a black substance in the human body which caused men to sin. After it was removed, Umayya became sinless. Mohammed copied Umayya's claim, but Mohammed said it was two angels who opened his heart and took away the "black al-a'laka,'" making him sinless.

Mohammed would often sit with Fari'ah, the sister of Umayya, because Mohammed was fond of her beauty. She used to recite many poems which her brother, Umayya, wrote. Mohammed incorporated many of them into the Qur'an. Mohammed, like Umayya, adopted the phrase "In your name, Allah, are them" which the Jinn-devil taught to Umayya.

The Arabian Jinn-devils spread the message that all the Arabian gods and idols were to be respected and honored. In this way, the Jinn-devils attracted Arabians to their gods. The term "In your name, Allah, are them" expressed their diabolic intention to compete with the Biblical concept of deity which prohibited anyone to honor any god except the Triune God.

The Hajj Proceeds to Muzdalifah where Pagan Pilgrims Worshipped the Moon

I would like to return to our discussion of what happened in the month of the Hajj. I mentioned that on the 9th day of the month of pilgrimage, called Du al-Hijjah, the pilgrims stand on the hill of Arafa until sunset crying, "Allah are them, I am here." After sunset, the pilgrims begin a journey to a place called al-Muzdalifah, where they pass the night and pray the prayers of evening. The second day, the 10th day of the month of pilgrimage, called Du al-Hijjah, they conduct Waqfa before dawn, which means they stand and cry to Allah.

When we study the books which contain the Hadith of Mohammed, and which give us an account of his life, we find that Muzdalifah was a place where pagan Arabians of the area of Mecca and Medina often went to pray. They prayed from the time the moon rose until it disappeared. The books of al-Bukhari and Sahih Muslim are two authoritative books which contain the Hadith of Mohammed. They quote the words of Abdullah, the servant of Asmaa, who was the sister of Aisheh, the youngest wife of Mohammed:

> Asmaa went to Muzdalifah, and started to pray. She prayed for an hour, then she said, "My son, does the moon disappear?" I answered "no." Then she prayed an hour and said, "Did the moon disappear?" I said "yes," and she said "depart," so we departed.[26]

Mohammed, in one of his Hadiths, also speaks about praying in Muzdalifah until the moon disappears.[27] These words tell us that Muzdalifah was located in a place where pilgrims of the Arabian Star Family honored and worshipped the moon. Therefore,

Asmaa worshipped at Muzdalifah while the moon was rising in the sky, and she could not stop her prayer while the moon was visible. She stopped only when she knew the moon had disappeared. It is clear to us that Muzdalifah was the place where the phase of the moon was right for the worship to begin during the Hajj. The fact that pilgrims had to leave Arafa after sunset indicates that they fulfilled their duties toward the sun in this stage of the Hajj, and that they didn't need to sleep at Arafa, the location dedicated to the sun in the Hajj. Perhaps, even before the Hajj was instituted, they were to reach Muzdalifah during the night when the moon was worshipped.

This discussion of the Hajj, and its Arabian pagan roots, is an attempt to help our Muslims friends understand the true nature of these Arabian rituals involving the Arabian Star Family, and to avoid considering them part of the worship of the true God. Even if Mohammed could have clothed the worship of his pagan ancestors with more claims, it does not make this kind of worship to be a legally, divine worship.

We already looked at the stations of the Hajj located near Mecca. In the pre-Islamic Hajj, each station had a place to invoke a member of the Arabian Star Family. We learned that pilgrims stopped to worship the sun at the station of Arafa, and they invoked the moon at the station of Muzdalifah. I will continue explaining the phases of the Hajj.

Different tribes gave more importance to some stations of the pilgrimage than they did to other places. In the past, we assume that these locations were disconnected. A tribe would dedicate each place to one member of the Arabian Star Family. Eventually, they unified and coordinated all of these worship sites, resulting in one great Hajj, accepted by all the tribes who previously venerated their own preferred star deity.

A Waqfa was a stop on the pilgrimage. Pilgrims made a Waqfa at Muzdalifah. They always stopped at Muzdalifah before dawn. This confirms that, before they unified the rituals, Muzdalifah was a place dedicated exclusively to the worship of the moon, and only the hours of the night before dawn gave worshippers the opportunity to spend several hours with the Arabian moon before it disappeared. They made at least two Waqfa, one during the night and the other before dawn, before the moon disappears.

At Muna, or Mina', they had a station in the Hajj dedicated to the worship of Manat, one of Allah's two daughters.

Pilgrims visited Muna before the sun rose to perform special rituals. First, they cast seven pebbles, or small stones, onto a small mountain; second, they made animal sacrifices; and third, they cut their hair, officially terminating the Hajj. Rituals conducted at this station are identical to rituals the Arabians performed when making pilgrimages to places dedicated to Manat, one of Allah's two daughters.

Muna, or Mina', is an important station on the pilgrimage. We see this by the way pilgrims cast the seven stones. Mecca was to be on their left side and Muna on their right side.[28] In the mind of Arabians, putting Mecca on the left side meant it had much less importance than Muna where they honored Manat, one of the two daughters of Allah, and a definite deity of the Star Family. The names for both Muna and Manat, the daughters of Allah, have the same meaning, which is "wish," or "aspiration." Manat was worshipped in many locations in and around Mecca and Medina. Medina was the city to which Mohammed emigrated. One of the worship locations was Mashlal, seven miles from Medina.[29] Also, there were many places for the worship of Manat between Mecca and Medina; one was Khadid,[30] and still others were along the seashore.[31] We assume that Muna, or Mina', was the main location on the pilgrimage to worship Manat, because Muna was named after Manat.

According to many Arabic historians who wrote about pre-Islamic Arabia, such as Ibn al- Kalbi, Khazraj and Oas were the two tribes whose worshippers were most attached to Manat.[32] These two tribes helped Mohammed wage war against the Arabians to bring them into submission to Islam. That's one of the reasons Mohammed incorporated the ceremonies of Hajj to Muna into the Islamic Hajj. In order for Mohammed to please

Khazraj and Oas, he adopted many of their religious laws and ceremonies. He kept Friday as the day the two tribes worshipped, and continued the pilgrimage between the two stones of Safa and Marwa, the ritual which was observed by these two tribes.

I previously mentioned Mashlal, the place which was seven miles from Medina where Khazraj and Oas lived. There was a temple there, built around a rock representing Manat. The temple had a Sidneh, or service, like the one observed in the temple at Mecca.[33] Another temple for Manat was at Khadid. Among the tribes who worshipped there were Khuzaa'h, the tribe that built Mecca.[34]

Manat was the deity to whom the Arabians would plead when they needed rain. At the end of their Hajj, they presented animal sacrifices to Manat.

Manat, originally a planet, was represented by a rock on which sacrifices to the various gods were made during the Hajj ceremonies. According to many narrators, this was due to two factors connected with Manat. First, the word Mana means "to shed blood," suggesting to some narrators that the rock of Manat received its name because of all the sacrifices made on the rock of Manat.[35] Second, because Manat means "wish or aspiration," it was a place where many tribes came to present their animal sacrifices, which represented their own aspirations and pleading for rain.[36] All this may shed some light on the origin and the motives of the Hajj, as it is still practiced by Muslims today. We see why sacrifices are presented only in the station of the Hajj called Muna. Different tribes in the region presented their sacrifices to their gods on the rock of Manat.

We also see that one of the purposes of the Hajj in pre-Islamic times was to plead with the gods for rain. That's why they dedicated their sacrifices and finished the Hajj in the place where Manat is worshipped because Manat was the god with whom they pled for rain. Aridity and draught are serious problems for Arabs. It seems that when the draught season lasted for several months, Arabian tribes in the areas around Mecca and Medina organized a special retreat to the hills, to invoke the members of the Arabian Star Family for the return of rain. The pleading terminated when they presented their sacrifices to Manat, the goddess whom they thought was capable of granting their wish for rain.

The Islamic Hajj is the same Hajj instituted by pagan Arabian tribes to plead to their gods to give them rain. When Islam came, Mecca was added to this Hajj, and other ceremonies were developed.

Ibn al-Kalbi, who wrote about the customs of Arabians before Islam, mentioned a kind of pilgrimage that the tribes of Khazraj and Aos, along with the tribes of Ozd and Ghassan, made to al-Mashlal, the place located seven miles from Medina and dedicated to the worship of Manat. He said:

> They used to make a pilgrimage and make "Waqfa," a religious stop, at various places. They would not cut their hair. When they finished visiting the various places of Hajj, they would come to Manat, where they cut their hair. They did not consider their pilgrimage as complete without doing this.[37]

This is exactly what happens today in the Islamic Hajj. After pilgrims visit the different places, they stop at the hill of Arafa, which we saw was the place where Arabians made "Waqfa" to invoke the sun. They went on to Muzdalifah, where they stopped to invoke the moon, then concluded at Muna, where they presented their sacrifices and cut their hair. Today, the Hajj of Islam surely reflects the same pagan rituals as it did in pre-Islamic times. The pagan Arabians were united in the efforts to plead with their gods, specifically the sun, the moon and Manat, three of the four members of the Star Family. This was before the planet, Venus, replaced the moon as the title for Allah. The Hajj, as I mentioned, most probably was for the purpose of pleading for rain. Since the presenting of the sacrifices and the cutting of their hair was the last phase of the pilgrimage which pagan Arabians performed, we know that the Hajj was terminated officially at the station of Muna. Everything that came later, and is practiced in

Islam today, was added to the old ceremonies of the Hajj practiced before Islam.

Mohammed added several things to the pagan Hajj. The Hajj returned to Mecca. The people circled the Kaabah of Mecca seven times. Those who didn't perform the Umra', or the small Hajj, had to make a course between the two stones of Safa and Marwa seven times before returning again to Manat where the state of consecration, called Ihram, stops. The pilgrims enter into a state of entertainment and amusement during the days 11, 12 and 13 of Du al-Hijjah, the month of pilgrimage. Pilgrims were instructed to throw stones in all directions. They were to drink water from the well of Zamzam and visit the tomb of Mohammed.

Later, three tribes returned to Mecca after performing the Hajj to Manat. Several ceremonies were added to the original Hajj.

The first ceremony is the return from Muna, or Mina', to Mecca. We find a key to this ceremony in the narrations of Arabic writers who wrote about the pilgrimage and the religious customs of tribes in western central Arabia. They tell us that the tribes of Khuzaa'h, Oas and Khazraj honored Manat in Mashlal, about seven miles from Medina. It was the main place where Manat was worshipped, and from Manat they returned to march around the Kaabah of Mecca.[38]

From this we see that the tribe of Khuzaa'h, which first built Mecca during the 4th century A.D., would go to the rock of Manat to present their sacrifices, pleading for rain. For Khuzaa'h, returning to circle around the Kaabah was understandable, because the Kaabah was their temple, built for them by the Himyarite leader, Abu Karb Asa'd, when he occupied Mecca. He reigned in Yemen from 410-435 A.D. Khuzaa'h had as its main deity, Venus, who was called "Allah," a title snatched from the moon. For Khuzaa'h, honoring Manat, the daughter of Allah, and pleading to her for rain without returning to her father, Allah, in his sanctuary at Mecca, would have meant disloyalty to the head of the Arabian Star Family. So they were instructed to return to the Kaabah and circle around it. This was not Quraish, Mohammed's tribe, who occupied Mecca and drove Khuzaa'h away. Quraish is not listed with the three tribes who returned from Manat's rock to circle around the Kaabah.

Mohammed added Mecca to the Hajj, to institute an occult custom of Aos and Khazraj in their Hajj called Umra', which was performed to two statues of the old priest of Jinn of Mecca.

Two other tribes, who used to visit Manat and return to Mecca, were Aos and Khazraj. These were the two tribes which helped Mohammed subdue the Arabians and make them converts to Islam through the sword. When we study the religious history and rites of these tribes, we understand why Aos and Khazraj would return to Mecca after making a Hajj to Manat. These two tribes conducted a special Hajj to the two statues which, according to tradition, were two priests of the Jinn-devils. The two priests were Asaf, a male, and Naelah, a female. Arabians around Mecca and Medina believed that these two priests committed fornication inside the Kaabah, and were transformed by gods into stones. These stones were revered over the two main stones, called Rukun, in the Kaabah of Mecca. Since the stones in a temple were the places where the main idols stood, we can understand the importance of Asaf and Naelah in the worship system of Mecca.

Oas and Khazraj, as well as the rest of the worshippers who revered the old priests of the Jinn-devils, Asaf and Naelah, had a special Hajj called Umra'. They began the Umra' Hajj by kissing the two statues of Asaf and Naelah at Mecca. But, instead, the tribes of Oas and Khazraj began by kissing copies of the statues which were placed on the shore opposite Mecca. Then they went to a hill near Mecca to the two rocks called Safa and Marwa, upon which were placed the other two statues of Asaf and Naelah. They were to walk seven times between these two rocks, then return to Mecca to kiss the two statues of Asaf and Naelah. The two rocks of Safa and Marwa were connected with occult worship.

To this Umra', or small Hajj, was added the drinking of water from the well of Zamzam, where other statues of Asaf and Naelah, the old priests of the Jinn-devils, were placed. Mohammed incorporated the small Hajj into the larger Hajj. Only three tribes would return to Mecca after finishing the great Hajj at Muna. They were Khuzaa'h, the builder of Mecca, and Khazraj and Oas, the two tribes of Medina.

I mentioned that the people of Khuzaa'h returned to Mecca after visiting Manat, to honor their god, Allah, or Venus. Oas and Khazraj returned to Mecca to fulfill their vows to pay homage to Asaf and Naelah, the statues of the famous priests of the Jinn-devils, before they continued the Hajj by going to Safa and Marwa, where the two statues of Asaf and Marwa were placed.[39] Then they proceeded to the well of Zamzam, which had no statues except Asaf and Naelah. This tour around the statues of Asaf and Naelah is a clear indication that those priests of Jinn were subjects of the Umra' Hajj, which was instituted to honor them.

The statues of Asaf and Naelah were placed at the well of Zamzam by Abdul Mutaleb, the grandfather of Mohammed, the man who first dug the well. Abdul Mutaleb was a worshipper of the religion of the Jinn of Arabia, and of Asaf and Naelah, so he placed their statues on the well he dug.

Today, we have seen through a study of history, that Mohammed incorporated the small Umra' Hajj which was, in pre-Islamic times, connected with the Jinn religion of Arabia, into the great Hajj. He did so to please the two tribes of Khazraj and Oas, who accepted him as their leader, and accepted his agenda to subdue the Arabians and convert them to Islam through many wars. But, prior to the pre-Islamic times of Mohammed, Mecca had nothing to do with the Hajj which was called Islam's great Hajj. Instead, Mecca practiced Umra', the occult Hajj of the Jinn religion of Arabia.

I would like to pose this question which should be important to my Muslim friends. Is the occult religion of the two tribes which helped Mohammed convert Arabians to Islam, and the pagan customs of a few desert tribes of central western Arabia which pled with their gods for rain, something to be maintained and professed by your mind and heart when you are thirsty for the truth of God?

The "Great Hajj" which was incorporated into Islam, was a pilgrimage made by only a few pagan local tribes who instituted it in the area around Mecca and Medina.

I previously mentioned that only three tribes returned to Mecca to circle around the Kaabeh after they made the Hajj to Manat, which was located near Medina. Those tribes were Khuzaa'h, Aos and Khazraj. This tells us that Mecca had special importance for these tribes in particular, but concluding the Hajj by returning to Mecca was not considered part of any Hajj for any other Arabian tribes. Although they were limited in number, a majority of the tribes who were involved in the original pagan Hajj around Arafa, Muna and Muzdalifah were tribes who lived in the region around Mecca and Medina. These three locations, Arafa, Muna and Muzdalifah, drew a small number of local tribes, which indicates that the Hajj was originally a local ceremony for the worshippers of the sun, moon and Manat, the daughter of Allah. None of the eastern, northern or southern Arabian tribes were involved in this Hajj, even though they were among the strongest tribes of Arabia.

We can tell which tribes began the Hajj prior to the advent of Islam by examining the kind of ceremony each tribe performed in each station of the Hajj. Each tribe honored its own preferred deity among the members of the Star Family. Quraish, the tribe from which Mohammed came, made Muzdalifah the central location for the Hajj. Muzdalifah was the place which was dedicated to honor and worship the moon in the ceremonies of the Hajj. Aisheh, the youngest and most beloved wife of Mohammed, reported many of Mohammed's Hadiths and described the customs of Jahiliyah. Aisheh said:

> Quraish, and all who follow the religion of Quraish, called Hummas, used to make the Waqfa, or primary stop, in the Hajj at Muzdalifah, while others stopped at Arafa. When Islam came, Allah ordered his prophet to come to Arafa and make it their main stop before continuing on to other locations on the Hajj, such as Muzdalifah and Mina.[40]

Quraish wanted to honor the moon, which was the head of the Star Family, so they instituted a Hajj which was designed to return to Mina' to plead for rain with Manat, the daughter of Allah. Another group selected Arafa as their Waqfa, or main stop. They did so to emphasize the importance of Ellat, who was the sun, and their preferred deity over the rest of the Star Family. We see that, before Islam, Arafa, which was among the hills where these Arabian tribes performed the Hajj, was the place where the sun was venerated and worshipped.

Prior to Islam, competition between worshippers of the sun and worshippers of the moon was obvious in the Hajj. Umar Bin al-Khattab, the second Caliph of Mohammed, and one of Mohammed's fathers-in-law, said:

> The pagans did not walk after their own Waqfa, unless the sun had risen. Mohammed had contradicted their custom, beginning his walk before the sun rose.[41]

We can understand the conflict between rituals when we realize that Ellat, the sun, was the main deity for many Arabian tribes in the region. They could not leave their Waqfa before sunrise. Because Beni Hashem, the clan from which Mohammed came, was part of the tribe of Quraish, it was more attached to the moon; thus, they had no problem neglecting the sunrise. In their tradition, the moon was more revered than the sun. Mohammed claimed that the moon looked on him with tenderness and affection when he was a child. Mohammed would hear noises from the moon when it prostrated itself before the throne of Allah,[42] because the family of Mohammed venerated the moon more than the sun.

The tribe of Sufa conducted their religious ceremonies from Arafa to Muna. It was at Muna where they conducted the casting of stones. A particular man of Sufa was designated to cast the first stones. No one could throw stones before he did.[43] This shows that Sufa initiated the first Hajj, or pilgrimage, which started at Arafa and proceeded to Muna. It seems likely that they were the

THE HAJJ AND RAMADAN

ones who developed the first laws and ceremonies, and routed the Hajj to those two locations. First, they honored the sun at Arafa; then they proceeded to Muna, where they pled for rain in ceremonies performed for Manat. The ceremonies included animal sacrifices made to Manat, the cutting of their hair, and throwing or casting stones. All this was initiated by the tribe of Sufa and performed at Muna.

Qusayy Bin Kilab, the 8th ancestor of Mohammed, encouraged participation in the local pagan Hajj after he occupied Mecca, although neither he nor any member of his family was responsible for its ceremonies.

Until Qusayy's time, Sofa led the ceremonies. Qusayy, the 8th ancestor of Mohammed, was also the one who gathered many families together to form the alliance which became Quraish, and occupied Mecca, driving away the tribe of Khuzaa'h, which had founded the city. Qusayy then fought the tribe of Sofa, who developed the Hajj which included Arafa and Mina.[44] When Qusayy Bin Kilab found some pagan Arabians conducting the Hajj as part of their pagan customs, he encouraged them to continue these rituals.[45]

Qusayy was of Yemeni origin, meaning that none of his ancestors ever took part in the Hajj. Even after Qusayy occupied Mecca, no one in his family led the ceremonies or the functions of the Hajj. In fact, we are told in the Tabari that, after Sofa was extinct, the clan of al-Safwan assumed responsibility for the Hajj.[46] All these historical facts show us that Quraish, the tribe to which Mohammed belonged, had nothing to do with the Hajj. Therefore, claiming that Quraish was a religious tribe which existed from the time of Ishmael, and were defenders of the faith who led religious ceremonies in Arabia, is unhistorical and preposterous.

Originally, the Hajj was conducted by two groups; one worshipped the sun, and the other worshipped the moon. Later, the two ceremonies were combined into one Hajj.

Udwan was yet another tribe which initiated the Hajj based on worshipping the moon at Muzdalifah. They made religious Waqfa at Muzdalifah; then they walked to Muna.[47] It is clear that they were mainly worshippers of the moon. The difference between where Sufa and Udwan began the Hajj shows that the Hajj in pre-Islamic times was not a united ceremony, but was specific to two groups – the worshippers of the sun and worshippers of the moon. But they held one similarity in common. The ceremonies of both groups ended with a visit to Mina', the nearest location to where Manat, the daughter of Allah and the goddess of rain, was honored. They both had the same goal : to plead for rain.

Quraish and the fanatic group, Hummas, followed Udwan on their ceremony to plead for rain, beginning at Muzdalifah and proceeding to Muna. Other groups followed Sufa, beginning at Arafa where they worshipped the sun, and concluding at Muna where they honored Manat, the goddess of rain. Even though the two ceremonies where later unified, each group continued to honor its own deity, making Waqfa, or stops, in the same places, and on the same hills they used to honor their specific deities. When he prevailed over the region, Mohammed took the old custom developed by the tribe of Sufa and imposed it on the others, making everyone's main stop at Arafa.

Muzdalifah, and the Occult Worship in Central Western Arabia

Now we turn our attention to Muzdalifah, and the occult worship in central western Arabia. The station of the Hajj called Muzdalifah was mentioned by Arabian authors who wrote about Arabian customs before Islam. They said that Muzdalifah was a place which had a mountain called Khazeh قزح , named after a devil.[48] Khazeh was a famous Arabian idol,[49] showing us that the worship of the devil, Khazeh, had spread into central western Arabia, especially around Mecca and Medina. Jawad Ali, an Iraqi scholar, believes that this idol was worshipped at Muzdalifah.[50] Arabian historians say that before Islam, the person who performed, or led the Arabians in the ceremonies at Muzdalifah, stood on the mountain of Khazeh.[51]

The religion of Jinn-devils in Arabia, and the Arabian Star Family Worship, became the two main religions in Arabia. The Kaabahs in Arabia often had Kuhhan of the Jinn religion serving as priests. Therefore, many of the ceremonies of both of these religions were combined or united. The Arabians considered the Jinn-devils as kindred to Allah. This tells us why Muzdalifah was important for the pagan Arabians of central Arabia before Islam. It was a place where both the devil, Khazeh, and the moon were worshipped.

Mohammed added another ceremony to the Hajj. People walked seven times between the two stones, Safa and Marwa. Mohammed did this ritual in spite of the hatred harbored by some of his followers, who saw it as a pagan ritual connected to Jahiliyah and practiced in pre-Islam times.

Walking seven times between the two stones, Safa and Marwa, was a custom of Jahiliyah, the pagan period before Islam. This is confirmed by Mohammed's biographers and the authoritative reporters of his sayings and customs. Ibn Abbas, one of Mohammed's most significant reporters, confirmed that walking between Safa and Marwa was Jahiliyah's custom.[52] Another important reporter of Mohammed's Hadith was Uns Bin Malek, who said:

> Asem has told us saying "I said to Uns Bin Malek, you used to hate to walk making a pilgrimage between the Safa and Marwa." He answered, "Yes," because it was from the pagan rituals of Jahiliyah until Allah inspired that "Safa and Marwa are from the rituals of Allah, he who makes a Hajj to the temple, or the Hajj of Umra', has no sin if he encompasses around them." [53] (quoting Surah 2:158)

The reason why some Muslim followers of Mohammed hated this pilgrimage involving Safa and Marwa was because it came from the pagan ritual of Jahiliyah. Without doubt, they were aware of its connections with occult worship. *Sahih Muslim*, another authoritative book of Hadiths, reveals that the majority of Muslims revolted against the tendency of a few Muslims to consider Safa and Marwa as part of the Hajj. Those who refused to appear before Safa and Marwa were armed with the knowledge that such worship belongs to the pagan Jahiliyah.[54]

But Mohammed claimed he was inspired to write a new verse of the Qur'an. Surah 2:158 states:

> Behold Safa and Marwa are part of the ritual of Allah. So, if those who visit the house in the season of Hajj, or make the Hajj of Umra' at other times, should encompass them, there is no sin in them.

This way the ritual of Safa and Marwa became a ritual of Allah.

This pagan Hajj, limited to a few Arabian tribes around Medina and Mecca, had become one of the main pillars of Islam, like the Jihad. Mohammed endeavored to attract the pagan Arabians by adopting their rituals and their Hajj to Arafa, Muzdalifah and Mina', where they worshipped three of the members of the Arabian Star Family. In addition, they engaged in occult worship at Muzdalifah, where ceremonies for the devil, Khazeh, were performed.

Though we know the names of the pagan tribes who instituted this Hajj, these rituals were later attributed, by Islamic tradition, to Abraham, even though he never set foot in central western Arabia. Connecting these pagan ceremonies with Abraham can deceive only those who accepted its claims without comparing them with the facts of history.

THE ORIGINS OF THE HAJJ CEREMONIES

The month the Hajj is conducted is called Du al-Hijjah. The Hajj, or religious pilgrimage, was a custom practiced by pagan

Arabians, in which they made a trip to visit their gods and sanctuaries. The month in which the Islamic Hajj is performed is the same month in which pagan Arabians performed their Hajj. Among inscriptions found in Arabia, the term "Du Hajjinin," which means "Du al-Hijjah," is the same month the pagan Arabians made their pilgrimage.[55]

Northern Arabians also had a month in which they visited their sanctuaries and honored their gods. Epiphanius speaks about this month during which the pagan Arabians perform their ritual of Hajj.[56] Muslims, today, perform their Hajj in the same month of Du al-Hijjah. While classical writers also wrote about the sacred months for Arabians, Photius wrote about the months which the Arabians considered as "Haram," in which they agreed not to fight. Scholars, such as Winekler, have identified those months to be the same months when Arabians did a Hajj, in addition to the month when they fasted, which they called Ramadan[57]. During the month of Du al-Hajjeh, each Arabian went to his sanctuary, or special hill, to worship his own god. There were many places where Arabians used to do Hajj.[58]

This helps us to see that the Hajj around Mecca was separately conducted by two groups during the same month of the Hajj. One group went to Arafa to worship the sun, the other group went to Muzdalifah to worship the moon. After making their religious stops to honor their own gods, both groups made stops to give homage to Manat and plead for rain. The rituals of the Hajj and Du al-Hijjah, the month of pilgrimage, were well-known among pagan Arabians, a fact which Islamic historians and writers confess[59].

The Ceremony of Casting Stones at the Hill

We already mentioned that at Muna, or Mina', the pilgrims cast seven stones at a hill. Islamic tradition claims this locality is where Abraham met with the devil and threw stones at him. History tells us that Abraham never visited Mecca, because Mecca was not in existence during Abraham's time. Mecca appeared later, after the 4th century A.D. Central western Arabia, where Mecca was later located, was uninhabited at the time of Abraham who lived in the 21st century B.C. It was a desert, unknown to the inhabitants of Mesopotamia, where Abraham was raised, and unknown to the country of Canaan, where Abraham went to live.

North Arabian cities, such as Dedan and Qedar, were built around the 9th century B.C. Cities like Yathrib were built after the route between Yemen and the Fertile Crescent flourished, around the 6th century B.C., but the route along the Red Sea between the northern cities of Arabia and Yemen was not developed until the 3rd century B.C., as attested to by Greek geographers. Although Greek geographers and classical writers tell us some stations appeared then, the area where Mecca was eventually built was uninhabited until after the Christian era. So, how could Abraham have abandoned his sojourn in the Land of Canaan, to come to a desert where no one had ever lived before?

Further, striking the devil with stones is an illogical myth because the devil is a spirit, not affected when material things are thrown at him. The devil does not have a material body to be injured by the stones. The same is true when stars are thrown at him. The Qur'an claims that meteorites were stars which Allah used to strike the devils. Rather, the casting of stones at the devil was a pagan ceremony practiced by various pagan sects in the Middle East.[60] Casting the stones was a ritual initiated in Muna by the tribe of Sofa who led the ceremonies on the hill of Arafa. The tribe of Sofa did not allow anyone to walk from Arafa to the next Hajj station before all the tribes had done so. No one was allowed to cast stones before they did.[61] This indicates that Sofa began casting the stones as part of their Hajj in that part of Arabia, and made it part of their tradition.

The Zoroastrian Rite of Casting Pebbles and Other Persian Customs Left an Impact on the Arabian Hajj

Zoroastrians also cast stones on the water and in bull's urine. The water and urine were prepared for ablutions and the purification of bodies and objects. Once they were cast, these stones, or pebbles, were deposited in holes in the ground, evidently to strike the insects and worms in the ground which were considered devils by the Zoroastrians. We read about this ceremony in many chapters of the *Epistles of Manuskihar*, part of the Pahlavi Texts, traditional literature for the interpretation of the Avesta, which are the sacred writings of Zoroastrianism.[62]

The concept behind making ablutions in Zoroastrianism was to expel, or drive away, the devil from the body. In the Zoroastrian books, such as the Vendidad, part of the Zenda Avesta, we find that the devil is driven away from a part of the body each time the water of ablutions reaches that part. Then the devil flees to inferior parts, until the water touches the toes of the feet, and the devil is driven away completely.[63] We find the same concept in the Pahlavi texts, such as in the "The Bareshnum Ceremony."[64] Also, in Shayast La-Shayast, Chapter XX, where we find written that, in order for the devil to flee from the body, man should perform ablution in water and bull's urine before the sunrise.[65] The water in Zoroastrianism is a god that cleans the soul and removes away the stain and effect of the devil. The Qur'an contains the same teaching concerning the importance of water: to clean the soul of the man and to drive the devil and his stain from the body. We read in Surah 8, called al-Anfal, verse 11:

> He covers you with drowsiness ... and he makes the water descend from heaven on you in order to purify you and to remove from you the stain of Satan.

The Zoroastrians believed in the power of bull's urine in purifying and healing. In the Zoroastrian literature called the *Epistles of Manuskihar*, Epistle I, Chapter VII, the urine is described as "well curative in performance."[66] In the Vendidad, the Zoroastrians claimed that Ahura Mazda, the main deity of Zoroastrianism, recommended to drink milk and bull's urine for curing diseases.[67] Mohammed borrowed this kind of treatment from the Zoroastrians, but he changed the use of the bull's urine with the urine of the female camel. He claimed that the urine of the female camel can treat all diseases. People who came to him with diseases were ordered by Mohammed to drink the female camel's urine.[68]

People used to drink Mohammed's urine in front of him, and he was happy, alluding that his urine was a curative for diseases.[69] We know how nocuous and harmful urine is, whether of the camel or humans, because of the germs that the body eliminates with the urine, besides other harmful acids and materials which the body removes.

We find other rituals in the pre-Islamic Hajj coming from Zoroastrianism. One of Zoroastrian's Persian gods was the fire. Qusayy, the 8th ancestor of Mohammed, came from Yemen and occupied Mecca. He lit a fire on Muzdalifah, the place where the moon was worshipped in the pre-Islamic Hajj. Al-Tabari wrote that this fire continued to burn during the time of Mohammed, and the three Caliphs who came after him.[70] We can understand how this Persian religious exercise became part of the Hajj, when we understand the influence of the Persians on Yemen and the southern regions of Arabia. In Yemen, there was a fire continually burning for years according to Persian worship.[71]

Another Zoroastrian custom calls on its followers to make good works and religious practices on behalf of dead relatives and friends.[72] We find Mohammed adopting the same rite. In a Hadith, reported by al-Bukhari, Mohammed advised a woman to make a Hajj for her dead mother.[73]

Phases through which the moon passes affect worship in the Middle East, especially in Arabia. The way in which the moon was worshipped in Muzdalifah in pre-Islamic times reminds us of the Persian worship of the moon. The moon in the Nyayis, a Zoroastrian sacred literature, is addressed three times a month: first, at the time when the moon is first visible; second, when it is the full; and, finally, when it is on the wane.[74] It reminds us of how Arabians worshipped the moon at Muzdalifah until the moon disappears. They concluded by fasting, and then feasting when the crescent moon reappears. In fact, the feast of Ramadan begins when the crescent of the moon reappears. The moon plays an important part in Islam today, as we see from the crescent which is Islam's identity symbol.

The rituals connected with the moon and its worship also have roots in Aryan worship. We read in the Apastamba, a sacred

Aryan book, that a feast is established when the moon's crescent appears. The religious man can't study, or do anything, for two nights.[75] This ritual is repeated in Ramadan. After a month of fasting, the Muslims feast when they see the crescent appearing in the sky.

We know that Ramadan was originally a Harranian ritual which took place in the city of Harran, on the border between Syria, Iraq and Asia Minor. The Harranians fasted for one month, beginning the first or second week in March, identical to Ramadan. This fasting was for Sin, the god of the moon. Some Arabic historians identified the fasting of the Harranians with the fasting of Ramadan. When the moon's crescent appeared, the Harranians ended their fasting and began a feast, the same way Arabians celebrate Ramadan each year. We assume the celebration of Ramadan was transferred from Harran to Arabia during the 6th century B.C. when Nabonidus, the Harranian King of Babylonia, occupied North Arabia from 556-539 B.C. For more on this topic, I refer the reader to the subject of Ramadan in Part V, Section 3.

The Third Ritual of the Hajj is Cutting the Pilgrim's Hair

The cutting of the hair was a habit practiced by some Arabian tribes after a pilgrimage to honor their gods. One of their gods was an idol named al-akyaser الأقيصر. They conducted a pilgrimage to the idol where they cut their hair, mixed it with flour and threw it in the air.[76] The same celebration was also observed by many pagan Yemeni tribes.[77] Tribes which emigrated to Medina, and the area around Mecca, came from Yemen after the collapse of the dam at Ma'rib, about 150 A.D. This helps us understand why the cutting of hair was the ritual which ends the Hajj.

I mentioned earlier that some Yemeni tribes honored Manat, the daughter of Allah. Manat was represented by a rock, to which these tribes went on their Hajj. At the end of the Hajj, they cut their hair. Ibn al-Kalbi, al-Azruki, and others wrote about the customs of Arabia. They tell us tribes, such as Aos, Khazraj, Ozd, and Ghassan, were all tribes of Yemeni origin which made the

Hajj to Manat. In many places, they made religious stops to honor their gods without cutting their hair until they reached Manat, where they ended their Hajj by cutting their hair. They didn't see their Hajj as complete unless they did so.[78]

You may remember that Manat was the goddess to whom they would plead for rain. After they performed the Hajj to their gods, they would come to Manat, cut their hair and present their animal sacrifices. Stations of the pre-Islamic Hajj included Arafa, the place where they would stop to worship the sun, and Muzdalifah, where they would stop to worship the moon. Then the Hajj would conclude at Mina', called Muna, the place dedicated to Manat, where they cut their hair and presented their animal sacrifices. In Mohammed's time, this same Hajj was transferred to Islam with the same rituals, including the ritual of cutting the hair at Manat.

The Ritual of Crying in the Hajj

Another ritual conducted during the great Hajj was to cry two things: "Allah are them, I am here" and "Allah is greater." Al-Ya'akubi, the Arabic historian, wrote that each Arabian would stop before his idol and cry "Allah are them, I am here." [79]

We find that when the Hajj was transferred to Islam, it presented the same religious words. When they came to the hill dedicated to the worship of the moon, they cried "Allah Akber," which means "Allah is greater." This is because the moon, who was Allah, was viewed as head of the Star Family and was greater than the other members, Ellat, the sun, and Manat and al-'Uzza, two of the planets. The cry "Allah is greater" is not an Islamic cry but, rather, a pagan cry which the worshippers of the Star Family used to say. Pre-Islamic Arabian poetry often honored members of the Star Family by emphasizing Allah as the head of the Star Family by repeating the words" Allah Akber." For example, Loas Bin Hagar, the Arabian poet of Jahiliyah, which was the pre-Islam period, said:

I swear by Ellat and al-Uzza and all who follow their faith, and in Allah, Allah is greater than they.[80]

Abdel Mutaleb, the grandfather of Mohammed, who was not a Muslim but was a worshipper of the Arabian Star Family also attached to the Arabian Jinn religion, used to cry the same cry, "Allah is greater."[81] They held this cry in common with all the worshippers of Star Family members. This explains why we find this cry in the rituals of the Hajj, which were originally dedicated to three of the members of the Star Family: the moon, the sun, and Manat, the daughter of Allah and the goddess of rain.

It seems that when the Hajj was initiated, the moon still enjoyed the title of Allah before the title was snatched by Venus. When pre-Islamic pagan Arabians would see the moon in its crescent, they would cry with a loud voice "Allah Akber," which is "Allah is greater." From ancient times, the moon was "Allah" to many Arabian tribes and, as such, was their visible deity. The moon in the form of a crescent, after it disappeared for a period of time, stimulated them to cry in worship to him.

Crying, and honoring the moon when the crescent appears, still has its impact on Islamic rituals today. Today, you will notice when Muslims see that the crescent appearing, they end their fasting and start the feast of Ramadan, following exactly the old rituals of the worshippers of the moon. For those worshippers, the moon was their deity and focus, and to the moon they initiated the fasting of Ramadan.

Conclusion

Al-Shahrastani, the Arabic historian, wrote about the pagan people of Jahiliyah. He says they often had the Hajj in months other than Du al-Hijjah, but they performed the same rituals as the Islamic Hajj, respecting the days of the month. They made the 10th of the month the day for animal sacrifices, just as Muslims today perform sacrifices on the 10th day of the month of Du al-

Hijjah. In other words, sometimes they selected other months, but followed the same rituals in the same places.[82]   With this evidence, we conclude that the Islamic Hajj was practiced by pagan Arabian tribes. The Hajj was initiated by a few tribes for their own gods. Later, the various elements of the Hajj were consolidated. Today, the Islamic Hajj presents rituals which were known to be practiced by pagan tribes around Medina and Mecca, founded by tribes who emigrated from Yemen, and performed these rituals to their gods.

Although Muslims claim that the Hajj was connected to Abraham, this Hajj was not connected with Abraham at all.

None of those tribes ever mentioned a connection between their pagan Hajj and Abraham or Ishmael, as Islam claims. None of the Arabian poets before Jahiliyah attributed their Hajj to Abraham or Ishmael. The Hajj, originally conducted around the Arabian Star Family, was attributed to Abraham only after Islam came on the scene.

For Muslims to go on a Hajj to where pagan Arabian tribes honored Star Family members will never connect them with the true God. This ritual is similar to many rituals performed by the pagans of the middle East and Asia.   Adding the name of Abraham to the pagan rituals of a few Arabian tribes around Mecca and Medina will never change the nature of their pagan ceremonies. Muslims, instead, need to study the faith of Abraham as it is told in the Bible. Abraham never fasted when the moon disappeared, nor cried and feasted when the crescent appeared. He never connected his worship with the movements of any of the bodies of the solar system, or with the stars, or with the rocks. Neither did he throw stones at the devil, or cut his hair in front of a stone.

We live in a tolerant society where people are free to believe what they want, and have the freedom of speech to solicit converts. Muslims today are seeking converts by propagating false teachings, and many are being deceived. Many people have assumed that Allah and God are the same, and it's not important which religion we embrace. However, today we have learned that

God and Allah are not the same. The doctrine of Allah in Islam was blended from many forms of pagan worship and rituals over many years. It was formed from worship of the moon at one point, and worship of Venus at another.

THE SMALL HAJJ CALLED UMRA' AND OCCULTISM AT MECCA

Historically, the Umra' Hajj was a ceremony of the Jinn religion of Arabia which revolved around two defiled priests' figures.

We will examine the small Hajj called Umra', and the occultism at Mecca which accompanied it. In the area around Mecca people practiced what was called Umra', or the "visit." It was a small Hajj, or pilgrimage, which dates back to pre-Islamic times. The Umra' was connected to the ceremonies of the Arabian Jinn religion, especially as they treated some of the stones and idols. Two of the idols were priests of the Jinn. One was male and was named Asaf, and the other was female and was named Naelah. According to tradition, they were priests inside the temple of Mecca, called Kaabah. Arabian mythology claims they committed fornication together in the Kaabah, and the gods transformed them into two stone statues.

There were many copies of the statues for people to worship. The most important statues were placed on Safa and Marwa, two stones on a hill near the well of Zamzam. Al-Shahrastani, an Islamic historian, claimed that Amru Bin Lahi had put the statues on the two stones of Safa and Marwa.[83] But Amru Bin Lahi is not a real historical figure. Muslim tradition endeavors to attribute all their Arabian paganism to him, accusing him of bringing all the statues, idols, and pagan worship to Arabia. This is an unhistorical excuse, since paganism and the worship of the stars and the moon in Arabia existed from ancient times, as attested to by the inspired writers of the Bible and by Assyrian inscriptions dating back to the 9th century B.C. They described the idols of many Arabian tribes who came in contact with the Assyrians. Greek historians who visited Arabia, starting from Herodotus in the 5th century B.C., also confirm what the writers of the Bible and Assyrian inscriptions relate. Therefore, it's absurd to think that Islamic tradition could separate Islamic worship and locations from their original pagan background and origins by attributing all of this to Amru Bin Lahi, a man for whom there is no evidence that he ever existed.

In pre-Islamic times, the Asaf and Naelah statues were placed on the main stones of the Kaabah of Mecca and on the two stones of Safa and Marwa. In the Umra' Hajj the pilgrims had to circle these statues seven times. This helps us understand the real worship at Mecca in pre-Islamic times, and the Umra' Hajj, which was connected with it.

The worship at Mecca was a combination of two creeds: Arabian Star worship and Arabian occult worship. Arabian Star worship was under the administration of the Kuhhan, the priests of the Arabian Jinn religion which was the only organized pagan religion in Arabia. There were no priests in Arabian Star worship. The Kuhhan dominated the various Kaabahs and temples where the Star Family was worshipped. The Kaabah of Mecca had Kuhhan who were responsible for the Kaabah activities. One of them was a famous priest of the Jinn named Wake'a وكيع . Wake'a recited a rhymed prose which is similar to the rhyming prose of the Qur'an.

There was also a serpent in the Kaabah which lived in the well of the temple where the worshippers threw their gifts.[84] The serpents were considered by the Arabians to be Jinn-devils.[85] This suggests that the serpents as Jinn were worshipped by pilgrims visiting Mecca. Their gifts were thrown to the serpent as signs of their worship, honor and fear because it was a Jinn-devil. This is the same thing we encounter in many Indian temples where a serpent is presented food and gifts because it is the main deity of the temple.

Our hypothesis about the Jinn worship in the temple at Mecca is supported by the fact that the name Allah, according to old Arabian writers, is derived from Allaha, the title given to the serpent.[86]

What was the True Religion of Abdul Mutaleb, the Man who Dug the Well of Zamzam to Venerate Asaf and Naelah?

The statues of Asaf and Naelah were placed on the well of Zamzam. Ibn Hisham, who edited the oldest book on the life of Mohammed, says these statues were worshipped at the well of Zamzam. He tells us that the worshippers sacrificed their animals to the statues there[87]. This suggests to us that the well of Zamzam was dedicated to the worship of the two priests of the Jinn, which the statues represented. It was Abdel Mutaleb, the grandfather of Mohammed, who dedicated the well of Zamzam to the two venerated Jinn priests and their statues. We draw this conclusion for many reasons. First, Abdel Mutaleb dug the well of Zamzam.[88] Second, Abdel Mutaleb was one of the worshippers of the statues of the two Jinn priests. He was so consumed by occult worship that he wanted to sacrifice one of his own sons at the feet of the two statues at Zamzam. That son was Abdullah, the father of Mohammed. When Abdel Mutaleb was at the point of killing Abdullah with his knife, Abdel Mutaleb's brother rescued the boy.[89]

The idea of sacrificing one's son to the Jinn or their representatives, the venerated leaders and priests, is known, not only in Arabia, but also in other parts of the ancient world. Even to this day worshippers in the occult religions sacrifice children to devils. The fact that Abdul Mutaleb chose to sacrifice his son before these two statues reveals that the religion of the Jinn of Arabia was the religion to which he was most attached.

The third reason for concluding that Abdul Mutaleb dedicated the well of Zamzam to the statues of the Jinn priests who were venerated in Mecca is that Abdul Mutaleb showed that he had a close relationship with the representatives of the Arabian Jinn religion. Those representatives, or priests, were called Kuhhan, the singular of which is Kahen. Abdul Mutaleb consulted the Kuhhan when he faced a problem. They were his counselors, and he used to travel great distances in order to meet and consult a famous Kahen. When a dispute between the tribe of

Quraish and Abdel Mutaleb occurred because of the well of Zamzam, Abdel Mutaleb chose a famous Kahinah of Jinn to rule in the matter. This Kahinah was the one who appointed two dangerous Kuhhan of the Jinn, Satih and Shak', to be priests of the Jinn after her death.[90] Al-Halabieh says about these two Kuhhan of the Jinn:

> They were the chiefs of the Kuhhan and the ones with knowledge about occultism and the priesthood to the Jinn.[91]

Ibn Hisham mentions about this Kahinah, "She was the Kahinah of the clan of Saad Hutheim."[92] When a dispute arose between Abdel Mutaleb and Beni Kilab, which means the clan of Kilab, Abdel Mutaleb went to a Kahen of the Jinn called Rabiah Bin H'thar al-Asadi to judge the matter.[93] Consulting the Kuhhan of the Jinn was something that the grandfathers of Mohammed practiced. Hisham, the father of Abdel Mutaleb, was known to consult a main Kahen of the tribe of Khuzaa'h.[94] Many examples such as these shed light regarding the affiliation of the family and the ancestors of Mohammed to the religion of Jinn in Arabia.

As if this were not convincing enough, two more considerations prove that Abdul Mutaleb was a leader in the Arabian Jinn religion. When Abdel Mutaleb dedicated his son Abdullah, who became the father of Mohammed, he did it through a Kahinah, a female Kahen, under the instruction of the Jinn to whom she was connected. The biographers of Mohammed, including Ibn Hisham, Mohammed's most authoritative biographer, tell us that Abdel Mutaleb took Abdullah to a Jinn priestess named Khutbah. She lived in the city of Khaybar located in north central Arabia.[95] When he visited Khutbah, Abdul Mutaleb expressed his readiness to kill his son if the priestess of Jinn ordered him to do so. It is clear that children born to the followers of occult sects were to be sacrificed to the malignant spirit connected with the medium or priest of the occult community. The spirit may ask that the child be killed as a sacrifice to the devil, or the priest may ask the child's parents to present dogs or other animals to the malignant spirit as sacrifices.

ISLAM IN LIGHT OF HISTORY

It is clear that, in the case of Abdul Mutaleb, we encounter the same occult phenomenon which is practiced among various occult sects. The spirits of Jinn-devils rule over the destiny of children who are born within the occult community. This was the reason many children were sacrificed to the devil.

We see the dedication of Abdel Mutaleb to the religious system which Khutbah represented. Abdel Mutaleb was ready to obey the decision of the Jinn-devil to whom Khutbah was a medium and a priest, in whatever the Jinn decided for his son. Ibn Hisham reports the answer the Jinn priestess gave to Abdel Mutaleb's request: "Return to me after one day until the one to whom I am connected comes to me."[96] By this she meant the Jinn-devil. The Jinn-devil came to her and told her that camels should be sacrificed instead of Abdullah, who became the father of Mohammed.

To decide the religion of any person, one needs only to look at where he consecrates his children. If he dedicates his children in a church, we know he is a Christian. If he dedicates them in a Jewish synagogue, we can be sure he is a Jew. If he dedicates them in a Sabian temple, then he is member of the Sabian sect. But when he dedicates his children in an occult ceremony by a medium of the order of a Jinn-devil, then he belongs to the occult sect that the medium or priestess represents. That's his religion. Not far from Mecca, there were many Christian churches, particularly in the city of Najran. There were also many synagogues near Mecca, but Abdul Mutaleb avoided all these and went to dedicate his son through Kahinah, a priestess of the Jinn.

Another thing to consider was his willingness to find a wife for his son Abdullah from among the priestesses of the Jinn. He introduced Abdullah to many young Jinn priestesses. On one occasion reported in the book of Halabieh, which contains the life of Mohammed:

When Abdel Mutaleb accompanied his son Abdullah in preparation for marriage, he passed by a Kahinah who was a priestess of Jinn from Tubbalah, a small town in Yemen. The name

of the woman was Fatimah, daughter of Mur al-Khathmieh
الخثعمية.[97]

Another priestess of Jinn to whom Abdullah was introduced was
Ruchieh Bint Naufal رقية. She was also a Kahinah priestess of
Jinn. Ibn Hisham, Mohammed's main biographer, showed that
Abdul Mutaleb encountered Ruchieh in the Kaabah, which
suggests that she was part of the occult functions that took place
in the Kaabah of Mecca.[98]

Khadijah, the First Wife of Mohammed, and her Cousin Waraqa

Ruchieh was the sister of Waraqa bin Naufal, the Ebionite occult
priest who was the cousin of Khadijah, the first wife of
Mohammed. Waraqa was the one who convinced Mohammed to
be a prophet. After returning home from the cave of Harra', where
he often went, Mohammed was frightened. He told his wife that a
spirit claiming to be Gabriel appeared to him and choked him
three times. Mohammed was convinced after this encounter that
he had a devil inside him. But Khadijah insisted that Mohammed
become a prophet of Allah. It's interesting to note that when
angels appeared in the Bible, they never threatened anyone or
imposed the prophetic role upon him.

Khadijah was married to Nabash Bin Zarareh Bin
Wakdanنباش بن زرارة بن وقدان, a visionary for the Jinn, before she
met Mohammed. The Jinn appeared to Nabash in the form of an
old man to give him information[99]. As a wife of a visionary of
Jinn, this gave Khadijah some prestige, because many Arabians
consulted Jinn visionaries, and gave them money. This also
explains why Khadijah was wealthy. She had caravans which
brought goods from Syria to Mecca. After Nabash died, she
employed Mohammed in her caravans, then married him,
although Mohammed was twenty years younger than she.

After the negative experiences which depressed Mohammed,
Khadijah sent him to her cousin, Waraqa, to convince him that
Mohammed was called to be a prophet of Allah. Waraqa
succeeded in his task and became responsible for most of the

Qur'anic verses at the beginning. Waraqa inserted Ebionite doctrines about Jesus in the Qur'an, stating that Jesus was a prophet, and that He was not crucified, but God made someone to resemble Jesus. That one was crucified because the crowd thought he was Jesus. This doctrine was first initiated by Simon, the magician from Samaria, who later founded a heresy which took his name, Simonianism. In reality, Simon created the root for such doctrine, before it was developed by the Gnostics in later times. Here, I present Simon the magician's idea about Jesus, which Hyppolytus reported in *"The Refutation of all heresies:"*

> Jesus Christ being transformed, and being assimilated to the rulers and powers and angels, came for the restoration (of things). And so (it was that Jesus) appeared as man, when in reality he was not a man. And (so it was) that likewise he suffered, though not actually undergoing suffering, but appearing to the Jews to do so.[100]

The idea that the people crucified someone whom God made to resemble Jesus was embraced by some heresy-believing groups which were known to have immoral values, such as free sex and connections with occultism. Waraqa belonged to one of these cults.

Waraqa was one of the founders of the group called Ahnaf. In the first narration of the life of Mohammed, written by Ibn Hisham in the 8th century A.D., we read:

> The Honafa', or Ahnaf, was a small group started when four Sabians at Mecca agreed. Those four were Zayd bin Amru bin Nafil, Waraqa bin Naufal, Ubaydullah bin Jahsh, and Uthman Bin al-Huwayrith.[101]

The four founders of Ahnaf were all related to Mohammed. They were descendants of Loayy, one of Mohammed's ancestors. Furthermore, Waraqa bin Naufal and Uthman Bin al-Huwayrith were cousins of Khadijah. We know this from Mohammed's genealogy presented by Ibn Hisham.[102] Ubaydullah Bin Jahsh was a maternal cousin to Mohammed. Mohammed married his widow, Um Habibeh. All this reveals the close connection between Mohammed and the founders of the group.

This group was unknown outside Mecca, but Umayya bin Abi al-Salt, a maternal cousin of Mohammed, is considered by some to be a member of the group. He lived in the city of Taif. We know many people joined them. They belonged to different religions, and thus had various doctrines. Each religion contained some form of polytheism, paganism and occultism. This makes them the most unlikely group in history to claim that they espoused the faith which Abraham and other prophets in the Old Testament professed and preached. It's ridiculous that Muslims would believe that this pagan group represented the true and devout faith.

The myths which they believed and incorporated into their poetry were also written into the Qur'an because Mohammed belonged to the group from the time he was a youth. He boasted that he believed in their creed, and he was known to have connections with many members of this group. He was influenced by their teachings, as well as by the immoral concepts and the use of slogans of sex to draw people to them, such as a paradise of free sex. All this reflects Mohammed's deep affiliation to this group. Mohammed used their ideas. In the Qur'an we encounter some of the same myths.

It was not known if this group called themselves Honafa' or Ahnaf, or if they were called this by the society as such, but they knew the terminology had a negative meaning and reflected negative behavior. The word *hanif* means "astrictive, confined, awry, biased and errant." The Arabic word comes from the verb *hanafa* which means "to become astrictive."[103] Although the Qur'an would convey a positive meaning to the term *hanif* today, it was not so at the time of Mohammed. Jawad Ali, the Iraqi scholar I referred to earlier, says, "The Hanaf is straying from the right way." Jawad Ali quotes many old Islamic authors who maintained this was the meaning of *hanif* at the time of Mohammed.[104] According to Jawad Ali, the word also is derived from an Aramaic word which means "atheist, guileful, hypocrite, infidel or perverted."[105]

No matter how you look at it, the term *hanif* was a negative one at the time of Mohammed, as we see it in the Arabic and Aramaic languages. This suggests that since the group's members were called by this term, not by themselves but by the society in which they lived, it is a reflection on their immoral conduct and the perversions in which they participated.

The Immoral Reputation of Ahnaf and its Impact on Mohammed

Their immoral behavior is seen in their poems, such as the poem composed by Waraqa Bin Naufal, one of the four founders of the group. He boasted of his own experience raping a girl in her home and enjoying sex with her. In his poem he encourages others to enjoy experiences like this.[106] Waraqa's immoral ideas left a special impact on Mohammed, who learned under him.

When Waraqa died, the biographers of Mohammed said the "inspiration cooled down or languished."[107] Because of this, Mohammed wanted to throw himself many times from a mountain. The narrators are in disagreement about the duration of such period in which he tried to kill himself; some claimed it was forty days, others say it was three years.[108] It took time before Mohammed found other resources for his verses.

How Should we Label the Grandfather of Mohammed who Dug the Well of Zamzam?

I mentioned that when Abdel Mutalib wanted to find a wife for his son Abdullah, the eventual father of Mohammed, he rejected many priestesses of Jinn before he selected a wife. Finally he selected a wife for Abdullah. She was Amneh, a niece of Soda Bint Zehra, the main priestess of the Jinn at Mecca. Al-Halabi, a biographer of Mohammed, states that the reason Abdel Mutalb took Amneh as a wife for Abdullah was due to her aunt Soda Bint Zehra.[109] Abdul wanted to be near the chief priestess and embrace the kind of dedication to the worship of Jinn which she represented.

An important test of the level of someone's dedication and his attachment to his religious convictions is the partner he has selected for himself or for his son to marry. If he's satisfied with any female of the sect, we might consider him a normal follower of his own religious system, but if he looks for wives only among women dedicated to his religion he ceases to be a simple follower of his religion, and becomes an activist and a fanatic. He shows that he desires to promote the religion by building a family totally dedicated to it, so that such family may have a leading role in his religious system.

This helps us to see the religious affiliations of the man who dug the well of Zamzam, and gives us the purpose for which he dug the well. It was a custom for Arabians to dig a well and dedicate it to the gods they worship and venerate. The fact that Abdul Mutaleb dug the well of Zamzam and erected the two statues of the priests of Jinn, Asaf and Naelah, on the well, is sufficient to convince us of the nature of his religion and the zeal he had to promote it. Because he considered killing his son, Abdullah, before those two statues, it indicates that the Arabian Jinn worship was his main religion, and he was fully dedicated to it.

The literature which gives us background to the life of Arabians at the time of Mohammed mentions the custom of some Arabians to present sacrifices to the Jinn-devils after they dug a well.[110] The fact that Abdul Mutaleb had erected the two statues of the priests of Jinn on the well of Zamzam, and that he was ready to kill his son at the feet of these statues, indicates that he wanted to bring a sacrifice to the Jinn, and that he dug the well of Zamzam for the express purpose of honoring the worship of the Jinn religion of Arabia.

How ironic it is to connect this occult place with Abraham! Muslims today receive no benefit from traveling so far to drink water from a well like the one at Zamzam. Neither do they benefit from performing rituals from this pagan occult system. Christ is the one who gives the true water of life. He gives the gift of the Holy Spirit and eternal life to each one who accepts Him as

413

personal Savior. Shouldn't our Muslim friends be among those who follow Christ?

THE UMRA' HAJJ WHICH IS INCORPORATED INTO ISLAM, AND ITS PAGAN AND OCCULT ROOTS

We want to look at the small Hajj, called Umra'. It was the occult Hajj of Mecca, and its temple. This small Hajj is different from the great Hajj which took place outside Mecca. Mecca had nothing to do with it. The small Hajj was incorporated into Islam by Mohammed, although it is historically documented that the ceremonies of this Hajj were closely connected with the Arabian Jinn religion.

The Islamic small Hajj, or Umra', which can be performed any time during the year, begins at the temple of Mecca by performing the "tawaf" where pilgrims walk in a circle around the Kaabah. Then they proceed to drink from the water of the well of Zamzam. Afterward, they walk seven times between the two stones, Safa and Marwa, where the two statues of Asaf and Naelah were erected in pre-Islamic times. Finally, they cut their hair at the Marwa stone.

The pre-Islamic Umra' was a ritual of the Jinn religion of Arabia which revolved around the statues of the two priests of Jinn and a statue of a wind-devil.

We want to see how this small Hajj was originally part of the Jinn religious ceremonies and had as its focus the venerating of four idols placed on four stones. Although the idols were later removed by Islam, the stones where the idols were placed continue to be the subject of Hajj and its worship. Those idols were the two statues of Asaf and Naelah. They were the most venerated priests of Jinn. Two other idols were placed over the two stones, Safa and Marwa. There were also two statues of Asaf and Naelah on these stones.[111] Safa and Marwa were located on two hills near Mecca, close to the place where Abdel Mutaleb, the grandfather of Mohammed, dug the well of Zamzam and erected the two statues of Asaf and Naelah as the deities of the well.

Muslims still go there in their small Hajj to venerate the two stones on the two hills.

Arabians venerated Asaf and Naelah because they considered them to be sacred priests of the Kaabah at Mecca in the service for the Jinn. They also were important symbols of Jinn religious worship. Tradition claims Asaf and Naelah became two stones.

Al-Ya'akubi, the famous Arabian historian and geographer of the 9th century A.D., who wrote about the life of Arabia before and after Islam, records that two idols were placed over the Safa and Marwa. The idol placed on the Safa was named Mujawer al-Rih' مجاور الريح, which means in Arabic "the shelter or place of sanctuary for the wind."[112] The wind at Mecca was considered as a Jinn-devil. We know this from the writings of many people. Many biographers of the life of Mohammed mentioned that Mohammed was visited by a priest of the Jinn-devils who came to embrace Islam. The name of the priest was Thamad al-Azdi. The book of *Halabieh* says:

> The delegation of Thamad al-Azdi who came to Mohammed was reported by Ibn Abbas: "Thamad came to Mecca and he was from Izd Shina't, which is the name of his tribe, and he used to cast spells or conjure through the wind which was a devil of Jinn. He greeted Mohammed embracing Islam."[113]

Thus, we see that the wind was one of the titles for the Jinn-devil at Mecca at the time of Mohammed. The Arabians believed that the wind was a Jinn. The storm was also among the devils worshipped at Mecca.[114] An idol named Khazeh was believed to cause storms, so he was placed in the Kaabah at Mecca. Many scholars believe Khazeh was a devil.[115] Previously, when we discussed the stations of the great Hajj, we saw that there was a place at Muzdalifah which had a mountain called Khazeh قزح, named after this devil. The person who led the ceremonies at Muzdalifah was to stand on this mountain. All this sheds light on the Temple of Mecca and its occult practices.

Arabian authors, such as al-Azruqi الازرقي, who wrote about Mecca before Islam, mentioned that the wind was worshipped at

Mecca, and there was an idol there named Nahik who represented the wind. People used to make a pilgrimage to see this idol[116]. The idol of the wind on Safa was called "the shelter or place of sanctuary for the wind." The idol of the wind was worshipped as part of a ritual for the worship of the Wind-devil on the hills of Safa and Marwa. The Wind-devil, along with the statues of Asaf and Naelah which were in the temple at Mecca, and over Safa and Marwa, was the subject of the pilgrimage for what became the small Hajj, or Umra'.

Further Proofs That the Safa and Marwa Were a Center of Worship of the Jinn Religion of Arabia

Other proofs support the idea that Safa and Marwa, the two stones near the well of Zamzam, became a center of Jinn worship. The Jinn had a special way to call worshippers. They played music similar to a clanging occult sound. It was heard at night as a drum or timpano. Ibn Abbas, the cousin of Mohammed, and the authoritative reporter of his Hadith, says: "The Jinn used to play all night between the two stones of Safa and Marwa."[117] These things demonstrate that the place between Safa and Marwa was an important center of worship in the Arabian Jinn religion . It had the following occult elements: the statues of Asaf and Naelah – the famous deified priests of Jinn – and the idol of the Wind-devil. These idols encouraged the Jinn worshippers to make the pilgrimage to Safa and Marwa. In fact, those worshippers connected their pilgrimage to the stones where the idol of the Wind-devil and the statues of Asaf and Naelah were placed. They visited the two statues of Asaf and Naelah, the venerated Jinn priests, and went to the well of Zamzam, which we saw was dedicated to the statues of Asaf and Naelah.

Proofs That the Umra' Hajj Revolved Around the Statues of the Two Priests of Jinn

The four stones over which the four idols were placed are still venerated in Islam today. I will discuss the connections of these idols with the old, small Hajj. We will also see that these idols, especially the statues of Asaf and Naelah, were the subject of the small Hajj of Mecca.

The venerating of Asaf and Naelah, the two statues of the priest of Jinn, was rooted in the worship of Mecca and the Kaabah. There are many proofs that lead us to conclude that the Hajj inside Mecca was dedicated to these statues. The Hajj was the main ceremony for worshippers of the Arabian Jinn religion. Al-Ya'akubi mentions that the statues of Asaf and Naelah were placed over the main sacred stones of the Kaabah. He goes on to say that people who performed the Hajj used to kiss these two statues before they proceeded with the Hajj. They went full circle by ending the Hajj with a return to the same statues of Asaf and Naelah[118].

Al-Ya'akubi shed light on the origin of the Meccan Hajj which became the Umra' Hajj. We can only conclude from his writings that there was a Hajj before the Islamic era which involved the two statues of the priests of Jinn. From his writings we can see that the stones called Rukun at the temple of Mecca were not the main worship elements of the temple. Because Asaf and Naelah were placed on the Rukun, it meant that they were significantly important. The custom of many pagan peoples was to put the gods they considered precious on stone platforms, rather than on the ground of the temple. This explains why Arabians who venerated the temple at Mecca put Asaf and Naelah on the two main stones of the Kaabah.

Another thing we can conclude from the description of the small Hajj in Ya'akubi's writings is that the course of the small Hajj was around the two priests of Jinn. Asaf and Naelah were worshipped and may be considered as intercessors between the worshippers of Jinn and the Jinn-devils themselves. The Hajj started from their statues and concluded when they returned to kiss the same statues.

This also explains why the statues of Asaf and Naelah were erected at the well of Zamzam. Arabians used to dig a well for each temple to which they went to sacrifice to the gods they worshipped. This would build Hajj around the statues of the gods. Among the ceremonies, they drank water from the well which was dedicated to the deity. The worshippers in the Arabian Jinn religion erected two statues on the well of Zamzam in honor of the two statues they represented. Ibn Hisham, the first book narrating the life of Mohammed, mentions that the Arabians presented sacrifices to the statues of Asaf and Naelah, which were erected at the well of Zamzam.[119] This confirms that Asaf and Naelah were the deities in whose honor the worshippers drank the water of the well of Zamzam, and to whom they made the ceremonies of the Hajj.

The two tribes of Medina that supported Mohammed in his plot to subdue their Arabian neighbors, and require them to embrace Islam, performed the same occult Hajj to Asaf and Naelah.

The fact that the Umra' Hajj to Mecca revolved around the two priests of the Jinn statues, and that it was part of a ceremony of the Arabian Jinn religion, is supported by other historical factors, one of which is the way Aisheh interpreted one verse of the Qur'an in Surah 2:158, called Al-Baqarah. The Qur'an says:

> Behold Al-Safa 'and Marwa are Allah's ceremonies. So those who visit the Kaabah in season or at other times, should encompass them around so that there is no sin in them.

Aisheh, the youngest wife of Mohammed, spoke about the rite to encompass the Safa and Marwa which Mohammed incorporated in the Qur'an. She said:

> Ansar, in pre-Islamic times, went to worship the two idols placed on the seashore. [By Ansar she meant the two tribes of Yathrib who helped Mohammed subdue the Arabians and require them to accept Islam by making war against them.] These idols were Asaf and Naelah. Then the two tribes came to encompass Safa and Marwa. Afterwards, they cut their hair. When Islam came, they were not as eager to encompass Safa and Marwa, as they did before Islam. Allah inspired the verse "Behold Safa and Marwa are Allah's ceremonies." As a result, the two tribes returned to the practice of encompassing the Safa and Marwa.[120]

Aisheh explained how and why many verses of the Qur'an came to be, and she reported many of Mohammed's Hadiths. Her words, quoted above, reveal and confirmed important facts. Concerning the occult religion of the two tribes, Oas and Khazraj, you may remember that these two tribes made a treaty with Mohammed in which they would say "there is no god but Allah, and Mohammed his prophet." In exchange, Mohammed promised to lead them in war against neighboring Arabian tribes, promising them special privileges. They were to enjoy the wives and daughters of the Arabians they conquered by making them concubines, enslaving their children, and taking their neighbors' possessions. From the words of Aisheh we understand that the two tribes used to worship Asaf and Naelah and go to Safa and Marwa, the two places which were at the center of Jinn worship, as we saw previously. There they would also worship the statues of Asaf and Naelah. This shows that the true worship of these two tribes was occult in nature. They worshipped the same elements as those revered by the Arabian Jinn religion.

The second thing we see is that they performed a Hajj which started with the same statues of Asaf and Naelah, and passed by Safa and Marwa. Then they cut their hair, showing that this is the same occult Hajj performed by other pre-Islamic Arabians mentioned by al-Ya'akubi. The difference is that the two tribes began their Hajj at the two statues of Asaf and Naelah on the seashore near Mecca, while the others started the Umra' Hajj from the statues of Asaf and Naelah placed over two stones at the temple in Mecca, then proceeded to the Safa and Marwa hills. The same ceremonies contain the same elements of Jinn worship, except one places the statues on the seashore and the other places them in the Kaabah at Mecca. They both encompassed Safa and Marwa, where they found the statues of Asaf and Naelah and the idol of the Wind-devil.

The reason the two tribes chose the statues of Asaf and Naelah on the seashore, and not at the Temple of Mecca, was because they considered the Kaabah to be a place of worship for the tribe of Quraish. They preferred to start the Hajj from the statues on the seashore. However, they did confirm that the Hajj had to begin from Asaf and Naelah, the venerated priests of the Jinn, the first element of worship to begin the Hajj of Mecca. The two tribes could not miss the other pillar of the Hajj of Umra', which was the same Safa and Marwa, which we saw as the center of Jinn activity, where the idol of wind which represented the Jinn was placed and worshipped, and where the same statues of Asaf and Naelah were placed as important figures in the leadership of the Jinn religion.

It doesn't make sense for Muslims to build monotheistic claims on an occult Hajj which clearly revolved around elements of worship of the Jinn religion. Today, Islam practices the same ceremonies of this occult Hajj at the same places, yet it attributes them to Abraham. What is the relationship between the faith which Abraham confessed and the Jinn-devils, who were at the center of the Jinn religion? Clearly, Mohammed wanted to unite elements that can't be united. God's worship cannot be included in ceremonies dedicated to the Jinn and its representatives. Mohammed confirmed the same occult Hajj practiced by the two tribes that supported him. This included visiting the well of Zamzam, which his grandfather dug in honor of the Jinn and his servants, Asaf and Naelah, which were the main subjects of the Hajj.

I previously quoted the words of Aisheh, Mohammed's wife, when she talked about the religious Hajj performed by the two tribes of Yathrib, Oas and Khazraj. Remember, they backed Mohammed and helped him use the sword to impose Islam on their neighbors. We also notice in Aisheh's narration that they performed the same ceremonies of the Hajj, including marching around the two stones of Safa and Marwa, and the cutting of their hair. When Islam appeared on the scene, the pilgrims encompassed Safa and Marwa seven times, then finished the Hajj by cutting their hair. This shows that Mohammed continued the ceremonies practiced in the Hajj which contained elements of the occult worship of the Arabian Jinn religion.

After Abdel Mutaleb, the grandfather of Mohammed, dug the well of Zamzam near Safa and Marwa, visiting the well and drinking of its water became part of the small Hajj called Umra'. We must, therefore, conclude that the well of Zamzam was dug explicitly to honor the deities for which the Hajj was called in the first place, namely to honor the Jinn and his famous and devoted servants, Asaf and Naelah. Our conclusion is based upon many facts. First, the well was dug near Safa and Marwa which, we saw, was venerated due to the statues of Asaf and Naelah which were placed there. The idol of the Wind, also considered as Jinn by those living in Mecca, was placed over one of the two stones. Other occult phenomena included Jinn activity on the two hills. Second, because Abdul Mutaleb was an elder of the Jinn religion, we conclude that the well of Zamzam was dug explicitly to honor Jinn deities. Third, because Abdul Mutaleb erected the two statues of Asaf and Naelah over the well of Zamzam, we see that the Hajj was connected with these deities. The Umra' Hajj began by kissing the copies of the statues of Asaf and Naelah placed on the main stones of the Kaabah, or by kissing the copies placed on the seashore near Mecca. Further, the two tribes of Yathrib also started the Hajj by kissing the statues. All this shows us that Abdul Mutaleb dug the well of Zamzam to honor the Hajj connected with the same Asaf and Naelah, Kuhhan of Jinn at the Kabbah. That is why the rite of drinking the water of the well of Zamzam, where the two statues were erected, became part of the Hajj ceremonies which adherents of the Jinn religion observed.

Worship rites of the Jinn religion of Arabia did not smoothly transfer into a religious ritual which claimed a monotheistic faith founded by Abraham. These claims were false and unhistorical. How, then, could the well of Zamzam be caused by the footprint of Gabriel, as Muslims claim? Ibn Ishak, chief Islamic biographer of Mohammed, claimed that the tribe of Jurhum covered the well with the Black Stone and a gazelle of gold. This was after Jurhum was defeated and driven from Mecca. How could it be possible for the only well in Mecca to be hidden from the inhabitants of Mecca and from the eyes of the Bedouins who walked miles to find water for their camels? Would they not have redug the well the same day it was buried? Surely if the well had existed when Islamic tradition claims, it would have become the most famous place in Mecca, and the main artery of life which would bring the precious water upon which they depended every day. Therefore, we suppose that they would have redug it the same day it was buried. How, then, as Islamic tradition claims, could the well be hidden for hundreds of years until a voice suddenly came to Abdul Mutaleb to begin digging? And how could a voice to dig the well come to a man who was known to be a worshipper of the pagan deities, Asaf and Naelah? How could the well be created, according to Islamic tradition, by the angel Gabriel? Does God ask the worshippers of the Jinn-devil to do sacred works on His behalf? If Abdul Mutaleb had really heard a voice from heaven telling him to dig a "sacred well "why did he erect the statues of Asaf and Naelah? Why would he want to sacrifice his son at the feet of Asaf and Naelah? Is not this enough proof to convince us that he dug the well to the same statues that he erected over the well, and to whom he showed reverence to the point he was willing to sacrifice his son to them? He wanted to provide a well of water to the Hajj, dedicated to the same Asaf and Naelah. It is common knowledge that Arabians used to dedicate wells of water to their gods.

All these questions should cause our Muslim friends to recognize how old Arabian occult rites were given new meaning when Mohammed founded Islam. He simply incorporated them in his new religion. Yet, historical facts connecting the ceremonies of the old pagan and occult religion of Arabia to the new Islam of Mohammed were not smooth enough to hide the original occult practices. To accept the stories they had to create in order to make the adjustments would require someone as naive as a child. People today, born with a neutral heritage, soon discover its inconsistencies.

What's the secret behind Khazraj and Oas, the only tribes who accepted Mohammed's offer to back him with military power to force Arabian tribes to accept Islam?

Knowing that Oas and Khazraj, the two tribes of Yathrib from al-Medina, had an occult Hajj which started from the two statues of

Asaf and Naelah, can explain why they were the only tribes which were ready to accept Mohammed's offer to help him subdue neighboring Arabian tribes and convert them to Islam. In return, you remember, he guaranteed to give them the females of those they conquered to become their concubines, and Mohammed gave them the conquered children as slaves and confiscated their possessions.

There is a connection between these two tribes and the Hajj of Asaf and Naelah. The Hajj proceeded toward a location in the hills of Safa and Marwa which was dedicated to the Wind-Jinn. This is significant in identifying their true religion, and their affiliation with the occult religion of the Arabian Jinn. The Kuhhan, who were priests of the religion of Jinn, backed and supported Mohammed. The two tribes, both adherents to the Jinn religion of Arabia, provided the military power of religion to stand with Mohammed in his plan.

Marching around the stones, Safa and Marwa, was a ritual hated by most of Mohammed's companions because they knew it was a pagan ritual. Yet, they still observed it because Mohammed claimed that Allah confirmed it.

Even the companions of Mohammed confessed that the Hajj to Safa and Marwa was a pagan rite from Jahiliyah, the pre-Islam period. Sahih al-Bukhari said:

> Asem told us that he said to Uns bin Malek, a companion of Mohammed, "You were hating to encompass around the Safa and Marwa." He answered, "Yes, because it was one of the pagan rites of Jahiliyah until Allah gave a verse that the Safa and Marwa are the rites of Allah. If one makes the Hajj to the Kaabah, he must encompass them. The person has no sin when he encompasses them." [121]

Even Ibn Abbas, the cousin of Mohammed, and the most authoritative reporter of his Hadith, speaks of encompassing the Safa and Marwa as was the custom of the people of Jahiliyah, meaning the pagan Arabians before Islam. His speech is reported in Sahih al-Bukhari.[122]

Muslims at the time of Mohammed knew the origin of this pagan rite just as they knew about many Arabian pagan rites which Mohammed incorporated in Islam. But they embraced it simply because Mohammed made the decision to incorporate it into Islam. Everything Mohammed said or wrote in the Qur'an became acceptable and sacred, even though his followers knew its pagan roots. It's sad that they didn't use their knowledge to judge Mohammed once they discerned how he built his religion. Instead, they allowed him to invalidate their discernment by following him. Mohammed annulled their knowledge, even though they knew how he selected the pagan, occult rites which many of them hated.

Mohammed Intended to Unify the Pagan Arabian Rituals Under One Religion

Mohammed planned to gather the laws and rites which Arabians before Islam were known to practice. His aim was to form a religion which would satisfy all Arabians. Al-Bukhari said:

> Pre-Islamic pagan Arabians walked in a circle around Safa and Marwa. So when Allah told us to encompass the Kaabah, he did not mention Safa and Marwa in the Qur'an. They said to Mohammed: "O prophet of Allah, we encompassed the Safa and Marwa. Allah sent a verse to encompass the Kaabah, but he did not mention the Safa and Marwa. Do we sin if we encompass the Safa and Marwa?" So Allah gave this verse: "the Safa and Marwa are rites of Allah." Abu Baker said that this verse pleased both parties: those before Islam who did not want to encompass the Safa and Marwa, and those who encompassed the Safa and Marwa before Islam, but were embarrassed to encompass it after Islam arrived. [123]

It is clear that Mohammed's intention was to satisfy all Arabians by including all their rites, especially the rite to march around Safa and Marwa, which was practiced by many members of the two tribes who supported him in raging wars against the Arabian tribes to impose Islam.

The rite was also practiced by him, since it was a rite of his grandfather who strengthened it by digging the well of Zamzam and erecting over it the statues of the two deities, Asaf and Naelah, which were the main elements for which the Hajj of Mecca was performed.

Mohammed himself was known to practice the rituals of the occult Hajj. He removed the idols which were the subject of the Hajj from over the stones, but he kept marching around the stones where the idols were placed.

Many years before writing it in the Qur'an, Mohammed encompassed the Safa and Marwa seven times because it was a rite his family and his grandfather observed. He conducted the Hajj starting at the Kaabah, encompassing it and kissing the two stones. Then he encompassed the two stones on the hills of Safa and Marwa.[124] As we have seen, Mohammed followed the same rites which we saw were adopted by adherents of the occult Jinn-religion who started their Hajj by kissing the statues of Asaf and Naelah placed in the Temple of Mecca. The statues were placed on the same stones which Mohammed continued to revere and to kiss.

They continued the Hajj by encompassing the same stones of Safa and Marwa, where the statue of the Wind-Jinn was placed, along with statues of Asaf and Naelah. Except with one difference: Mohammed didn't consider the statues to be part of the Hajj ceremonies. Although he fought to destroy all kinds of statues, he worshipped the stones where the idols had been placed before he removed them. So what difference did Mohammed make when he adopted the same pagan occult rite, venerating the stones where the idols were placed and just removing the idols?

To make the same tour around the stones where the statues revered by the Jinn religion were placed, and to conduct the same rituals which the worshippers of the occult sect performed, could never bestow new meaning to the old pagan occult worship, even though Mohammed performed it himself. Our Muslim friends should avoid falling into this dangerous trap. It's aimed to distract them from the faith which God has announced in the Bible. The Scriptures, alone, lead the soul to Christ, the true Creator and Savior of the soul.

THE ROLE OF THE TEMPLE AT MECCA IN THE JINN RELIGION AND IN THE ARABIAN STAR FAMILY.

We continue our study of the occult influence on the temple at Mecca. We will look at the occult ceremonies and their influence on the Islamic ceremonies and on the Qur'an.

We've talked about the history of the Kaabah. It was a temple were the two statues of Asaf and Naelah, the famous Kuhhan of Jinn, were located. The Hajj began there and progressed to the statues of Wind-Jinn. Copies of the statues of Asaf and Naelah were placed over the hills of Safa and Marwa. One cannot fail to observe the role of the Temple of Mecca as a place of worship for the Jinn religion, as well as being a place for the worship of the Arabian Star Family.

Another element which helps us to understand the role of the Temple of Mecca is that it united the two main religions of Arabia: the Jinn religion, and the Star Family religion. In the Star Family religion, Allah was the biggest star. His wife was the sun, and his daughters were Manat and al-'Uzza, each representing a planet. The Kuhhan, who represented the Jinn religion to Arabians who practiced other pagan religions, such as the worship of the Arabian Star Family, were accepted by the people who considered the Kuhhan to be gods. The tribe of Quraish considered Iblis – another name for the devil – and Allah to be brothers.[125] They said that between Allah and the Jinn, there is great kinship.[126] They believed that the angels were daughters of Allah, and that the mothers of the angels were the daughters of the "Jinn's lord."[127] The Jinn were viewed as superior to the angels. Pagan Arabians gave this exalted position to the Jinn because they believed the Jinn were in close relationship and kinship with Allah. Because the Jinn replaced the angels, they left their fingerprints on the Qur'an.

The Jinn-devils Replaced Angels in the Qur'an, Just as They Replaced Angels in Literature and Poetry of the Jinn Religion of Arabia

The Qur'an represents an Arabian literature developed before Mohammed; such literature attributed artistic works to the Jinn.[128] In the Qur'an, we find the spirit of the Arabian Jinn religion. We see devils as ingenious workers for Solomon in Surah al-Anbiya'. Quoting from Surah 21, verses 81 and 82:

> For Solomon, the violent wind flowed under his command to the land which we had blessed, for we do know everything. And among the devils were some who dived into the sea for him, and did other works besides, and we protected them.

Verse 81 refers to Solomon claiming that he had the wind as his servant. Under his command, the wind would go to the land which Allah blessed, called the land of Harran, as we understand from other sources. The wind as a servant of superior gods and deified kings is a habitual theme in ancient religions of the Middle East.

Al-Sabuni, a modern expositor of the Qur'an in Saudi Arabia, commented on verse 82:

> The devils dived for Solomon, entering the depths of the sea in order to get jewels and pearls. They made great buildings for Solomon, including the construction of his palaces.

The devils are portrayed in the Qur'an as very useful agents for Solomon and for the prophets. They are pictured as true agents of God, which He placed into Solomon's service.[129] This teaching is derived from the Jinn religion which elevated the devils in the eyes of the Arabians so that the devils would become venerated and be worshipped. These Qur'anic verses implied a relationship between God in the Old Testament and the devils, to the point that God would have protected them. This is contrary to the teaching of the Bible, where the devils are condemned creatures, and there is no partnership between God and devils.

Other verses of the Qur'an also show the influence of the Jinn religion on the Qur'an. Surah 38, called Surah S'ad, in verses 37-39, is directed to Solomon: "The devils, which included every kind of builder and diver, is our bounty, so thank us, and no account will be asked." The devils are portrayed as gifts of God to Solomon, who was required to thank God for them. This false allegation was taken directly from the Arabian Jinn religion, which gave the devils a high position and treated them as treasured gifts to the prophets of the Old Testament. Such allegations are contrary to the teaching of the Bible. The Bible warns us about devils, and presents them as a curse, and as enemies of God and man. The Bible warns us not to have any relationship with devils.

Not only in the Qur'an do we find the idea of devils working for Solomon, but we see it also in pre-Islamic poems by men who were known to have a relationship with the Jinn. For example, we find in the poems of al-Nabighah النابغة that the Jinn worked for Solomon, building the city of Tadmur in the Syrian desert for him[130]. Another example is found in the writings of Al-Aasha', a pre-Islamic Arabian poet. Al-Aasha' named the Jinn-devil who inspired his poetry. He called the Jinn-devil Musahhal المسحل, and described him as his " beloved one." Al-Aasha' says: "My brother, the Jinn, has greeted me. My soul is dedicated to him."[131] This shows al-Aasha' was one of the many poets dedicated to the Jinn religion of Arabia. These poets considered the Jinn to be brothers, and they tried to unify men with the Jinn. Mohammed also expressed similar thoughts. He claimed to go to heaven where he encountered Allah who delegated him for a mission to the humans and to the Jinn. Mohammed defined his people as originating from the Jinn and from humans.[132] He often claimed that the Jinn became Muslims,[133] and he referred to them as brothers.[134]

Al-Aasha' wrote in one of his poems that the "Jinn were working for Solomon, building arches."[135] Mohammed copied the same idea into Surah Saba 34, verses 12-13. Speaking of Solomon, he wrote:

> Among the Jinn who worked with him, by the leave of his lord, they worked for him as he desired, building arches, statues, and basins as large as reservoirs and cauldrons fixed in their places. Work you sons of David with thanks.

The Qur'an portrays God as asking the sons of David, like Solomon, to thank God because He sent the Jinn to do such artistic works. This is a false assertion about God. This idea of holding the Jinn in high esteem as good workers sent by God was an idea promoted by the Kuhhan in Arabia, to make the Jinn appreciated and venerated by the Arabians. It further sought to cause the Arabians to come to the Kuhhan as representatives of the Jinn and seek counsel from them.

Ancient Roots of the Arabian Jinn-Devils Which Were Highly Regarded as Descended From the Gods

The teachings of the Arabians about the Jinn-devils being related to Allah, and their daughters being mothers for the angels, has its ancient roots in Arabia. The Akkadians, who came from Arabia to Mesopotamia, claimed that seven devils were sons of the Mesopotamian god "An," who represented the sky, and his wife "Kai," who represented the earth. According to the Sumerians, An and Kai were married. The Akkadians introduced the idea that the devils were related to the main gods of Mesopotamia and assisted them in creating and governing the universe[136]. The Akkadians worshipped a devil named Girru, whom they claimed was of the line of the god, "An," and was formed from fire.[137] In the Qur'an we find that the Jinn-devils were also formed from fire.

The roots of ancient Arabia show that thousands of years before Mohammed the religion of Jinn-devils gave them an exalted position, making them a dynamic force in pagan worship in the temples of Arabia, especially in Star Family worship. The Kuhhan became the religious class, a hierarchy responsible for the various temples of Arabia. This enabled the Kuhhan to introduce the rites of the Arabian Jinn religion in the temples, such as the Umra' Hajj which revolved around the Jinn and the famous servants of Jinn, Asaf and Naelah. We saw how this Hajj became an official Hajj which started at the Kaabah of Mecca. The Kuhhan caused the revered figures of the Jinn religion to be the focused sacred elements in the temple. The statues of Asaf and Naelah were placed over the main stones of the temple at Mecca.

Since the early construction of the Temple of Mecca, the Kuhhan of the Jinn were its official priests. This explains how they made their occult Hajj into a ceremony of the temple.

The Temple of Mecca was governed by the Kuhhan of the Jinn. We see this from the presence of the two statues of the Kuhhan on the stones which, without doubt, became sacred because of the two statues placed there. The fact that the statues continued to be located there for a long time tells us that the hierarchy of the temple was contained in the Kuhhan line. They considered Asaf and Naelah to be the pioneer servants to the temple. It's similar to a priest in a Catholic church putting the image of the first bishop or priest who served the church in the main corner of the sanctuary.

We conclude that the rites in the Kaabah of Mecca were conducted by the Kuhhan of the Jinn, and they were responsible for its religious functions. There are other famous Kuhhan who were known to be responsible for the Kaabah at Mecca. Among them was Wake'a Zuhair al-Iyadi. Ibn al-Kalbi, an Arabian historian and author who wrote about the pre-Islamic era, says that Wake'a was responsible as the Kahen of the Kaabah in those times.[138] According to the old Arabian authors, Wake'a was known to have rhymed prose like that of the Kuhhan.[139] This confirms his affiliation with the Kuhhan of the Jinn religion. His rhymed prose was considered equal to the Qur'an. We also find many of his phrases copied by Mohammed and incorporated into the Qur'an. Excerpts of the sayings of Wake'a are found in old Arabic literature, such as Majma' al-Amthaal written by al-Maydaani.[140]

All this confirms the sovereignty of the Kuhhan of Jinn over the Temple of Mecca, making them the true religious class of the temple. This also explains how many of their rites, such as their Hajj to the main elements of the Jinn religion in the city, became a main ritual of the Temple and for the worshippers of the Arabian Star religion.

They Worshipped a Serpent in the Temple at Mecca, and the Arabians Thought it was a Jinn-devil

The true ceremonies of Kaabah, and their connection with the Jinn religion, is shown by the worship of a serpent in the Kaabah. The writings of Tabari, the famous Arabic historian who wrote about pre-Islamic Arabia, tells us that a serpent lived in the well of Kaabah, where the inhabitants of Mecca threw their gifts.[141] It seems that the gifts were offered to the serpent. Arabian historians who wrote about pre-Islamic Mecca said that the term "Allaha," from which the name Allah was derived, was applied to the "big serpent."[142] Arabians worshipped serpents, considering them to be serpent-devils. One of the titles for the devil around Mecca was "Azab," who was believed to be a serpent.[143] Historians also said that the Jinn is a white serpent,[144] whom they believed heard and distinguished between languages. Poets, like al-Nabighah and others who were known to have a relationship with the Jinn, such as Umayya bin Abi al-Salt and Adi bin Zayd, promoted such ideas.[145]

Because the serpent in the well of the temple was worshipped, and because he received their gifts, we can see that the Temple of Mecca was an important center for the worship of the Jinn. They worshipped the Jinn through worshipping the serpent in the well of the Kaabah, and they called the serpent "Allaha." Remember that the idol "Kozah" was placed in the Kaabah. The people believed he caused rain and thunderstorms, but many scholars think he was a devil.

In structure and ceremony, the Kaabah, in many ways, was identical to the temples of the Jinn religion of Arabia.

The Arabians had temples which they called "Taghut"طاغوت , a title for Marid of the Jinn مارد الجن, which means a giant Jinn. In subsequent times, the Kuhhan of the Jinn were also called Taghut,[146] showing us that the Taghut were the temples of the Jinn religion. Authors who wrote about Arabia in the pre-Islamic period mentioned the similarity between the Kaabah of Mecca and the Taghut. Taghut had the same construction as the Kaabah from the inside, and they had the same ceremonies, such as marching around them like the pagan Arabians who had encompassed the Kaabah.[147] This suggests to us that the temple at Mecca was much like the Taghut, united with other various temples of the Jinn religion. In ceremonies and structure, there was an affinity between the temples built for the Arabian Star Family and those of the Jinn religion. This is understandable, since the Kuhhan of the Jinn governed the religious functions in most of the temples built for Star Family worship. The Kuhhan governed the worship of the Star Family temple in the same way they governed the temples of the Taghut, which were dedicated to the worship of Jinn. The Temple of Mecca was one of the temples of Arabia which practiced the worship of the two main pagan religions of Arabia : The Arabian Star Family Worship and The Jinn religion.

The two priests of Jinn, Asaf and Naelah, were assumed to have been buried in the Kaabah of Mecca. The Kaabah was a place of immoral ceremonies, which supports the idea that it was a sanctuary for the Jinn religion. In pre-Islamic times, the tombs of some of the Kuhhan became sacred places where Arabians visited to get a blessing. Pagan Arabians made their sanctuaries into places of security and shelter. If anyone entered the sanctuaries, he would became invulnerable, and no one could harm him.[148] This was also observed at the Temple of Mecca. This may suggest that the Kaabah originally was a place where the two Kuhhan, Asaf and Naelah, were buried. Then tribes from Yemen built a temple there, sharing the same purpose for the Kaabah between

432

the Jinn religion and the Arabian Star Family Worship which Yemeni tribes embraced.

Also, the authors who wrote about Mecca in pre-Islamic times spoke about the ceremonies which occurred in the Kaabah which are practiced today only in the temples of Satanism. For example, according to the authoritative book of al-Bukhari, when they encompassed the Kaabah, the marchers were to be naked, including the women.[149] Also, according to the book Halabieh, the Kaabah was a place of fornication. If someone wanted to commit fornication, he could do so at the Kaabah.[150] This reminds us of the fornication which occurred in the temples belonging to devil worship, and which supports the affiliation of Kaabah with the Jinn religion of Arabia. Arabic writers who tell us about Mecca describe the fornication of the women of the city.[151] It seems these immoralities in the Kaabah had influenced the city.

The history of occult practices in the Kaabah of Mecca rule it out as a temple of the true, holy God, since He is opposed to Satanism and any form of the occult. All the ceremonies and the personalities who governed the ceremonies, including the idols which were worshipped and the stones which were venerated, confirm that the Kaabah was a local expression of paganism and occult worship in Mecca. This defilement was worse than what occurred in any other pagan temple known to the ancient world, whether in the Middle East or in Asia. These practices failed to have even a trace of the character of worship worthy of the true God as we encounter Him in the Bible. The worship of the God of the Bible exposes every source of the occult. It is totally bound up with the Scriptures which God inspired and gave to the prophets to be conserved for all ages. The Bible was honored in every sanctuary where the people worshipped God, something we did not see in the Temple of Mecca at any point in history. In the Temple of Mecca we see only the occult and the pagan Star Family tradition. How can Islam claim that the temple of Mecca was the historical center of monotheism throughout history?

433

3 _____

RAMADAN AND ITS ROOTS

Ramadan has Pagan Roots in India and in the Middle East

Ramadan, the ninth month of the Islamic calendar, and the rigid observance of thirty days of fasting during the daylight hours, has pagan roots developed in India and in the Middle East. The observance of fasting to honor the moon, and ending the fast when the moon's crescent appears, was practiced with the rituals of the Eastern worshippers of the moon. Both Ibn al-Nadim and the Shahrastani tell us about al-Jandrikinieh, an Indian sect which began to fast when the moon disappeared, and ended the fast with a great feast when the crescent reappeared[152].

The Sabians, who were pagans in the Middle East, were identified with two groups, the Mandaeans and the Harranians. The Mandaeans lived in Iraq during the 2nd century A.D. As they continue to do today, they worshipped multiple gods, or "light personalities." Their gods were classified under four categories: "first life," "second life," "third life" and "fourth life." Old gods belong to the "first life" category. They summoned deities who, in turn, created "second life" deities, and so forth.

The other group, considered as Sabians, were the Harranians. They worshipped Sin, the moon, as their main deity, but they also worshipped planets and other deities. The Sabians were in contact with Ahnaf, an Arabian group which Mohammed joined before claiming to be a prophet. Ahnaf sought knowledge by going to northern Iraq, where there were many communities of Mandaeans. They also went to the city of Harran in the al-Jazirah district in northern Syria on the border between Syria, Iraq and Asia Minor.

In Mecca, the Ahnaf were called Sabians because of the doctrines they embraced. Later, when Mohammed claimed to be a prophet, he was called a Sabian by the inhabitants of Mecca because they saw him performing many Sabian rites which included praying five times a day; performing several movements in prayer that were identical with the Mandaeans and the Harranians; and making ablution, or ceremonial washing, before each prayer. In the Qur'an, Mohammed called the Sabians "people of the book," like the Jews and Christians.

Ramadan was a pagan ceremony practiced by the Sabians, whether they were Harranians or Sabians. From the writings of Abu Zanad, an Arabic writer from Iraq who lived around 747 A.D., we conclude that at least one Mandaean community located in northern Iraq observed Ramadan[153].

Ramadan was Originally an Annual Ritual Performed at the City of Harran. Similarities Between the Ramadan of Harran and the Islamic Ramadan

Although the fasting of Ramadan was practiced in pre-Islamic times by the pagans of Jahiliyah, it was introduced to Arabia by the Harranians. Harran was a city on the border between Syria and Iraq, very close to Asia Minor which, today, is Turkey. Their main deity was the moon, and in the worship of the moon, they conducted a major fast which lasted thirty days. It began the eighth of March and usually finished the eighth of April. Arabic historians, such as Ibn Hazm, identify this fast with Ramadan.[154]

Ibn al-Nadim wrote in his book, al-Fahrisit, about various religious sects in the Middle East. He says in the month in which the Harranians fasted for thirty days they honored the god Sin, which is the moon. Al-Nadim described the feasts which they celebrated and the sacrifices they presented to the moon.[155] Another historian, Ibn Abi Zinad, also speaks about the Harranians, saying that they fast for thirty days, they look toward Yemen when they fast, and they pray five times a day.[156] We know that Muslims also pray five times a day. Harranian fasting is also similar to that of Ramadan in Islam in the fact that they fast from before the sun rises until the sunset, just as the Muslims do during

435

the days of Ramadan.[157] Still another historian, Ibn al-Juzi, described the Harranian fasting during this month. He said they concluded their fasting by sacrificing animals and presenting alms to the poor.[158] We also find these things in Islamic fasting today.

Mythological roots concerning Harran's celebration of the moon explained the disappearance of the moon after it joined with the star cluster, Pleiades, in the constellation of Taurus. It occurred during the third week of March. The people prayed to the moon, pleading for its return to the city of Harran, but the moon refused to return. This is thought to be the explanation for why they fasted during this month. The moon did not promise to return to Harran, but it did promise to return to Deyr Kadi, a sanctuary near one of the gates of Harran. So after this month, the worshippers of Sin, the moon, went to Deyr Kadi to celebrate and to welcome the return of the moon.[159] According to Ibn al-Nadim, the historian mentioned earlier, the Harranians called the feast al-Feter عيد الفطر , the same name by which the feast of Ramadan is named[160].

In addition to the feast during Ramadan, the Harranians had five prayers which they repeated day and night. Each had to be preceded by ablutions, which were ceremonial washings.[161] The same system of five prayers each day, preceded by ablutions, was embraced by Mohammed.

The fasting of Ramadan spread from Harran into Arabia. This may have occurred after the occupation of Nabonidus, the Babylonian king, to the north of Arabia, around the year 552 B.C., during his sojourn in the city of Teima. Nabonidus was from the city of Harran. He was a fanatic worshipper of the moon, Sin, and his mother was a priest of Sin. He disagreed with the priests of Babylonia who considered the god, Marduk, as the chief of the gods of Babylonia. Nabonidus was eager to spread the worship of Sin, the moon, as the main deity. So he left his son in charge of Babylonia and went to live in Teima in North Arabia.

In pre-Islamic times, Ramadan became a pagan Arabian ritual and was practiced by the pagan Arabians with the same features and characteristics as the Islamic Ramadan.

Ramadan was known and practiced by the pagan Arabians before Islam. Al-Masudi says that Ramadan received its name because of the warm weather during that month.[162]

The pagan Arabians in the pre-Islamic Jahiliyah period fasted in the same way Muslims fasted, as originally directed by Mohammed. Pagan Arabian fasting included abstinence from food, water, and sexual contact – the same as practiced by Islam. Their fasting also was done in silence. There was to be no talking, not even for a short period of time such as one day, or a longer period of time of a week or more.[163] The Qur'an points to the same kind of fasting when, in Surah 19, it describes God instructing the Virgin Mary to say that she vowed to fast before God, which also meant she couldn't speak to anyone[164]. The Arabian practice of keeping silent during the fast noticeably influenced the customs of the Qur'an. We are told that Abu Baker approached a woman among the pagan worshippers in Medina. He found her fasting, including abstinence from speaking.[165] Fasting was a serious matter for the Arabians, enforced with laws requiring severe penalties for failing to abstain from talking. Ramadan in Islam is a continuation of this kind of fasting.

Mohammed imposed on his followers many religious rituals from the two tribes of Medina who backed him in subduing the Arabians to Islam. Among such rituals was Ramadan.

It seems that Ramadan was practiced in many cities in North Arabia where Nabonidus, the Harranian king of Babylonia, ruled. One of the cities he occupied was Yathrib, which later became al-Medina. Mohammed imposed Ramadan fasting, as well as the ritual of praying toward Mecca instead of Jerusalem, after he emigrated to al-Medina, whose Arabian tribes used to pray toward Mecca, just as it seems they used to fast during Ramadan.[166] Mohammed adjusted his ceremonies to fit the religious rituals and customs of Oas and Khazraj, the two tribes from al-Medina who backed Mohammed in his wars against the Arabians. One of their ceremonies was a weekly religious feast each Friday. Mohammed made this day the religious day of Islam.

Muslims Can't Gain the Favor of God by Practicing Religious Ceremonies Such as Ramadan.

Ramadan is not true fasting, because the participants still eat their meals during the night. Since the ritual allows them to eat while it is dark, they simply eat a large meal in the late evening and wake up early in the morning for another big meal. In other words, they simply change the time of their meals from daylight to darkness.

The hypocrisy continues during Ramadan in the kind of meals they eat. Rather than simple meals which they have during the year, they arrange for elaborate meals, spending sometimes triple or more money on food during Ramadan than in any other month. In reality, it's not true fasting, but an excuse for eating extra in the month they claim to be fasting.

Fellowship with God is not based upon arduous or deceptive religious practices. Neither is fellowship with God granted through religious practices. A criminal who is required to appear before a court to receive justice doesn't gain the judge's favor by practicing religious rituals. Being religious doesn't annul the criminal act he committed. In the same way, as a sinner, man doesn't obtain the favor of God by doing religious rituals or by fasting. He can't avoid the justice of God and the condemnation that awaits him because of his sins. A holy God refuses to have fellowship with sinners, even though they perform many religious practices.

However, God has provided salvation to mankind when He sent His Son in human flesh to die on a cruel cross in order to pay the penalty demanded for sin. The only way for a person to have fellowship with God is to believe in the redemptive work of Christ. In so doing, the repentant sinner finds that his sins will be removed, and the righteousness of Christ will be imputed to him. Then the Spirit of God is given to him so that he can fellowship with God spiritually, and for eternity.

REFERENCES AND NOTES TO PART V

[1] *Sahih Muslim*, 9, page 100

[2] *Bukhari*, 2, page 141; *Sahih Muslim* 9, page 119

[3] Al-Biruni,op.cit.,page 318 (cited by *The Knowledge of Life*, Sinasi Gunduz, Oxford University, 1994, page 183

[4] Ibn al-Nadim, *al-Fahrisit*, page 322

[5] Ibn Kathir, *Al Bidayah Wal Nihayah*, Dar Al Hadith, (Cairo, 1992), 2 : 243

[6] Ibn Darid, *Al-Ishtiqaq* 84; Qastallani Ahmad ibn Muhammed, *Irshad al-Sari*, 6, page 171 ; Ibn Kathir, *al-Bidayah Wal Nihayah* 2, page 244; Ibn al-Atheer, *Asad al-Ghabah Fi Maarifat al-Sahabah* 2, page 231

[7] M. A. al-Hamed, *Saebat Harran Wa Ikhawan al-Safa*, (al-A'hali-Damascus, 1998), page 199

[8] *Tarikh al-Tabari*, I, pages 156, 157

[9] Ibn Habib, *Munammaq*, page 275; cited by Patricia Crone, *Meccan Trade*, Princeton University Press, 1987, page 173

[10] Muhammad Ibn Habib, *Kitab al- Munammaq*, page 196

[11] Azruqi, *Akhbar Mecca*, page 132

[12] Wellhausen, *Reste*, page 83; cited by Patricia Crone, *Meccan Trade*, Princeton University Press, 1987, page 174

[13] Patricia Crone, *Meccan Trade*, Princeton University Press, 1987, page 175

[14] (Ibn Saad, *Tabaqat,* 1, page 216); *Ibn Hisham*, page 281 ; Cited by Crone, page 175

[15] *Ibn Hisham*, page 286; (Ibn Saad, *Tabaqat* 1, page 217; Cited by Crone, page 175

[16] Ibn Habib, *Kitab al-Muhabbar*, page 315

[17] Jawad Ali, *al-Mufassal*, vi, page 328

[18] Ibn Habib, *Kitab al-Muhabbar*, page 313

[19] al-Kalbi, *al-Asnam*, Dar al-Kutub al-Masriyah, Cairo-Egypt, 1925, 14; Yaqut al-Hamawi, *Mujam al-Buldan*, 8: 169; Azruqi, *Akhbar Mecca*, I, page 73

[20] al-Kalbi, *al-Asnam*, Dar al-Kutub al-Masriyah, Cairo-Egypt, 1925, pages 13, 15; Yaqut al-Hamawi, *Mujam al-Buldan* 8, page 169

[21] *Al- Bukhari*, 2, page 166

[22] *Tarikh al-Tabari*, I, page 553

[23] *Tarikh al-Tabari*, I, page 553

[24] *Bukhari*, 3, page 181

[25] *Al-Aghani*, by Al Asfahani, 4, pages 122-195

[26] *Sahih Muslim* 9, page 39; *Bukhari*, 2, page 178

[27] *Bukhari*, 2, page 178

[28] *Suhih Muslim* 9, pages 42 and 43

[29] *Taj Al Aruss* 10, page 351; *Tafsir al-Tabari,* 27

[30] Al-Tabarsi al-Fadl ibn al-Hasan, *Majma' al-Bayan fi tafsir al-Qur'an*, 9, page 176; Yaqut al-Hamawi, *Mujam Al Buldan* 2: 944; Jawad Ali, vi, page 246

[31] Al-Ya'akubi , I, page 312

[32] al-Kalbi, *al-Asnam*, Dar al-Kutub al-Masriyah, Cairo-Egypt, 1925, pqge 14 ; see also Yaqut al-Hamawi, *Mujam Al Buldan* 8; page 169

[33] *Tafsir al-Tabari* 27, page 35

[34] *Tafsir al-Tabari* 27, page 35

[35] *Tafsir al-Tabari* 27, page 32

[36] *Tafsir al-Tabari* 27: 32; Al Zamkhari al- Khawarismi, *Al Kashaf* , 3, page 144

[37] Al Azruqi, *Akhbar Mecca*, 1, page 73; Al Kalbi, *Alasnam*, page 14; Yaqut al-Hamawi, *Mujam al-Buldan*, 8, page 169

[38] *Tafsir Ibn al-Kathir* 4, page 252

[39] Al Shahrastani, *Al Milal Wa Al Nah'el*, page 578

[40] *Sahih al-Bukhari*, 5, page 158

[41] *Sahih al-Bukhari*, 4, page 235

[42] *Halabieh*, I, pages 127 and 128

[43] *Ibn Hisham*, I, page 100; *Tarikh al-Tabari*, I, page 507

[44] *Tarikh al-Tabari*, I, page 507

[45] *Tarikh al-Tabari*, I, page 508

[46] *Tarikh al-Tabari*, I, page 508

[47] *Ibn Hisham* I, page 101

[48] *Taj Al Aruss* 2, page 207

[49] Jawad Ali, *al-Mufassal Fi Tarikh al-Arab Khabel al-Islam*, vi, page 384

[50] Jawad Ali, *al-Mufassal Fi Tarikh al-Arab Khabel al-Islam*, vi, page 384

[51] *Taj Al Aruss* 2, page 207

[52] *Sahih al-Bukhari*, 4, page 238

[53] *Sahih al-Bukhari*, 2 , page 171

[54] *Sahih Muslim* 9, page 23

[55] D.Nielsen, *Die Altarabischen Mondreligion* (Strassburg, 1904), S. 86; Jawad Ali, *al-Mufassal Fi Tarikh al-Arab Khabel al-Islam*, vi, page 348

[56] *Shorter Encyc.of Islam*, page 124; quoted by Jawad Ali, vi, page 348

[57] Winekler, ALF., II, Reihe, Ibd., S.336; quoted by Jawad Ali,vi, page 349

[58] Wellhausen, *Reste, Arabischen Heidentums*, Berlin, 1927, page 84; quoted by Jawad Ali, vi, page 351

[59] Al Masudi, *Muruj Al Thahab*, II, pages 212 and 213

[60] Alessandro Bausani, *L'Islam*, Garzanti Milano, 1980, page 61

[61] *Tarikh al-Tabari*, I, page 508; Ibin Hisham, I, page 100

[62] *Epistles of Manuskihar*, Epistle I, Chapter VII, 16, *Pahlavi Texts*, Part II, Translated by E.W. West, *The Sacred Books of the East*, Volume 18, Published by Motilal Banarsidass, page 308; *Epistles of Manuskihar*, Epistle II, Chapter III, 12, ; Epistles of Manuskihar, Epistle I, Chapter IX, 6; *Appendix- The Bareshnum Ceremony, Pahlavi Texts*, Part II, Translated by

E.W. West, *The Sacred Books of the East*, Volume 18, Published by Motilal Banarsidass, page 447

[63] *Vendidad*, Fargard VIII :41-71, translated by James Darmesteter, *The Zenda –Avesta* part I , *The Sacred Books of the East*, Volume IV, pages 105-110

[64] *Appendix- The Bareshnum Ceremony, Pahlavi Texts*, Part II, Translated by E.W. West, *The Sacred Books of the East*, Volume 18, Published by Motilal Banarsidass, page 437

[65] *Shayast La-Shayast*, Chapter XX, 5, *Pahlavi Texts*, Translated by E.W. West, Part I, *The Sacred Books of the East*, Volume 5, Published by Motilal Banarsidass 1970, page 394

[66] *Epistles of Manuskihar*, Epistle I, Chapter VII, 17, *Pahlavi Texts*, Part II, *The Sacred Books of the East*, Volume 18, Published by Motilal Banarsidass, page 309

[67] *Vendidad*, Fargard VII:66

[68] *Sahih al-Bukhari*, 5, pages 64 and 70

[69] *Halabieh*, I, page 86

[70] *Tarikh al-Tabari*, I, page 512

[71] Al-Nuwayri, *Nihayat al-arab fi funun al-adab*, I, page 109; Alusi al-Baghdadi Mamud Shukri, *Bulugh al-arab fi ma'rifat ahwal al-arab*, 2, page 102

[72] *Dadistan-I Dinik*, Chapter VIII, 1, *Pahlavi Texts*, Part II, Translated by E.W. West, *The Sacred Books of the East*, Volume 18, Published by Motilal Banarsidass, page 26

[73] *Sahih al-Bukhari*, 8, page 150

[74] Comment on *Nyayis, The Zenda –Avesta* part II, translated by James Darmesteter, *The Sacred Books of the East*, Volume 23, page 349

[75] *Apastamba*, Prasna I, Patala 3, Khanda 9, 28, *Sacred Laws of the Aryas*, Part I, Translated by Georg Buhler, *The Sacred Books of the East*, Volume 2, Published by Motilal Banarsidass, Delhi, page 35

[76] al-Kalbi, *al-Asnam*, Dar al-Kutub al-Masriyah, Cairo-Egypt, 1925, 18; Yaqut al-Hamawi, *Mujam al-Buldan*, 1, page 341

[77] Yaqut al-Hamawi, *Mujam al-Buldan*, 1, page 341

[78] Azruqi, *Akhbar Mecca*, I, page 73; Yaqut al-Hamawi, *Mujam al-Buldan*, 8, 169; al-Kalbi, *al-Asnam*, Dar al-Kutub al-Masriyah (Cairo, Egypt, 1925), 14

[79] Al-Ya'akubi, I, page 225

[80] al-Kalbi, *al-Asnam*, Dar al-Kutub al-Masriyah (Cairo, Egypt, 1925), page 11

[81] *Ibn Hisham* I, page 118

[82] Al Shahrastani, *Al Milal Wal Nahel*, page 590

[83] Al Shahrastani, *Al Milal Wal Nahel*, page 578

[84] *Tarikh al-Tabari*, I, page 525

[85] *Taj Al Aruss*, I, pages 147 and 284

[86] *Taj Al Aruss*, 9: 410

[87] *Ibn Hisham*, I, page 69

[88] *Ibn Hisham,* I, pages 117 and 118

[89] *Ibn Hisham*, I, page 126; *Halabieh*, I, page 58

[90] *Halabieh*, I, page 121

[91] *Halabieh*, I, page122

[92] *Ibn Hisham,* I, page 119

[93] Al-Nuwayri, *Nihayat al-arab fi funun al-adab*, 3, page 133

[94] Al-Nuwayri, *Nihayat al-arab fi funun al-adab*, 3, page 123

[95] *Ibn Hisham* I, pages 126 and 127

[96] *Ibn Hisham*, I, page 126; *Halabieh*, I, page 58

[97] *Halabieh,* 1, page 63

[98] *Ibn Hisham,* I, page 128

[99] Ibn Darid, *Al-Ishtiqaq*, pages 88 and 89

[100] Hyppolytus, *The Refutation of All Heresies,* book VI , Chapter xiv

[101] *Ibn Hisham* 1, page 242: quoted by Jawad Ali, vi, page 476

[102] *Ibn Hisham*, first part; pages 63 and 76

[103] *Al-Munjed*, Arabic dictionary, page 158

[104] Jawad Ali, *al-Mufassal*, vi, page 451

[105] Jawad Ali , *al-Mufassal*, vi, page 454

[106] Al Asbahani, *Al-Agani* 3, page 118

[107] *Sahih al-Bukhari*, 1, page 4

[108] *Halabieh,* I, page 421

[109] *Halabieh,* I, pages 73 and 74

[110] *Al-Lisan*, 13, page 213; quoted by Jiwad Ali, *al-Mufassal*, vi, page 720

[111] Al Shawrastani, *Al-Milal Wal Nahil*, page 578

[112] Al-Yaa'kubi 1, page 224

[113] *Halabieh*, 2, page 39

[114] *Taj Al Aruss*, 5, page 367

[115] *Encyc. Religi.,* I, page 661; quoted by Jawad Ali, *al-Mufassal,* vi, page 287

[116] Al Azruqi, *Akhbar Mecca*, I, page 73

[117] *Taj Al Aruss*, 6, page 197

[118] Al Yaa'kubi, 1: 224

[119] *Ibn Hisham*, I, page 69

[120] *Sahih Muslim*, 9, pages 21 and 22

[121] *Sahih al-Bukhari*, 2, page 171

[122] *Sahih al-Bukhari*, 4, page 238

[123] *Sahih al-Bukhari*, 2, pages 169 and 170

[124] *Sahih al-Bukhari*, 2, pages 170, 146 and 181; *Bukhari*, 8, page 128; *Sahih Muslim,* 9, pages 8 and 23

[125] *Tafsir al-Tabari*, 23, page 69

[126] *Tafsir al-Tabari*, 23, page 69

[127] *Sahih al-Bukhari*, 4, page 96

[128] Al-Jaheth, *al-Haiwan*, 6, page 187; quoted by Jawad Ali, *Al-Muffassal*, vi, 723

[129] Sabuni, *Safwat al-Tafasir*, 2, page 270

[130] Al-Jaheth, *Al Haiwan*, 6, page 223; quoted by Jawad Ali, *Al-Muffassal*, vi, 723

[131] Al-Tha'alibi, Abd al-Malik ibn Mohammed, *Kitab Thimar al-qulub*, pages 69 and 70

[132] *Halabieh* 2, page 130

[133] *Sahih al-Bukhari*, 5, page 227

[134] *Halabieh* 2, page 63

[135] *Taj Al Aruss,* 9, page 165

[136] Jeremy Black and Anthony Green, *gods demons and symbols Ancient Mesopotamia*, page 162

[137] Jeremy Black and Anthony Green, *gods demons and symbols Ancient Mesopotamia*, page 88

[138] Alusi al-Baghdadi Mamud Shukri, *Bulugh al-arab fi ma'rifat ahwal al-arab*, 2, page 260

[139] Alusi al-Baghdadi Mamud Shukri, *Bulugh al-arab fi ma'rifat ahwal al-arab*, 2, page 260; Maydaani, *Majma' al-Amthaal*, 2, page 81

[140] Maydaani, *Majma' al-Amthaal*, 2, page 81

[141] *Tarikh al-Tabari*, I, page 525

[142] *Taj Al Aruss*, 9, page 410

[143] *Taj Al Aruss*, I, pages 147 and 284

[144] *Taj Al Aruss*, 9, page 165

[145] Al-Jaheth, *Al Haiwan*, 4, 203; quoted by Jawad Ali,vi, 726

[146] Raghib al-Isfahani, Abu al-Qasim al-Husayn ibn Muhammed, *Mufradat al-Qur'an*, page 307; al-Kalbi, *al-Asnam*, page 6; *Taj al-Aruss*, 10, page 225

[147] *Ibn Hisham* I, page 64 ; *Hamish Ala Al Rauth Al Anf*, I, page 64; quoted by Jawad Ali, *al Mufassal*, vi, pages 401 and 402

[148] Jawad Ali, *al-Mufassal*, vi, page 448

[149] *Sahih al-Bukhari*, 2, page 164

[150] *Halabieh* 1, page 15

[151] Ibn Al Muja'wir, Descriptio, 1, 7; quoted by Patricia Crone, *Meccan Trade*, Princeton University Press, 1987, pages 106, 107

[152] Ibn Al Nadim, *Al-Fahrisit*, page 348

[153] Abdel Allah ibn Zakwan Abi al-Zanad. See Ibn Qutaybah, op. cit.page 204; Cited by Sinasi Gunduz, *The Knowledge of Life*, Oxford University, 1994, page 25

[154] Ibn Hazm, I, page 34; quoted by Sinasi Gunduz, pages 167-168

[155] Ibn Al-Nadim, *Al-Fahrisit*, pages 324-325

[156] Quoted by Rushdi Ilia'n, *Al Saebiun Harraniyen Wa Mandaeyn*, Bagdad, 1976, page 33

[157] Quotation from Arabic historians by M.A. Al Hamed, *Saebat Harran Wa Ikhwan Al Safa*, Damascus, 1998, page 57

[158] Ibn Al Juzi , *Talbis Iblis* , prepared by M. Ali, Kher, page 84; Quotation by M.A. Al Hamed, *Saebat Harran Wa Ikhwan Al Safa*, Damascus, 1998, page 57

[159] Dodge, B., *The Sabians of Harran*, page 78
[160] Ibn Al Nadim, *al-Fahrisit*, page 319
[161] Ibn Al Nadim, *al-Fahrisit*, page 319
[162] Masudi, *Muruj Al-Thaheb*, 2, page 213
[163] Jawad Ali, *al-Mufassal*, vi, page 342
[164] al-Allusi, *Ruh' al-Maani* 16; page 56 ; *Tafsir al-Tabari*, 16, page 56
[165] Qastallani Ahmad ibn Muhammed, *Irshad al-Sari*, 6: 175; Ibn Hagar, al-Isabah 4:315
[166] Al Masudi, *Muruj Al-Thaheb*, 2, page 295

Part VI

The Rise of Islam

1_____

THE EARLIER FOLLOWERS OF MOHAMMED AT MECCA AND JINN AS MUSLIMS

Before discussing how the rise of Islam happened, I will discuss how Mohammed claimed that the Jinn- devils became Muslims, how they knew about the Qur'an, and what myths Mohammed used to make the devils partakers and authors of one chapter of the Qur'an. This is important in order to see the part that the religion of Jinn-devils of Arabia had in the rise of Islam.

Mohammed imitated the Persian Zoroastrian myth about the meteorites as stars which strike the devils during the period of inspiration.

I direct your attention to Surah al-Najm, which means "chapter of the star" in the Qur'an. In this Surah, or chapter, Mohammed claims that a star came down to him, giving him inspiration. We can understand this Surah more fully if we understand the circumstances behind it. When the prophets of the great Star of Arabia saw meteorites lighting up the night sky, they thought the meteorites were stars. The meteorites' purpose, they thought, was one of two possibilities: the meteorites were to strike the devils who spy on the sky when the gods send inspiration to a prophet, or they were to inspire the oracles spoken by the prophets.

This concept is also followed by Zoroastrians who venerate the star, Tistrya, as the lord of the stars. According to the Zoroastrian creed, Tistrya uniquely appears on the tenth of August each year to inspire the people. When this happens, fierce fighting is accompanied by an increased number of meteorites striking the devils who endeavor to spy on this inspiration.[1]

Mohammed copied the Zoroastrian myth. In Surah 72, called al-Jinn, he stated that meteorites increased when the Qur'an was carried by the angel Gabriel through the seven layers of heaven and through the "ceiling of the sky," so that it might be brought to Mohammed. The increase in the number of meteorites was attributed to the number of devils who were spying on the ceiling and were struck by the stars hurled by angels.

The way in which Mohammed introduced the Jinn-devils as authors of part of the Qur'an fooled some naïve people of his time.

Mohammed claims that the same Jinn, or devils, found him under a tree, believed his words and became Muslims. In turn, they authored one Surah, called Surah al-Jinn, which is Surah number 72. In verses 8 and 9 of this Surah, they tell how they discovered the Qur'an while they were spying the ceiling of the sky: "We pried into the secrets of heaven, but we found it filled with stern guards." According to other verses of the Qur'an, these guards are the stars, or meteorites. "We used to, indeed, sit there, the Surah continues, to steal a hearing, but anyone who listens now will find a meteorite watching him in ambush."

When Mohammed introduced the devils, or Jinn, as Muslims and authors of part of the Qur'an, he only fooled people who were especially naïve, such as the people called Jahiliyah, who were the ignorant people at the time of Mohammed. Every day for many years before his reported encounter with the devils under a tree in the desert, Mohammed recited verses from the Qur'an. How, then, could the devils first encounter the Qur'an when they were struck on their heads with the stars hurled by the angels of Allah?

Another thing our Muslims friends need to ponder is where the devils were always sitting. According to the Qur'an, they sat on "the ceiling of heaven to spy." If that were true, did they not see the angel Gabriel coming down each day through the ceiling of heaven? Could they not follow him to see if he went to the house of Mohammed? Could they not build a direct connection with Mohammed without risking being struck on the head with stars?

Mohammed shared the mythological views and ways which the priests of the Arabian Jinn Religion promoted in order to draw attention to their oracles.

Following Gabriel from the "ceiling of heaven" to the house of Mohammed would have been easy since, according to the Qur'an, the news and spiritual directions come down from heaven carried by angels. The devils hear some of the news and steal it to communicate it to their priests on earth. This is the idea supported by the Arabian religion of Jinn. Khater was a priest of the devil in Arabia before the birth of Mohammed. We see Khater describing how an angel struck a devil who was spying "the ceiling of the sky." The strike on the devil's head caused him to drop the information which he had stolen from the angels who were talking together.[2]

The priests of the Arabian devils were called "Kuhhan." They spread the myth about their devils spying in the ceiling of heaven at the risk of being struck with the stars hurled by the angels. The priests told this in order to convince their Arabian customers to consult with them about the information the devils collected at great risk to themselves. The teachings of the Jinn religion in Arabia are similar to what Mohammed himself believed. Mohammed said: "The news came down from one heaven to inferior heavens until it reached the heaven of the world. The devils spy until they find news, then they steal it, and bring it to their Kuhhan priests."[3] By "the heaven of the world" he meant "the ceiling of heaven," which he described in the Qur'an. Mohammed embraced the concepts held by the Kuhhan priests of the Arabian Jinn religion; to make his Qur'an seem important, he claimed the Qur'an was also spied upon by devils when the angel Gabriel descended through the ceiling of heaven in order to reach Mohammed and give him the verses of the Qur'an. This idea was of Zoroastrian origin, and was promoted by the Jinn religion of Arabia, and was used by Mohammed.

Analysis of the Group who Followed Mohammed Before his Accord With the Tribes of Oas and Khazraj

Our Muslim friends need also to ponder the critical importance of the occasion on which the Jinn-devils are said to have met Mohammed. This was after Mohammed failed to convince the citizens of Mecca that he was a prophet. At the time, his followers totaled about eighty people, many of them outlaws and criminals who raped people in passing caravans. Al-Bukhari, the authoritative book which contains Mohammed's sayings and biography, mentions Abu Basir, an outlaw criminal and gang leader. Abu Basir became Muslim and camped outside Mecca, ambushing caravans of Mecca each day to steal from them. We read in al-Bukhari, that:

> Abu Jandal, a man who became Muslim, joined Abu Basir, and forced every man who embraced Islam to join Abu Basir, till they became a gang. Every time they heard of a caravan coming out of Mecca bound for Damascus they ambushed it and killed the people of the caravan, taking their money.[4]

Most of the early followers of Mohammed were from a group called Saalik. They envied the people of Mecca because those people became rich from their commerce with Syria, Palestine, Iraq and Yemen. The Saalik were lazy, not willing to work but willing to enjoy the riches of others. They were known for their raids on others for spoil. Among their leaders was Urwah Bin Zayd al-Uzedi who was also Arraf عراف, that is, a diviner, or soothsayer, for the Jinn-devils.[5] The Saalik being led by a soothsayer reveals that they were part of an occult sect. This may explain one of the reasons why they followed Mohammed, as Mohammed also announced that he was a prophet to the humans and Jinn–devils,[6] and considered the so called Muslim Jinn-devils as brothers. He claimed that the Jinn-devils became Muslims, and he called them " your brothers, the Jinn."[7]

449

The Saalik also believed in free sex. That's why they attacked houses in Mecca and raped the women there. The Saalik followed Mohammed, viewing Islam as an excuse to steal from the caravans. They discovered the doctrine of Mohammed which said that followers were limited to four wives each, but they could enjoy whatever number of concubines they could gain; they considered war an appropriate means to reach their goals.

These facts concerning the followers of Mohammed at Mecca are clearly seen in the Islamic authoritative books which narrate the life of Mohammed. For example, we read in the book of *al-Bukhari* that Mohammed emigrated to al-Medina and was supported by the two tribes of al-Medina. When he wanted to enter Mecca with his followers on a pilgrimage, the inhabitants of Mecca sent Urwa Bin Masud, a respected leader, to negotiate with Mohammed. As Urwa learned about the followers of Mohammed, who were from the city of Mecca, he recognized dangerous criminals among them. One was al-Magirah, whom Urwa rebuked for his perfidy and treachery. Al-Magirah had crafted friendships with some people in Mecca, killed them, and took their money. Then he joined Mohammed as a Muslim in order to flee from justice.[8]

One of the Arabian leaders told Mohammed, "those who followed you are the thieves who steal the pilgrims."[9] Those thieves followed Mohammed without having repented from their crimes. On the contrary, in following Mohammed they found a false "legalization" of committing major crimes, and of spoiling the possessions of others (and their females) under the excuse of religion.

When Mohammed Failed to Spread his Religion Through Convincing People, he Changed Strategy, Offering a Filthy Bargain

When Mohammed saw that only groups like Saaliks would follow him, he changed strategy by trying to make a concession to the Arabian tribes. He visited their cities and settlements with a strange offer. The tribes had to believe that Mohammed was the prophet of Allah, and they had to be committed to fight with Mohammed and his group to impose Islam over every Arabian tribe. In return, Mohammed would guarantee that the children of the tribes they conquered would become their slaves, and that the women and daughters of the conquered tribes would be at their disposal. Also, money and possessions would go to the victors.

It is interesting that the Arabian tribes refused Mohammed's offer. They considered it to be shameful to wage wars against other tribes in order to take their wives as concubines and their children as slaves. Among the tribes which Mohammed visited was a tribe called Baker Bin Wael. Mohammed's message to them was reported by the biographers of his time. One biographer wrote:

> You exalt Allah over you until you occupy their houses, enjoy their wives and make their children your slaves. The only condition is that you bless Allah thirty times and laud him thirty-three times and say "Allah is great" thirty-three times.[10]

The core of Mohammed's offer was that the victors would take the women and houses and make the children their slaves. Mohammed did not announce a doctrine to follow, but presented a despicable bargain wrapped in religious words. Thankfully, Mohammed's offer was refused by the Baker tribe.

The Moment in Which the Devils Showed up to Back Mohammed

The story is told that one day Mohammed went to the tribe of Thaqif in the city of Taif to present the same offer he had presented to the Bakers. When the Thaqifs refused to hear him, Mohammed returned to Mecca, discouraged by this refusal. On his way back to Mecca, he sat under a tree in the desert. His biographers say the Jinn came down in the tree which, in turn, informed Mohammed of the presence of the Jinn. Mohammed recited verses from the Qur'an to the devils, and the devils said, "this is the Qur'an that we could not hear because we were struck with stars in order that we could not hear it." They soon believed Mohammed and embraced Islam.[11]

The Jinn were also called devils in the Arabian language at the time of Mohammed. Al-Jaheth, an ancient Arabian writer, told about the beliefs of the Arabians at the time of Mohammed. He said that they described devils and they called them "Jinn-devils," "devils," or just "Jinn."[12] Jarir, a famous Arabian poet, says in one of his poems that he has a devil who makes incantations, and this devil was of the Jinn.[13] Al-Tabari expresses the same thought that Satan was one of the Jinn, and chief of them.[14]

The Qur'an also treats the Jinn as devils. In Surah 18, called al-Kahef, verse 50, the Qur'an says that Satan was one of the Jinn. In the books that narrate the life of Mohammed, Satan is described as "the father of the Jinn."[15] We can only conclude that if Satan is chief of the Jinn, it's clear that the Jinn are, indeed, devils.

And why, if Allah intended to make Muslims of the devils, would he strike their heads with stars or meteorites while they were spying and listening to the Qur'an as Gabriel was descending through the "ceiling of heaven?" Allah should have been happy for them to hear the Qur'an while they were up on the ceiling of heaven. They could have become Muslims there. Striking them on their heads with meteorites makes no sense.

Was not Mohammed known to the devils every day while he was reciting verses of the Qur'an at Mecca? If the kingdom of the devil is united, and devils watch everything happening on earth and report it to Satan, why wouldn't the Jinn-devils learn about Mohammed before that day when he sat under the tree, discouraged and disappointed because the Thaqif tribe rejected him? Doesn't this incident teach us the that devils were acquainted with Mohammed's message from the beginning? Wouldn't they want to keep him from getting discouraged, and wouldn't they choose this critical moment to encourage and support him?

The Jinn-devils immediately began authoring a chapter in the Qur'an equal in language to the rest of the Qur'an, attacking the Sonship of Christ and boasting to be righteous. Finally, the Qur'an would have us believe that the Jinn, immediately after hearing the Qur'an, became authors of one of its chapters. Jinn are transformed in just one moment to be authoritative authors like Allah. The chapter of Jinn is the chapter of devils. In it they attack Jesus Christ as the Son of God. They represent the inspiration and authority of the Qur'an, establishing doctrine. In the Surah, attacking the Sonship of Christ, they claim some of the devils are righteous.

To justify the absence of miracles in his claims, Mohammed said the Arabic language of the Qur'an was a sign of his prophetic role. Mohammed claimed that the Qur'an was given to him in a high Arabic grammatical form which even the Jinn couldn't imitate. However, the style of the devils' chapter is the same Arabic style as the rest of the Qur'an.

People are deceived because they do not read the Bible, where they can learn about the tricks of the devil.

According to the Bible, the Devil is a liar and never will be righteous. He was removed from the presence of God forever. Remember, also, that the Devil can appear to be religious in order to deceive people without true Biblical knowledge, but he will never be a creature who loves God or is transformed into something righteous, as the devils claimed in the Qur'an's chapter of the Jinn. In the Book of the Revelation, the Bible warns about the "depths of the devil," through which he tries to deceive people who do not study the Bible. Only the Bible, the true Word of God, exposes the ways of Satan and provides those who study it with the means to deal with the tricks of the Devil. The more we study the claims of Islam, the more we see how gullible the followers are expected to be.

The Reputation of Mohammed was Bound With the Bad Reputation of the Group who Followed him at Mecca

The relationship of Mohammed with the group who followed him, which was known in making raids and pirating the caravans, and raping the women and girls at Mecca, bound the reputation of Mohammed to the reputation of this group.

Al-Halabi, a biographer of Mohammed, reports on the reaction of the Arabian tribes toward Mohammed's offer to them to embrace Islam. If they would do this, Mohammed guaranteed to give them the children of the Arabian tribes they conquered as slaves, and their wives and daughters as concubines. Al-Halabi wrote:

> No one has accepted him among those tribes, and they said, "The people of the man know better about him. Do you think a man can be fitting to us, after he corrupted his people?"[16]

In other words, the rejection of Mohammed by the Arabian tribes was based on the principle that Mohammed claimed to be a religious reformer, yet he abused and corrupted his people. I personally believe that their view was based on the fact that Mohammed was allied with a certain group at Mecca, which was known for their beliefs on sexual dominance and their willingness to take the riches of others. Many of them, when they embraced Islam, began to attack the caravans on the route from Mecca toward Syria.

2

THE FILTHY BARGAIN

The Nature of the Two Tribes Which Accepted the Offer of Mohammed

One day a group of two savage tribes from the city of Medina, the Oas and the Khazraj, came to the area of Mecca. The names in Arabia reflect the character and costumes of the one who is called with such name. Oas, according to the biographers of Mohammed, means "wolf" or "coltish," "gamesome" and "people of frivolity."[17] These terms reflect the true nature of these two tribes which inhabited Medina. Treason and treachery, which characterize the wolf, was applied to these tribes. Their members were known for their lives of frivolity and violence. They were known for being lazy, not willing to work, and living from freeloading off others. On the other hand, Beni Kharithah and Beni Nathir were two Jewish tribes who also lived in the city. They were known to cultivate the land and plant trees – mainly dates. They built commerce between Syria and Arabia. On the contrary, while Oas and Khazraj had no agricultural or commercial activity, they lived, instead, as interlopers sponging off the riches of others.

Although Mohammed's offer was refused by other Arabian tribes, it was viewed by Oas and Khazraj, the two tribes who met with Mohammed at Mecca, as an easy booty and spoil opportunity. Mohammed's offer was a perfect match for their background and behavior, because they were known for their frivolity and thievery. They saw the offer as a way to spoil the riches of the Jews in Medina. What actually happened was that within a brief time, Mohammed was received by the two tribes and emigrated to the al-Medina. Once in power there,

Mohammed drove the Jewish tribe of Beni Nather from the city. He besieged their settlements, took their houses and prohibited food from reaching them. The lack of food made them yield to him. So Mohammed took their houses, furniture and fields and all their gold, money, and weapons. Once deported from the city, the Jewish tribe of Beni Nather went to Syria.

Later, Mohammed besieged the second Jewish tribe, Beni Kharithah, and prohibited food and water from reaching them until they were compelled to yield to his judgment. Mohammed claimed that the judgment of Allah was on them. All the males over ten years of age were killed, and the males under ten became slaves. The houses, and the females of the tribe, were divided and given to Mohammed's followers, Oas and Khazraj, and to the Muslims who followed him from Mecca. When it came to killing the males over ten years of age, Mohammed ordered trenches to be dug. The males were fettered and brought in groups to the trenches, where they were beheaded and buried. He then divided the females and gave them as concubines to the members of the two tribes, Oas and Khazraj, and to his followers who emigrated to Medina with him. As Mohammed promised, the children became slaves, and the money and houses were divided among his followers. Older women with small children were sold as slaves in Damascus. As was his custom, Mohammed took one-fifth of everything for himself – that is, from all the spoil of the females; of the children as slaves; and of the money, houses and lands.

With the money obtained from selling the older women and the children as slaves, he built an army and equipped them with body armor and shields. Now he was prepared to wage war against other Arabian cities and to subdue them.

The Filthy Tune of Mohammed Found the Fit String Through Which Mohammed Will be Heard by Force by the Rest of the Arabians

What happened in the Medina helps us understand why Mohammed's offer found willing listeners, first by this group of eight persons who was visiting Mecca. Thus, the tune of

Mohammed, which was refused by the Arabian tribes, which required them to say "Allah is great, and Mohammed his prophet." In return, they would obtain the females of others, beside their money and their children as slaves. I say that this tune seemed now to this group of eight persons as a means for the two tribes to fulfill what they were unable to achieve without a leader who would embody these illicit abominations explicitly, expressly, and openly. That is, a leader who would place their covetousness, carvings and aberrations into a religious context would justify what they already practiced openly. In fact, they used to practice these aberrations, and they were characterized with, in their history. Within this context, they thought they had the excuse to kill the two rich tribes in their city and other cities, and rape their daughters and wives, and loot their houses, lands and money, and enslave their children.

Mohammed had played on this filthy string, the only string that allowed him to play his filthy tune, through which he would be heard in Arabia. This string was Oas and Khazraj, the two rancid and vile tribes of Arabia. Mohammed knew the character of those two tribes; in fact, once he said to his youngest wife about them, "that those two tribes are licentious."[18] He knew they liked frivolity and licentiousness, so he was shrewd enough to offer them the things that goes with their immoral desires.

Mohammed Proposes Killing the Creditor and Helper so as to Get Rid of the Debts and Then to Take the Spoil

Before the attack on the Jewish tribes, there had been peace in the city. Living side by side with Oas and Khazraj, the Jewish tribes had loaned them abundant amounts of money through a peaceful alliance. But Mohammed had other ideas. He considered the possibility of killing these two rich Jewish tribes and taking all their money. This language of getting rid of the two Jewish tribes, who were helping the Oas and Khazraj and giving them continuous loans, created greediness and covetousness in the Oas and Khazraj to betray the alliance with the rest of inhabitants of their city. Thus, they could get rid of their creditors and spoil their riches, houses, and females; and enslave their children.

457

Mohammed initiated this strategy when he met with a group of eight people from the tribe of Khazraj. Authoritative Islamic books which narrate his life quote Mohammed as saying:

> "Who are you?" They said, "A group of Khazraj," and he said, "Are you those who are in alliance with the Jews of Medina, Kharithah and Nather?" (Mohammed knew they were in alliance to defend each other against attacks from the outside, and to refrain from attacking each other.) They said, "yes." And he said, "Why not sit down so I may talk to you?," They said, "Yes."[19]

We can only speculate on the rest of the conversation Mohammed had with this group, but it must have been similar to the tribe of Wael Bin Baker which we examined earlier. They were to bless the name of Allah thirty-three times and, in return, they would have the females and money of others, and they would enslave the children. This became the foundation of Mohammed's message to the Arabian tribes after he failed to make proselytes of them by convincing them of his religious claims. Why would we expect his message to Oas and Khazraj to be any different? Mohammed was simply searching for a tribe to help him wage war against the Arabians in order to subjugate them to himself as their prophet.

The inhabitants of Mecca understood Mohammed's message to the two tribes, as it really was a treaty to make war against the inhabitants of Mecca in order to take away their liberty and their riches. The events which followed confirmed the kind of message Mohammed had proposed. Mohammed's message was contrary to the custom of the Arabs who respected their neighbors and would not betray them, be disloyal, or destroy them. This message found the people who are deprived from the human conscience embracing it. Mohammed knew the circumstances of these two tribes. He knew about their alliance with Beni Nather and Beni Kharithah which provided security and safety in the city. Because there was no national government in Arabia, security was achieved only through alliances between the main tribes in each city. Alliances demanded respect and cooperation among the tribes. For example, they cooperated in the way they handled criminals to be judged, and in the way they defended the city when an external attacker became a threat.

Mohammed presented the same message to each group he met, not as a religious, peaceful message, but as a proposal to put an end to security in the city, and allow for the ability to trample human rights. He presented an opportunity for greediness and covetousness, based on betraying one's neighbor and conspiring against him in order to kill him. The message of Mohammed cancelled covenants and pledges between neighbors, destroying the principles of security which had been followed for hundreds of years. Each neighbor became a victim, and his wealth and family members became the possessions of those who accepted the schemes of Mohammed.

Is Mohammed the Right Example to Follow?

In evaluating a philosophy or a creed, we can't ignore how the founder behaved. What were the results of his actions in his own time? The founder's example will always be the paradigm, or model, which generations to come who embraced his teachings will use to examine and imitate his teachings. Violent people in radical Islam have found an example in their founder and leader, Mohammed. It is little wonder that the Islamic radicalism in Sudan prepared a Jihad, or holy war, attacking the Christian villages of the south. Just like the tribes of Oas and Khazraj, they killed the males and distributed the females to those engaged in Jihad.

What would have happened if one quarter of the world had embraced the Nazism of Hitler? Would that exempt us from evaluating the acts of Hitler, exposing his atrocities, and opposing the danger of Nazism to the human society? I advise my Muslim friends to ponder this. God established goodness, and bestowed the privilege of being a family to mankind. Would God deprive a man of that by killing the man and giving his wife and daughters to another religious group to be their concubines and slaves?

I urge you to compare the life of Jesus Christ to that of Mohammed. Jesus went to the Cross for you. He was attacked, beaten and crucified, but "he opened not his mouth." There was "no guile found in him." Jesus never waged war, never violated the rights of those around him, nor incited his followers to rape and enslave others. Jesus even urged his followers to feed their enemies and do good to those who despitefully used them. Isn't there a difference?

What was Perceived from the Representatives of the Two Tribes was not a Religion but a Specific Plan

Although his offer was rejected by the other Arabian tribes, it appealed to the members of the two most cruel tribes in the history of Jahiliyah, or pre-Islamic times. In Mohammed's offer, the eight representatives of these two tribes saw a way for tribe members to get rich quick, and they saw a large pool of women to fulfill their expectations for frivolity and sex. In addition, they saw a way to rid themselves of the debts they owed their neighbors. They would inherit their neighbor's gold, houses and land, and they would benefit financially from making slaves of the children and selling them in the markets. And, all this was to be done under the cover of religiosity.

The representatives of these two tribes saw that Mohammed's offer was not a religion, but a specific plan to conquer Arabia. And Mohammed was ready to apply it personally by emigrating to Medina to lead the two tribes to carry out his extermination program and fulfill their sexual passions. From here, we see the eight people have returned to their city, Al Medina, with a specific plan, which was the same plan Mohammed presented to the tribe of Baker and to other Arabian tribes. Mohammed proposed that he would become the leader for the two tribes in order to carry out his genocidal plan.

They promised to convey Mohammed's message to the two tribes – which consisted in the acceptance of the leadership of Mohammed for what he promised, which amounted to treason of their neighbors; depriving them of their money, wives and daughters; and enslaving their children. After talking to Mohammed, the eight representatives returned to their city, al-

Medina, with Mohammed's demonic plan which they conveyed to the two tribes. In their actions, we see a willingness to convey Mohammed's genocidal message. We see them expressing their preference to follow Mohammed over their own tribal leadership, and to fulfill the plan Mohammed displayed. Ibn Hisham, Mohammed's biographer, quotes their own words: "May they be gathered to you. We will come to them and call them to your order. If they agree to it, nobody is preferred over you." Another of Mohammed's biographers, al-Halabi, agrees with Ibn Hisham when he tells us: "May they be gathered under you. If their words will be united toward you and they follow you, nobody is preferred over you."[20]

We can clearly see that the matter is not of a religious nature, accepted individually, but it's a commitment to a plan whose subject was well known, since Mohammed had already presented it to the rest of the tribes.

The treaty between Mohammed and the two tribes was called "the treaty of Akaba." Mohammed gained the advantage when the two tribes accepted his bait, by making them come under his bondage and enslavement.

Mohammed's program spread through the two tribes. After a short time, they sent a delegation of twelve people to him who spoke officially for the tribes. They made a commitment to defend Mohammed with the same vigor with which they would defend their own children. They accepted that Mohammed would emigrate to them, indicating that the tribes had accepted his program, which consisted of the following: that Mohammed would take the leadership of the two tribes and would begin the piracy which he previously proposed, which would guarantee their dominance over Medina by exterminating the rich Jewish tribes who lived in the city. Then he would wage wars against neighboring Arabian tribes.

This treaty was called "the treaty of Akaba." Mohammed's biographers said he told the representatives of the two tribes:

"I pledge allegiance with the condition that you defend me as you defend your wives and sons." So they pledged their allegiance to Mohammed under these terms, and they accepted that he would emigrate to Medina with his followers.

Mohammed added more conditions. He must have:

"their obedience in times of perspicuity as well as in troublesome and difficult times," said one of his biographers. "They must be loyal to him in the days that are encouraging and in the days of hated events. They shall not contend with him and his command."[21]

Ibadah Bin al-Samet عبادة بن الصامت was one of the leaders selected to represent the two tribes before Mohammed. He said:

"We pledged allegiance to Mohammed to completely listen to him and obey him, in our easy, normal times as well as in our difficult times, when the days were in our favor and when the days were not in our favor."[22]

This means they were to be obedient to Mohammed in all circumstances, whether they liked it or hated it. Mohammed had fettered them in severe bondage. They fell into his trap and took the bait, anticipating free sex, and the money and possessions which would be theirs.

Mohammed expected blind obedience, in which they relinquished their right to object to his actions or to hold differing opinions, no matter how much they hated it. Mohammed built his scheme on their desire to enjoy the women they conquered, and experience a continuous life of extravagance, wantonness and licentiousness, even if it meant they had to sacrifice their own liberty. Mohammed put them in the worst kind of bondage ever imposed on mankind. Even today Muslims are subjected to the same bondage. They are not free to choose their own faith, and they face death if they doubt Mohammed's claims or abandon him.

The followers of Mohammed have become human tools whom he humiliated in order to increase his authority and extend his domain. He had no regard for them, so he pushed them into suicidal wars. Compare what Mohammed did to the behavior of Jesus Christ who, instead of fleecing His followers, offered Himself as a ransom for them.

Mohammed placed his followers in bondage, to the extent that he threatened to excommunicate anyone who would speak with loud voice before him. Mohammed turned his face away from such a person. He would not respond to his salutes, and avoided any conversation with him. Then Mohammed ordered his followers to treat the excommunicated person in the same manner, and thus separate him from his own household. Mohammed separated him from his wife, prohibiting his wife to serve her husband or to remain in the home with him. He did this in order to humiliate the person. After this, Mohammed used to claim that the repentance of such an excommunicated person had been announced to Mohammed from Allah. Mohammed used to claim such things after he had humiliated the excommunicated person and changed him into a lowly humiliated slave.

When we study the names of the early representatives who pledged themselves to Mohammed, we discover that most of them were killed in the piracy expeditions which Mohammed waged against villages, cities and tribes in Arabia. Biographer Ibn Hisham treats these issues in his book about Mohammed. Mohammed's actions enslaved his followers to their excessive and abnormal lusts, and he founded his kingdom and domain on their bodies.

Mohammed's Selfish Behavior in Pushing People to Suicidal Wars for his own Exaltation, in Contrast to the Loving and Caring Behavior of Christ

Mohammed's behavior stands in stark contrast to the behavior of Christ, who was not concerned about His own personal suffering, but rather kept from exposing His disciples to the harmful treatment of others.

We see this in the Gospels. For example, in John 18:4-10, the rulers of the Jews came with their soldiers to arrest Jesus while He was with His disciples in Gethsemane. John tells us in his Gospel:

Jesus therefore, knowing all the things that would come upon Him, went forward and said to them, "Whom are you seeking?" They answered Him, "Jesus of Nazareth." And Jesus said to them, "I am He."... Now when He said to them, "I am He," they drew back and fell to the ground.

Then He asked them again, "Whom are you seeking?" And they said, "Jesus of Nazareth." To which Jesus answered, "I have told you that I am he. Therefore, if you seek me, let these go their way," that the saying might be fulfilled which he spoke, "Of those whom you gave me I have lost none."

Jesus didn't want to forfeit any of His disciples. Instead, He gave Himself as a ransom for their salvation and for the rest of the world.

On the other hand, Mohammed saw those who followed him (and were deceived by his bait) as tools without value or importance, as firewood to be burnt only to facilitate Mohammed's desire to gain dominion over the Arabian tribes. Mohammed offered nothing to his generation except a horrible example, pushing people to suicidal wars for his own exaltation. He made devious bargains to fulfill his plans. How can he possibly be of spiritual benefit to either his own generation or to subsequent generations?

There is no one worthy of being the Savior other than Jesus Christ, who proved to be a loving leader. Being in the form of God, He didn't consider it robbery to be equal with the Father in the Godhead, but He made Himself of no reputation, taking on Himself the form of a servant in the likeness of a man. Appearing as a man, He humbled Himself and became obedient to the point of death, even the death of the Cross. In contrast to Mohammed, Jesus is a true leader, as well as the Savior of the soul. His example of humility and unselfish love need to be followed today. God the Father has selected no leader other than Jesus, the one who reflects God's humbleness in human form, and God's love. He is the One who gives immediate salvation for every one who asks Him by faith.

Are you following God's appointed leader, or have you fallen for the deception so cleverly perpetrated many years ago? If you do not follow Jesus, I urge you to seriously consider His life and His teachings. It is a matter of eternal consequence.

The two most vicious and ferocious tribes in all Arabia took Mohammed's bait, only to suffer the severest of shame, humiliation and bondage.

Ibn Maktum, also called Amru, was a cousin of Khadijah, who was Mohammed's first wife. Mohammed sent him to Oas and Khazraj. [23]

It is difficult for us to understand how the two tribes were ready to accept Mohammed as their boss and leader after only eight of them met with Mohammed for only a few minutes. Further, they agreed to host a group of outlaws at Mecca. There is no answer to such a question, except that the saliva of the tribesmen flowed smoothly toward the sex-motivated and destructive scheme presented by Mohammed.

We need to look past that short discussion and hasty decision. Sitting with eight of their members for only a few minutes could not have been sufficient time to plant religious thoughts in their hearts. Rather, it took only a short time for Mohammed to announce his specific plan that called on the tribes to kill their neighbors, seize their money, houses, lands and females. When Mohammed's abusiveness and tyrannical language told them to betray their neighbors, friends and allies, he began to court them and seduce the souls of the two tribes who were the most beastly of all the Arabian tribes.

Concerning their immorality, the two tribes of Oas and Khazraj were similar to the group who followed Mohammed at Mecca. They refused to work, and they lived in indulgence and extravagance, envying other tribes who had money and enjoyed the respect of others. In Mohammed's plan, they found a religious excuse to attack their Jewish and Arabian neighbors, and easily subdue them to become their leaders, pirate their money, and control their women.

They had no understanding of what Islam was all about, since only eight people met with Mohammed, and they met with him for only a few minutes. This couldn't possibly allow enough time for them to understand any of the religious claims of Mohammed. But it did give them enough time to understand Mohammed's plan, which became an obvious slogan to everyone who visited the area around Mecca. Mohammed endeavored to influence his visitors, hoping that his proposition would find a response with one or more of the tribes, and that his immoral schemes would bear fruit among tribal chiefs who had been inclined to perversion.

Finally, Mohammed found that the tribes of Oas and Khazraj were ready to respond to the filthy satanic tune which he played for them. When Mohammed noticed that the poison which he had placed in their minds had spread to the tribal leadership, he imposed cruel conditions on them, and required a high and costly price from them, which was to pledge their blind obedience to him. We can see this in the terms of the treaty Mohammed had with them. It read that they pledged

> Their obedience in times of perspicuity, as well as in troublesome and difficult times. In the days that are encouraging and in the hated events. And that they shall not contend with him and his command.[24]

Even though they knew what fate awaited them, the two tribes agreed to be subject to him on those conditions. They did it in order to obtain other conditions which had greater appeal to them.

The treaty was known for its strict terms. No other religious man in history was ever called by a group of people to be recognized as reformer in their midst, without first having lived among them for many years in order to gain their confidence and persuade them that his promise was genuine. But here we find two tribes willing to go along with eight of their members who had an accidental and shallow meeting with Mohammed. The entire membership of the tribes was ready to make Mohammed the master of their souls in severe blind obedience.

What aspect of the treaty made these aggressive tribes undergo complete subjection? What made them imprison their souls under the bondage of a man without having the opportunity to object to what he decided? The thing that made them totally surrender to Mohammed was what he promised them – the spoils of war: wives, daughters, lands and houses. Therefore, the quick, unlawful and illicit riches led frivolous leaders to submit to cruel shame and humiliation. Their wills became completely enslaved to the point where there was no freedom of thought, and no objection to whatever Mohammed imposed on them. They were unable to express themselves or make the slightest suggestion.

This was, perhaps, the worst humiliation ever imposed on a people. This is the same kind of covenant the Devil makes with human beings today. He places the belt of authority tightly around his victims, fettering their minds and their personalities. He steals their wills and their personal liberty. He insists that everything be yielded to him and to his representatives. Even today, each person on whom Mohammed imposes his ideas suffers from the same consequence. Objection to Mohammed's thoughts are not acceptable. The Muslim who thinks independently faces the maximum punishment, which is death. This is true today in any Muslim country. Muslims who dare object to the ideas of Mohammed, the diviner of Mecca, face capital punishment.

The immediate adoption of Islam by the two tribes was made by the tribal chiefs. This was to expedite the application by Mohammed of the rest of the articles and terms of the treaty.

The entrance of the two tribes into Islam was not through personal or individual religious persuasion or personal conviction of the people, but was made solely on the decision of the tribal chiefs. Mohammed sent Mesab Bin Amir with the tribal leaders as part of the treaty. Mesab encouraged the tribal chiefs to bring the two tribes into Islam before Mohammed's arrival at Medina.

Therefore, the process of indoctrinating the chiefs into Islam, and then quickly bringing their members into the religion, came without any preparation, teaching, or taking into consideration anyone's point of view, or any individual's decision. Accepting Islam was required as part of the accepted plan which Mohammed displayed to their representatives who met with him at Mecca. Therefore, when the leaders wore the garments of Islam, it was something spontaneous and automatic. They also imposed Islam on the members of the tribes in only a brief moment, without anyone understanding anything about the religious doctrines of Mohammed. We see this in the examples of Saad Bin Maath سعد بن معاذ and Usaid Bin Hutheir اسيد بن حضير, who were the leaders of the tribe of Beni al-Ashhal, a major branch of one of the tribes.[25] We find Saad imposing Islam on the members of his tribe when they accepted the articles and terms of the treaty with Mohammed. Mohammed's biographers said:

> When Saad stood to speak to them, he said, "Sons of Abed al-Ashhal (al-Ashhal was the head from whom the tribe descended), how did you see my order to you?" They answered, "You are our lord, and you have the best opinion among us, and your order is blessed." He then said, "What you say to your wives is illegal and illicit until you believe in Allah and his prophet." After he said this, none of the members of the tribe of Beni Abdel Shahal remained without becoming Muslim that evening. All the men and women became Muslims on the same day.[26]

We see that the people themselves were not persuaded by the religion of Mohammed. Instead, it was a political move in the hands of the tribal chiefs to expedite the program promised by Mohammed. The process of accepting Islam was completed without delay or desire to understand what Islam really was. The leaders saw that quickly imposing Islam on tribal members would guarantee the acceptance of the terms of Mohammed's accord. They did this in order to achieve their goals in becoming the truly rich people of Medina and the cities around it, instead of the chiefs of Quraish. In addition, they would soon take the wives, daughters, and the possessions of the Jewish tribes that they had lived with for generations.

As mentioned earlier, a short time after Mohammed came to the Medina, he drove away the Jewish tribe of Beni Nathir and took their money, houses and lands. Then he besieged the houses and settlements of the second Jewish tribe, Beni Kharithah, until they yielded to him. Mohammed then ordered his followers to cut off the heads of any male over ten years of age. Next, they dug trenches and buried their victims. Mohammed then distributed the females they conquered to the tribal chiefs and the tribal members, exactly as he had promised. Mohammed divided their houses and fields, apportioning them to the two tribes and to those who followed him from Mecca. He sold all the children under ten into slavery.

This same example, set by Mohammed, has been followed by Muslims throughout history. Islam has spread by imposing itself on the masses who never understood what the religion was all about.

The ultimate goal of the Qur'an is to force the world to embrace Islam through humiliation and the sword, and to exterminate those who do not accept Islam.

After Mohammed died, the very tribes on which Mohammed imposed Islam by force withdrew from Islam and expressed the desire of everyone to choose his or her own faith. But their rebellion did not last for long. Abu Baker, the first Caliph of Mohammed, waged wars against the rebelling tribes, subduing them to Islam and killing those who refused to embrace this religion. He did this in accordance with the Qur'an which orders all Muslims to fight all those who don't believe in Mohammed's claims. The Qur'an incites Muslims to fight "unbelievers" or "infidels." In Surah 8:39, the Qur'an says: "fight them on, until there is no seduction, until this religion is only the religion of Allah." Another verse, Surah 9:12, says: "fight the chiefs of infidelity that they may be exterminated." And in Surah 9:36 we read that Muslims are to "fight the infidel all." It is clear from the study of these, and many other verses of the Qur'an, that the requirement of the Qur'an is to fight all non-Muslims. If they don't accept Islam, Allah gladly wants them to be exterminated, because the goal of Jihad, or holy war, is to make the whole world embrace one religion: Islam.

The followers of Mohammed put these verses into practice. After they dealt with backsliders in Arabia, they waged many wars in the Middle East to impose Islam on different nations. In a sense it worked for Mohammed's followers. The religion spread in the areas they occupied. If people would not convert willingly, they imposed it through the sword. In some countries, like North Africa, the inhabitants faced death if they did not embrace Islam. As a result there were numerous martyrs. In other countries, such as Syria, Palestine, Egypt and Jordan, they imposed a heavy tribute, called Jizyah جزية, on those who failed to convert to Islam. There is a verse in the Qur'an, Surah 9:29, which says that infidels, such as Christians and Jews, are targets of Mohammed's anger:

> Fight those who believe not in Allah ... from the people of the book (he meant the Christians and Jews) until they pay the Jizyah [the tribute] by their hands, humiliated.

According to Qur'an, the tribute paid by Christians and Jews included personal humiliation. For example, Muslims applied this teaching during the 7th century A.D. in Christian countries by spitting in the faces of those who paid the tribute but refused to become Muslims. Often they beat them while they were paying the tribute. They had no tolerance for either Christians or Jews. Rather than kill them immediately, Muslims imposed heavy tributes on them, always paid with some kind of humiliation. This was intended to put pressure on non-Muslims so that most of them would be compelled to yield to Islam.

The ancestors of most Muslims in the Middle East were nominal Christians who, because of the heavy tribute and humiliation imposed on them, yielded to Islam, even though they were not convinced of its doctrines. Today, many of their descendants still aren't able to liberate themselves from Islamic bondage. They are still paying a heavier price than the tribute their ancestors were required to pay. Today, Muslims must pay the tribute of blood if they seek religious freedom.

Christ respects the individual freedom to choose to believe in Him, in contrast with Mohammed's behavior which forcefully imposed his creed, killing the one who doubted it.

Christianity, led by Jesus Christ, stands in stark contrast to the Islam of Mohammed. Mohammed used every illicit and abusive way he could to force people to consider him as a prophet. Mohammed carried force to such an extent that he exterminated those who refused to believe in him. On the other hand, we find Jesus refusing to be Lord over people who don't come to Him by their own choice and refuse to place their faith in His true identity as God incarnate. The Bible records that Jesus refused the Jews who wanted Him to be their king after He performed a creative miracle and fed 5,000 people in the desert. He multiplied the five loaves and two fish. Jesus wasn't looking to be a king over people who didn't recognize His identity through faith. He didn't want to dominate people who were attracted to personal interests, rather than building a loving relationship with Him by acknowledging His perfection, perfect love and holiness as God.

Jesus never denounced anyone who doubted His divine identity. Do you remember Thomas who doubted Jesus' resurrection, and declared that he would not believe unless he saw the prints of the nails in His hands and put his fingers into them and into Jesus' sword-pierced side? Jesus didn't fight against Thomas, but He appeared to Thomas and allowed him to trace the prints of the wounds in His hands and side. Because Jesus allowed the facts to create faith, Thomas was able to say to Jesus, "My Lord and my God." While Mohammed used the sword and imposed heavy tribute to enforce untruthful claims upon people who were not convinced of them nor believed in him, Christianity simply presents the facts, enabling the soul to recognize its true Creator and God.

My friend, if you are a follower of Islam, living under the control of its false claims, you need to think for yourself. Compare the claims of Jesus Christ to what you believe and make an educated choice. It's worth anything it may take to break away from the delusion of Islam to follow Christ.

PAGAN RITUALS FROM TWO TRIBES LIVING IN MEDINA BECAME THE MAIN RITUALS OF ISLAM

Did you ever wonder why Muslims worship on Friday, while Jews worship on Saturday and Christians worship on Sunday? The answer may surprise you. When Mohammed emigrated to Medina from Mecca, he had to deal with two tribes, Oas and Khazraj, who had their pagan rituals, many of which they weren't willing to abandon. Mohammed found it necessary to incorporate these rituals into Islam. One ritual concerns the day of Friday, the pagan religious day celebrated by Oas and Khazraj. They called the day "Urubah," but it corresponds to our Friday. Ibn Abbas, the cousin of Mohammed, tells us:

> The Ansar, a title for the two tribes, said, "There is a day for the Jews to meet every seven days, and for the Christians there is also a weekly day. So, let us make a day in which we meet and call on the name of Allah and pray." So they made it the day of Urubah.[27]

They chose the same pagan day which they celebrated before they became Muslims. It was the day they worshipped idols. They sent for Mohammed before he emigrated to Medina to ask his permission to use their pagan day of Urubah for their weekly worship. Mohammed allowed it,[28] and the pagan day of the two tribes became the sacred day for Muslims. The incident shows that in the early years, Mohammed had no fixed religious rituals to present to his contemporaries. His main goal was to satisfy the Arabian tribes, so he adopted their existing rituals.

Friday, or al-Jummah as it is called in Arabic, was named by Kaab Bin Luay, one of the two tribal chiefs. He called the day Jummah, which in Arabic means "meeting" or "gathering." For pagan Arabians, Friday is called Urubah, which means "mercy."[29] It was their pagan weekly feast when the two tribes met on Friday before the emigration of Mohammed to Medina.[30]

Mohammed Followed the Rituals of the Two Tribes When They Contradicted his Rituals

The two tribes not only imposed their pagan weekly day of worship on Mohammed, but they dictated the direction which they were to face when they prayed. In Arabic they called it "Khublah." Before his alliance with the two tribes, Oas and Khazraj, Mohammed used to face Jerusalem like the Jews did when praying, but the two tribes were non-compliant and disagreed with the direction Mohammed faced. Kaab Bin Malek said:

> We made a pilgrimage with our people who were pagan. Our chief, Albraa Bin Maarur, was with us. When we left Medina, Albraa said, "Oh, I have an opinion, but I do not know if you agree with me or not." We asked, "What is this opinion?" He said, "I decided not to pray with the Kaabah behind me, but instead, I'll pray facing it." We said, "In the name of Allah, we heard that our prophet always prayed facing toward Damascus (meaning the temple of Jerusalem), and we do not want to contradict him in this." He said, "I am going to pray toward the Kaabah." So when the time of prayer came, we prayed facing Damascus with the Kaabeh behind us. When he prayed he faced Kaabah with Damascus behind him.[31]

Here we find before his alliance with Oas and Khazraj that, in Mohammed's mind, the Kaabah was not a building that was superior to the Temple of Jerusalem which he thought existed then. If he really believed that Abraham wanted to sacrifice his son Ishmael on the Black Stone of Mecca, why did he neglect the Kaabah until the chiefs of Oas and Khazraj imposed it on him?

Another conclusion we draw from this incident is that deference was given to the pagan rituals of Oas and Khazraj of Medina. If they differed from Mohammed's rituals, they took precedence. We see the two tribal chiefs were indifferent to what Mohammed practiced. As we saw in the case of Albraa Bin Maarur, they had their own rituals which they inherited from their pagan fathers, such as Friday worship, and facing their

Khublah toward Mecca where the two statues of Asaf and Naelah resided. (Asaf and Naelah were the two priests of Jinn whom they venerated.) The statues stood on the shore in Mecca while copies of them were on the main stones of Kaabah. They also conducted a Hajj to the hill of Safa and Marwa where copies of the two priests of Jinn were placed. The leaders of Oas and Khazraj could not accept the plans of Mohammed to pray facing toward Jerusalem. Mohammed wanted to make a connection with the faith of the Old Testament, but they showed they were not ready to abandon their pagan rites. Although they had accepted Mohammed's program which enabled them to exploit the women and seize the money of their Arabian neighbors, they were not ready to abandon the rituals of their original pagan religion. Their real intention was to have a religious appearance like that of Mohammed which would enable them to meet the conditions of the accord with him because they wanted to have sex and the material possessions of those they conquered. But they insisted in continuing their own pagan rituals, with or without Mohammed's consent. For example, we saw Albraa Bin Maarur insisting that he continue his prayer ritual facing Mecca, rather than assume Mohammed's custom to pray toward Jerusalem. Albraa did not care that the rituals of Mohammed contradicted his own rituals.

Here we see Mohammed was obliged to give up his own rituals when they contradicted those of Oas and Khazraj. Mohammed was ready to accept their rites, such as worshipping on Friday, and circling around Safa and Marwa which Oas and Khazraj practiced during their occult Hajj to the statues of Asaf and Naelah. Many Muslims objected to these rites, knowing that they were the pagan rituals of Jahiliyah. Uns Bin Malek said:

> Asem has told us, "I said to Uns Bin Malek, 'You used to hate to
> walk making a pilgrimage between the Safa and Marwa.' He
> answered, 'Yes,' because it was from the pagan rituals of
> Jahiliyah. Allah inspired Mohammed to recite a verse in the Qur'an
> which says, 'Safa and Marwa are from the rituals of Allah. He who
> makes a Hajj to the temple or the Hajj of Umra' has no sin if he
> encompasses around Safa and Marwa,'" quoting Surah 2:158.[32]

This verse pleased Oas and Khazraj, the two tribes of Medina. The same thing happened in the case of "Khublah," which is an Arabic word meaning the direction one must face when praying. The Khublah to Mecca in prayer was more important to Oas and Khazraj than any religious ritual Mohammed used to establish a connection with "the people of the book." By book, he meant the Bible. Mohammed quickly changed his Khublah from being toward Jerusalem to being toward Mecca, in order to please the chiefs of those two tribes.

Mohammed quickly adjusted his rites to satisfy the tribes, but he did so with verses of the Qur'an so that he would remain the main channel of legislation and the maker of all the laws which were inspired by Allah.

Mohammed Incorporated the Customs and Rituals of Oas and Khazraj with the Excuse that Allah had Praised Them.

We read in the biography of Mohammed:

> Allah inspired a verse of the Qur'an which says, "Men liked to purify their bodies and themselves." Then Mohammed called them and asked, "What is this purification that Allah made a compliment to you because of it?" They said, "O prophet of Allah, none of us, neither women or men, evacuate the bowels or defecate without a thorough cleaning." Mohammed answered, "This was it."[33]

Mohammed noticed that the two tribes had special customs, such as thorough cleansing with water, or with stones from the fields, after defecation. So he asked them about the details of these customs. Then he ordered them to do this as part of the Islamic law.

This reveals to us that Mohammed wanted to copy the customs of the two tribes, but in a way that made it look as though Allah had ordered him to do so. Mohammed wanted the tribes to continue their customs, but under the pretext that Allah liked the customs and commended them. Then Mohammed imposed the customs of the two tribes upon all Muslims. We read in the biography of Mohammed: "It was characteristic of the prophet of Allah to make a law for his nation that they clean themselves with stones after relieving themselves."[34] However, civilized people, such as the Byzantines at the time of Mohammed, used to clean themselves with more hygienic material than stones of the desert. Stones are contaminated with germs and worms that easily enter the body through this primitive method of cleaning.

When Mohammed entered Medina, he gave a speech in which he emphasized his determination to put into practice the terms of the articles of his agreement with the chiefs of the two tribes, Oas and Khazraj. He said, "I was ordered to have Medina eat up the other towns," meaning to conquer other cities and take their money and steal their women.[35] Without a doubt, when Mohammed entered Medina, he quickly emphasized and confirmed the purpose of his program. He announced the rallying cry through which he attracted for the first time eight of them at Mecca, which then spread quickly in the souls of the chiefs of Oas and Khazraj, and they accepted him as a leader who would put this program into practice. Mohammed could not enter the city of Medina without repeating his call to arms. It is like a man elected as the president of a nation because of his specific agenda. His first declaration will focus on his determination to apply the program which brought him to power. So when Mohammed entered Medina, he didn't have speeches filled with religious slogans, but he repeated the catchwords he used to initiate the filthy bargain he made with Oas and Khazraj, when he was called to power and was given authority over these two tribes. No other language could have pleased the ears of those who called him because of the open and frank manner in which he made his previous offer. Therefore, Mohammed enforced these things in the minds of these savage tribes.

Mohammed was accepted as the leader by Oas and Khazraj without any analysis of his doctrine. In fact, the two tribes held nothing in common except for the rallying cry to eat up the nearby towns and enjoy their women. There was nothing that Mohammed could stress when he entered the city except the old program he had presented to the two tribes. Had he come with thoughts of piety and religion, no one would have received him. His donkey would have continued to wander in the town with Abu Baker, his assistant. No one would have been excited at the sayings of the one who rode the donkey. The same thing happened in Mecca when Abu Baker promoted the claims of Mohammed. Few were attracted to his speech. Nabash Bin Zarareh Bin Wakdan, the husband of Khadijah (who became the first wife of Mohammed), was the visionary of Jinn: the Jinn appeared to Nabash in the form of an old man to give him information[36]. Abu Baker was his most important disciple. Abu Baker remained a close friend of Khadijah, eager to obey her when she declared Mohammed was the prophet, instead of her former husband.

When Mohammed changed his language from what appeared to be religious to what now consisted of "eating up the villages," he was followed by a group at Mecca which was looking for these degrading experiences, and who were envious of the people of Mecca and covetous of their riches. These groups found Mohammed to be the one who played to their aspirations with a loud and daring voice under the excuse of forming a new religion.

Therefore, not any recitation would fit the occasion when he entered Medina in pleasing the two tribes who responded to his sayings, which he made their representatives at Mecca to hear.

3

TO WHAT MORAL CATEGORY SHOULD MOHAMMED BE ASSIGNED?

Offering sex as a Bribe to Oas and Khazraj was Openly and Publicly Promoted by Mohammed

Mohammed's first campaign was to enlist a tribe to which he had not previously presented his claim to see if they would accept or refuse it. When he moved into their settlements he found women in the camp. He took the women and returned to Medina, giving orders to the members of the tribe to enjoy sex with the females whom he stole.[37] He did this because he wanted the members of the two tribes to have confidence that he was serious about what he had promised, which was part of the covenant he had with them.

Where did all this happen? Thaniat al-Wada'a was located in the suburbs of Medina. The biographers of Mohammed indicate that this place was used by Mohammed for public fornication and immorality. The book of Halabieh says:

> When the companions of Mohammed returned to Thaniat al-Wada'a from Khaybar, they called the females with whom they enjoyed free sex in Khaybar.[38]

Al-Wada'a was a place set aside for sex with the women stolen in their campaigns with Mohammed. We see that Mohammed encouraged immorality on a large scale, to the extent that the females of an entire city were dragged there for sexual gratification. I ask the question, "Throughout history, which of the world's religions, other than the religion of Mohammed, were

478

founded on sexual pleasure?" This is a unique characteristic of Mohammed's religion among the known religions of the world. Anthropologists tell us that this kind of public behavior of free sex and orgies is something common among the occult sects which openly worshipped the devil. Our Muslim friends need to know that the God of the Bible is a holy God who abhors sin and immorality. The licentiousness and immorality on which Mohammed founded and established his religion places his religious teachings on the same level as the occult groups which adopted these practices for their abnormal and perverted adherences.

Truth cannot be found within the life and teachings of a man who founded his religion on such abominations. Nor can we imagine that such a person could have had any relationship with a holy God. Nor can anyone improve upon a religion which was founded on these practices. The only way our Muslim friends can avoid eternal damnation is to come out of this system and return to the holy God who was expressed in Jesus Christ. His true essence and character is seen through His perfect holiness, conduct and teaching.

Mohammed planted hatred in the hearts of his followers in preparation to conduct Jihad, or holy war, against all those who were not Muslims, even members of their own families.

After emigrating to Medina, Mohammed prepared his followers for the task of Jihad. Muslims were ordered not to reside in territories which were not Muslim.[39] His followers were told that they should emigrate to Medina, leaving their spouses and sons who are not Muslims. The motive behind these orders was to separate the Muslims from their societies, in order that Mohammed could control them. As instruments in his hand, he could easily enlist them in the wars and piracies which he planned to wage against the tribes and cities of Arabia.

Mohammed undermined family relationships, and ordered his followers not to show kindness toward the members of their families who were not Muslims. He says in the Qur'an, Surah al-Mujadilah 58:22:

> You will not find those who believe in Allah and the last day to love and be kind with those who ignore Allah and his prophet, even though they are their fathers, their sons, their brothers, or members of their tribe.

In Surah 9, called Tawbah, verses 23 and 24, Mohammed says:

> You who believe, do not give consideration to your fathers and brothers, if they preferred to be infidels rather than embrace faith. The one who relates to them will be unjust. If you favor your father, your son, your brother, your wife or your kindred, or if the wealth you gained, the commerce you are afraid to lose and the houses you enjoy, are dearer to you than Allah, his prophet and the Jihad for him, then wait until Allah brings about his decision and order.

Through these verses Mohammed laid a foundation for his followers to be hostile toward the members and relatives of their own families and the society in which they lived. He did so in order to prepare the ground for his followers to make Jihad against family members and kindred who remained in Mecca and refused to become Muslims. In verse 24, he taught that Jihad must be dearer to them than their families. He did this to prepare them to fight against their families who refused Islam. After Mohammed sowed hatred in the heart of his followers against their fathers, brothers, wives and kindred, he included a verse in the Qur'an in which he sanctioned their slaughter. The verse is 123 of the same Surah 9. It says:

> You who believe, fight those who are related to you among the infidels, and let them find in you hostility and harshness.

The Arabic word for the phrase "related to you" in this verse is "Yalunakum." According to the Islamic expositors of the Qur'an, it means "those in your family who are close to you, such as fathers, sons, brothers and cousins." Al-Sabuni, a modern Saudi expositor of the Qur'an commenting on this verse, says:

> They had to start fighting those who were the closest family
> members until they reached the ones who were more distant in
> their relationship.[40]

After Mohammed (in verses 23-24 of Surah 9) prohibited
displaying kindness to fathers and other family members, he did
something even worse. In verse 123 we read that Mohammed
authorized the slaughtering of fathers and other family members,
under the excuse that they were infidels who refused to become
Muslims.

Fathers are Killed by Their Muslim Sons Who, in Turn, are Forbidden to Regret or Show Sadness

After Mohammed prepared his followers to show hate and
hostility toward members of their families, and to fight them, he
then led his followers in expressing a diabolic hatred
unprecedented in human history. Mohammed led his followers to
attack the caravans of Mecca, to steal their property, and to kill
their leaders. When the people of Mecca saw that the riches of
their city were being confiscated, and that law and order were
being threatened by Mohammed and his followers, they came out
to defend what was theirs. Then Mohammed encouraged his
followers to fight the inhabitants of Mecca who came out to
defend their caravans.

But when Mohammed saw that many of the people of Mecca
were the fathers of his followers, he intentionally ordered his
Muslim followers to wrestle with, and fight, their own fathers.
Mohammed knew the fathers would not kill their sons, even
though they (the sons) joined Mohammed and sabotaged the law
and the security of the city. Mohammed knew this, and he saw
that he would gain an advantage in battle when he selected sons to
fight their own fathers. As a result, many fathers were killed by
their own Muslim sons during the battle. It was in the battle of
Uhud that Abu Ubeideh Bin al-Jarrah killed his father and
eventually became a leader and one of Mohammed's commanders.

Not only did Mohammed promote the slaughter of fathers by their own sons, but he prohibited the sons to show any regret for killing their fathers. He would not allow the sons to show any sadness after the killings. Abi Hatheifah ابي حذيفة killed his father in battle. Afterward, Mohammed began disposing of the dead bodies by throwing them into a large well. Abi Hatheifah saw the dead body of his father whom he had killed as it was thrown in the well. When Mohammed noticed the expression on Abi Hatheifah's face, Mohammed said to him, "It seems you still have some feeling toward your father?"[41] Abi Hatheifah understood that if he showed any sympathy or regret at his father's death, this might bring the wrath of Mohammed on him. So he said, "I don't mourn for my father. But in the name of Allah, I knew my father to be a man with a good mind, showing clemency and favor. I desired that he should become Muslim."[42] Today, I ask my Muslim friends, "Is it right for a son to kill his father?" His son who murdered him attested to the good qualities of his father. Were not those qualities befitting a man with a good mind, clemency and favor? Did not these qualities place him above those who killed him, including his son and the mastermind who planned these atrocities? Never before has history recorded atrocities like this!

Many people who disagreed with Mohammed were betrayed and killed by their close Muslim friends and relatives.

When anyone disagreed with Mohammed, he deceived him and then killed him. Often Mohammed sent a Muslim who was a relative of the victim to do the job, sending the would-be killer at night while the victim was sleeping at home. Mohammed knew the intended victim would open his house to a relative. For example, because Kaab Bin al-Ashraf occasionally criticized Mohammed, Mohammed sent two men at night to kill him. One of them was Mohammed Bin Muslima who was a close friend of Kaab, and the other was Abu Naelah who was a brother of Kaab. Both brothers were wet-nursed by the same woman. Arabians consider unrelated brothers suckled by the same woman as real brothers.

Both Mohammed Bin Muslima and Abu Naelah came to Kaab asking for him. Al-Bukhari, Mohammed's biographer, said:

> Kaab called them to enter his well-fortified yard. The wife of Kaab said to him, "Where you are going at this hour of the night?" He said, "It's for the sake of Mohammed Bin Muslima and my brother Abu Naelah." Then one of the brothers said, "When I draw near to him to kiss his head you kill him." So they killed him and reported this to the apostle of Allah.[43]

On many occasions Mohammed sent Muslims to decapitate poets and intellectuals who criticized Islam or disagreed with him. Mohammed's custom was to have them killed at night and have their heads brought to him. He usually selected friends or relatives of the victims whom they allowed to enter their homes at night, assuming they would not harm them.

The followers of Mohammed were taught to deny their friendships with infidels. Another example is Abdel Rahman Bin 'Auf عبد الرحمن بن عوف. He had a close friend, Umayya Bin Khalef. When Muslims began killing those of Mecca who came to defend their caravans, Umayya was surrounded by many Muslims who struck him with swords. Umayya cried to his old friend Abdel Rahman for help, but Abdel Rahman ignored him and abandoned him. Umayya died with his son by blows from the swords.

Teaching Love and Forgiveness Comes From the True God, not From Mohammed who Taught Hatred and Betrayal

Killing fathers and brothers, and betraying friendships as taught by the Qur'an and instructed by Mohammed, stands in stark contrast to the teaching of the New Testament. Jesus said in Matthew 5:43-44:

> You have heard that it hath been said, "Thou shalt love your neighbor, and hate your enemy." But I say unto you, "Love your enemies, bless them

that curse you, do good to them that hate you, and pray for them which despitefully use you, and persecute you."

In Luke 6:28, we read, "Bless them that curse you, and pray for them which despitefully use you." The teaching of the New Testament expresses the character of the loving God who wants humanity to live in harmony and peace by loving each other and forgiving each other. Yet, we read the Qur'an and can't help but notice Mohammed's example, sowing hatred in families and among close relatives. Readers are encouraged to kill fathers and other family members just for being infidels. We find atrocities committed by the enemy of humanity, the Devil, of whom Jesus said in John 8:44, "He was a murderer from the beginning." He has schemed to kill and incite people to commit heinous crimes since the beginning of the creation of man.

4 _____

ISLAM AS THE NEWBORN OF THE JINN RELIGION OF ARABIA

Negative Spiritual Forces Stand Behind the Atrocities of Mohammed and his Followers

Betraying friends and relatives in their own homes by Muslim relatives whom Mohammed commissioned is beyond reason. Recruiting a Muslim son to kill his own father is something so horrible which only hell can scheme and promote. What led to this kind of behavior? Studying the rise of Islam confirms that behind Mohammed were the forces of the Arabian Jinn religion.

The Jinn-devils of Arabia wrote poetry and rhymed prose to influence the Arabians. Because the Arabians were fond of poetry and sentimentality, they were easily influenced. The devils were known to present the cries of poetry, called Hawatef, which is heard by those who practiced occultism and were in contact with devils. After Mohammed emigrated to Medina, the Jinn-devils recited many Hawatef in praise of the chiefs of the two tribes who made the original accord with Mohammed.[44] Hawatef, attributed to the Jinn-devils, were recited in order to praise and encourage chiefs like Mohammed and Saad Bin Maath from the Oas tribe, and Saad Bin Ibada from the tribe of Khazraj.[45]

Another thing that reveals the relationship of Mohammed to the Kuhhan is that Mohammed continued to consult the Kuhhan and the Jinn religion of Arabia even after he claimed to be a prophet. One of the Kuhhan was Saf Bin Sayyad who claimed "that his devil brought him information about hidden secrets and news of the earth."[46] He used to augur, or foretell the future, through his devil. Sayyad claimed to be a prophet of Allah, like many of the Kuhhan claimed in Mohammed's time.[47] The books which narrate the life of Mohammed report that Mohammed returned to this Kahen of the devil to consult him. We are told that Mohammed searched until he found Saf Bin Sayyad in order to consult with him.[48] This demonstrates that Mohammed was seeking direction from Saf Bin Sayyad, knowing that Sayyad had a devil who provided him with advice and gave him direction.[49] This shows how much Mohammed depended on the representatives of the Jinn religion of Arabia for direction. *Al-Bukhari*, the authoritative book which contains the Hadith of Mohammed, reports a visit which Mohammed and some of his followers paid to Saf Bin Sayyad.

The Jinn Religion of Arabia Used Monotheism to Confront Christianity

At the time of Mohammed, many Kuhhan of the Jinn religion of Arabia claimed to be prophets of Allah. Their occult religion sought to confront and oppose Christianity. Many Kuhhan dedicated themselves to become prophets spouting "monotheistic slogans" contrary to Biblical monotheism, which had became a threat to them. The monotheism of the Jinn religion is based on Allah, known in Arabia to be the greatest star that appears in the third part of each night. Mohammed also said, "Our lord appears in the horizon of the sky in the third part of each night."[50] Today we know that star is actually Venus. So we see that the Jinn religion of Arabia adopted star worship to confront Biblical monotheism. The Jinn became important agents in service to Allah. The concept of the Jinn-devils as useful agents of Allah are actually found in many of the Surahs of the Qur'an.

We find these Kuhhan who claimed to be prophets endeavored to support each other. Mohammed, after consulting Saf Bin Sayyad, asked him if he believed that he (Mohammed) was a prophet, and Saf answered "yes." Then Saf Bin Sayyad asked Mohammed if he believed that he, Saf bin Sayyad, was a prophet of Allah. Mohammed answered, "I believe in Allah and his prophets," an answer that does not exclude the faith of Mohammed in Saf Bin Sayyad as another prophet of Allah.[51]

Umar Bin al-Khattab, who later became second Caliph in Islam, asked Mohammed to allow him to hit the neck of Saf Bin Sayyad because he claimed to be a prophet of Allah like Mohammed, but Mohammed answered Umar, "If he is a prophet of Allah, you can't have authority over him,"[52] showing that Mohammed respected Saf Bin Sayyad. He believed in the probability that Saf Bin Sayyad was a prophet of Allah, and warned Umar not to hurt him. This also reveals that Mohammed, at the beginning of his claim to be a prophet, believed in the kind of monotheism practiced by the Saf Bin Sayyad with which the Jinn religion in Arabia allied themselves. The Jinn religion of Arabia presented many Kuhhan as prophets to this form of monotheism. Mohammed's support from the Kuhhan proves that Mohammed was one of those prophets whom the Jinn religion has dedicated to such monotheism.

The Kuhhan Upheld Mohammed and Promoted Islam

The Islamic books which narrated the life of Mohammed confessed: "Some of Kuhhan of Arabia had an important influence and role in preparing their tribes to embrace Islam." [53] Among the famous Kuhhan who supported Mohammed was the Kahen of the Jinn-devils named Khater Bin Malek. He was the most famous Kuhhan in the tribe of Beni Lahib.[54] Another dangerous Kahen of the devils who promoted the claims of Mohammed was Satih. [55] Al-Halabieh says: "Satih was as one of the chiefs of the Kuhhan, who was a man of great knowledge about occultism and the priesthood of the Jinn."[56]

Among the Kuhhan who backed Mohammed was Swad Bin Khareb al-Dusi, a famous Kahen of Arabia. He had a devil who appeared to him, and he was famous in augury, or foretelling the future, through his devil. The Arabian custom was to test the devil of the Kahen before consulting him. Every time his devil was tested he was presented with a riddle, like a secret word, and then he asked the Kahen to guess the word through his devil. Swad would immediately guess the word.[57] We can easily see the Kuhhan, through their devils, were agents who promoted the claims of Mohammed.[58]

After Mohammed emigrated to Medina, many of the Kuhhan fought side by side with him. They accompanied him in his war against the Arabian tribes, trying to convert them to Islam. Among the Kuhhan who fought alongside Mohammed was Amru Bin al-'hamiq عمرو بن الحمق .[59] This reveals how important it was for the Jinn religion of Arabia to seek Mohammed as a successful representative of their strategy to confront Christianity by spreading a form of monotheism based on Allah, which was borrowed from the monotheistic Star Worship of Arabia.

The Jinn Religion of Arabia Unifies its Efforts Behind Mohammed's Islam, Which was the Newborn Occult Religion of Arabia

In the past, the religion of Jinn of Arabia named many of its Kuhhan to become prophets of Allah. But with Mohammed's military campaigns to convert Arabian tribes to Islam, the religion of the Jinn changed its strategy, unifying all its efforts and activities under Mohammed. This can be demonstrated by many incidents. For example, early Islamic literature refers to a famous Kahen, Khanafer Bin al-Taua'm al-Humeiri خنافر بن التوأم الحميرى . He was the chief of his people, very rich, and bodily strong. Delegations from Yemen came to Mohammed as the result of threats against them. Wars and the pressure to embrace Islam took their toll. Every year, they were required to pay the Jizyah, a large amount of money, exacted as tribute from those who refused Islam. Their wives and daughters became concubines, and the death penalty was enforced on their sons over ten years of age. This Kahen came out with his people and camped in a valley. He allied himself with another chief, Jodan Bin Yahya al-Ferthami جودان ابن يحي الفيرضمي, against Mohammed. But his devil, called Shassar, came to him and ordered him to embrace Islam.[60]

The Jinn religion played a fundamental part in supporting Mohammed, including support through its poets who received their poems from the Jinn-devils. The Jinn inspired people through their poems. Early Arabian narrators said inspiration came through special encounters between people and Jinn.[61] The capacity of the Jinn to inspire rhymed prose and poetry was indisputable in Arabia. Al-Mirsabi, born around 900 A.D., gathered poems inspired by a Jinn named al-khin'ur الخينعور.[62] Their prose and poetry were superior to those of the Qur'an, both in language and smoothness, or volubility.

Arabs have fifteen kinds of rhymes used in their poetry. The Jinn had thousands of rhymes which Arabs at the time of Mohammed were unable to imitate.[63] Therefore, Arabians considered the prose and poems which the Jinn inspired to be miraculous acts that humans were unable to imitate. Kuhhan, who claimed to be prophets in Arabia, used their rhymed prose, inspired by their Jinn, to convince others they were prophets. They claimed Jinn of other Kahen were unable to produce the same level of rhymed prose. Mohammed also claimed, in Surah 17, verse 88 of the Qur'an, that the rhymed prose of the Qur'an is a miracle no human or Jinn could imitate. But in reality, the Qur'an is inferior to many of the rhymed prose of the Kuhhan. There is a complete Surah, called the "Surah of Jinn," which is in the Qur'an which claims that the Jinn are officially the authors. It claimed that the Jinn believed in Mohammed and became Muslims. The language of this Surah doesn't differ in any way from the rest of the Qur'an. Since the Jinn's writing is the same as the rest of the Qur'an, we can only conclude that the claim "the rhymed prose of the Qur'an was miraculous" means it is the same quality as the rest of the rhymed prose of the Kuhhan, which came from their Jinn.

Some of the Arabian poets up to, and including, the time of Mohammed give us the names of the devils who inspired the poetry. The poet al-'Aasha said the name of the devil who inspired him was "Musahhal" مسحل, and al-'Aasha often praised his devil in his poems.[64]

Hassan Bin Thabet, Mohammed's poet and his closest companion, used to praise Mohammed through his poems and defend him. Hassan confessed that a devil inspired his poems. He said his devil was from "Beni Shasban," one of the chiefs of devils.[65] It seems that "Beni Shasban" was the name of a legion of devils responsible for the religion of Jinn of Arabia. Many of the Islamic poets sought help from devils to inspire their poems. Among them was the famous Islamic poet, Jarir, who said his devil was "Iblis of the devils."[66] Iblis, in Arabic, means Satan. So we see that devils openly supported the claims of Mohammed.

These things and other proofs confirm that the religion created by Mohammed was born from the religion of the Jinn in Arabia. We saw previously that Mohammed was a Kahen. In fact, I mentioned that his uncle Abu Taleb praised Mohammed, showing that he was a Rachi, equivalent to a shaman – a man who cured diseases through sorcery. Rachi was a profession practiced by the Kuhhan in Arabia. Abu Taleb boasted that Mohammed cast spells on patients at the cave of Harra' before he claimed to be a prophet.[67] We saw also that Mohammed's claims were sustained by the Kuhhan in the beginning. We saw also that Mohammed's first wife, Khadijah, was married to Nabash Bin Zarareh Bin Wakdan نبـاش بن زرارة بن وقدان, a visionary for the Jinn, before she met Mohammed. The Jinn appeared to Nabash in the form of an old man to give him information.[68] She promoted the idea of prophethood for Mohammed, at a time when Mohammed was passive and accused the devil of creating his negative experiences.All these facts prove that the Jinn religion of Arabia conceived the same kind of "monotheism" which Mohammed proclaimed similar to the "monotheism" proclaimed by other Kuhhan, who said that they were prophets of Allah who lived when Mohammed lived.

Evaluation by the Human Conscience

Mohammed's assistants, who committed many crimes including the decapitation of innocent people, became heroes in Islam. Some of them killed their fathers, such as Abu Ubeideh Bin al-Jarrah who was honored by Mohammed as an important leader. Mohammed called him "Amin al-Ummeh," which means "the faithful of the nation," and Mohammed entrusted him to lead many of his expeditions. Abu Ubeideh Bin al-Jarrah was also entrusted by the Caliphs, Abu Baker and Umar, to lead the

Islamic army in Syria. Therefore, those who killed their fathers were given great honor in Islam.

But the inevitable question remains: "Is the radical Islamic militia today, and its violence against innocent people, any better than the violence created in Mohammed's time when his followers killed their fathers as infidels and decapitated their relatives?" Or, are they any better than those who followed the command of Mohammed to cut off the heads of their relatives after entering their homes as friends betraying them. How different are today's terrorists, who beheaded one person or more, than Mohammed who ordered trenches to be dug and beheaded the heads of the tribe of Beni Kharithah from age ten years and over, and buried their bodies?

Mohammed set an example for today's Muslim. He wrote verses in the Qur'an that encouraged Jihad, or holy war, against infidels who do not follow Islam. His hatred in the Qur'an is the motivator for radical militias, and the justification for the violence they create. What they teach and practice takes the lives of many innocent people in many parts of the world today.

Many non-Muslims today are asking how militant Islamic groups can blow themselves up as suicide bombers. How can they pledge themselves to suicidal operations? Today's violence is nothing new. Mohammed insisted that his followers shake hands with him to pledge what he called the "pledge of death," meaning that they entered battle as a suicide pact with the intention to die in a jihad. Ibn al-Akwa', a companion of Mohammed, confirmed that when Muslims pledged to Mohammed in a pledge called "the pledge of Radwan" in a place near Mecca called al-Hudiebeh, they "pledged to death," meaning that they pledged to enter the battle to die. Then Mohammed wrote a verse in Surah 48, verse 9, claiming that "Those who pledge to you, also pledge to Allah." Al Sabuni says this verse came when Mohammed pledged death in Al Hudiebeh.[69] What the radical Islamic militia is doing today is only an imitation of what Mohammed practiced and proclaimed.

As we saw in the previous parts of this book, Islam is based on historically false claims growing from pagan and occult worship of Arabia attributed to Abraham and the Bible.

Islamic radicals today base their military strategy on the old plans of the Jinn religion of Arabia, which they used to conquer Arabia and the Middle East. They endeavor to subdue the world through violence. As long as the Qur'an and the example of Mohammed are taught in schools and mosques, it will attract recruits who are willing to give their lives to accomplish it. Will Muslims today continue to believe in the Qur'an and trust Mohammed, who initiated this plan in the first place and established its principles, or will Muslims look for the truth which the Bible announced in hundreds of prophecies, which included the coming of the Savior, His death on the Cross, and His resurrection?

The teaching of the Bible is not the violence encouraged by Islam, but peace which Christ's teaching and example create in the heart of all who accept Him and His teaching. His truth creates love for one's enemies and forgiveness for all. Instead of hatred and killing innocent people, Christ died to change the hearts of men and women. He is worthy of consideration by every Muslim.

REFERENCES AND NOTES TO PART VI

[1] *Tir Yast* V:8, see also the footnote number 4 - the comment of Mr. Geiger , *Zend Avesta* part II, page 95

[2] *Halabieh* I, page 337

[3] *Bukhari*, 4, page 79; *Halabieh* I, page 339

[4] *Bukhari*, 3, 183

[5] Al-Masudi, II, page 182; Al-Asbahani, *Al Aghani*, 3, page 73

[6] *Halabieh* 2; page 130

[7] *Halabieh* 2, page 65

[8] *Bukhari* 3: pages 179, 180, 183

[9] *Bukhari*, 4; page 158

[10] *Halabieh* 2, page 158

[11] *Halabieh* 2, pages 59-61

[12] Al-Jaheth, *al- Haiwan*, 6: 190; quoted by Jawad Ali, *al-Mufassal*, vi, page 709

[13] Al- Shebli, *Ahkam al- Jinn* , page 114

[14] *Tarikh al-Tabari* I, pages 56 and 61

[15] *Halabieh* 2, page 65

[16] *Halabieh* 2, page 158

[17] *Halabieh* 2, page 159

[18] *Bukhari*, 6, page 140

[19] *Ibn Hisham* 2, page 53 ; Halabieh 2, page 159

[20] *Ibn Hisham* 2, page 54; *Halabieh* 2, page 159

[21] *Halabieh* 2, page 162

[22] *Ibn Hisham* 2, page 73

[23] *Halabieh* 2, page 163

[24] *Halabieh* 2, page 162

[25] *Ibn Hisham* 2, page 59; *Halabieh* 2, page 170

[26] *Ibn Hisham* 2, page 60; *Halabieh* 2, page 171

[27] *Halabieh* 2, pages 168 and 169

[28] *Halabieh* 2, page 169

[29] *Halabieh* 2, page 169

[30] *Ibn Hisham* 2, page 58

[31] *Ibn Hisham* 2, pages 60 –61; *Halabieh* 2, page 172

[32] *Bukhari*, 2, page 171

[33] *Halabieh* 2, page 238

[34] *Halabieh* 2, page 239

[35] *Halabieh* 2, page 240

[36] Ibn Darid, *Al-Ishtiqaq*, pages 88 and 89

[37] *Bukhari* 3, page 122 ; *Halabieh* 1, page 590 ; 2, page 588; *Sahih Muslim* 10, page 10

[38] *Halabieh* 2, page 235

[39] Al-Sabuni, *Safwat al-Tafasir*, third edition(1981), 2, page 469; depending on verses of the Qur'an

[40] Al Sabuni 1, page 568

[41] *Halabieh* 2, page 430

[42] *Halabieh* 2, page 30

[43] *Bukhari* 5, page 26

[44] *Halabieh* 2, page 229

[45] *Halabieh* 2, page 229

[46] *Sahih al-Bukhari,* 7:113,114, 215 ; *al-Raud al-anf* 1, page 137

[47] *Al-Bukhari* 7, pages 113,114; *al-Raud al-anf*, 1, page 137; Introduction to Ibn Khaldun 1, page 95

[48] *Al-Bukhari* 7, pages 113,114; *Zad al- Muslim* 2, page 104

[49] *al-Raud al-anf*, 1, page 135

[50] *Sahih al-Bukhari*, 2, page 47

[51] *Sahih al-Bukhari*, 7, pages 113, 215

[52] *Sahih al-Bukhari*, 7, page 114

[53] *Al Raud al-anf* 1, page 137; Al-Nuwayri, *Nihayat al-arab fi funun al-adab*, 3; page 124 ; Tashkibri Zadeh, *Miftah Al Saadeh* 1, page 113; *Subuh Al Aasha* 1, page 398

[54] *Halabieh* 1, page 139

[55] *Al Raud Al-anf* 1, page 18

[56] *Halabieh* I, page 122

[57] *Al Raud al-anf* 1, page 139 ; *Nuzhat al-Jalis* 1, page 177

[58] *Ibn Hisham* 1, page 166

[59] Ibn Darid, *Al-Ishtiqaq*, page 279; Ibn Hajar, *al-Isaabah* 2, page 526

[60] Ibn Hajar, *al-Isaabah* 1, page 456; *Taj Al Arus* 3, page 192; *Al- Amali*, written by Al Khali 1, page 134

[61] Alusi al-Baghdadi Mamud Shukri, *Bulugh al-arab fi ma'rifat ahwal al-arab*, 2, page 350

[62] Bint al-Shatea', *Risalat al-Ghufran*, page 291

[63] Bint Al Shatea', *Risalt Al Ghufran*, page 291

[64] Al-Jaheth, *al- Haiwan* 6, page 225; quoted by Jawad Ali, *al-Mufassal*, VI, page 734

[65] Al-Tha'alibi Ahmad al-Malik ibn Muhammed, *Kitab Thimar al-Qulub*, pages 55, 69

[66] Al-Tha'alibi Ahmad al-Malik ibn Muhammed, *Kitab Thimar al-Qulub*, page 69

[67] *Ibn Hisham* 1, pages 189, 218

[68] *Taj al-Arus*, 6, pages 197, 287; Ibn Darid, *Al-Ishtiqaq*, pages 88 and 89

[69] Al-Sabuni, *Safwat al-Tafasir,* 3, page 220

Index

495

498

500

501

505